Halifax N

Gregory Brown & Basil Spiller

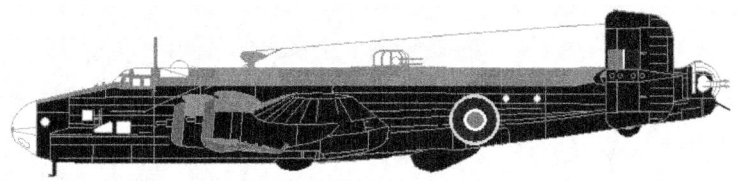

On the 1st of October 1941, with the war in Europe and northern Africa entering its third year and Japan threatening to invade Australia, Basil Spiller, on his eighteenth birthday, joined the RAAF in Brisbane. In May 1942 he was called up and began observer training. In March 1943 he embarked for Britain where he was trained as a navigator. Basil joined No. 102 Squadron, a heavy bomber squadron, operating from RAF Pocklington in Yorkshire. With four other Australians and two Englishmen he formed a Handley Page Halifax crew of exceptional quality.

During his nineteenth operation, a bombing mission over France, Basil was severely wounded but continued to navigate his plane and crewmates to safety.

Basil and his crew flew the last of the thirty-five operations required to complete their first Tour of Duty on the 18th of November 1944. When the war ended, he and three of his original crew had also completed eight operations of a second Tour together.

Basil Spiller participated in forty bombing operations over occupied Europe and Germany. He was promoted to Flying Officer and was awarded the Distinguished Flying Cross for courage, devotion to duty and his exceptional abilities as a navigator.

This is Basil's story of his years at war.

Front cover photograph: A Handley Page Halifax Mk 3 bomber silhouetted against target indicators. RAF night attack on a flying bomb site at Biennais, France, at 3.38 am on 5/6th July 1944.
Back Cover photograph: Evening sunlight shines on a Handley Page Halifax Mk 3 bomber, during an attack on a flying-bomb site in the Pas-de-Calais, France.

Gregory Brown
Tasmanian Stories
35 Bingley Street, Howrah, Tasmania, Australia 7018
greg.brown18@bigpond.com

First published August 2013

Copyright © Gregory Brown 2013

All rights reserved. No part of this publication may be reproduced, stored in a retrieval system, or transmitted in any form or by any means, electronic, mechanical, photocopying, recording or otherwise, without the prior written permission of the author.

National Library of Australia
Cataloguing-in-Publication entry:

Brown, Gregory, 1952-
Halifax Navigator: an oral and extended history of Basil Spiller's years at war.

 Written by Gregory Brown. Story told by Basil Spiller.

 ISBN-13: 9781490599960 (paperback)
 Includes bibliographical references.

 1. Spiller, Basil.
 2. Australia. Royal Australian Air Force - Airmen - Biography.
 3. Flight navigators, Military - Australia - Biography.
 4. World War, 1939-1945 - Europe - Aerial operations, Australian.
 5. World War, 1939-1945 - Personal narratives, Australian.
 6. World War, 1939-1945 - Participation, Australian.

 940.5442094092

Published at CreateSPACE/Amazon
https://www.createspace.com/

Every attempt has been made to credit copyright holders of materials used in this book in the accompanying research and background notes, and to contact holders of copyright for permission to reproduce material in the book. Copyright holders who have been inadvertently omitted please contact the author at the email address above. Changes will be made in subsequent editions.

Acknowledgements

The diaries and recollections of several men who were in 102 Squadron with Basil Spiller have been central to the development of this narrative. Bill Rabbitt, Basil's pilot, kept a war diary, and after Bill died, his family sent the surviving crew members a copy. The diary allowed Basil's memories of his war years to flow and gave his oral history form and shape. Bill's two sons, Andrew and Michael, sent me copies their father's flying log and war photographs. Don McLean, Basil's bomb aimer on their first tour of duty, also kept a war diary, which his son, Mike, lent me, along with Don's flying logs. Harry Brabin's wartime memoir also helped structure this work. Harry was Basil's wireless operator. I am very grateful to Sandy Concannon, Basil's first tour rear gunner, for sharing his wartime recollections and reading a late draft of the book, prompting several important changes. Basil's hut-mate, Bob Selth, whose Halifax was shot down by a German night fighter, shared his memories about the incident and gave me the wonderful stories about him and his mate Rex "Chicken" Lathlean. Bob is not too well at present and I wish him well.

The accompanying research notes list websites that have provided background material for this work. In particular, I am indebted to the National Library of Australia's brilliant "Trove", and the online services of the Australian War Memorial, Canberra, and the Imperial War Museum, London. I also salute the quick and helpful access to knowledge and starting points that Wikipedia provides.

Five primary texts have given body and depth to the story. They are: *The Halifax File* by R. N. Roberts; *The RAF Pocklington & RAF Elvington War Diaries* by Mike Usherwood; *It's Suicide But It's Fun* by Chris Goss; *Flyers far Away* by Michael Enright and *The Bomber Command War Diaries: An Operational Reference Book, 1939-45* by Martin Middlebrook and Chris Everitt.

Friends close to home have also supported *Halifax Navigator*. Thanks to Keren Keegan for the photocopying and binding and to Duncan How and Courtney Jones for editing the book. Thanks also to Terry and Jacqui Chapman (Basil's daughter) for their final edit of the narrative and their work on Bill's and Don's diaries. Special thanks must go to my daughter Gabriella and my wife Sue for the cover design, patience and support. Lastly there is Basil Spiller who, as he approaches his 90th birthday, is doing it a bit tough. Thanks Basil for your friendship and for taking me flying with you in your Halifax.

Greg Brown, August 2013

Author's Note

In February 2011, my wife Sue and I accepted a luncheon invitation from our friends Jacqui and Terry Chapman. Jacqui's father, Basil Spiller, was visiting from Brisbane and they wanted us to meet him. When we arrived, Jacqui and Basil were in the garden examining her latest additions and improvements. Sue walked down to join them and I went inside to find Terry. He and I stood at the window watching Basil, Jacqui and Sue as they moved around.

Terry said, "You wouldn't believe that old bloke down there was a war hero, would you?"

"What do you mean?" I asked.

"He was a navigator in the Second World War. He did a tour of duty on Halifaxes and started a second tour. He did forty bombing missions by the end of the war. They gave him a DFC."

"Jacqui's Dad?" I asked. "She's never mentioned it."

"Yeah! He was badly wounded and nearly got killed."

Not long after that, they came inside and I was introduced to Basil.

"When are we going to write your war story?" I asked.

"Eh?" he said.

"Your war story. When are we going to write it?"

"What would you write about," he said.

"Forty bombing missions. Your DFC. Nearly getting killed. Just to start," I said.

Basil hesitated and said, "Would you want to?"

"I will if you will," I said.

That's where *Halifax Navigator* started. A few weeks later in early March, Basil returned to Tasmania and we began to record his oral history. More recordings followed - in June 2011 and January 2012 at his retirement village unit in Cleveland, and in May 2012 on Stradbroke Island. Each recording was transcribed, photocopied, bound and sent to Basil. I've lost track of the number of phone calls we've had, and the number of times Basil has resolutely tried to explain the triangle of velocities, the art of air navigation, to a non mathematical brain. New memories were jogged, others drifted in from the ether and just when we had it 'finished', new material arrived – Sandy's stories, Bob Selth's stories, Don's diary, Bill's flying log. (Just yesterday, on the phone, Basil explained how, after touching down and realising that N-Nan had no brake pressure, Bill Rabbitt was still able to stop the plane.)

Here is Basil's story!

This book is dedicated to Betty Spiller who waited for me to come home, while I served in Bomber Command during World War 2.
Basil Spiller, August 2013

"When we got to Sandgate there was a big crowd and a welcoming committee – the Lord Mayor and parliamentary dignitaries. Through the crowd, I could see my own, personal welcoming committee. Betty was there!

.... I can remember that Betty had on a pink, woollen dress that she had knitted. She looked very beautiful.

....Can you imagine what it was like? Coming home! The tickertape parade through the city! Arriving in Sandgate! Looking into the crowd! And there's Betty!"

Part 1

Training in Australia

"Coming? Then hurry!"
RAAF Recruitment Poster, World War 2.

Chapter 1: Enlistment

I was born at Menapi, a coastal village in the Territory of Papua, where my father, Hobart, and my mother, Dorothy, owned a coconut plantation. I was an Australian citizen because Papua was an Australian territory administered by the Queensland government.

My mother died of septicaemia from an infected mosquito bite the day after my first birthday. Nine months later my father took my sister, Leila, and me to Perth in Western Australia to be raised by my mother's parents, the Richardsons. I cannot remember Leila because she died in a terrible accident on my grandparents' property when she was four years old and I was still a toddler. It happened on the 7th of September 1925. Leila was chasing a kitten when she accidently fell into an underground tank and drowned. I understand that we had been living with my grandparents for just six weeks when she died. At the age of eleven, I returned to live with my father at Menapi but when the long school summer holidays finished each year, I would travel to All Souls School, an Anglican boarding school at Charters Towers in Queensland, for my education. There were only a few day students there. You could count them on one hand.

I began working in Brisbane at Burns Philp, soon after I passed my senior examinations. They were big shipping wholesalers with plantation and shipping interests in coastal Australia, Papua and New Guinea. My father had worked for them when he emigrated to Australia from New Zealand before the First World War. That was the way he got to Papua. He arranged for my job with the company. On my eighteenth birthday I enlisted in the airforce at the RAAF recruitment office in Eagle Street, Brisbane. Initially I was interested in the navy because of my experiences with small boats in New Guinea, but the navy wasn't interested in me because they were not recruiting at the time so I decided to join the airforce. Because I was under age I had to send my enlistment papers to Papua for my father's signature. They arrived back in a couple of weeks with his signature attached.

At the time of my enlistment I had ingrown toenails in both my big toes. Knowing that I would be subject to drill on the parade ground I had them treated and they were healed up by the time I went into the airforce. At the medical examination I had an infected tooth and a cyst behind my left ear. The medical officer insisted that I get them treated at my own expense. I can remember going to work with a bloodied bandage around my head when I had the cyst removed at seven o'clock one morning at a private hospital.

When I enlisted, I was placed in the Airforce Reserve aircrew and given a badge which I wore in my left lapel. Every week I attended Morse Code and aircraft recognition classes.

In late January 1942, while I was doing this and awaiting call up, my father began quite a remarkable journey from New Guinea. When the Japanese invaded Rabaul the order to evacuate came over the radio. He and his native crew left the coconut plantation at Menapi on the "Iavara", our forty foot launch. He headed south-eastwards across Goodenough Bay and Milne Bay and sailed past the administrative centre of Samurai before turning westwards into the Coral Sea. He then sailed the last leg of his journey inside the calmer waters of the Papuan Barrier Reef along the south coast of Papua, before entering the Gulf of Papua and landing in Port Moresby. The Iavara had sailed over four hundred miles.

He was in Port Moresby for the first air-raid by the Japanese on the 3rd of February 1942. He intended to sail on to Brisbane and take his crew with him but the authorities would not let the natives travel to Australia. Dad gave them the Iavara so they could return to Manapi. On their way home the launch was sunk by the Japanese but most of the crew escaped. Shortly after his arrival in Port Moresby, Dad was asked to lead a flotilla of three boats, filled with Australian women and children, around the Gulf of Papua to Thursday Island nearly 350 miles away. He was the only man available who could read a compass and had any seamanship skills. They left Port Moresby and travelled right around the Gulf of Papua to Daru and then they crossed Torres Strait to Thursday Island. After arriving at Thursday Island Dad caught the coastal steamer "Wandana" to Brisbane and I met him at John Burke's wharf. He arrived to find me enlisted and doing classes as part of the Airforce Reserve. Then in May 1942 I was called up and told to report to the Initial Training School at Sandgate.

Dorothy Esther Spiller

Mainly About People
"Franziska"
    ....The engagement is announced of Miss Dorothy Richardson, second daughter of Mr. and Mrs. J. Richardson, of North Perth, to Mr. Hobart Spiller, of Papua, British New Guinea. The marriage is to take place shortly at Townsville, and the bride-elect will then pay a visit to Perth before taking up her residence in British New Guinea.
The Daily News **(Perth, Western Australia). Tuesday 18 May 1920**

Spiller. - On October 2, 1924, at Menapi, Papua, after short illness. Dorothy Esther, beloved wife of Hobart Spiller, mother of Leila and Basil, second daughter of Mr. and Mrs. Richardson, Uralia, Northam; sister of Mrs. Howden, Harold and Eric Richardson, aged 25 years.
Western Mail **(Perth, Western Australia). Thursday 13 Nov. 1924**

Leila Dorothy Spiller

Child Drowned in Tank
Northam. Sept. 7.

Shortly before noon yesterday the police received a message that a child had been drowned in an underground tank at West Northam. Sergeant Buttle proceeded to the spot, and ascertained that a little girl, Leila Spiller, aged four years, living with her grandparents, Mr. and Mrs. Richardson, in Wellington-street, had fallen into an underground tank.

The infant was pulled out by a man named Ross Dunstan, of Duke-street, and a number of neighbours had applied artificial respiration. Dr. Aberdeen was in attendance and removed the child to the public hospital, where further efforts were made to restore life, but without success. The Coroner (Mr. F. M. Read) decided that an inquest was unnecessary.

The West Australian (Perth, Western Australia). Tuesday 8 September 1925

Spiller. - On September 6, at Wellington-street, Northam, accidentally drowned, Leila Dorothy, beloved daughter of H. Spiller (New Guinea), granddaughter of Mr. and Mrs. J. Richardson, of Northam, aged 4 years 3 months.

The West Australian (Perth, Western Australia). Wed. 9 September 1925

First Japanese Air Raid on Port Moresby, Papua

Port Moresby harbour 1942. A Japanese bombing raid on a convoy of ships carrying Australian troops and supplies. The bow of a ship can be seen behind the wall of explosions.

Dr. William Gibbs, a member of the RAAF Meteorological Service was based in Port Moresby at the time of the first Japanese air raid and later wrote:

"Our first Japanese air-raid occurred on the night of 3 February 1942. I can recall much discussion among my fellow officers regarding the air-raid precautions we should take. Some felt we should shelter in the slit trenches or more elaborate sand-bagged shelters, all of which contained considerable water underfoot in this, the wet north-west season. Some of us decided to stay in the open and take cover if the noise of the aircraft indicated they were coming in our direction. The Japanese aircraft, which I believe were Kawanisi 'Mavis' flying boats, flew singly in wide circles, dropping the occasional bomb at random. The loud droning of their engines kept us awake and out of bed for long periods. I cannot recall any anti-aircraft fire or searchlights. There were no RAAF or USAAF fighters in Port Moresby at that time. Eventually the Japanese flying boats departed and we returned to our beds and a somewhat fitful sleep. The Japanese flying boats paid another visit on the night of 5 February with a similar routine, the primary objective of which appeared to be to deprive us of sleep."

Aircraftman AC2

Basil Spiller.
Aircraftsman 2, RAAF, May 1942

Chapter 2: Sandgate and Kingaroy

Developments in Air Force
Four States Affected.
Canberra, Tuesday. - Ten Royal Australian Air Force establishments will be formed or extended immediately in four States under important developments in the Empire air training scheme building programme, announced by the Minister for Air (Mr. McEwen) tonight.

A radio air gunners' school and an air navigation school will be established at Maryborough (Q.). The elementary flying training school which was to have been established there will be located at an aerodrome yet to be selected. Three new units will form at Sandgate (Q.) on Monday. These include an initial training school to enable Queensland pilots, observers, and air gunners to receive preliminary ground instruction within the State, an embarkation depot and a station headquarters to administer two units at that centre.

In South Australia the elementary flying training school at Parafield will be expanded to a full school, involving the provision of more living quarters. Instruction rooms at Parkes (N.S.W.) will be increased by the establishment of an air gunners' school within a few months. Extensions are being made to hospitals at the R.A.A.F. station, Laverton (Vic.) and the Engineering School, Melbourne.
The Mercury **(Hobart, Tasmania). Wednesday 11 December 1940**

Sandgate was the Initial Training School for RAAF aircrew in Queensland. When I was called up in May '42 I reported there. The base was located at Redcliffe, close to the beginning of the Hornibrook Highway right on the waterfront, a fair way from the Sandgate railway station. After the War it was converted to an old persons' home which is still there.

Upon enlistment I became an Aircraftman AC2 and was given my uniform. It had a dark blue forage cap with a white flash on the front to differentiate the aircrew from the ground staff AC1's. I wore it all the way through my training until I qualified for aircrew at Parkes and got my wings and sergeant stripes.

Air Force life at Sandgate mainly comprised lectures and drill. It was pretty full on. At the lectures we were instructed in the art of aerial navigation, trigonometry, aircraft recognition, Morse code and gunnery. We learned to strip a Browning machine gun. We also studied meteorology but mainly it was maths and trigonometry. I can remember permutations and combinations and logarithms as part of aircrew training. I did very well at this and topped the class in the final examination because it was pretty much like the mathematics I had been doing in my studies at All Souls.

Every Friday night at five o'clock we were given leave and required to be back in the barracks by twelve o'clock on the Sunday night. I was intent on saving as much money as I could so I didn't drink at all in those days and I didn't smoke. In fact I was disgusted by the blokes who used to come home at eleven o'clock on Sunday night, turn all the lights on in the sleeping quarters and play merry hell. There were some that did that. I was teetotal in those days. Drinking came later when I got to Canada.

Most of the recruits would take leave on Friday and be back in time on Sunday evenings. I stayed in Brisbane with my father who was boarding at a private hotel near the Fortitude Valley side of the Storey Bridge. He had a room there and I'd spend the days with him.

One Monday morning, not long before I arrived at Sandgate, the recruits left their huts to find a B17 Flying Fortress on its belly in the playing fields attached to the base. It was just there! It had happened on the weekend when they were away. They thought it had probably flown out from the USA and had run out of fuel while it was on its way to the Flying Fortress base at Archerfield near Brisbane. The pilot had attempted to touch down in an entirely inadequate space. Apparently there were no casualties so it must have been a remarkable feat of flying. They cleared the way and made a makeshift strip, and it took off a few days later.

One day while I was there, we were buzzed by a United States Army Air Force P39 Airacobra. The pilot made three or four passes, buzzing the RAAF facility for kicks. He was showing off. I presume that he knew there were trainees in the lecture huts below. His sweeps took him out over Moreton Bay and then he would turn and came back in past all the huts getting lower and lower with each pass. We were becoming more restless in the lecture rooms until finally we couldn't contain ourselves any longer and all poured outside. We arrived just in time to see him turning back towards the base for another go. He was flying so low, coming towards us but this time he was too low. His wing tip hit the sea and the plane cartwheeled over and over across the shallows of Moreton Bay. I actually saw its wingtip clip the water. We all ran down to the bay. It was low tide and the remains of the plane were sticking out of the water. Some of the guys waded out to see if they could do anything for the pilot but he was dead already. They came back festooned with belts of ammunition and other souvenirs but our authorities promptly confiscated it all.

Later that afternoon we were hanging about on the parade ground when we heard another plane in the sky. I looked up. It was another Airacobra. The pilot did not buzz us like the first one did. Instead he flew the plane up really high and then, in the blink of an eye, it plummeted straight into the water as if the pilot had committed suicide. It was a controlled dive straight into the water, very close to the other wreck in the bay - probably within one hundred metres of it. I have my own theory about what happened and there are others who thought the same. I thought the pilot must have been a special mate of the pilot who had died earlier in the day and that he had committed suicide because his mate had been killed. It was quite a remarkable thing to witness.

After our final examination, we had an aptitude test to see if we were suited to become pilots or not. The test consisted of following a dot on a screen using a joystick and the pedals of a simulated plane. I failed miserably but because I had done so well in the exam, they decided that I'd be suitable for training as an observer which was a mixture of navigation, bomb aiming and gunnery. So I had finished my initial training and was due to be posted to an air observers' course.

In the meantime the authorities decided that they would terminate the Initial Training School at Sandgate and transfer it to an aerodrome at Kingaroy. They loaded us onto a train and sent us there in the middle of winter. It was a cold hole. My memories of Kingaroy are of deep frosts all night and guard duty outside sitting before a roaring log fire to keep warm.

Eventually we were posted to the navigational school at Cootamundra and granted a week's leave. I can remember when we left Kingaroy. It was still the middle of winter. We were loaded onto a cattle truck on a train at nightfall and we travelled to Gympie. It was so cold that we begged the engine driver to allow us to ride on the plate of the locomotive. He let a couple of us do it and we had the advantage of the coal fires of the locomotive. In the early hours of the morning at Gympie Railway Station we froze again waiting for the Brisbane mail train. I had a week's leave with my father in Brisbane and then went to Cootamundra.

Flying Fortress Emergency Landing at Sandgate

On Saturday the 18th of April 1942, B-17E Flying Fortress, #41-2435, made an emergency landing on reclaimed land (now Decker Park) situated at the southern end of the Hornibrook Bridge (now Houghton Highway) at Sandgate. It became bogged in the soft ground beside the RAAF Sandgate huts.

On the 21st of April 1942, the Brisbane Courier-Mail newspaper reported the incident:

"Bomber May Be Saved

An attempt will be made within a few days to fly a heavy bomber off a recreation area on which it made a forced landing at a Queensland coastal town. Fencing at a nearby air station is to be pulled down to provide the bomber with the biggest possible runway. The pilot of the plane made a skilful landing on a reclaimed area which had been built up from swamp, the machine coming to a standstill when one wheel became bogged."

Onlookers had seen the Flying Fortress circle the area several times before its pilot, Captain G. A. Montgomery, made the decision to land. The B-17 had flown through violent weather and was lost and desperately low on fuel. After touching down, the plane raced onwards with its wheels sinking deeper into the wet clay, until finally one wheel became bogged causing the plane to lurch to one side and "groundloop". Remarkably the plane suffered only superficial damage.

After inspection, the decision to create a makeshift runway and attempt a takeoff was made. The plane was jacked up, railway sleepers were placed underneath and it was dragged back to a position close to the road behind. Trees were cut down, fences were dismantled, holes were filled and a runway of sorts was constructed, ending at the sea wall some five hundred feet from the plane, pointing eastwards towards Moreton Bay.

The Flying Fortress was made as light as possible and given only fuel enough for the short flight to Archerfield airbase, Brisbane, the headquarters of the USAAF Fifth Air Force.

At 4 pm on Tuesday 21st of April, three days after the emergency landing, a large crowd gathered to witness the spectacle of the takeoff attempt. With its engines revving to full power, the brakes were released and the B-17 surged forward bouncing over the uneven ground. After about one hundred metres, the pilot lifted the plane's nose.

It rose sluggishly, suddenly veering left towards power lines and trees at the edge of the cleared area. The crowd watched in silence as the underbelly of the plane cleared the trees and power lines with only inches to spare. Relieved, the crowd cheered and applauded.

The plane gained height, circled the area once, and headed towards Archerfield.

B-17E Flying Fortress, #41-2435, bogged on reclaimed land after its emergency landing near RAAF Sandgate Initial Training School. This photograph was taken by RAAF Sergeant Jack Woodward, then based at Sandgate, with a camera concealed in his great coat, and shielded by four of his fellow sergeants, after American military police had told the inquisitive crowd that anyone caught taking photographs would have the camera "confiscated and charges laid" against them.

Airacobras Crash at Sandgate

In this chapter, Basil Spiller recounts the story of two Bell P-39 Airacobras crashing into Moreton Bay in separate incidents on the same day near the Initial Training School at Sandgate. Both planes were from USAAF 80th Pursuit

Squadron which had moved to nearby Petrie Airfield in May 1942. The two crashes occurred on Wednesday the 15th of July, five days before the squadron left for Port Moresby to begin operations against the Japanese.

Australian based USAAF Bell P-39D Airacobras in flight.

That morning, a crowd from the RAAF station watched as the pilot of the first Airacobra, 2nd Lieutenant Travis Ferguson, made several sweeps over them from Moreton Bay, joyriding and doing a low level "beat up" of the training school, getting lower with each pass.

Womens' Auxiliary Air Force (WAAF) Sergeant, J. C. Craig who witnessed the crash said: "We had become accustomed to this since our American Force friends had moved on to the Strathpine airfield, and used the Sandgate Camp as a target for 'shooting up' the enemy. On this occasion the pilot did a couple of low runs across the base, coming in from the west, very low across the parade ground, making a turn out over the water, and coming at us again. However on one of these turns he was so low that when he banked to come around, his wing hit the mud, the tide being out. There, before our very eyes his plane nose dived into the mud, killing the pilot." Her account is similar to Basil Spiller's account of the crash.

The crash of the second Airacobra occurred later that same day at 4pm. Astonished onlookers believed that the pilot, Lieutenant Joseph Cole, committed suicide by placing his plane into a controlled dive from a high altitude, deliberately crashing it into the shallows near the wreckage of the Airacobra which had crashed earlier that day, its wreckage still in the shallows. The USAAF investigation team reported that the crashes were unrelated and that the men had no close association. That the two Airacobras were from the same squadron and the second plane nose dived into the bay alongside the first plane, strongly suggests that Lieutenant Cole and Lieutenant Ferguson were more than pilots from the same squadron but were in fact close friends. It is too coincidental to believe otherwise.

Chapter 3: Cootamundra

Air Training Schools Begin On Monday
First Intake of 293 Pupils in Scheme.
MELBOURNE, April 26. Air training schools established under the Empire air scheme will open on Monday throughout Australia. The first intake of 293 pupils will begin training as pilots, air observers, and radio air gunners.

Of the total of 144 pilots to begin training, 48 will enter the initial training school at Somers, Victoria, and 96 will begin work at elementary flying schools in the various States.

All of the 69 observers will enter the No. 1 Air Observers' School at Cootamundra, and 80 radio air gunners will be trained at the No. 1 wireless air gunners' school Ballarat.

The Minister for Air (Mr. Falrbairn) said today that all members of air crews selected up to the end of February this year would be training by July 27. From Monday on there would be intakes of air crew personnel every four weeks. Men selected during March would begin training in August or early September.

Twenty-two pilots and 38 gunners will arrive in Melbourne from other States on Monday. They will be met by pilots from Victoria and Tasmania, and they will all be taken to Somers. The remaining 12 pilots from Western Australia and South Australia will arrive in Melbourne on Tuesday.

Victoria's quota of observers will leave for Cootamundra on Sunday.
The Advertiser **(Adelaide, South Australia). Saturday 27 April 1940**

I arrived at No. 1 Air Observers Station Cootamundra on the 21st of August 1942 and was there until the 5th of December. Cootamundra was an important railway junction roughly halfway between Melbourne and Sydney on the western side of the Blue Mountains. It was an ideal place to run an air observers' course because it was dead flat country and ideal flying conditions. I was in 28 Course.

When I arrived the first thing they did was organise our bedding. They took us to a big room that was filled with straw and issued us with a hessian palliasse which we filled with the straw. That was our bed for the next three months. We slept on our "mattresses" on the floor.

A lot of our time was spent listening to lectures on aerial navigation and meteorology, the two main things. We also did some Morse code but not much of that.

Every morning we'd have to go on parade and we were inspected to see whether we had had a shave or not. We were issued with one new blade every payday - every fortnight. The old blade would be pretty blunt by then. If we hadn't shaved and were caught, the penalty was to clean out an Avro Ansons which were usually filled with dust and vomit and engine glycol. It was not a pleasant task. I was shaving at that time but I used to try and get away with it without success. The penalty was pretty dreadful for not shaving because the young inexperienced recruits would vomit everywhere in the Ansons.

After we had been there for a couple of days we were sent out on flying exercises. My first flight was on the 25th of August. Our Avro Ansons were obsolete twin engine British bombers with retractable undercarriages that the students had to wind up manually after takeoff. We flew at an altitude of two to three thousand feet all over western New South Wales on cross countries, taking bearing and distance, learning the art of drift and how to offset our course to achieve a certain track over the ground. That occupied all of our remaining time at Cootamundra. Eventually we did only flying, no lectures or "square bashing" drill. Celestial navigation came later at Parkes.

I was issued with my "RAAF Observer's Air Gunners and W/T Operator's Flying Log Book" at Cootamundra and, like all airmen, I took it everywhere with me while I was in the RAAF - wherever I was posted in Australia and Britain. That book has been with me for over seventy years now. I entered the details of every flight I went on, training flights and bombing operations with 102 Squadron at Pocklington, and every flight I did when I was between Tours at 42 Base, ferrying aircraft to other squadrons, "assimilating" French crews and running the top brass around. We had to hand it in for checking, usually at the end of every month, and whenever we were given a new posting. My navigation and air gunnery assessments are in there too.

It shows that while I was at Cootamundra I went on thirty-nine flights, twenty as first navigator, fifteen as second navigator and four as third. My average flying time was about an hour and a half but four flights were over three hours in duration. All up I did over fifty-four of daytime flying and just over eight hours of night flying. We flew all over south east New South Wales, on the western side of the Blue Mountains.

I was interested in girls at that stage but I was too shy to do anything out of line. I got my first girlfriend there. I used to walk her home after she finished work at the local café. I remember that she always smelt of boiled cabbage because that was what she had been cooking all day. I saw more of her at the café too. I didn't dance then so we didn't go to many dances. I used to take her mainly to the pictures.

I remember going to church every Sunday night at Cootamundra because they used to put on a big supper for the visiting air servicemen but also because they had a very good choir. I don't know what church it was. I didn't care. One of the ladies had a beautiful voice. I was interested in singing. I had been a boy soprano at boarding school. I entered eisteddfods and I was always a member of the All Souls School choir. So I used to go to church to be fed and entertained. It was very different from Bill Rabbitt, Don McLean and Sandy Concannon, the pilot, bomb aimer and rear gunner from my Halifax bomber crew over in

England, who were all devout catholics. I was not a catholic but I reckon that some of their religion might have rubbed off on me and saved my life over there.

I had leave in Sydney a couple of times for the weekend. I used to stay at Airforce House alongside the Commercial Travellers' Association building in George Street. I used to go on the harbour cruise at night and try to pick up girls. I was not part of a team. Once when I was in a café, I picked up the menu and there were girls' phone numbers on it. The next time I came to Sydney I had a mate with me. I rang one of these girls up. and arranged to meet her with her girlfriend in the foyer of the Australia Hotel. It was a favourite meeting point in Sydney. We met these girls but they must have been very disinterested in us because they excused themselves to go to the toilet and we never saw them again. They must have been very impressed!

A month after I arrived at Cootamundra I saw a terrible thing happen. One of our staff pilots who used to ferry us around the country was posted to Wagga, a Beaufighter OTU (Operational Training Unit). One day he decided to fly back to Cootamundra and show us how skilful he was. He killed himself and his navigator by doing a low circuit of the aerodrome and clipping the wing of his Beaufighter into the ground and they cartwheeled to their deaths across the 'drome. There was always a fair bit of playfulness and showing off going on. I saw a lot of that. Pilots were a breed of their own. They could get away with murder. For seventy years I could not remember his name but recently I have learned that he was Flight Sergeant John Jenkins, from South Australia and his navigator was Sergeant Vivian Suthurst.

I got the mumps just before I was due to sit for my final exam, so I did the exam in the hospital on the base. Luckily I passed. There were thirteen subjects and I scored seventy-seven percent. Because I was sick I was separated from the 28 Course group trainees, who were all posted immediately after their exams. I was put back to 29 Course which graduated a month later. After leaving hospital, I was given a week's sick leave to recuperate and I went back to Brisbane to stay with my father.

One of the other tenants at the guesthouse in Brisbane was in charge of the allocation of seats on aircraft flying between Sydney and Brisbane. To save me a day's leave he arranged for me to fly back instead of going by train. I can remember going out to Archerfield aerodrome, me a lowly LAC (Leading Aircraftsman) in tropical uniform, surrounded by Air Vice-Marshals and Group Captains. I am sure they looked at me and said to themselves: "Why has he got priority to fly back to Sydney?" It's not what you know, it's who you know!

My log book shows that I qualified as an Air Observer Navigator on the 11th of November 1942. When I got back after my week in Brisbane I had to wait three weeks for my new course group to finish. I was still really three weeks in advance of them because I had already passed my final exam. To while away the time and give me something to do, I was put on guard duty at a petrol dump on the outskirts of Cootamundra. By then it was summer and I used to swim a lot at the local pool. I met my second girlfriend there. I used to swap guard duty and take her out. I would come back at about 11 o'clock from the pictures and go on guard duty 'til dawn.

Eventually I left Cootamundra on the 5th of December. I was given another week's leave and posted with my new 29 Course mates to the No. 1 Bombing and Gunnery School at Evans Head.

The Empire Air Training Scheme

Avro Anson aircraft of the RAAF Number 1 Air Observer's School at Cootamundra in flight formation over a wings parade for training course graduates. 27 April 1944.

Pre-war planning for the Second World War in Europe had determined that each year a minimum of fifty thousand trained airmen - pilots, navigators, radio operators, engineers and air gunners - would be needed to man the aircraft of the Royal Air Force and conduct the air war against the German Luftwaffe. It was believed that Britain could train twenty-two thousand airmen but this was well short of the number needed. As well, Britain was not an ideal place to train large numbers of aircrew because of the danger of attack. RAF airfields were crowded and busy and were needed to launch attacks into Germany and occupied Europe. Training overseas would help alleviate these problems.

Britain turned to British Empire members for support and put forward a plan for Canada, Australia, New Zealand and South Africa to increase airforce recruitment and provide initial aircrew training. Australian and New Zealand aircrew usually travelled to Canada for more advanced training before travelling to Britain where they would join operational training units the last stage before bombing operations with the RAF.

On the 17th of December 1939, in Ottawa, Canada, Australia joined the Empire Air Training Scheme. Australia agreed to provide twenty-eight thousand airmen to the RAF by 1943. This was thirty-six percent of the aircrew to be trained by Empire nations under the scheme. Training began in Australia in April 1940. Initial training, pilot, air observer, bombing and gunnery, and wireless operator schools were established around the nation. On the 14th of November 1940, the first graduates of the scheme left for Canada. It was initially proposed that once aircrew from each country arrived in Britain they would serve in national squadrons but as the war progressed many RAAF aircrew flew in mixed squadrons.

In March 1943 the agreement was renewed. Recruitment in Australia was however gradually being wound down because of an oversupply of aircrew in Britain. The war had begun to turn in the Allies' favour. Through 1944, the effectiveness of the Luftwaffe and German ground defences gradually declined. The USAAF had also taken a leading role. The horrific loss of life sustained by the RAF from 1940 to 1944 had been stemmed and the need for aircrew was reduced. By October 1944 recruitment in Australia had all but stopped. The scheme officially closed on the 31st of March 1945. Some 37,000 Australians had been trained under the scheme.

Flight Sergeant John Jenkins and No. 31 Squadron RAAF

In the above chapter Basil Spiller relates the story of the death of Flight Sergeant John Evan Jenkins, who had been a pilot at No. 1 Air Observers School flying trainees on navigational exercises. He was from Terowie in South Australia.

At the time of his death, John Jenkins was training for operations against the Japanese. He was based at No. 31 Squadron at RAAF Base Wagga where the squadron had been reformed on the 14th August 1942, just five weeks before Jenkins's death. Crews were flying the newly acquired Bristol Beaufighters which were to be used initially in a "heavy" fighter role against Japanese positions in the Dutch East Indies and Portuguese Timor. Overshadowed by the legendary De Haviland Mosquito in the European theatre, Beaufighters were used to devastating effect by Australian squadrons against the Japanese, who nicknamed them the "whispering death" because of their speed, quiet engines and heavy firepower. These fast and robust fighter bombers were also capable of carrying a bomb load of two thousand pounds.

On the 21 September 1942, John Jenkins and his navigator, Vivian Suthurst, flew to Cootamundra. In high spirits they decided to buzz the airfield at low level. Basil Spiller and the other trainees watched as Flight Sergeant Jenkins brought the aircraft closer, curving low towards the runway. The plane's wing tip clipped the ground, sending the aircraft cartwheeling across the field. Both pilot and navigator were killed. They are buried at the Cootamundra General Cemetery.

.

No. 31 Squadron ground crew busily servicing a Bristol Beaufighter at Morotai Island in the Dutch East Indies on the 10th of January 1945.

The squadron went on to serve Australia with great distinction in the western Pacific theatre of war. From Wagga, it relocated to RAF Bachelor airfield, near Darwin, in October 1942, before beginning operations from RAF Coomalie Creek airfield. Its first operation was against Japanese positions in East Timor on the 17th of November. Perhaps the squadron's most famous raid was on the Japanese airfield at Penfoei near the coastal town of Koepang, West Timor. In a surprise raid, Beaufighters from 31 Squadron attacked forty Japanese aircraft on the ground, destroying eighteen and damaging many more without loss to themselves.

As the war turned against the Japanese, 31 Squadron followed the Japanese retreat northwards through the western Pacific moving its base first to Moratai, in the Celebes Islands, and then to Tarakan on the east coast of Borneo. The squadron returned to Australia in December 1945.

Chapter 4: Evans Head

Seven New Air Force Bases
Melbourne, Wednesday.
　　Seven additional Air Force establishments required under the Empire Air Training Scheme will be formed within the next few weeks. An official R.A.A.F. statement issued today said that the new establishments will comprise two elementary flying training schools, a bombing and gunnery school, two schools of technical training, an embarkation depot, and a stores depot.
　　No. 1 Bombing And Gunnery School will be at Evans Head, in the New South Wales Northern Rivers area, and will be formed early in August. Elementary flying training schools will be No. 6 at Tamworth (N.S.W.), and No. 7 at Western Junction, Tasmania. The two new schools of technical training will be No. 5 at Perth and No. 6 at Hobart. Another establishment to be formed during August will be No. 2 embarkation depot at Bradfield Park (N.S.W.). No. 2 stores depot is to be formed at Waterloo, Sydney.
　　　　　　The Courier-Mail **(Brisbane, Queensland). Thursday 25 July 1940**

Evans Head was the home of the No. 1 Bombing and Gunnery School (BAGS) situated on the north coast of New South Wales, about thirty kilometres south of Ballina. I was posted there from the 11th of December 1942 until the 2nd of March 1943.

We were flying Fairey Battles. They were clapped out early World War 2 British bombers powered by Rolls Royce Merlin engines. They'd been chopped up badly in the early battles in France and withdrawn from active service. At Evans Head, they were prone to breaking down repeatedly. They had a bad record of serviceability. I think it was due to the fact that the beach sand used to get into the air intakes of the motors and render them unserviceable.

At Evans Head there were not many lectures but plenty of practice bombing and gunnery. One of the courses was air to air gunnery. A pair of Fairey Battles would take off together. One of them would have two trainees in the back seat with a single machine gun and the other would tow a drogue, a canvas tube, behind it. The two planes would alternate overtaking and being overtaken. When we were firing the machine gun at the drogue we had to allow for deflection. I was hopeless at it. My scores are at the back of my log book. There are three of them. It says: "Successfully carried out the following exercises: "Fr.B.T. 4%; Fr.B.R.S.T. 6%; Fr.U.T.T. 3%".

The three scores are for firing from different positions in relation to the drogue. Fr.B.T was a firing beam test. Fr.B.R.S.T. was the firing beam relative speed test and Fr.U.T.T. was the firing under tail test. The important thing is the percentage hits to rounds fired for my best attempt - four percent, six percent and three percent. It doesn't read too well does it? I was rated "below average" even though my log book says my gunnery was "successfully carried out". It is very difficult to fire accurately when you are scared stiff. I had to stand up in the "Battle" to fire the gun. If you look at a photograph of one you can see that there is no turret, just a free standing, gas operated Vickers machine gun poking out from the rear of the cockpit. It was hairy! I had to stand up, without a harness, half in the plane and half out in the slipstream, and be expected to hit the target. No wonder so many Fairey Battles were shot down in France and sent out to Australia for aircrew training!

We also had to drop practice bombs on the bombing range at Evans Head and I was not very good at that either. Four bombs were carried under each wing. They were painted white and were about two to three feet long and six inches in diameter. They weighed about ten pounds and had fins so that they would drop accurately. They were designed to test your accuracy in bombing so they were fully aerodynamic. The bombs were released by pressing a teat when the target came into the bomb sight. They were not filled with explosive but when they hit the ground there would be a puff of white smoke. We would bomb a big circular target that looked like the bulls-eye on a dart board. My log book also has my bombing record at Evans Head. I was rated as an "average" bomb aimer. My best two attempts were one hundred yards and ninety-seven yards respectively from the target with fifteen bombs. That was the closest I got to the target so there were quite a few outside that. In my log book it says: "Two hundred and twenty-four (yards) average error". That wasn't the greatest, was it? So I wasn't a great gunner or bomb aimer. That's why they made me a navigator.

The Fairey Battle was a notorious aircraft to drop bombs from. The bomb aimer's position was under the centre section. There was a sliding panel in the floor of the fuselage just behind the engine. As soon as you opened it you got a blast of hot air from the exhaust of the motor and it used to fry you up. It also stank of glycol. I had to lie on the floor and settle down, staring into a one metre by half a metre gap of nothing but open air in front of me, apart from a rudimentary instrument panel and a tail drift bombsight. No wonder I went so badly. I was always hanging on for dear life.

One feature of my time at Evans Head was the compulsory surfing parade every afternoon. We would assemble on the parade ground in our togs and march down to the local beach and have a couple of hours of compulsory surfing. It was heaven!

I can remember that the food was good there too. We had oodles of milk to drink. It was on tap in big urns in the mess hall. We used to get leave every weekend. You'd wonder if there was a war on because we were always on leave. We used to go on leave from five o'clock on

Friday and had to be back at midnight on Sunday night. I can remember that the last bus from Lismore to Evans Head, about thirty miles away, would arrive at a quarter to twelve on Sunday night and it was always packed.

We were forbidden to travel to Brisbane that Christmas. I don't really know why but it was the height of the Japanese scare campaign and they may have wanted to keep everybody at Evans Head just in case things got bad. American troops had started to arrive and were moved by train so the trains were always full. It was a really serious time. In February 1942 air-raids started on Darwin and by mid to late 1942 things were going badly in the Solomons and in New Guinea.

So we spent Christmas '42 at Evans Head but we were allowed to travel up to Ballina, a beautiful town about twenty kilometres further up the coast. We used to go down to the local telephone exchange and chat the girls up while they were answering calls. It was a manual telephone exchange and manned by three or four girls all the time. I didn't take any of those girls out. I went down there with my mates so I wasn't alone prowling around like a lone wolf anymore.

Modern Training for RAAF Men

"Another step upwards in the intricate and specialised training of airmen for the Empire Air Scheme and the Royal Australian Air Force. An air-gunner trainee entering the cockpit of one of the modern bombers used at No.1 Bombing and Gunnery School, Evans Head (N.S.W.)."

The Courier-Mail **(Brisbane, Queensland). Thursday 9 January 1941**

The Fairey Battle

The Fairey Battle was a single engine, two-seater light bomber. It entered service with the RAF in 1937. Although it exceeded Air Ministry specifications, it was already considered obsolete at that time but paradoxically it was ordered into mass production because of the increasing strength of the German Luftwaffe and the possibility of conflict.

The 'Battle' had a crew of three - the pilot, navigator/bomb aimer and rear gunner. They were the first planes to be equipped with Rolls Royce Merlin engines, made famous as the power-plant for the legendary Supermarine Spitfire.

'Battles' were 12.9 metres in length and had a wingspan of 16.5 metres. They had a maximum speed of only 257 miles per hour (410 kilometres per hour) with a loaded weight of almost 10,800 pounds at an altitude of 20,000 feet. Fairey Battles were armed with a mounted 0.303 inch Vickers K machine gun operated by the rear gunner and a Browning 0.303 inch machine gun in the starboard wing. They had two small bomb bays in each wing, each carrying a 250 pound bomb. As well three smaller bombs, weighing about 80 pounds, could be mounted on racks beneath the wings. When production ceased in September 1940 more than 2,201 Fairey Battles had been built.

Fairey Battle aircraft at RAAF Evans Head, NSW. 1941

On the 20th of September 1939, during the period known as the *Phoney War*, a Fairey Battle shot down a Messerschmitt Bf109, the first RAF 'kill' of the war. Despite this, mounting losses proved what was already well known, that the Fairey Battle was at the mercy of the faster, more powerfully armed and manoeuvrable German fighter planes such as the Messerschmitt Bf109E, which had a cruising speed of 300 miles per hour (480 kph) and a maximum speed of 350 miles per hour (560 kph).

During four terrible days in May 1940, 107 Fairey Battles in France were sent on operations against the advancing German army and sixty were shot down, predominantly by Messerschmitt Bf109's but also by ground fire. On the 15th of June 1940 the remaining Fairey Battles were withdrawn to England and by the end of 1940 they had been completely removed from front line service.

The remaining aircraft played an important role on coastal patrol duties and in the Empire Air Training Scheme where they were used as training aircraft for pilots, navigators, wireless operators and gunners. As part of this scheme, 739 'Battles' were sent to the RCAF in Canada and 364 were sent to the RAAF in Australia - half of the total number of Fairey Battles produced – even though the RAF was critically short of combat aircraft at the time.

Evans Head Surfing Parade

S.A. Airman Drowned in Surf
Others Have Narrow Escapes
Sydney, March 9.

Leading Aircraftman Murray Horwood, 23, of North Unley, S.A. was drowned in the surf at Evans Head today after he and seven other Air Force trainees had been swept several hundred yards out to sea by a strong undertow.

Five of the men reached the beach unaided, but Horwood and Leading Aircraftmen McIntosh and Goldby, also of South Australia, were carried farther out. McIntosh and Goldby were rescued with difficulty and are now in the Air Force hospital at Evans Head suffering from severe shock.

Horwood disappeared before the rescuers could reach him. His body was found later in the day floating in the breakers, half a mile from where he and the other trainees had entered the sea, opposite the Evans Head bombing and gunnery school.

Horwood and Goldby only arrived at Evans Head station from South Australia yesterday afternoon.

***The Advertiser* (Adelaide, South Australia). Monday. 10 March 1941**

Chapter 5: Parkes

New RAF School at Parkes
Melbourne Monday: The Minister for Air, Mr. McEwen announced today that training at Australia's second wireless-air gunners' school, which was formed at Parkes (New South Wales) on January 9, would begin on February 6.
Wing-Commander H. R. Harding would command the school and its opening would complete the originally planned installation at Parkes of a station headquarters, an air navigation school and a wireless-air gunners' school."
The Sydney Morning Herald **(New South Wales).** Tues. 21 January 1941

The No. 1 Astro Navigation School at Parkes was the third leg of the air navigation course. I was posted there from the 6th of February to the 4th of March 1943. They trained navigators and wireless-air gunners for the Empire Air Training Scheme. We mainly studied celestial navigation through sightings of the stars in the southern sky. It was very concentrated, only lasted a month and we were granted no leave. During the day we had lectures about celestial navigation. Then we had to be on the station every night so that after dinner we could gather on the parade ground and study the heavens. We studied star maps of the southern sky and learned to identify various stars.

When they were satisfied that we knew the stars intimately we were introduced to the bubble sextant which would give us, in conjunction with various almanacs, a position line based on the latitude and longitude and time of day. Then, after they were satisfied that we were ready, we flew at night and attempted to get fixes and obtain position lines in the air from the bubble sextant and various stars. We flew Avro Ansons. With the pilot were two or three observer trainees and we'd take it in turns to obtain star sightings.

The bubble sextant was an instrument with which you could measure the angle of a star from an "imaginary" horizontal line. Sailors could use the horizon as their line of reference, but when an aircraft is flying at night, you can't see the horizon. The bubble sextant works like a spirit level and makes an "horizon" so that you know when the sextant is level. I would select a suitable star – one that I knew - either fore or aft through the canopy and sight the star through an eyepiece of the sextant. By turning a knurled knob on the right hand side of the sextant I could place the star in the middle of the bubble. It was like a circle – a lighted circle. When I was satisfied that it was in the circle, I pressed a button and it would record sixty one-second sightings of the star angle relative to the horizon. It would give me an average reading of the sixty sightings which would be shown printed on a little lighted screen. This was the angle of the star to the horizon. I would repeat this process for three different stars. Then I would refer to tables in special almanacs which were used throughout the British navy. They were the gospel as far as celestial navigation was concerned. I would use the angles of the stars and the tables in the almanacs to determine the latitude and longitude of where our plane was located on a "line of position" I had drawn on my chart.

The accuracy of this system was about forty percent and it was obsolete before we left Australia. It was superseded by radar assisted navigational aids and it wasn't used at all by Bomber Command in Britain. Fighter pilots didn't use celestial navigation either. They were skilled at map reading and they were in contact with ground controllers who would give them a course on which to set their compass and fly back to base. They didn't fly the distances that we did and would usually have a good idea about where they were. During the war celestial navigational aids might still have been used up in the Pacific islands where they had no radar coverage. So when I say it was obsolete, it was obsolete in the European theatre of operations.

On the 4th of March, after a month at Parkes, they gave us our assessments. In my flying log, my proficiency was rated as "average". They granted us our wings and either commissions or sergeant stripes. I was given sergeant stripes. There was no ceremony associated with receiving them. There was just a list posted on the notice board of those who had been granted a commission and those who were made sergeants. Ten percent of the intake received commissions straight off the course. Bill Rabbitt, our pilot through the war, was granted a commission after he had finished flying school.

I received my sergeant stripes and a Brevet with one wing – a pilot's brevet had two. I had to sew them onto my uniform myself, just above the left breast. Well, you wanted to get them up as soon as possible for pride sake and there was nobody else to sew them on for me. Maybe I pinned them up temporarily 'til I could get to a lady friend to sew them on neatly. I wasn't given a new forage cap so I unpicked the flash from the front of the one I had

The Avro Anson

Avro Ansons were in service with the RAAF from 1935-1955. Most finished operations with the RAAF soon after the end of the Second World War. Some 1,028 Avro Ansons served with the RAAF during this period. This light bomber was the first of Australia's low wing monoplanes with retractable undercarriage.

With war fast approaching, the Anson became rapidly outdated. In Australia they were initially used for maritime patrol and general reconnaissance but this role changed to that of gunnery and navigational training aircraft as part of the

Empire Air Training Scheme. During the war Ansons were also used in anti-submarine patrols off the east coast of Australia.

Avro Anson bombers from RAAF No. 3 Squadron.

Thousands of young Australian men like Basil Spiller, were trained on Avro Ansons. They then made their way to join aircrews particularly in the UK. As a training aircraft the Avro Anson made an invaluable contribution to the Allied war effort.

A In Australia, number of Avro Ansons continued to fly in various civil roles until the early 1960's including the Royal Flying Doctor Service, the police forces in several states, and scientific research bodies.

Chapter 6: Return to Sandgate

After Parkes I was posted back to Sandgate which by then was only an embarkation depot. Sandgate in reality was just an address where aircrew went every Monday morning to report their whereabouts. Then they could leave again. I was there for several weeks waiting to be sent overseas on a draft just like everyone else.

Because my father was at work during the week I stayed at Sandgate and lived with him at weekends. It was continual leave and we could move freely around and go into Brisbane whenever we liked

December 1944. RAAF Base Sandgate. Photograph taken towards the west of the base's buildings and grounds from Bramble Bay. To the right of the base is Pine River.

In that time my relationship with Betty started. She and I had worked in the same office at Burns Philp. We were both seventeen. I was smitten from the word go and by the time I was getting ready to go overseas, she had shed her previous boyfriend, Sydney. I remember that Betty's father did not approve of him because he was a Mormon. Every Saturday afternoon I took her to the pictures. After the pictures, I would put her on the train and she would go home to Wynnum, a suburb of Brisbane.

I was eventually granted ten days pre-embarkation leave to get everything in order. This was the real thing. I knew that ten days later I would be on the draft overseas, so I spent the remaining time with my father. I remember one day going with Dad to a professional studio to have a photograph taken of the two of us together. I look like a young boy in that photograph. I was nineteen.

When I returned to Sandgate after my leave, a fellow who had been posted back to the islands committed suicide. He had served in the Pacific area before, and whether he was on leave or on sick leave I don't know. He didn't want to go back and they were getting ready for embarkation again. He cut his throat in the latrine. I did not witness it but I was in the latrine at the same time and saw the resulting commotion. There were about five or six cubicles between me and him. I came out of a cubicle and saw the other men milling around. There was a lot of blood around and naturally I was glad that I did not see more than I did.

Pre-embarkation Leave Photograph

Basil and his father, Hobart Spiller. Photograph taken in late February 1943 during Basil's pre-embarkation leave.

Part 2

Embarkation

Colombo Race Course Rotary Club, Ceylon, *War Funds* poster, 7th January 1941. Basil Spiller's squadron at RAF Pocklington was given the official title of "No. 102 (Ceylon) Squadron" in honour of fundraising for the squadron in the former British colony.

Chapter 7: The Mormacsea

In early March 1943, at the end of pre-embarkation leave, we assembled at Sandgate and we were sent immediately to Clapham Junction, a railway marshalling yard in south Brisbane, and boarded a train. We travelled overnight to Sydney and were escorted to the Bradfield Park embarkation depot. There we were issued with a second blue uniform and an extra kitbag and bedding for the night. The next day we were assembled again. We handed back the bedding and got on the train and returned to Brisbane. Believe it or not!

They did this to fool Japanese spies because they were paranoid about security at that time. In 1942, the Japanese had invaded Rabaul and Papua and New Guinea and bombed Port Moresby and they weren't driven out until October/November 1942 after they lost the Battle of the Kokoda Trail. You have to remember that at this time Papua and New Guinea were Australian territories. When it was invaded, Australia was invaded. The Japanese bombed Darwin on the 19th of February 1942 and they bombed north-west Australia over sixty more times. On the 31st of May 1942, three Japanese submarines attacked ships in Sydney harbour. That was striking right at the heart of Australia. Everyone knew that the Battle for Australia was on. The Americans knew too. General MacArthur had his headquarters in Brisbane. It was alive with Yankee troops. You couldn't move for them at night time because there were so many of them on leave in the city. Subsequently, we arrived back in Brisbane and were immediately taken down to the wharf and got on a ship where we waited for three days. Then at night we slipped our moorings and crept into Moreton Bay and out into the open sea. The authorities were worried about submarines. They had every right to be so cautious because on the 14th of May, just a month after we weighed anchor, the hospital ship Centaur was torpedoed off Stradbroke Island by a Japanese submarine.

The ship I was on was a modern, refrigerated cargo ship called the Mormacsea. It was all steel construction with no wooden decks. It was a vessel owned by the More-McCormack Line, which specialized in transporting refrigerated fruit from South America to the east coast of the US. It was a fast, empty ship and there were only the crew and forty of us Aussies on board. As we approached the tropics it got hotter and hotter so we used to sleep on the open deck and get hosed off by the crew every morning. We were pretty roasted and brown by the time we got to San Francisco. When we crossed the equator the voice on the tannoy said: "We will be crossing the equator in a couple of minutes and you will feel a slight bump!" One peculiar habit the American crew had was at dusk when a voice would come over the tannoy stating that "the smoking light is now out". That was the order for no smoking. In the morning they would announce "the smoking light is now lit" so you could smoke.

It was all American food and it was strange to us but it was very good. Jam came with our meat and vegetables and we had different cereals for breakfast. The difference in food is the main thing I remember, not the details of what food they gave us. We had salt water showers and we were introduced to salt-water soap which was specially designed to lather in salt water. There were open toilets with water running down them all the time, which was the same on all troop ships,. You just sat on a log of wood and did your business. We didn't sight any land across the Pacific and the weather was perfect the whole time. There was nothing to do. I can't remember how we filled in our days. We probably read and played Crown and Anchor. One night we witnessed the sinking of another cargo ship by a Japanese submarine but it was way out on the horizon, just on dusk. We saw the distress signal go up but we didn't stop. Had we stopped we would have been a target too. But it was March '43 and we were heading for San Francisco!

A couple of days out of San Francisco we ran into a southerly squall and it became very rough. We were detailed to go down into the cold room and shovel out all these broken eggs and it was a most unpleasant job as you can imagine. It was about a foot deep in egg yolks. There must have been hundreds of dozens of them – all broken. They had all tumbled out of the fixtures and smashed onto the floor because of the bad weather and the heavy pitching of the ship. We got buckets and shovels and shovelled them up. We tipped them overboard and then hosed out the cold rooms.

We arrived at San Francisco early one morning and docked at about nine o'clock. On the way in we passed the island prison of Alcatraz and it looked like quite a forbidding place. We had been on the Mormacsea for three weeks and were glad to get off but it was all just ho-hum for the American crew. At the dock we were told to report at six o'clock that night to the ocean-going ferry pier at the bottom of Market Street, so we were out all day. San Francisco was quite a busy place – very hilly. Market Street is the main street. It climbs up a hill. We went on one of the cable cars. That is the tourist thing to do. We talked to American civilians and had lunch and in no time it was six o'clock. We assembled at the pier and boarded a ferry and were taken across the harbour to the Northern Railway terminus in Oakland, a city almost as big as San Francisco. We were bundled onto a train and headed north along the west coast of the US. This was the first experience I had of Pullman Cars. They folded down the seats and porters let down bunks from the ceiling.

They curtained it all off and "bingo!" - they had converted a day carriage into a sleeper. We were treated like kings really and we slept like logs. The next morning we were in the redwood forests of northern California and the ground was littered with snow from late winter snow falls.

As we travelled up the west coast of the US we called in at Portland and Seattle and finally arrived at Vancouver in Canada. The west coast of the US is very scenic country – beautiful country - and it was a thoroughly enjoyable trip. We had experienced American hospitality and Pullman Cars and had porters to wait on us. They brought us beer and indulged us. They really looked after us. We were enjoying the scenery and living the high life. It was like a second holiday!

In Vancouver we changed trains immediately to a Canadian-Pacific train. The same thing happened with the sleeping arrangements on the Canadian train. Once again we had porters who looked after us and looked after us well. We went through the Rockies, Banff, and Lake Louise, stopping only for refuelling and water, and reached Calgary in Alberta. We travelled through Calgary and ended up in Edmonton.

The SS (Steamship) Mormacsea

Starboard side view of the troopship SS Mormacsea, taken on the 15th of February 1943. There are anti-aircraft guns aft, on the superstructure, and in the bows.

After the USA entered the Second World War following the bombing of Pearl Harbour by the Japanese, the Moore-McCormack Line's large fleet of ships was placed at the service of the United States defence forces.

The Moore-McCormack Line's contribution to the war effort included the operation of 707 different ships that made 2,199 voyages and moved over 20,400,000 tons of war supplies. These ships performed many roles during the war including that of troop transport.

The SS Mormacsea weighed 7,886 tons. It was built by Moore Drydock Co. in Oakland, California. It was an ex-Sea Panther standard type C3-M built for the

United States Maritime Commission in 1941. Its conversion to a troop transport ship was completed on the 2nd of September 1942.

In 1946 the Mormacsea was returned to the Moore-McCormack Line. In October 1968 it was scrapped at Baltimore.

In his account of the journey across the Pacific Ocean on the Mormacsea, Basil Spiller says that they set sail in March 1943. The photograph below taken from a website dedicated to the Mormacsea is of a 1935 One Dollar Silver Certificate which was signed by the crew of the Mormacsea after crossing the Equator on March 30, 1943. This was most probably the voyage from Brisbane to San Francisco that Basil Spiller described in the chapter above.

The 1935 One Dollar Silver Certificate signed by the crew of the Mormacsea after crossing the Equator on March 30, 1943.

Chapter 8: Edmonton

We arrived in Edmonton on a Saturday. From the railway station we were escorted to a huge airforce base built on the rodeo and agricultural showgrounds which had been commandeered by the Canadian airforce. We were put in huts together. There were about six thousand Canadian airforce guys there and only forty of us Australians. No wonder we got lost!

As soon as we arrived, we were allocated a Scottish/Canadian sergeant to look after us. His idea of looking after us was to form us up outside our hut and march us out through the main gate, turn right and halt. The next thing he would say was, "See you tomorrow morning guys." That used to happen every day. We slept at the base and every morning he would dismiss us and say "see you in the morning". We were in Edmonton for six weeks and had the whole time off. As far as the RAAF was concerned we had disappeared from the radar screen and nobody was looking for us.

By the time we got to Edmonton, in April 1943, I had formed a friendship group with Eddie Norman and Hal Slader. Hal was born in Longreach and went to All Souls School in Charters Towers with me. His father worked for the railway at Jericho, out in western Queensland. Eddie was born at Herberton on the Atherton Tableland in Far North Queensland. He was a cynical person and he was a master at questioning and doubting everything he heard. They were my closest friends out of the forty others. We did everything together.

On the first evening, we were in the sergeants' mess having a drink. The bar steward answered the phone and said out loud, "Would three Australian sergeants be available for a date with three girls tonight?" So we put our hands up. I don't know why the girls asked for Australians or how they knew Australians were there but they stipulated Australian servicemen. Maybe we were the only three Australian sergeants in the mess at that time. We fell on our feet. We arranged to meet the girls at about 7.30.

We got out of the tram and there were three girls waiting for us at the tram stop. Two were in uniform, Canadian army girls, and one was a civilian. They took us to the civilian girl's home where we met her father and mother. She had a younger sister. They gave us a slap-up meal and we spent the evening in their company. Then at about 11 o'clock we took the two army girls back to their barracks. I arranged to meet one of the army girls, Florence, the following night.

The civilian girl's family home was our port of call for the next six weeks in Edmonton. They gave us open house. We could go there any time. Her mother was of Scottish descent and had a quaint Scottish/Canadian brogue. Her father was a railway man who worked on the Canadian Pacific Railway. I don't think he was a manager or anything out of the ordinary. I never really knew. Their house was an ordinary house and they were an ordinary family. We called in there a lot over the next few weeks and made the house our rendezvous because the family knew the families of the two army girls who made it their weekend rendezvous as well because they only got weekend leave – Friday, Saturday and Sunday night's leave. We used to take them to dances and whatever – and to the pictures. Afterwards, I would walk Florence to the army school where she was based. The route back took us past Blatchford Field, the Royal Canadian Air Force aerodrome in Edmonton. We would cut across the grass and say goodbye at the gate.

Alberta had strange liquor laws. You had to queue up to get a liquor licence, so that's the first thing we did. Teetotallers gave their liquor licences to guys who drank but I started to drink in Edmonton so I kept mine. We'd take our licences to a government liquor store and that would entitle us to a dozen bottles of beer and a twenty six ounce bottle of spirits per month which wouldn't last long so we used to treasure it and hold onto it wisely. Every one of us had an allocation. We didn't drink at the house.

Our drinking habits were like this.... We'd go to a little underground bar and dance floor, an American type "speakeasy" located invariably below street level. You went down a flight of stairs into this place where there would be booths and a dance floor and we'd dance to jukebox music. This was a completely new thing for us.

The first thing we would do was call for a bowl of crushed ice and a bottle of "Canada Dry Ginger Ale", as big a bottle as you could get. "Canada Dry" was a famous brand. In the meantime we had our bottle of spirits stashed between our legs and we would fill our glasses with crushed ice and a suitable amount of Canada Dry and top it up under the table with a liberal amount of scotch or rum or whatever. You could not buy alcohol at the speakeasy. We didn't drink much, just enough to enjoy the dancing. Hal, Eddie and I took the three girls. We paired up with them for the six weeks that we were there. There had been previous drafts of Australians to Edmonton so we weren't the first. They were used to Australians and they probably felt that they were doing their bit for the war effort too.

Bowling alleys only came to Australia in the 1960's but they were in every Canadian and US city in the early 40's. So I learned to ten-pin bowl in Edmonton. It was another favourite spot and we would often spend the night bowling.

One night I was there on my own and a Canadian sailor approached me. He said, "Are you on your own?"

I said, "Yes."

He said, "Would you be interested in going out with my sister for the night? We're going to go to a speakeasy to drink rum."

I said, "Yes."

He said," No hanky-panky mind you. She's engaged to a Canadian sailor."

I said, "Okay."

We poured ourselves into a big American sedan which he had borrowed from his father and drove out to his parents' place. His father and mother were out for the evening and he climbed in the window and pinched a bottle of his father's over-proof rum. That was my introduction to Jamaican rum. Potent stuff! We spent the night at the speakeasy and danced to the jukebox and I got thoroughly drunk. I had not experienced inebriation before. They poured me out of the car at the entrance to the station and I went to bed. I was in an upstairs bunk and immediately I lay my head down I got violently ill and I can remember chucking up out of the window. The next day I had a colossal hangover and I never touched rum for thirty or forty years until I discovered it again over at Straddie (Stradbroke Island). Now it is one of my favourite drinks – rum and ginger beer – "Dark and stormy"! That's what we call it in Queensland.

I can remember one night back at base in Edmonton when I got pretty drunk and I had to go to the toilet. I hooked my money belt up amongst the bend in the toilet cistern and forgot about it. It was late at night and I climbed into bed and suddenly remembered my money belt. I was really worried and hot-footed it back to the sergeants' mess and found it in exactly the same position as I left it. I was very lucky.

After about six weeks, all the Australians, except me, realized that they were fast becoming broke. I had plenty of money because I had drawn out a hundred pounds from my bank account before I left Australia and I had taken it all with me - my entire life savings. Most of the other forty blokes depended on payday and we hadn't been paid for months – from when we got on the ship. Because we queried why we hadn't been paid, we found out that the authorities had lost our papers completely and they didn't know we were at the station in Edmonton. So there was hell to pay. They had lost us from the time that we had boarded the Mormacsea. There were forty Australians out there in the world somewhere, enjoying themselves, having a good time - bowling and drinking and getting liquor and taking girls out.

Inevitably, there was a rude awakening for us. A couple of days later, probably after telegrams had been sent between Canada and Australia, they decided that we would undertake additional training. They lined us up and issued us with full flying kit but something must have happened overnight because the next day they lined us up and we handed it back again. The following day we were on a train heading for Halifax, Nova Scotia. We didn't even have a chance to thank the three girls and say goodbye. We were bundled off in secret.

They may have moved us on quickly to disguise the fact that they had forgotten about us. We had been there for six weeks and our training had consisted of giving us flying gear on our second last day and then demanding it back again. It could have been because the authorities decided that they wanted more aircrew in the UK, so instead of extra training for Coastal Command in Canada, we were shipped off to Halifax and fast tracked to go on the next draft to the UK. Then again, it wasn't until almost a year later that I flew on my first bombing operation.

Altogether, it took six days to cross Canada. The train trip was just as good as the last one but it was longer. We had to go from one side of Canada to the other and we ended up in Halifax, Nova Scotia.

We whiled away the time on the journey by playing the American dice game "craps" on the floor of the carriage. We played that and not "Two Up". It was the natural thing to do in Canada because Canadians were mad about craps. Later on when we got to Halifax there was a craps game on twenty-four hours of the day in the men's toilet on the airforce base. You could bet on the side. You didn't have to handle the dice at all. You could bet whether or not the roller would make his "point". I was pretty lucky in craps and I added to my stash of money. That may have been why I was charged £10 for my share of the car that my crew bought later on at 102 Squadron. They may have been thinking, "There are times when we don't have any money but Basil's always got money!"

But that is another story.

Blatchford Field, Edmonton

Blatchford Field was an RCAF aerodrome five kilometres from the centre of Edmonton. The airfield was built during the First World War and in the 1920s and 1930s played an important role in the development of Canada's North West Territories. During the Second World War, Blatchford Field became an aircrew training station as part of the British Empire Air Training Scheme, home to the No. 16 Elementary Flying Training School and the No. 2 Air Observers School. The flying training school closed in 1942 but the observers' school was not closed until 1944.

In 1944, the station became RCAF Station Edmonton and Canadian squadrons were located there. During the war it was also used by the USAAF.

Being so close to Edmonton, the airfield was gradually crowded in by the expanding city, and could not accommodate the rapid increase in wartime air traffic and larger aircraft.

Exterior view of the barrack huts at RCAF Blatchford Field, Edmonton, after a snowfall. Basil Spiller spent six weeks in huts like these at the Edmonton showgrounds as a guest of the RCAF and forgotten about by the RAAF in Australia.

In a wartime agreement with Canada, the USAAF used Blatchford Field extensively to give protection to Alaska and the Aleutian Islands after the Japanese attack on Pearl Harbour. It also became a transport hub to facilitate the construction of the Alaskan Highway which joined Alaska by road to the 48 U.S. states south of Canada. The limitations of the airfield were well realised and the Americans constructed a new aerodrome at Namao, thirteen kilometres north of the city. After the war Nameo became the new RCAF Station Edmonton.

Since then, the old Blatchford Field has been run as a commercial aerodrome by the Edmonton municipal council.

Chapter 9: Halifax to Liverpool

Halifax was the embarkation port for troops to the United Kingdom and the trans-Atlantic convoys with their war cargo left from there.

Halifax was the end of the earth! It was midsummer and it rained every day. It was a dreary place and the sun never came out. The only other thing I can remember about Halifax was the twenty-four hour crap game situated in the men's toilet. Every time you took a leak you were able to roll the dice. It did not stop.

For two weeks we never did anything in Halifax. We got no leave and stayed at the camp. It was a dreary couple of weeks. For somewhere to go we walked down the main street and back again. Nothing ever happened there.

In the First World War an ammunition ship, fully loaded, had blown up in Halifax harbour and devastated the town. So we were very apprehensive that it might happen again because the harbour was filled with ships that came back to Canada empty, were loaded again with troops, weapons, ammunition, food and supplies for the war effort, and left to join convoys, where they were given naval protection on their way to Britain. It was a very big port.

After two weeks we boarded a French ship called the Pasteur. It was a large modern passenger liner of about thirty thousand tons that had been converted into a troop ship and was being used for ferrying troops to England. It seemed huge to us. It was fully equipped with mess decks. We lived and slept and ate in confined quarters with about seven foot ceilings. We were allowed to go to the latrines twice a day. The food was always stew or things that they could ladle out of a big urn that they brought around. The sleeping quarters consisted of a mixture of hammocks that were permanently slung and mattresses on the floor. I had a mattress on the floor. It was a pretty miserable existence. The threat of U-boats was constantly in our minds. We were well below the water line and we would have had no hope of survival if we had been torpedoed. We were thinking about that all of the time. On one occasion we were allowed on deck and we found the whole of the five thousand odd troops were there at the same time. It was crowded and there were Crown and Anchor and Craps games being organized by the hard-headed sergeants who were only interested in making money by taking money off the poor unsuspecting troops. It was a con game. Nobody wins except the organizer of the game in Crown and Anchor.

The ship went flat out and we zigzagged all the time. We were continually leaning one way and then the other. The ship would only go on a certain course for five minutes and then it would keel over violently to the other side and go in another direction. They were worried about U-boats so they were making it hard for them to torpedo us. It was May/June '43, the height of the U-boat campaign. The Pasteur was a new ship. It was one of the fastest ships in the world so it was unescorted on its way across the Atlantic. The faster ships never had escorts. Like the Pasteur, the Queen Elizabeth and the Queen Mary would have been unescorted when they were carrying American troops to England from New York. A U-boat would only have torpedoed one of these ships by accident. German battleships would have been a different story.

Eventually after four days we arrived in the Irish Channel and steamed into Liverpool. We were in England!

The TSS (Turbine Steam Ship) Pasteur

The ocean liner and freight transport ship, TSS Pasteur, was built by the French shipping company Compagnie de Navigation Sud-Atlantique. Construction began in 1938 at St. Nazaire. It was named Pasteur in honour of the brilliant French chemist and microbiologist, Louis Pasteur. As fate would have it, the ship was launched in August 1939, just one month before the start of the Second World War.

TSS Pasteur (left) at anchor, Halifax, Nova Scotia, World War 2.

Because of the war, the Pasteur was laid up in St Nazaire. It was not until 1940 that ie sailed on its maiden voyage, carrying two hundred tons of gold from Brest, in France, to Halifax, in Canada. When Germany invaded France, the Pasteur was seized by Great Britain. During the war its operation was overseen by the Cunard-White Star Line. It was used primarily as a troop transport and hospital ship. The TSS Pasteur weighed 29,253 tons. Its length was 212.4 metres, its width was 26.8 metres and it was 93 metres deep. It had eleven decks that were converted to "mess deck" spaces for soldiers. When it was launched, the Pasteur was the third fastest passenger ship ever built. It could operate at 50,000 horsepower and reach speeds of 26 knots.

Speed was the Pasteur's major defence. Had it travelled as part of much slower North Atlantic convoys with a naval escort, its speed advantage would have been lost and its precious human cargo put at greater risk. Its speed made it an extremely difficult target for German U-boats to hunt, find and attack. So the Pasteur made her crossings rapidly and alone.

The war service of the TSS Pasteur was exceptional. During World War 2 it travelled extensively through the North and South Atlantic Oceans, the Indian Ocean and the Pacific Ocean. It transported over 250,000 troops, and travelled 370,000 miles.

The TSS Pasteur was awarded the Croix de Guerre, France's highest military honour. In 1957, there were angry protests in France when the ship was sold to a German shipping company.

Part 3

Training in Britain

Vickers Wellington Mark I bombers of 9 Squadron RAF, in formation, 1939.

Chapter 10: Brighton

In June 1943, we docked at Liverpool. We disembarked from the Louis Pasteur and were transferred straight to a train. We travelled overnight and ended up at the RAAF's Personnel Despatch and Receiving Centre at Brighton on the south coast of England. We were billeted at the Grand Hotel on the waterfront. It is a magnificent hotel. We were still on our perpetual holiday. We were on the top floor, the sixth floor. When my wife, Bett, and I visited the UK after the war I took her to see the hotel.

Previously the RAAF was billeted at the Metropole Hotel at Bournemouth just down the coast but the Jerry had bombed the hotel in May and six Australian airmen were killed.

In Brighton, the RAAF had been given two hotels - the Grand and the Metropole - for their use. The forty of us who left Australia were still together, all billeted at the Grand. There were many more airmen there as well.

Air-Raid

On the first night we were there Jerry laid on an air-raid. Focke Wulfs came over and tried to bomb our hotel. We didn't bother to go down to the air-raid shelter. We sat on the windowsills of our sixth floor rooms and watched it and we had a good view of all that was happening. Every couple of yards along the waterfront there was a Bofors guns and they were pumping out tracer shells. The whole of the beach was lit up by them and there were a couple of searchlights trying to latch onto the Focke Wulfs. We didn't see any German planes but we were fascinated by the tracer bullets that the Bofors guns were throwing up and the searchlights that were crisscrossing the night sky. The Germans dropped some bombs but they landed a couple of miles away. Maybe they were looking for the marshalling yards which were a favourite target. Anyway they missed us.

So we've arrived in Liverpool, got on the train and gone to Brighton and bang! Air-raid! First night! Now we were in the thick of the war. Up until then it was plain sailing and we had been treated well with a bit of luxury laid on along the way but now we were into it. We felt exhilarated because we were young and foolhardy. We lived for the day. We weren't scared, otherwise we would have gone into the air-raid shelter instead of sitting on the windowsill of the sixth floor and watching it all happen. It was a bit foolhardy sitting out there like that but we didn't care. We didn't worry about being killed. From the start we adopted a fatalistic attitude that it "might happen to him but it won't happen to me". That was our attitude when we were flying over Germany too - "Look at those poor bastards. They got shot down but I'm all right. I won't get hit." It's the age-old attitude. That's the way it was. I don't know if everyone felt like that, but that's the way I felt.... until I was wounded and then my attitude drastically changed and I was scared from that point on. Even though I nearly died, I did another twenty odd missions and volunteered for a second tour. It was madness but I had an affinity with my crew.

Money

I have already mentioned that on my pre-embarkation leave I drew all my savings out of the bank and put it in a money belt which I purchased when I joined up in Australia. Perhaps I may not have been expecting to come back home. So I carried a considerable amount of money around my middle. In Canada I had a lot of luck at craps so I was well endowed with money when we got to England.

I opened a post office savings account and deposited all my savings in it and got rid of the belt. I had a savings book and wherever I went to in England I could go to the local post office and draw out money so it was very handy.

I still had the hundred pounds that I left Australia with and more because we were well paid and I didn't need to send any home. There was just Dad. I used to draw the whole lot out and bank it. As well, I probably won about fifty pounds sterling playing craps on the way over, so I had plenty of money during my two years in England. I was never broke. I reckon my crew knew I was never broke too.

Ice Hockey

One day on a bit of a sightseeing visit in Brighton I found an ice skating rink and discovered that ice hockey was played there every Sunday afternoon. The next Sunday I wandered down to have a look. I probably would have gone to ice skating at the rink in the normal course of events anyway because I was a good skater. I hadn't seen ice hockey when I was in Canada because it was summer when I was there. It was summer in England when I arrived there too but this old rink was still open.

I started going there to watch ice hockey matches between units of the Canadian army who were billeted in the south of England. Every Sunday afternoon they would play a championship match. It was my first introduction to ice hockey and I found it a fast and furious and fascinating game. I spent five or six afternoons there. I wouldn't miss it for anything. Ice hockey for a spectator is one of the best sports in the world. It gets you right in. It is one of the world's great spectator sports. Even now, almost seventy years later, I sometimes watch it on the sports channel.

The Grand Hotel, Brighton

The Grand Hotel in Brighton. On their first night in Brighton, Basil Spiller and his friends watched a German air-raid from his 6th floor balcony, the top left balcony in this photograph.

Bournemouth Air-Raids

From mid-1940 until mid-1944, Bournemouth was subjected to regular German air-raids. On the 23rd of May 1943, some 26 German Focke Wulf 190 fighter planes attacked Bournemouth from airfields in the Cherbourg Peninsula region of France. Each plane was carrying a 500 pound bomb. It would appear that there was no specific target for the intruders but the intention was obviously to cause as much damage to key buildings and create panic in the community. Hotels were targeted because it was well known that British Empire aircrew personnel were being accommodated in the coastal resort towns of southern England

In the attack eighty-one civilians and forty-eight service personnel were killed and many more were wounded. Fifty-nine buildings were destroyed. The Metropole Hotel in Landsdowne Circle was hit directly by a bomb and suffered massive damage. The hotel was the Personnel Despatch and Receiving Centre providing for Australian and Canadian aircrew while they were awaiting assignment to operational training units.

Bournemouth, England, 23 May 1943. The Metropole Hotel in ruins.

Seven Australian and eleven Canadian airmen were killed in the attack and they are buried at Bournemouth North Cemetery. Australian newspapers widely reported that six Australians had died in the attack but the number was in fact seven. Flight sergeant Allan Kerrigan of Merrylands, New South Wales, had also been killed but his name was omitted from early reports.

Bournemouth Air-raid – Newspaper Report

6 RAAF Sergeants Killed In Air-raid

When enemy fighter-bombers raided Bournemouth, on the south coast of England, on Sunday, May 23, 6 RAAF sergeants were killed. There were also heavy civilian casualties. The sergeants, who were members of air crew and who were trained in Australia, were:

Vivian Lewis Pope, 19, of Waikerie, SA; George Arthur Mills, 23, of Dubbo, NSW; John Francis McMahon, 28, of Oakleigh, Vic; Neil Morton Gray, 19, of Mascot, NSW; Colin Bernard Crabbe, 23, of Strathfield, NSW; Ronald Franklin Fenton, 20, of Glen Innes, NSW.

The Argus **(Melbourne, Victoria). Thursday 10 June 1943**

Chapter 11: The Lady Ryder Scheme and Mrs Reid's

In the Grand Hotel there was an RAAF administration office. At breakfast time officers would often announce that there would be a general assembly of aircrew at 10 o'clock in such and such a room. Everyone went. We were regimented and obeyed orders. At one of these assemblies a couple of days after we had settled in, they offered us a week's leave and suggested that we might take advantage of the Lady Ryder Scheme.

Lady Ryder was a titled "Lady", the daughter of the Earl of Harrowby. She'd organized a system of leave where Australian and other airforce bods could go and register and say, "I want somewhere to go on leave". They would give us a name and an address and say, "Go and see him or her and they'll put you up for a week." I was given the name and address of a Mrs Reid in Rednal, a suburb of Birmingham, on the outskirts of the city, about ten miles from the CBD. Birmingham is still the second biggest city in England. It is in the West Midlands county, next to Warwickshire.

Eddie Norman, Hal Slader and I went on leave at the same time but we didn't go to the same Lady Ryder billet. On the first night the three of us stayed in London at the Regents Palace in the heart of Piccadilly right near the traffic island with the boarded up and sandbagged memorial fountain and Eros statue in the middle. It would not have survived a direct hit from a bomb but it would have been well protected from shrapnel and flying debris.

Piccadilly was a real eye opener. Naturally we went to the pub because that is what you did. We had a few noggins and then left at "10 o'clock Closing". That was the wartime closing time. In Britain the pubs opened at 12 o'clock and closed at 2 pm and they opened again at 5 and closed at 10 pm, so there was an afternoon session and a night session. The afternoon session only lasted for two hours and the night session lasted five. When we came out of the pub, the place was swarming with prostitutes – hundreds and hundreds of them – and we had to fight our way back to the hotel. Luckily none of us succumbed to their wiles. Looking back now, I don't know if I was lucky!

The next day I caught a train to Birmingham and I arrived at Mrs Reid's by double-decker tram. I had no trouble making my way. I had a tongue and could ask directions. The bus passed through a suburb called Longbridge which was the home of the famous Austin Motor Works where all of the Austin cars and trucks were built. The aircraft manufacturing side of the company built Hawker Hurricane fighters, and Short Stirling bombers earlier in the war and when I went to Rednal they were building Avro Lancasters. All the way from the centre of Birmingham to Rednal, for ten miles, I could see devastation from German carpet bombing and there was mile after mile of derelict housing. Obviously they were after the Austin Motor Works but I don't think they ever hit it. For the two years I was in Britain, and all the times I went back to Rednal, I never heard of them hitting the Austin Motor Works.

Mrs Reid was a Scottish lady with a grown-up family who had left home, and a teenage son who was still at school. She treated me quite royally, just the same as the family in Canada had treated me. She fed me well and I was able to rest and relax.

When the people in charge at Brighton gave us our rail pass they also gave us food coupons for the week and I handed mine over to Mrs Reid which is what we had to do. I think that collectively, because she had people staying with her, she had more coupons and could barter with her providers more successfully. That's the theory behind the whole thing. If you were on your own or there were just two of you, you'd only have ration tickets for one or two. It would be a lot harder than if you had ration tickets for three or four.

Mrs Reid took me to meet her friends and guided me to various places. I walked around the suburbs and found out where the pubs were and generally explored the area. It was my first week in England. I found out there was a golf links just over the road from her house and on later visits I took advantage of that.

I had my own room and I was usually the only airman there. I always travelled there on my own and I didn't play up at all. At the end of that first week's leave I went back to Brighton but I returned to Rednal many times because I had made that welcoming link. As soon as I arrived I always gave Mrs Reid my food coupons. I probably offered to pay something as well but it was refused. She was a very generous lady and treated me very well. I became very fond of her.

My holiday that started when I left Australia had continued for nearly eight weeks while I waited for a posting in England. Except for a week's leave when I went to Rednal, near Birmingham, I had stayed at the Grand – most of that summer! Not bad eh! But things were about to change.

Towards the end of August 1943 I got called before a crew classification board. There were half a dozen RAF ex-flying types looking through my results. They came to the conclusion that I was a dud bomb aimer and a dud gunner! So they classified me as a navigator because my results for navigation were better. And that's when I officially became a navigator.

In late August, I was posted to No. 27 Operational Training Unit at RAF West Freugh in south west Scotland. I left Brighton on about the 29th of August because my posting at West Freugh began on the 31st.

The Lady Ryder Hospitality Scheme

1925 portrait of Lady Frances Ryder (1888-1965), organiser of the "Lady Ryder Hospitality Scheme".

The Lady Ryder Hospitality Scheme initially provided hospitality and accommodation for Allied servicemen from British Empire countries while they were on leave in Britain. Having graduated from the Empire Training Scheme in their home countries, airmen like Basil Spiller travelled by troopship to the United Kingdom, leaving family and friends behind. As the war continued, the scheme supported men who had fled countries such as Poland and Czechoslovakia, intending to join the Allied forces.

Lady Frances Ryder, the daughter of the 5th Earl of Harrowby, and her good friend, Miss Celia MacDonald of the Isles, had conducted a similar scheme for students from British "Dominion" countries during the 1920's and 30's. Indeed, Lady Ryder and her mother, Lady Harrowby, had provided placements for Australian and other "Dominion" officers when taking convalescent and general leave during the First World War.

When the Second World War began, the hospitality scheme focused on the provision of suitable accommodation for airmen and extended its network of host families in towns, villages and farms around the UK.

Volunteers for the Lady Ryder Scheme made every attempt to match the men with compatible families who had registered with the scheme.

The often stated aim of the scheme was to provide men "with a measure of home life" to hopefully prevent them from being lonely and homesick while they were so far away from home.

Piccadilly Circus

Piccadilly Circus, London, during the Second World War. The site of the famous memorial fountain and Eros statue can be seen in the foreground, sandbagged, boarded up and being used as a billboard for war posters.

Chapter 12: West Freugh

I was posted to the No. 4 Air Familiarization Unit (AFU) at West Freugh from about the 31st of August until the 27th of September. As the name says, it was all about familiarizing aircrew with English flying conditions which were vastly different to western New South Wales where we did our previous cross-countries. In Australia where there might be fifty to a hundred miles between towns, you could run down a railway line and find where you were very easily. In England, the land was thickly populated and the villages were close together, and we had to familiarize ourselves with map reading under English conditions.

It was very difficult to know what we were looking at down below. We had to map read very cautiously and meticulously and be more serious about things at this stage otherwise we could get lost very easily. I had to be much more focused in my early AFU training and there were people looking over my shoulder much more. Everything was scrutinized.

We flew Ansons at West Freugh and we flew longer and much more serious trips, including night cross-countries. The weather was foul over the Irish Sea even though it was mid summer. We didn't get days like in Australia where the sun came out and stayed out for days on end. We mostly flew in drizzling rain, below cloud level at two thousand feet. It was bumpy and we had to have our wits about us to know where we were. West Freugh was quite a rude awakening to English flying conditions.

All my flights are covered in my log book. Three hours fifteen, three hours thirty minutes, four hours, three hours ten, three hours thirty-five. They were all cross countries over the Irish Sea. Sometimes we flew over Northern Ireland but never over Eire, the Republic of Ireland. They were staying neutral but we were still worried that they would shoot us down. They were unfriendly to everybody who flew over their territory.

I did five daylight and four night time flights and a total flying time of twenty-nine hours and five minutes at an average of well over three hours per flight. We had a pretty comprehensive time there. In a little over three weeks we had done a lot of flying. On these cross-countries I was map reading, navigating and setting tracks. I made charts and worked with them, setting directions and telling the pilot what to do.

Although Australian and British Ansons were structurally the same, the British ones had a retractable undercarriage. On Australian ones, the trainees had to wind them up manually and it was a routine job which we hated. We had to rotate a handle about half a dozen times. It was stiff and hard to do.

Harry Brabin and Don McLean

Not much of my time at West Freugh stands out but three more things are worth mentioning. The first thing is that I met Harry Brabin, a fellow Australian, there. Harry was from Manly in Sydney and he had been training as a WAG – a wireless air gunner. first at Bradfield Park, near Sydney and then for nine months at No. 2 Wireless School at Calgary in Canada. His training had been very different to mine. We were only at West Freugh for a month and we were pretty preoccupied with flying all the time. In his memoirs, *Diary of a WAG*, Harry says that we met because the WAAFs we were dating were friends.

There wasn't much to do at West Freugh but we used to go down to the NAFFI hut at night time and do a lot of fraternizing with the WAAFs over coffee. I was a pretty shy boy then. I was only nineteen. Harry was probably twenty, about a year older than I was, and a lot more confident. The place was lousy with WAAFs. Harry got entangled with a little WAAF from Northern Ireland. Her name was Vera. He talks about her in his book. One day, out of the blue, she asked him: "Should we call the padre over to discuss our marriage?" Harry figured it was time to cut and run. Harry and I became good mates and we decided to crew up together if we could. We ended up flying together right through the war.

I also remember that one day they took us in a bus trip up to a town call Girvan in Ayrshire, about thirty-five miles north. They kitted us out in full flying gear, flying suit and boots and mae-wests and we had to practise jumping fully clothed into a pool and operating the mae-west to satisfy ourselves that the mae-west really worked. That was the first time I had used one.

The third thing about West Freugh was that Don McLean, who became our bomb aimer when we crewed up at Lichfield immediately after leaving West Freugh, was there at the same time as Harry and me but we didn't meet him there. Don's log shows that his course went from the 25th of August until the 27th of September which was roughly the same time as us. I can't remember meeting him there but not long after we left we crewed up together at Lichfield. It was not surprising that we hadn't met before then because most of our flights were on different days.

Don's training was different from mine too. Mine was all navigating. Don did thirteen flights averaging less than two hours a flight. Three were gunnery exercises and the rest were bombing exercises in which Don did particularly well. In the three final exercises he dropped real bombs from an altitude of ten thousand feet and his average error was only seventy-nine yards. That's excellent! His assessment in his log book says: "Above average. A very consistent B/A (bomb aimer). Should make a first class B/A." They weren't wrong!

West Freugh lasted less than a month and it was pretty full on. My log book shows that I only did nine flights but that was a fair few considering the foul weather that we had that month.

In my flying log the West Freugh chief instructor's stamp is dated the 27th of September 1943. That's the date Harry and I left. We were posted to No. 27 Operational Training Unit (OTU) at RAF Lichfield and we travelled there immediately. An OTU was exactly as the name suggests. We were going there to join a flight crew which would be trained to operational standard, on Vickers Wellington bombers, for bombing operations over Germany and occupied Europe.

The Vickers Wellington

The Vickers Wellington was a two engine bomber which entered service with the RAF in October 1938. Seven years later, on the 13th of October 1945, when the last Wellington was rolled out of the factory, 11,484 had been built, more than any other British bomber of the Second World War. The Wellington was the only British bomber in production for the entire war. They were officially retired from service with the RAF in 1953, outlasting all other wartime bombers.

Many variations of the Wellington were made. The most significant changes were due to the revolution in engine technology that occurred during the war years resulting in the production of more powerful and reliable engines. This was driven by Bomber Command's constant demand for better engines for its expanding bomber force.

Increased numbers of engines were required for the new four engine "heavy" bombers and there was constant need for replacements for those lost or badly damaged in combat. The percentage loss of aircraft in 1943 was 4.1 percent on each operation. At that rate, without replacements, the entire bombing force would have been destroyed in just twenty-five operations – less than a month. In the war the British aircraft construction industry flourished.

Over 2,600 of the first production line Wellingtons, the Mark 1C, were built. They had two Bristol Pegasus Mark XVIII engines, each providing 1065 horse power. Maximum takeoff weight was some 28,500 pounds and its maximum speed was 235 miles per hour at 15,500 feet. It had a range of 2,500 kilometres with a full bomb load of 4,500 pounds.

Defensive armament was six .303 Browning machine guns, two in the nose turret, two in a rear turret and two in waist gun positions. There was a six man crew structure of pilot, radio operator, navigator/bomb aimer, observer/nose gunner, waist gunner and rear gunner.

The first significant variant of the Mark 1C was the Wellington B Mark III of which some 1,500 were built. This new version was equipped with four machine guns in the rear turret but the biggest change was to the power-plant with two 1,375 horsepower Bristol Hercules III engines being used, delivering twenty-nine percent more power.

The most widely produced version was the Wellington B Mark X which was basically the Mark III with a bigger power-plant. Some 3,800 were built. They were equipped with the new 1,615 horsepower Bristol Hercules VI or Hercules

XVI motors with 1675 horsepower, increasing power by over twenty-two percent compared to the Mark III.

It is estimated that during the war Wellingtons flew over forty-eight thousand bombing sorties, dropping over forty-two thousand tons of bombs with a loss of some 1,300 aircraft. Despite ongoing improvements, Wellingtons would never rival the heavy bombers which outperformed them in speed, range and manoeuvrability, and with four engines could carry at least three times the bomb load.

Vickers Wellington Mark I's from No. 9 Squadron based at RAF Honington, Suffolk, in flight,1939. On the 4th of September 1939, No. 9 Squadron flew the first RAF bombing raid of the war, attacking German shipping in the Baltic Sea, losing two aircraft.

From the start of bombing operations, the slow and cumbersome Wellingtons suffered alarming losses on daytime raids over occupied Europe and Germany. On the 18th of December 1939, twenty-two Wellingtons were detailed to bomb the German port city of Wilhelmshaven. The raid was a disaster. German radar tracked them and fighter planes from a nearby airfield intercepted the flight seventy kilometres before it reached the target. Unable to find cloud cover, the Wellingtons were easy targets and twelve were lost. Losses in the order of fifty-four percent were unsustainable, and shortly afterwards Bomber Command decided that future bombing operations would be conducted at night.

In 1942, the Wellington was still Bomber Commands' main bomber, although heavy bombers were being increasingly supplied to the squadrons. On the 30th/31st of May 1942, when Bomber Command launched Operation Millenium the first "one thousand" bomber raid on a German city – Cologne, some 602 aircraft from the bombing force of 1,047 were Wellingtons. In contrast there were only 131 Halifaxes and 73 Lancasters. To reach the magical number of "one thousand" aircraft for the raid, Nos. 91 and 92 Group OTUs supplied 299 aircraft with crews of men in the latter stages of their training, as well as ex-operational instructors who had previously been "screened", and who believed that, having completed a tour of duty, their operational life was over.

The arrival of the heavy bombers resulted in the gradual decline of Wellingtons on bombing operations. In 1943 Wellingtons flew 7,261 sorties in contrast to 15,194 Halifax sorties and 27,812 Lancaster sorties. Loss rates for 1943 are also worth comparing. In the twelve months, 393 Wellingtons were lost at a rate of 5.27 percent. There were 702 Halifaxes lost during the same period at a rate of 4.62 percent. 919 Lancasters were lost at a rate of 3.3 percent. These figures show that during 1943, Lancasters became Bomber Command's preferred aircraft. When Basil Spiller's crew began operational training at Lichfield in October 1943, Wellingtons had virtually been removed from bombing operations and had become the chief training aircraft. In December 1943, Wellingtons flew a total of just thirteen bombing sorties.

Nevertheless the Wellington continued frontline service with the RAF and operated in diverse roles including: countermeasures, reconnaissance, anti-submarine, anti-shipping and minesweeping roles with Coastal Command. Although superseded in Europe by heavy bombers, Wellingtons continued to play a valuable role in operations over the Middle East and India.

Sergeant James Ward, VC, No. 75 (New Zealand) Squadron RAF

Many acts of bravery were no doubt done on Wellingtons but there were none braver than that carried out by co-pilot Sergeant James Ward of No. 75 (New Zealand) Squadron, during a night time bombing operation to Münster on the $7^{th}/8^{th}$ of July 1941.

While flying over the Zuider Zee, in the Netherlands, his Wellington was attacked from below by a German night fighter, which in turn received a burst of machine gun fire from the Wellington's rear gunner, and was seen falling away in flames.

The night fighter attack caused a fire near a ruptured fuel pipe behind the starboard engine. As the crew prepared to bail out over enemy territory, Ward tied a rope around his waist and, carrying a canvas engine cover, crawled through the small astro-hatch and down onto the wing where he was buffeted continually by the turbulent wind stream which threatened to blow him off. He kicked holes in the plane's fabric skin for foot holds and after reaching the engine was able to smother the flames with the canvas. With great difficulty he crawled back inside the aircraft.

The danger was averted and although the ruptured fuel tank continued to leak, Ward and the pilot were able to eventually land the plane at RAF Newmarket. For his act of selfless bravery James Ward was awarded the Victoria Cross.

Summoned to meet Winston Churchill, a nervous James Ward was put at ease by the Prime Minister who said: "You must feel very humble and awkward in my presence?" The young New Zealander replied: "Yes, sir." Churchill then said: "Then you can imagine how humble and awkward I feel in yours."

James Ward was killed on the 15th of September 1941, when the Wellington he was piloting was hit by flak over Hamburg, during just his eleventh operation. He is buried in the war grave cemetery at Hamburg, Germany.

Sergeant James Ward of No. 75 (New Zealand) Squadron RAF, standing in the cockpit of his Vickers Wellington Mark IC, L7818 'AA-V', at Feltwell, Norfolk.

Chapter 13: Lichfield.

Lichfield is in the county of Staffordshire about fourteen miles north of Birmingham. I was there from the 28th of September 1943 until the 19th of January 1944. This was an Operational Training Unit solely for Australian aircrew trainees. It was the only all-Australian OTU in the UK. The commanding officer was Group Captain Patrick Heffernan. Everyone referred to him as "Paddy" – Paddy Heffernan. He was regarded as quite a man and held in high regard. I never met him at Litchfield. As CO he was dealing with more important things than the sergeants on the base. We did meet, however, in August 1944 when we were both patients at RAF Ely, an RAF general hospital in Cambridgeshire.

27 OTU was equipped with Vickers Wellington bombers and we were to be trained on them to operational standard. When we arrived at Lichfield, Wellingtons were being phased out of bombing operations. In September 1943 they only did about three hundred sorties for the month. By December this had dropped to thirteen and by the time we joined 102 Squadron at Pocklington they had stopped altogether. The OTUs were equipped with clapped out ex-operational aircraft. It was to be expected because the more modern planes went straight into the squadrons for bombing operations and other frontline duties. We always knew that we were being trained for either Lancasters or Halifaxes – the four engine bombers. There was a lot to learn and practise. Wellingtons at Lichfield had a five man crew – pilot, navigator, bomb aimer, wireless operator and rear gunner. On operations they had six man crews by adding a waist gunner who operated port and starboard guns mounted half way down the fuselage.

Crewing up, 30th September 1943

The first thing that we did was crew up. We were about to choose five of the seven man crew who would go on operations together over Germany and occupied Europe in four engine heavy bombers. This was the first stage of building a close knit group.

There are two other versions of how we crewed up – one in Bill Rabbitt's diary, *The Perilous Sky* and the other in Harry Brabin's memoir *Diary of a WAG*. Bill became our pilot and Harry became our wireless operator. Bill didn't do the selecting and Harry didn't do it either. I'll give you my version.

I have already said that Harry and I, because we were pals, decided at West Freugh that we would fly together, I as a navigator and Harry as a WOP (wireless operator) - by then air gunners had been separated from the wireless position.

One morning soon after we arrived, we were told to assemble in an empty hangar. The Commanding Officer said something like: "We want you to form crews amongst yourselves". We were told that we needed a pilot, a navigator, a bomb aimer, a wireless operator and a rear gunner in each crew. Mid-upper gunners and flight engineers were not needed because Wellingtons didn't have them. We understood that they would join us later when we converted to heavy four engine bombers, either Lancasters or Halifaxes. This method was the standard procedure for selecting the crew that you were going to be with on bombing operations. I suppose they could have just posted crew lists on the notice board but it would not have been any better. At least with this method, there was a chance that friends like Harry and I could stay together.

When we arrived the hangar was full of all the categories of aircrew - pilots, bomb aimers, navigators, wireless operators and rear gunners. Most of them got straight into it. There was a lot of excited chatter. Harry and I went to the toilet. We were having a pee when in walked a tall bomb aimer, named Don McLean and a little pilot, named Bill Rabbitt. Bill said, "Are you looking for a pilot and a bomb aimer?" We replied, "Yes we are." And Bill said, "How about linking up with us because we are looking for a navigator and a wireless operator." He could tell we were a navigator and a wireless operator because we had our breves up. He didn't know anything about us and we didn't know anything about him. It was all done in the toilet while all the rest of them were out milling around in the hangar. Harry and I weren't that concerned with trying to work out who the best pilot was or anything like that. We were casual about it. How would you know? You wouldn't! It may have been that we decided to have what was left. Maybe we did. Maybe we didn't know how to go about acquiring a crew. You wouldn't know who was who. It was just the luck of the draw.

Out in the hanger the others had got into the act and were actively crewing up. I don't know what method they adopted but the four of us adopted the "toilet" method and it worked. We pulled off a coup, I think, because we turned out to be an excellent crew. Bill told us that he'd already sorted out our tail gunner, Sandy Concannon, who was coming to the OTU that night. He and Bill had known one another back in South Australia. They must have talked over the phone and Sandy said, "I'll be your rear gunner." Bill was also hoping that Mick McCarthy, another friend of his from South Australia, would become our mid-upper gunner when we moved on to a Heavy Conversion Unit (HCU) the next stage after Lichfield. Bill fought very hard with the authorities to keep him and he stayed around for a while but in the end the policy was only one rear gunner per crew and they would not budge.

So we had our crew of five for Vickers Wellingtons. Sandy the tail gunner, Don the bomb aimer, Bill the pilot and Harry and I filled in the last two places. When the crew was finalised, Bill would have registered the names of his crew members. He would have gone to the pilots' chief instructor and told him the names of his crew. I presumed that he did that because from thereafter we were known as "Bill Rabbitt's Crew". That was the term everyone else used.

Vickers Wellingtons didn't need engineers because the pilot could operate the fuel system with only two engines. Halifaxes and Lancasters were four engine bombers. They were bigger, heavier and carried more fuel in more tanks. They needed an engineer to supply petrol from self sealing tanks to the engines, emptying them in sequence before changing over to the next one. With night fighter attacks and flak bursting everywhere there was twice the chance of one of engines being hit in a four engine bomber so an engineer would be needed to shut it down and seal it off while the pilot had more important things on his mind like keeping the plane airborne and getting them out of there. Lancasters had three large fuel tanks in each wing. That was one of the main safety problems with a Lancaster. If a tank was hit there was a bigger fire as well as the loss of a third of the fuel in that wing. Halifaxes had seven smaller fuel tanks in each wing. If one was hit it was still a shaky do but the fire would be smaller and only one seventh of the fuel would be lost. So there was a better chance of the fire being contained. In an emergency like that, the flight engineer came into his own, sealing off holed tanks, keeping ailing engines running and redistributing the fuel to keep the plane balanced.

Bill Rabbitt

The photographs of our crew show that Bill was not a tall man. He was five foot four. I was five foot six and a half and I towered over him. So he was a little guy. But he was an exceptional pilot. For a while there was doubt about whether they would allow him to pilot a multi-engine plane but by Lichfield he had crewed up and he must have liked the look of us, because he fought tooth and nail to be retained as a multi-engine pilot. He went up for special tests, sitting on a flat cushion with another one behind him so that he could sit more forward to operate the pedals of the Wellington, and he passed with flying colours. Harry Brabin in his book says Bill would have been more suited to flying smaller planes. This was no doubt a reference to his height but take it from me, Bill was a wizard pilot. After Lichfield, when we were posted to the HCU at Marston Moor we crashed our Halifax at Lichfield and it was really only Bill's flying skill that saved our lives. His assessment at the end of our first tour speaks for itself. In his diary entry on the 20th November 1944 Bill writes about his assessment: "Received my assessment as a Bomber pilot today and have been awarded the highest possible, also the most coveted – 'exceptional'."

Ground Training

My last flight at West Freugh had been on the 26th of September and I did not fly again until the 22nd of October, almost a month later. Upon arrival at Lichfield we began ground training which was made up of lectures, instruction and practice to prepare us for what lay ahead.

Bill Rabbitt found this time frustrating. In his diary on the 1st of October, soon after our arrival, Bill writes about swotting away. This would have been for exams he was required to sit probably about the workings of the Wellington bomber. Pilot's business! Then there was the question of his height hanging over him. On the 2nd he had interviews with the Chief Ground Instructor and the Medical Officer about his height and his ability to reach the foot pedals from the pilot's seat. He would have been anxious to start flying but he had to do his ground training too. Anyway, there was little flying done at the OTU in those first three weeks of October because the weather was crook. Fog and low cloud hung around all day. Weather at Lichfield was particularly bad because of the industrial haze and smog from Birmingham and Wolverhampton, two nearby industrial cities, which added to the usual problems of rain, fog and thick cloud.

As a crew we had instruction and practice in parachute, dinghy and crash landing drills, as well as in the operation of the Vickers Wellington 3's fuel and oil systems. We had to be certified as qualified in all these. Individually we had lectures and training in our own specialized areas. Bill did pilot business. He mentions such things as "intelligence talks" and on the 11th of October he did an exam in Airmanship and Signals. On the 12th of October he had another exam in Practical Airmanship. After doing his ground training with the rest of us, he finally did his flying tests and proved his suitability for flying bombers. I was doing navigation and was introduced to the GEE navigation system. Sandy practised at the gunnery butts with browning machine guns. Harry was with the wireless operators and Don would have been with the bomb aimers. There was a lot to do. Bill's diary entry on just the 4th of October says: "Lectures have now increased to twelve per day. The game is on."

Flock of birds

On the 4th of October 1943, not long after we got to Lichfield, we watched a Wellington bomber crew taking off but just as they were airborne a flock of birds flew up from the ground and shattered one of its laminated wood propellers. The propeller disintegrated and the pilot did a great job by cutting the motor and doing a slow, low half circuit of the aerodrome at an altitude of about a hundred feet and landing the plane with one motor on the runway that he'd just taken off from. The whole crew was saved. I was amazed with what I saw. I had actually seen a Wellington stay up on one motor! I didn't know if they could do that normally but after witnessing it I knew they could. It was a wizard piece of flying because the pilot didn't have much time to react. The undercarriage was going up when they hit the birds because the pilot didn't have time to put his undercarriage down again and the plane crash landed on its belly and went skidding along the runway. It was a bit hairy. We didn't run over and help them out or anything like that because the fire wagon and the ambulance were in attendance.

Six months later, on the 4th of April 1944, at our next posting to RAF Marston Moor, we were taken on a visit to the F. Hills & Sons propeller making factory. It was a former confectionary factory in York where they made a brand of chocolates called Terry's – Terry's Chocolates or Terry's Lollies or something like that. The propellers were made of laminated wood and then turned on a lathe and shaped. The Halifaxes that we were being trained on were equipped with steel propellers so I don't know why we visited a factory that only made wooden propellers. It was probably just a day out for us but I found it most interesting.

Flight plans and fixes

At briefings, every time we went up, the navigation section leaders would have a flight plan already written up on the blackboard for us and the navigators would have to copy it down exactly into their log and follow it religiously. Flight plans were calculated using met force winds - forecast winds from the meteorology department. Sometimes the forecasters blued and they were way out but you had to work through that. We did separate exercises from the other crews so we might be the only crew doing an operational training cross-country on a particular evening.

It is important to get accurate "fixes", otherwise you can't determine an accurate wind speed and direction. A "fix" is an accurate location of where you are at a particular time on the ground. But in a plane that position was probably not where I wanted to be on the flight plan because the wind would always make us drift off course. The flight plan already had the line of the direction we should be heading I would draw a line from the last fix to the new fix and then have a line representing the direction we really headed. The angle between the two lines represented our "drift", the degree to which the wind had blown us off course. I could then use the angle of drift to get us back on track by telling Bill to turn the plane more into the wind by so many degrees to get back on track. It is simple mathematics really – a vector diagram. They call this the "wind vector" or the "triangle of velocity". As soon as I did that calculation I had to get another fix and do it all over again every six minutes. I was constantly checking and constantly getting Bill to make adjustments to our direction. This method of navigation is what is known as "dead reckoning" - the navigators' bread and butter. This explains why getting fixes is so important. Anything that helped you get a fix was worth its weight in gold. At the start of the war, navigators had to rely on dead reckoning and celestial navigation. But there was always a serious problem at night time or when the weather was really dirty because you couldn't see anything so sighting was useless. Breaking through cloud is always dangerous if you do not know what is underneath your plane. You might be flying into fog and rain and not be able to see your drome, or a hill, or it might be a balloon barrage which once happened to us. What good is celestial navigation if the navigator wasn't very good at reading the stars? Luckily when I arrived at the OTU they were using GEE, and when we moved on to 1652 HCU, at Marston Moor, they had H2S and the Air Position Indicator as well, which was fortunate because by then the Germans had learned to jam GEE over the French coast.

GEE

"GEE", "H2S" and the "Air Position Indicator" (API) were vital navigational aids that I was able to access from my navigator's position. There was another one called "Oboe" which was top secret and installed in Pathfinder Force Mosquitos which were directed by Oboe controllers back in England and would follow a curved track to the target. They would lead us to the aiming point after we rendezvoused with them. It nearly got us killed once and I'll get to that later.

GEE and H2S gave accurate ground positions – fixes. The API was used to give a correct latitude and longitude air position. At Lichfield I began my training in GEE but every now and then I'd strike an aircraft that didn't have it so I'd still have to rely on pin point sighting information, usually from the bomb aimer, to get fixes for my calculations to navigate the plane. It was not ideal if you had a plane without GEE and you were relying on other crew members for fixes. I was lucky to have Don McLean right next to me in the bomb aimer section. Don had initially trained as a pilot before retraining as a bomb aimer and navigator. Few crews were that lucky. Without GEE all I had was dead reckoning and my flight plan but Don could always assist with his observation and map reading skills. Luckily we had GEE most of the time. Training to use it was so important.

GEE was a radio navigation system with transmitters across the UK sending synchronised radio pulses at precise intervals to GEE box receivers in our planes. By comparing the slight time difference between the arrival times of each pulse, we could check our specially prepared charts and calculate our position very accurately. The appropriate charts were given to us before each flight depending on the track we had to fly. The main reason for using GEE was to get accurate fixes so that we could make adjustments to keep our planes on track. Navigators also homed on GEE to get their aircraft back to base safely. I learned to set the co-ordinates for our airfield and I'd tell Bill to fly on a particular course. Two lines would appear as blips on my oscilloscope and drift over the screen. When they lined up vertically the aircraft was directly over home base. On clear days and nights we could look down and see our airfield. We could even break through ten-tenths cloud safely knowing that the drome was beneath us. This was "GEE homing". It was one hundred percent accurate flying around Britain but once we crossed the coast into mainland Europe on bombing operations it was useless because the Germans jammed it. I was not taught GEE homing before our first bombing operation and on return we got lost but I will talk about that later too.

Oxygen Masks

When we got to the OTU at Lichfield we were going to be doing cross countries in Wellington bombers at heights exceeding ten thousand feet. To operate efficiently at ten thousand feet and above you have to breathe pure oxygen. Included in our training was a decompression chamber exercise. On the 25th of October 1943, we all went into the chamber. The air was pumped out to simulate various heights in a plane. We were provided with pencil and paper and at various times we were instructed to write our names. When the equivalent of twenty thousand feet was simulated in the chamber all of us wrote unintelligible scrawl. When we looked at it later it proved to us that we had impaired capabilities through lack of oxygen. That absolutely convinced us that we had to use oxygen over ten thousand feet. Until then it had been our practice to clip on our oxygen masks only when we began climbing to ten thousand feet but after our exercise in the decompression chamber, we always wore oxygen masks from the deck up so we wouldn't be guilty of forgetting about it. In his dairy for this decompression chamber exercise Bill wrote:

> "Went into a decompression chamber. Basil and self went up without oxygen. Bas passed out at 26,000 feet and I could not use my muscles after 27,000 feet, although I was more or less conscious. Mick and Don took their masks off at 29,000 feet and soon passed out. Went into Lichfield and had a few beers at the Prince of Wales."

When we got to the squadron on operations we had our masks over our faces from the moment we took off. After takeoff we stayed at different altitudes and climbed on various legs according to the flight plan but it was usually not going to be long before we got up over ten thousand feet anyway. Each crew member had an oxygen mask. It was part of the flying helmet that we wore. When we finished a mission we took our oxygen masks with us and walked off with them.

Dinghy drill

One of the important exercises that we did was dinghy drill. On operations over Europe we always had to fly over the Channel or the North Sea. If our aircraft was damaged and we had to ditch it into the sea we had to be able to vacate it in as short a time as possible and climb into a dinghy to avoid drowning.

At Lichfield they had a Wellington fuselage in a hangar, minus the wings. The escape hatch was two thirds of the way down the fuselage and we had to climb up a ladder to vacate the aircraft. The pilot called out the words, "Dinghy! Dinghy! Prepare for ditching." By then all the crew were lying in crash positions behind the main spar with our hands behind our heads, bracing ourselves against the spar. Then he would say, "Go!" and we would all charge for the escape hatch and be out and into the dinghy in as short a time as possible. We got it down to eleven seconds. Whenever we had dinghy drill we did that same time again and again. We did a lot of dinghy drills. Bill's diary says that we did drills on the 5th, 6th, and 12th of October '43 and we had our test on the 13th. In the test we took twelve seconds to launch the dinghy and get into it. Then on the 25th of September, a really foggy day when there was no flying, we did another dinghy practice. They really drilled it into us because it was so important.

First flights at Lichfield

Bill's flying log shows that his first flight at Lichfield was on the 20th of October when he flew with Flight Sergeant Lawrence, an instructor. Bill would have started exercises to see whether he was suitable or not. It sounds like he had a rough first trip because in his diary he says that the weather was very bad with very strong cross winds.

He flew again the next day. Visibility was poor and there were strong cross winds again. When he was returning to base he had to ready the plane for a crash landing. He had been trying unsuccessfully for an hour to get the undercarriage to lock into place. He says that "all the crew were in crash landing positions". This was not our crew. Bill must have been up there as second "dickie" with another crew. He was lucky. While the ambulances and fire wagons waited, the undercarriage somehow held in position. Bill says it held because of his "wizard landing". He was very casual about it. Crash landing was a dangerous business and yet afterwards Bill played billiards with his friend Mick McCarthy, he joined us at the camp concert and even commented in his diary about the quality of the program. That's Bill for you! That landing probably helped his bid to get his pilot's ticket.

On the 22nd of October, I had my first flight at Lichfield. I was second navigator on a Wellington flown by Flight Sergeant Thomas. It was a four hour flight from base to Cambridge, Catterick, Elsham, back to Cambridge and then home. It was also the day that Bill finally "went solo". This means that he was the only pilot on the plane he was flying. The flight is recorded in his log and the word "solo" is underlined but the flight is not recorded in my log book, so the "crew" he flew with was not ours.

Our first flight as a crew with Bill Rabbitt as our pilot was a cross-country on the 27th of October 1943. Bill had satisfied the chief ground instructor and the medical officer about his ability to control Wellingtons and had satisfactorily completed his daylight circuits and bumps excercises because this flight was a three and a half hour cross-country. We flew to Woodhall, Bishops Stortford, Trowbridge, Wittering, Ragdale, Baggots Park and back to base.

The 'Link' Trainer

By the time he had arrived at Lichfield, Bill had accumulated a lot of flying hours but it was still mandatory for him to spend time doing flying exercises in the Link Trainer which was a flight simulator invented by Edward Link, an American. They were nowhere near as sophisticated as modern flight simulators but during the war they provided important training for pilots. We used to refer to it simply as "Link". Link Trainers were standard equipment at pilot training schools. It was basically a cockpit set up in a special room. It wasn't the real thing of course but it was the next best thing. It had full flight instrumentation, joystick and pedals and they could turn, pitch and roll.

I never saw one in action but it was common practice for the pilots to "go to Link". Bill used them a bit when he joined the RAAF back home in Australia, and after he arrived in England he used them a lot at RAF Ludsgate Bottom, his first posting. In his log he was certified as having completed four hours and forty minutes of Link training exercises there and finishing the course. At Lichfield he did Link when we weren't flying but when we were posted to Marston Moor it stopped because by then pilots had to know it all.

Gunnery practice

Sandy, our rear gunner, did separate training. Gunnery Flight had machine guns set up in a suitable out of the way place on the aerodrome. While I was at navigation exercises in the lecture room, he'd be down at the gunnery butts practising deflection shooting from turrets which were just like the ones in the planes. Sometimes Sandy was down at gunnery practice while we were on flying exercises.

Every now and again on our cross countries, we would descend to about a hundred feet and drop a flame-float into the sea to give Sandy some gunnery practice.

The first time we did this was on the 30th of October. It was our second flight as a crew. We would stay low, circling 'round and 'round and Sandy would be blazing away at it all the time. When you are circling an object, the deflection changes all the time and Sandy would be continuously correcting for changes in deflection. It was vital practice for him. After the flame-float exploded in a plume of smoke we would climb up to operating height and resume our cross-country. It was all part of the training. As we were heading back to base, this same cross-country exercise almost ended in disaster.

Derby balloon barrage

One of the dictums that they drilled into aircrews was: "Never break cloud unless you know where you are". When we were heading back to Lichfield the countryside below us was covered in ten-tenths cloud and we ignored that dictum. We ended up in Derby's balloon barrage and "all shits was trumps" that day because nobody ever wanted to get caught in a balloon barrage. They were so dangerous. The balloons looked like zeppelins. They were filled with hydrogen and a thick steel cable tethered them to the ground. Imagine your propellers hitting that! It could stop a plane in its tracks or take a wing off. They had winched the balloons up over Derby and they were flying just below the cloud base and when we broke cloud we were in the middle of them. Bill describes it very vividly in his diary:

> "October 30th 1943: Briefed for X-country today. Weather still filthy. Decided to take off. Did cross-country at 10,000 feet. Beautiful above the clouds. Went close to Irish coast. Had a good look at Isle of Man. Did firing at a flame float into the sea. Came back across Wales. ten-tenths cloud all way back to base. Decided to descend through cloud. 1196 U/S. (Radio transmitter unserviceable.) Stooged into Derby balloon barrage. Everybody "packing them". Balloons all around us. I was sweating like mad when we eventually got out of them. Everybody was speechless. So was I. Still cannot understand how we got out alive. Homed on QDM's. Bang on base. Made my best landing ever in Wimpey Z170. Went to Lichfield to celebrate. Met Betty Cunningham. Very nice too. Good show."

Derby was not far from Lichfield. When we got to the end of our cross-country I would have said to Bill: "I think we are there" but because we were above ten-tenths cloud we couldn't see anything. We decided to break cloud against the rules and have a look. And look where we ended up! We were right in the middle of the balloons! Bill had to weave in between them. He began a fully rated climb and climbed out of the balloons, through the clouds and broke through a couple of thousand feet higher up. If we had been caught we would have crashed. It was quick thinking and a very good bit of flying to get us out of it. It proves what a wonderful pilot Bill was. This was only our second flight together as a crew and he was able to do that in a Wellington he had just started to fly. Not too bad for a pilot they thought was too short to fly a bomber!

My position in the Wellington was different from what it was later in Halifaxes. In Halis, I was up the front of the fuselage behind the bomb aimer in the perspex nose, but in the Wellington, I was back with the wireless operator near the middle of the plane so we didn't see any of this at all. I can only go on what Bill and the others who were looking out said about the balloons. We were connected by intercom all the time. Bill said, "Balloon barrage!" and reacted immediately. He probably said more than that too! I remember the plane being tossed this way and that and the steep climb. In his diary, Bill says that everybody was speechless. We were speechless all right! When we landed we headed straight for the pub in Lichfield.

That was the only time we got caught in a balloon barrage and it taught us a salutary lesson – never to break cloud unless we knew where we were. It was always dangerous to break cloud but more so over in the UK because there were high tension wires everywhere, and the weather was so foul that we often had to fly in low cloud and fog and blinding rain, and you could always go straight down onto a mountain. It was very hard flying and if you wanted to survive you never broke cloud unless you knew where you were.

After our near disaster we still had to get back to base and we couldn't see anything. Bill says that "we homed in QDMs. Bang on base" which means that Harry brought us home on a wireless bearing. Harry would have been in touch with base, and base was notifiying us on the course to fly back on. Harry would have held the Morse Code key down and Lichfield would have taken a bearing from that and notified us of the course to take by sending a Morse Code signal back to us. That was a QDM. We did not have GEE on that Wellington. I had been relying on pin points from the countryside from Don our bomb aimer for navigation but there are no pin points in ten-tenths cloud or above cloud. No wonder we got lost. You have to rely on your flight plan and if you can't do that you are in trouble.

A few days later on the 3rd of November, we went on another cross-country for five and a half hours. We flew out to a sea position 5500N and 0000E, about sixty miles off the coast from the Tyne River, and dropped a float. Then we dived at it while Don McLean, our bomb aimer, and Mick McCarthy each shot a thousand rounds at it. Bill at this stage was still hopeful about getting Mick into the crew as our mid-upper. Sandy Concannon, our rear gunner, would have been on gunnery training somewhere else. Anyway we flew back over Cambridge, stooging around, having a look at the university, but as we approached Coventry, Bill saw barrage balloons again and "sheared off" because as he says in his diary he did not "want to get too familiar with these things". We had well and truly learnt our lesson.

Circuits and Bumps

The first phase of practical training for a pilot was inevitably Circuits and Bumps. Whenever we trained on a different aircraft the pilot had to satisfy the instructors that he could handle the takeoffs and landings.

My log book shows that we didn't fly with Bill on any of his daylight circuits and bumps at Lichfield but we had to when we graduated to night takeoffs and landings.

In contrast, when we got to 1652 Conversion Unit at Marston Moor we had to crew every one of Bill's circuits and bumps. There is a full page of these exercises in my log book. It is quite a contrast, isn't it? By then things were hotting up. We were getting more and more ready to begin operations.

We did six night time circuits and bumps exercises at Lichfield. On the 18th of November at eight o'clock, we went up in a Wellington piloted by Warrant Officer Webb. Bill would have been second dickie. We flew for one and a half hours. On the 22nd we did three flights. Flight Sergeant Lawrence was the pilot for the first one. Bill says the pilot was W/O Webb but my log says otherwise. The other pilot was there to instruct Bill and to 'screen' him. This means that he was giving Bill instruction about night takeoffs and landings as well as assessing Bill's ability to take off and land the plane.

Bill piloted the second flight that night but it is interesting that Flight Sergeant Lawrence flew the plane on the third exercise that night. There would have been something else that he wanted to show Bill.

We had two more night time circuits and landing exercises on the 24th and 26th of November and Bill piloted the Wellington both times. I did not have to navigate. How could I? There was nothing to navigate. We would take off, circle the airfield, land and do it again. It was pilot training. The rear gunner, bomb aimer wireless operator and navigator all went along for the ride.

Confiscated logs and charts

On every flight I was doing constantly doing my calculations, working on my charts and telling the pilot where to go. That was the object of cross-country. Every time we set out on a cross-country we had a flight plan which might entail one, two, three, four, five, six changes of course and changes of height. I was pretty proficient by this time. It was all training for bombing operations later where we were always trying to confuse the German radar operators and their night fighters and gunners. On Ops. we never flew a direct flight from base to the target. Instead we always flew doglegs and had frequent changes of course.

This was about the time when I had a brush with the navigation instructors. They were suspicious because my charts and logs were exceptionally neat and they thought I was doing them after we landed. On landing after one flight they confiscated my log and chart and took it away for perusal to satisfy themselves that I wasn't doctoring it when I got back on land. When you think about it, I was up in a plane that was being knocked all around the place by the wind and everything and it's shaking and I'm churning out neat handwritten things. With the plane bouncing around all over the place it was hard but that's the way I did it. I used pencils on my logs and charts and I always looked after them. I went into the second hand shops at Birmingham and I found those metal covers that they used to have for pencils and bought one for every pencil I had. My practice was to get a dozen full size pencils and sharpen them to a very fine point. I never used a pencil more than once. When it got to what I considered blunt I would discard it and get a new one out. That way I could use a new sharpened pencil and this was one of the reasons why I was able to do such neat work even in a plane that was rocking all around me, not like the planes of today. I was meticulous. You can see how neat it is from my flying log book and the log and chart of the Stuttgart raid which I still have. I was obsessed with neatness in those days. That's the sort of person I am.

Escape Exercises

Every now and then they laid on an "escape exercise" where we were transported by lorry out into the wilds of England at night time and dumped at some remote place from where we would have to find our way back to base. We weren't allowed to talk to any of the locals that we came across. Of course we bent the rules straight away. We always knew where we were and we headed for the nearest pub and spent the afternoon there. Then we'd get the local bus back and get the driver to dump us about a hundred metres short of the base and we'd wander in. Generally we treated it as a joke because it could never be the same as being shot down in Germany. You face that if and when it arrives.

I remember that on one of the escape exercises we did while we were at Lichfield, we spent the afternoon in the pub near Burton on Trent. We were drinking, talking to the locals and playing darts. Maybe they had a pool table too. Darts mainly, I think. When we left we got the local bus back to the station. We were naughty boys!

Bill's and Don's diaries

I did not know that Bill and Don were keeping diaries all the time they were away at war. It was a surprise a few years ago when I received a copy of Bill's in the post. His family had photocopied and bound it and sent copies to Bill's surviving crewmates. Don's 1944 diary came to light early in 2013 after I sent a draft of my book to Don's family as a Christmas present. Unfortunately his 1943 diary has gone astray. It would have been good to have that one because it would have jogged my memory a bit more about West Freugh and Lichfield. Both diaries give a lot of interesting insights into what was going on and how Bill and Don were both feeling at the time.

RAAF Plane Kills Spectators. Swansea, Tasmania, 1936

Stunting Over Town? Allegations at Swansea Inquest.
"Drome too small"

Hobart. Monday. Allegations that the Hawker Demon aeroplanes which visited Swansea for a demonstration flight on February 6 were performing aerobatics at a very low altitude over the township were made by residents who gave evidence at the resumed inquest at Swansea today on the bodies of Mrs Louisa Kate Cotton and Miss Jean Cotton, who were killed when one of the machines, in the charge of Pilot Officer E. V. Lansell, failed to rise clear of the spectators at the aerodrome.

Josiah Archibald Cotton, pastoralist, of Swansea, said there were about 80 or 90 persons present at the demonstration, and when the machines departed the first appeared to become airborne after a run of about 250 yards. It rose a few feet and remained at that height till about 50 yards from the spectators. Then it rose gradually. The second machine did likewise, but the third rose several feet, and then appeared to drop slightly, with the undercarriage about two or three feet from the ground. It remained at that height till the accident happened. Then it rose very sharply. From the sound of the engine he would say that it was functioning perfectly.

Christopher William Bush, boot-maker, said that the vibration created by one machine shook the building in which his premises were situated, and an almanac which was tacked on the window frame was dislodged.

Officer's Denials

Flight-Lieutenant Patrick George Heffernan said he had been seven years in the R.A.A.F., flying several different types of aircraft. He was in charge of the flight of the three Hawker Demons which visited Swansea. The three machines arrived in flight formation at a height of about 1500 feet. He gave the signal to break formation, and dived his machine in front of the Bay View Hotel, along the beach. At no stage was his altitude less than 100 feet. Witness denied that any of the three machines performed aerobatics or dived over the township. The closest his machine had been to the group of school children was about 200 yards. As he was taking off his machine was bumped into the air. He levelled it and flew parallel to the ground for several seconds. When he elevated the plane it was about 50 or 100 yards from the spectators. When he passed over them his altitude was about 30ft. He had no difficulty in passing over the crowd. He noticed that Lansell's machine did not become airborne as quickly as his had done.

Aerodrome Unsafe

The runway at the Swansea aerodrome, Flight-Lieutenant Heffernan continued, was considerably smaller than that used at Air Force landing grounds. He regarded it as unsafe for machines like the Hawker Demons.

The Coroner: Then why did you come here?

Witness: We were ordered here by headquarters.

The Coroner: Would you be acting against orders in flying low or diving over a town?

Witness: Orders state that a machine must not be flown over a populated area unless at such a height that it can glide to a point outside the area.

The Coroner: You came here to give a demonstration?

Witness: Yes.

The Coroner: Is not the aerodrome the proper place to perform aerobatics?

Witness: Our regulations state that aerobatics must not be performed over an aerodrome unless at a height of at least 6000ft. and a distance of three miles from the aerodrome. That would be useless from the viewpoint of a demonstration.

The Coroner: Because you were invited to give a demonstration you consider you were entitled to dive and zoom over the township at a low altitude?

Witness: No. It would not be done at a low altitude.

The inquest was adjourned to March 4.

The Courier Mail (Brisbane, Queensland). Tuesday 25 February 1936

Chapter 14: Bill Rabbitt's Crew

Except for the time we were attending lectures in our specialized fields, the crew did virtually everything together as a group. Don, Sandy, Harry and I were all sergeants. On the base we shared a hut and spent many hours in the sergeant's mess together.

Bill Rabbitt was an officer so he had his own quarters, serviced by a batwoman, and an officers' mess to go to. Off base we sometimes did our own thing but usually we all went out together. We drank, danced, partied, had fun and chased girls.

I did not keep a diary of my time at war and it is interesting to read Bill's diary about this period at Lichfield. It occurs to me that our lives at the OTU and afterwards were arranged to make us bond together as a team. It made sense because our lives were in each other's hands.

Within a fortnight of our arrival at Lichfield we started going off base together as a crew and getting up to mischief. Bill writes on the 13th of October 1943:

> "This evening took my crew in and we had a great time in Lichfield. We all had a few drinks. Met some decent Yanks. Lost them later. Struggled along to a dance. Talent available rather poor. Had a few more drinks. Met some WAAFs and they were beauties. Sandy, Basil and myself were the three lucky ones. Don and Harry then went somewhere else. Sandy walked into a bike and brought the unfortunate rider flat on his back. The fellow was pretty hostile but his anger was lost on us."

That was the first of many nights out together. In the three and a half months we were at Lichfield Bill's diary says that we went off base together at least eighteen times. We used to drink a lot at the local pubs. Then we would head off to a dance looking for girls. I remember going to a dance that was organized by the WAAFs.

I also remember that we headed straight for the pub at Lichfield when we narrowly escaped crashing into the Derby balloon barrage, and going to the pub again when we farewelled Mick McCarthy after Bill was unable to keep him in our crew as a mid-upper gunner.

It had always been touch and go for Mick staying with us because our five man crew was settled. Bill's plan was to keep Mick with us until we were all transferred to the HCU where he could grab the mid-upper spot. I remember that Mick came with us when we took leave in London. We had some photographs taken at a professional studio but we weren't happy with them because the photographer made us all look like angels.

The Lichfield Crew on Leave, London

The Lichfield crew with Mick McCarthy in London, 8 December 1943. (Left to right): Basil Spiller, Don McLean, Bill Rabbitt, Mick McCarthy, Harry Brabin, Sandy Concannon.

In his diary on the 4th of November Bill mentions that we all attended a 21st birthday party. He says that Harry and I "put on a good show". I cannot remember what we did but we might have had a few too many. We would either walk to Lichfield or ride bikes. There were many accidents on those bikes when we were heading home after a night on the beer.

Every now and again we would go on leave to Birmingham on a forty-eight hour pass which was equivalent to a long weekend. You could go wherever you liked for two nights as long as you were back at a certain time on the third day.

We used to go into Birmingham because that was the nearest big city. There was also an ice-skating rink there. We could all roller-skate so we found it easy to change over and we used to have a session of ice skating before we went to the pub. We always wound up at the pub!

On one occasion, on the 26th of November, I got tangled up with a shiela in the bar and she wangled me outside and her friends came outside as well – two blokes in civilians clothes. My crew was awake to this and they came out at the same time and it all fizzled out. All I knew was that I was heading outside with a young lady. I didn't know that she had mates and she had ulterior motives. They were going to rob me of my hard-earned money and leave me for dead. She and her friends just melted away when my crew appeared. In his diary Bill says:

> "Flew last night for 3 hours and everything was OK. Harry went into hospital today with flu. Don, Bas, Sandy and self went to Birmingham today. Saw a couple of shows, had a few beers and managed to prevent Bas from having his roll taken by "Sharpers". Wonderful bed at hotel."

On our way home from Birmingham the next day we stayed in Lichfield because flying was scrubbed at the base. So we went to the pictures and then to a dance.

Sometimes we would just go out to the pictures in Lichfield together. We saw movies such as *The Crystal Ball* and *Tales of Manhattan*. Afterwards we would go to the YMCA for supper. On the base there was always something to do for recreation. Sometimes we spent the evenings in the mess or the NAAFI – the Navy, Army Air Force Institute hut. Every base had one. It was open to all ranks. They didn't serve alcohol, only tea coffee and cakes. They might have sold packets of biscuits. They had entertainment and bands played there every night. The NAAFI was always packed with aircrew, maintenance staff, administration staff and WAAFs. I used to go down there quite a bit.

If we wanted to have a beer on the base we went to the mess. There were four messes – the officers' mess, the sergeants' mess, the WAAFs' mess and the other ranks' mess. For most of our first tour we would go to the sergeants' mess. Then we received our commissions and went to the officers' mess.

In the mess we had our meals in a separate eating area. There was a bar so we socialised and drank there. There was a nice billiard table and we could play table tennis and darts. There was also a lounge area with comfortable chairs and a sofa. The NAAFI and the messes were quite large because there were a lot of people on the base. Then there were camp concerts which we attended. They were a lot of fun.

Good mates

On the day that I was almost robbed in Birmingham, Harry was admitted to hospital with the flu. He was really sick. He was in there for eight days. We all went to visit him. On the 29th of November Bill wrote in his diary: "Harry still in hospital so we are still not flying." That says it all about building mateship in the crew. We were a crew and if one member could not fly then none of us flew. There were other wireless operators around but Harry was "our" wireless operator so we could not fly. Harry was then given seven days' leave to recuperate so we were all given seven days' leave and headed for London.

We played golf a couple of times at Richmond and had dinner in the clubhouse. We had a lot to drink at Codgers Bar and the Boomerang Club, ate steak and chips at Smokey Mick's Café and had fun on the tube going back to our digs at the Strand Imperial Hotel.

We went to the Prince of Wales theatre and saw a comedy play called *Strike a New Note* and to the Carlton Picture Palace where we watched the new movie *For Whom the Bell Tolls*. On the 11th of November we headed back to base a little worse for wear. We had had a great time. We were a team. We were five really good mates, and we'd live or die together.

Paddy Heffernan and the Command Bulls-eye

Near the end of their training, all crews had to do a "Command Bulls-eye" exercise which was a simulated air-raid on a big city like London. They were a good way to test the night time bombing skills of the inexperienced crews in the training units.

As far as we were concerned they were purely bombing and navigational exercises but the ground defences would also use them to test their searchlights and the set up of their anti-aircraft guns. When the CO was satisfied that a crew could do a Command Bulls-eye successfully they were judged ready for posting to a heavy conversion unit. My log book shows that our last flight at Lichfield, on the 12th of January 1944, was a night time Command Bulls-eye in a Wellington. Don and I got the plane to London, then Don did a photographic bombing run on a designated park or landmark. Green Park in London was one of our Command Bulls-eye "targets". Then we navigated back to base.

There was no problem with friendly fire when we were doing Command Bulls-eyes because the ground defences would know in advance that the exercise was going to happen. We were equipped with IFF (Identification Friend or Foe). In the nose of a Halifax there were twin dishes about as big as saucers. They were built into the perspex and emitted a radio signal that the ground defences picked up. All Allied aircraft were fitted with IFF. It was the navigator's job to turn it on, so immediately I entered the aircraft I switched it on and logged the time. It was standard procedure. The chances of us being fired at were pretty remote. Later, our first Command Bulls-eye at HCU was in broad daylight so our plane could be easily identified by the RAF roundels painted under each wing.

Paddy Heffernan was the very popular RAAF Group Captain in charge of Lichfield. He was a qualified pilot but he was considered too old for operations. He was probably in his late thirties or early forties but he loved to fly. He had a cushy job administering RAF Lichfield 27 OTU. Every now and then he would fly on a Command Bulls-eye.

On the night of the 6th/7th of November 1943, Paddy had a very attractive little WAAF section officer as a passenger. Her name was Karin Hughes. He smuggled her on board. It was against regulations but who was going to argue with him. He was the station CO. It ended in tragedy because on his way to London his plane was involved in a mid-air collision with a Halifax bomber from another training unit - 26 OTU. The news raced all around Lichfield the next day. Bill Rabbitt mentions it in his diary:

> "Heard this morning that "Grouper" had "bought" it - also Ian Stoeckel an SA (South Australian) boy. "Grouper" is the only one who got out of the collision alive so I heard a few minutes ago."

So Paddy Heffernan hadn't 'bought' it. He had managed to bail out. He was the only one that survived out of the two crews. The young woman was killed too. Two planes, two crews and the little WAAF bought it but he survived.

Eight and a half months later, I was in hospital at Ely, after I was seriously wounded during a raid on Forêt de Nieppe in France. Paddy Heffernan was a patient in the same hospital as me. He had a long recovery because he was still suffering from broken bones in his legs. His injuries must have been terrible. He came to see me. I told Bill and Don and they met him too.

Lichfield was virtually an Australian station so Paddy Heffernan's crew were Australians like all of us. They were very experienced. They were Pilot Officer Lorraine Quaite, the navigator, from Cairns, Queensland; Pilot Officer Jeffrey Parker, the observer, from Kensington Gardens, South Australia; Pilot Officer Colin Finch the wireless operator from Epping, New South Wales and Sergeant Alexander Anderson, a rear gunner, from Northam in Western Australia.

Two collisions in one night

As strange as it may seem, Paddy Heffernan's plane wasn't the only Wellington from our OTU to collide with another plane that night. You have to remember that at any time there were hundreds of aircraft buzzing around at night – heading off on bombing raids into Europe, coming back from operations, aircraft from OTUs going here and there and we did not have an air traffic control system like we have today. Then there was the weather to complicate things. The RAF at this stage of the war only bombed at night time so all aircrews had to be trained in night flying.

On the 6th of November 1943, No. 27 OTU Lichfield lost a second plane. It was Wellington X3637. It was on an evening cross-country doing navigational exercises. It took off at 1940 hours and about an hour and a half into the flight it collided with Short Stirling R9192 from 214 Squadron.

The Stirling pilot, Vern Scantleton, an Australian, saw the other plane and pulled back on his control column. His plane climbed but not fast enough and the tail of the Wellington smashed into the port side of the Stirling just behind the bomb aimer's position and the Wellington went corkscrewing towards the ground and crashed killing all the crew.

The Stirling had a big hole on the port side of the nose but all the crew were safe and they were able to fly back to base. The story of how they made it back is quite remarkable. You can read about it on the internet.

The Wellington had eight men on board – all Australians. Eight is a big number because crews at the OTU like ours usually flew with only five. The war records say that there were five "pupil" crew members and three "screened" crew members on board – three experienced men and five trainees. The screened bods would already have done a tour of duty with Bomber Command. A tour then was thirty bombing operations. After a tour you would be assigned roles as instructors. That's why there were eight. The trainees would have made a full crew on their own later. They were all there – pilot, navigator, wireless operator, bomb aimer and gunner - but it was not to be. The plane crashed into a farm near Little Walden in Essex and they are all buried at the Brookwood Military Cemetery in Surrey. It is very sad.

In his diary Bill mentions Ian Stoeckel. He was on the Wellington that collided with the Stirling. Ian was his middle name. He was named after his father Oswald and used his middle name instead. He was the "pupil" navigator in the crew. Bill mentions him because he was a South Australian too. He came from Glandore, an Adelaide suburb near the airport. He was just twenty years old. Bill might have struck him in training along the way. His diary entry sounds as though Bill thought Ian was on the plane with Paddy Heffernan. I thought there was only the one collision that night for a long time too.

Wellington and Stirling Collision, 6 November 1943

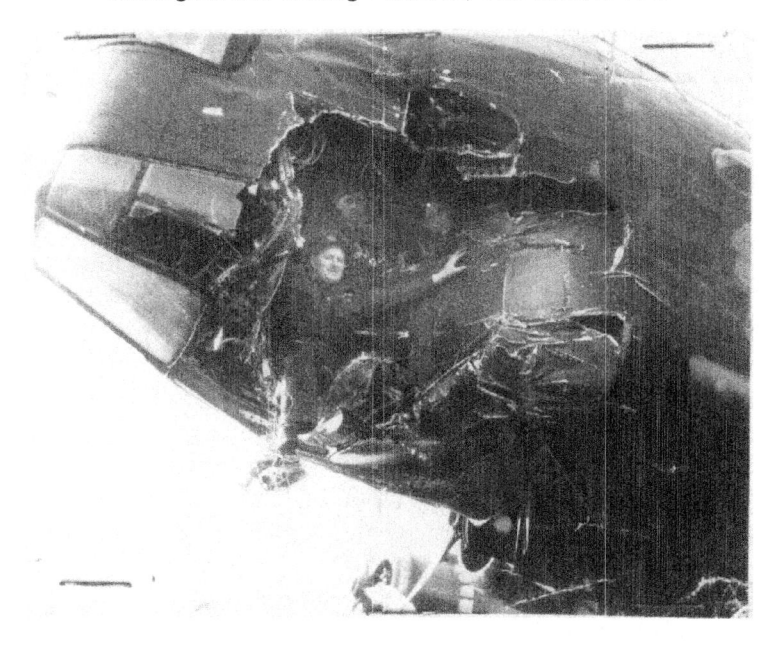

Three crew members sit in the damaged nose of Short Strling R9192 which collided with a Vickers Wellington X3637 from 27 OTU on the 6th November 1943.

WAAFs on board

We all used to take passengers up in the planes with us every now and then. We'd take the girls up! Yeah, we did! And the ground crew! We weren't allowed to but we did, just to impress the girls! They would have been able to twist Bill around their little fingers to get a flight.

Bill was a man for the girls all right and they all wanted to fly. We only did that on the squadron when we got our own plane because there was too much supervision on the OTUs. There was less on the squadron where it was all laissez-faire, with very relaxed discipline. As long as you were there to fly, you could do what you liked.

Bombing practice

In his diary Bill also describes our cross-country flight on the 7th, the day after Paddy Heffernan's collision:
"Did the same cross-country again today. Icing index very high. Rather a good day - good visibility. Dropped ten bombs

at Cannock. Ireland looks very nice from the air. Saw Dublin in the distance. Bas was navigating extra well today. Saw two very large convoys making for Liverpool. Visibility deteriorated towards end of trip. Landing three-pointer - very pleasant. Sandy came with us today. He has just finished in Gunnery Flight - very good show. Temperature down to four below today."

We flew over to Northern Ireland but first the flight plan took us over the Cannock Chase bombing range in Staffordshire. It was the bombing range attached to Litchfield OTU. Practice bombing was part of what we did. It was good training for Bill, Don and me. I had to navigate the plane to the target. Bill had to fly it there and hold it on the bombing run while Don was over the bomb site giving him instructions. We would take photos of the bombing and when we got back to Driffield they would be analysed for accuracy.

Nickelling Paris

When a crew finished their course at the OTU they had to do a "nickel" which was a dangerous practice bombing exercise, dropping propaganda leaflets, usually over occupied France. This was an initiation into flying over enemy territory.

During the "phoney war", the early days of the war before things became deadly, the RAF only did nickel raids on Germany. The powers that be were foolishly trying to convince the German population to turn back from their path to war.

Our last trip from Lichfield was a leaflet raid on Paris. It was the first time we had been over enemy territory. We did this trip on the 20th December 1943. Takeoff was late in the afternoon at 1615 hours and it lasted four hours fifteen minutes so we arrived back at base at about 2030. It was in the middle of winter and the days were short. We were getting shot at by flak so it was pretty eventful. Night fighters were also buzzing around. Bill described the nickel pretty fully in his diary. He is obviously very excited and it is one of the longest entries he made:

"Today is probably one of the greatest days of my life. Today marks my first active participation in Word War No. II. We had our first trip over enemy territory and nickelled Paris. We were told that we did an excellent job and heads here were very pleased. We arrived at position bang on time. Spent one hour over enemy territory and experienced concentrated "flak". The enemy gunners were pretty accurate and we felt the effects of two that went off underneath us. Operational height was 17,000 feet. We left here at 10,000 and made for Reading. From there we went to Selsey Bill (headland) and then across the Channel to France at 17,000 feet. Once inside France we could see a few lights. Then the flak commenced but we kept it on our starboard most of the time. All at once the ground below was a maze of lights all dotted around, spaced in no definite pattern, but as we tracked over them they would go out and reveal our course to any night fighter by visual methods. We nickelled okay and then set course to get out south of Le Havre and Honfleur which were reputed to be heavily defended. Two bursts of ack-ack shook us but we eventually got out south of track after one hour in enemy territory. On arrival back at the English coast the searchlights coned us for fifteen minutes. There was a raid on at the time and needless to say we cursed those searchlights a treat. Arrived back at base half a minute off ETA. At the interrogation they said we did a pretty good show and were good enough for the new instruments on the Lancaster. Father Commane gave us supper."

Going over continental Europe for the first time made me feel scared and apprehensive naturally. I can remember that trip well, especially the crew remarking – Bill and Sandy particularly – how poor the blackout was in France. They claimed that the lights would go out as we passed over them and that they were signalling our track to the German night-fighters.

I don't know if that's true or not. I wouldn't have seen any of the lights or flak because I was at my position inside the aircraft near Harry, Bbut Bill would have seen it all. We were getting shot at for the first time. There was flak bursting all around us. It was scary in that plane.

Flak bursting goes WOOF! When you are able to look out you see a puff of smoke where it exploded. I didn't feel the plane shaking more with the flak bursting all around it or any extra turbulence in the air that it was flying through. The plane was always vibrating and quivering. For me down there it was pretty much life as normal. I didn't see anything because I didn't look out. I was too engrossed in my work and I was flat out the whole time.

Bill's diary says that we got to Paris "dead on time" and we arrived back at base "half a minute off ETA" and in a way you could not ask more of a navigator. My memory about the trip is that I wasn't happy with my navigation. I felt that I was too apprehensive and I let it affect my judgement. But I did get everyone to Paris and back to base.

Handley Page Halifaxes

On the 19th of January 1944 we received our assessments. We were assessed as "above average". We were also told that we were being posted to a Halifax conversion unit which meant that we were going to be changed over "converted" from Wellingtons to Handley Page Halifaxes. Most crews at the OTU were hoping to be flying Lancasters.

Bill writes that we were all "terribly disgusted and disappointed". It was a pilot's thing about Lancasters being better than Halifaxes. Lancasters were the glamour plane at the time which explains why Bill was disappointed, but as far as I was concerned it was just a posting. By the time we started operations Bill had changed his mind completely and he was completely enamoured with Halifax Mk IIIs.

Chapter 15: Driffield

We left Lichfield on the 20th January and travelled to RAF Marston Moor where 1652 Heavy Conversion Unit was located. "Heavy" was the term used for four engine bombers. The HCU was equipped with Handley Page Halifaxes. Here we would do the "conversion" from old fashioned Wellingtons to operational Halifax Mk IIIs.

The next morning we found out that we were being transferred to the army station at Driffield to do a "battle" course until Marston Moor was ready for us. They had too many crews and were not prepared for another intake. We weren't the only crew affected. A number of crews had come with us from Lichfield.

This was when our mid-upper gunner from the RAF volunteer reserve joined us. His name was Charlie Hood. He was a young Englishman from Plymouth. Like us, he had been told to report to Marston Moor to be crewed up for training on heavy bombers. So now we were six. We left Marston Moor for RAF Driffield, where the army had set up a holding base for 4 Group aircrew and we resided there until there was room for us at Marston Moor.

RAF Driffield was in east Yorkshire about ten miles from the coast near Bridlington. Early in the war the Luftwaffe had bombed it heavily. The last squadron to use it before we arrived was 466 Squadron RAAF, an Australian squadron. They were relocated in December 1942 so that the runways could be rebuilt and they returned in June 1944 flying Halifaxes. During the time they were away, because all the facilities were still there, the British army moved in and set up a battle course and made it a training centre.

We arrived at Driffield on the 21st of January. It was only five months before "D-Day" and the army would have been flat out training for it. I don't know what the Army thought about aircrew being sent there to be trained in army techniques but they obviously went along with it. The army was probably helping out. I don't think the RAF or the Army took it seriously. There were forty-two days between when we left Lichfield and when we finally joined 1652 HCU at Marston Moor. During that time we were given twenty days leave and both times we applied they gave it to us that same day. We didn't take it very seriously either. We treated it more as a holiday and took it easy because we knew we were filling in time. Remember too that we were all sergeants, and probably flight sergeants by then, so we held rank on most of the army bods we had to deal with, which meant that they couldn't push us around like they did to their soldiers.

Assault course

On our first day we learnt about camouflage and watched a few army films in the morning. Then in the afternoon we went on a route march. But the next day we were right into it. Rifle drill in the morning was easy because we had all done it back home but in the afternoon we did the assault course and that was a different matter. We had rifles and helmets and jumped over ditches and ran about, climbing up and over barriers. We waded through a creek and a lake and we had to crawl through a hole full of water and come up on the other side about twenty feet away. Every one of us was tired and soaked to the bone and covered with mud. It was a real shock to the system for boys who had travelled in luxury through Canada in Pullman Coaches.

We did route marches and bayonet drills, threw hand grenades on the assault course and did night field exercises based on army techniques, crawling on our stomachs through mud and slush, carrying rifles and bayonets. One day they drove us twenty-five miles to RAF Elvington and made us do a bayonet charge on the airfield to test their defences. I can't remember ever doing drills on the Driffield parade ground in nice straight lines like you see soldiers doing on television. That would have been more our style!

Battledress

We wore battledress nearly all the time. It was a rich navy blue, airforce blue, Australian blue and the English battledress was a drab grey/blue. Our battledress comprised a set of trousers, just like suit trousers, with patch pockets on either side on the front of the thighs with buttons on the top. The jacket was a full blouse type with epaulettes and full sleeves with your sergeant stripes or whatever were your commissioned emblems of rank on them. They had patch pockets with flaps that buttoned down on both breasts and it had quite voluminous inside pockets. You could slip things into the inside pockets and nobody would know what you were carrying. The waist was drawn up by a strap that extended around the waist and it was drawn up by a belt buckle. When you tightened it up it ballooned up and you could carry a lot of stuff. That was our battledress.

We wore battledress on operations too. We wore normal shoes around the squadron and when we went out but on the plane we had flying boots. If you were not commissioned, on your head you wore just a forage cap. If you were commissioned you wore a cap with a little visor. We wore battledress all the time unless we were going to evening meals. We weren't allowed to wear it to the evening meal at the officers' or sergeants' mess. For that we had to dress in our dress uniform.

Food parcels

Every now and then crew members would get food parcels from their mothers or sisters, sweethearts or wives. They were usually manufactured back in Australia for the local department stores – McWhirters or Myer – and they were packed and sewn in calico. Food parcels from Australia were about a foot square and about seven inches deep and they were filled with things like fruit cake, tinned peaches, pears, cream, sardines, herrings and tomato sauce – all of the things that we didn't get in our rations in England. There was Nestles' full cream milk and cake in little tins. Family and friends would go to the local store, pay their money and give the name and address of the serviceman, and the store would do the rest. It was a service. The parcels would then have headed to England on boats like the Mormacsea. The common practice was to take the food parcels on leave and give them to the hosts in the Lady Ryder scheme but because I never got them I took nothing to Mrs Reid's place when I was on leave.

I never got a food parcel because I didn't have a mother or sisters to send them to me but Bill used to get them frequently from his mother. I was in regular correspondence with Betty and occasionally she would send me a fruitcake, purchased from a department store but I never got tins of peaches and cream or packets of biscuits from Bett. I used to send her air letters and Betty would send air letters to me. They were specially made from airmail weight paper and could be purchased from the local post office. We would write a reply to each letter every couple of months.

On escape exercises where they dropped us off and told us to find our own way home, they didn't give us rations or food packs so just to be on the safe side our crew smuggled the contents of their latest food parcels down their battledress. They would be loaded up with tins of sardines and sliced peaches or pears, and full cream milk and fruit cake. Then we had something to use to bribe the people at the local fire brigade or police station into giving us a cup of tea in the early hours of the morning.

Pigs and horses

I remember that at Driffield we shot through on several training exercises. Bill's birthday was on the 26th, Australia Day, and instead of being the defenders in an outdoor exercise we spent the day in the pub.

Another time we were dropped fifteen miles from Driffield and told to make our own way back and evade the sentries who would be waiting for us. We immediately headed into Bridlington and had a good day at the pictures, the Spa and playing billiards. We got back late and evaded the guards. They had probably given up and gone to bed. On a third exercise we were dropped off at a little hamlet called Market Weighton and told to stop another lot from getting through. It was so cold that we gave up when we found a nearby army camp and arranged for bed and breakfast for the night. These three escape exercises were not much better than the one we did at Lichfield which was a joke but on the night of the $2^{nd}/3^{rd}$ of February we went out on an escape exercise that wasn't a joke.

It was in winter and it was bitterly cold. That evening, they loaded us into a truck and drove out onto the Yorkshire Moors. At about one o'clock in the morning they dumped us fifty miles away in the middle of nowhere and told us to get back to base somehow. We weren't to contact any civilians. We must have been dropped off from the lorry somewhere near a village called Sleights. We then headed west through Grosmont and Egton before we turned south towards Pickering and Malton and Wharram le Street. The weather was really bad. By the time we were dropped off and worked out what we were doing, it would have gone 2 am. It was snowing and raining and the wind was bitterly cold. We weren't equipped for weather like that. Off we tramped along a country road and eventually came to a farmhouse where we found a barn filled with pigs. We kicked out the pigs and lay down where they had been sleeping and tried to get warm. The pigs weren't happy about it either. It was bitterly cold and we couldn't sleep. In the end we left the barn to the pigs and tramped on for three or four hours. Next we found a horse stable and had a rest for about an hour or so in a stall and then moved on again. We had to keep walking to stay warm.

At dawn we found ourselves on the outskirts of a little town called Old Malton. We walked into the town and it had barely started to stir. Bt then we had walked nearly thirty miles and there were still twenty miles to go. We were so hungry and cold. We had to have something to eat and get warm. The first thing we did was check ourselves into a café and order bacon and eggs with some money we had hidden on us. We talked to the locals even though we were forbidden to. Then we waited for the local bus which took us through Wharram le Street to Driffield. We walked to the station and checked in. We just wanted it to end. That was what we thought of escape exercises. We were all dog tired and had an early night. The next day Bill wrote in his diary: "Pretty tired today so bludged all day. Crew also feel a bit done up." We were knackered. Nobody told us the airforce would be like that!

Leaving Driffield

On the 21st of February our posting to Marston Moor came through. We were to report there on the 4th of March. Bill applied for leave straight away. He always liked going on leave and he was always very quick to put in for it. As captain of the crew it was always his prerogative. They gave us twelve days effective immediately which took us up to when we had to report to Marston Moor. We hurried to get packed and go, knowing we wouldn't be going back to Driffield. Technically we were still posted there but effectively our time in the army ended that day.

It had probably finished well before that. We had taken eight days leave on the 7th of February and when we returned we didn't do any more army training at all. Bill's diary that week says that we attended a night vision lecture and that was it. For the rest of the time there was nothing else on. Our time at Driffield can be summarised like this: seven days were full on. There were four days when we had either a morning or afternoon session. There were twenty days leave and the rest was a bludge. It was demanding at the start but it wound down as time went on. At Marston Moor things got very busy!

RAF Marston Moor

RAF Marston Moor was situated at Tockwith, thirteen kilometres west of York. It was the home of No. 1652 Heavy Conversion Unit (HCU) where crews completed heavy bomber training before beginning bombing operations over Europe. After opening in November 1941, it became one of the four 41 Base airfields operated by Bomber Command's 4 Group as training centres near York. The other three airfields were RAF Rufforth, home of No. 1663 HCU, RAF Riccall, home of No. 1658 HCU and nearby RAF Acaster Malbis which had only a minor training role.

The HCU's were the final stage before postings to operational squadrons. Trainee airmen, like Basil Spiller, had previously "crewed up" into five man crews at an OTU, and trained on two engine bombers, usually Vickers Wellingtons. Prior to that each man had undergone specialist training in his "trade" - pilot, flight engineer, bomb aimer, navigator, wireless operator and gunner, at schools in Britain, or overseas as part of the British Empire Training Scheme. Thus aircrew training was a progression. Crews were put through an exhaustive series of flying exercises to familiarise them with the four engine bombers they would be flying on operational tours. Luckily, as Basil Spiller's training on ex-operational Handley Page Halifax Mark II's drew to a close, 4 Group was being re-equipped with the excellent Handley Page Halifax Mark III.

RAF Marston Moor's layout was typical of Bomber Command airfields. It had three runways which formed a "triangle", enabling aircraft to take off and land from six different directions. The main runway was over one mile long and ran southwest to north east. Fearing attack by enemy aircraft, airfields were naturally well dispersed.

There were four large hangers for aircraft maintenance and thirty-six dispersal sites, "pans", spread around the perimeter, where planes were parked, fuelled and maintained by ground crews. The bomb store was situated on farmland well away from the main airfield.

Bill Rabbitt's Crew at Marston Moor, March 1944

"Bill Rabbitt's Crew" soon after their arrival at Marston Moor. Left to right: Basil Spiller, Harry Brabin, Sandy Concannon, Charlie Hood, Don McLean. Absent: Bill Rabbitt took this photograph and John Allen had not yet joined the crew.

Running the airfield was a big operation. At any time there were over two thousand RAF personnel living and working there in a self contained community, with its own operations centre, sleeping quarters, shower blocks and latrines, separate messes for WAAFs, officers, sergeants and ground crew, NAAFI hut and medical centre. In the above chapter, Basil Spiller and his pilot, Bill Rabbitt, are far from complimentary about the facilities they encountered.

Basil complains that he had to trudge through mud for "a mile between (his) sleeping quarters and (his) sergeants' mess" and says that it was "a totally bad place to get posted to". Bill describes the facilities as "piss poor". Nevertheless the long distances between living quarters, amenity blocks and communal and operational areas was a deliberate part of RAF airfield design.

RAF Marston Moor was closed when war ended in 1945 and although much of the site has since been converted into an industrial estate, the runways and most of the original buildings have been preserved.

Bill Rabbitt's Crew at Marston Moor, March 1944

"Bill Rabbitt's Crew" soon after their arrival at Marston Moor. Left to right: Basil Spiller, Harry Brabin, Bill Rabbitt, Sandy Concannon, Charlie Hood. Absent: Don McLean took this photograph and John Allen had not yet joined the crew.

Chapter 16: Marston Moor

Bill met up with me at York on the 3rd of March and we "had a few" in Betty's Bar. We stayed at a hotel overnight and the next morning reported to RAF Marston Moor. The CO was Group Captain Leonard Cheshire. He was a real war hero. He became a Master Bomber when he left Marston Moor and resumed bombing operations.

When we arrived, John Allen, a flight engineer from Bristol, was assigned to our crew and moved into the hut with us. John came from Bristol. He entered the Royal Air Force as a sixteen year old apprentice engineer. He trained on aircraft motors but when Bomber Command moved into four-engine bombers, they needed flight engineers to look after the motors, so he re-mustered as aircrew.

We were lucky to have John allocated to our crew as a flight engineer. He was very good. He knew as much about our engines as the ground crew and could talk to them about everything. This finalised the crew for our Tour of Duty which was going to be thirty-five bombing operations over Germany and occupied Europe. Our crew had two Englishmen and five Australians.

John and Charlie Hood were immediately part of the fold - Charlie, when he came with us to Driffield and John as soon as we arrived at Marston Moor. John fitted into the crew from the moment he appeared except that he would often go home to Bristol when we were granted leave. John was awarded a commission when we were and later a DFC at the same time as us too.

Charlie went home to Plymouth. He was in everything at the start too. He had a different personality and was more of a remote type of character. He gradually did less and less with the rest of us. He didn't like the dancing, going to the pub and chasing girls like the rest of us did.

Just after our arrival we went for a walk in the country and took some photographs on a fence and a bridge but John is not in them. He may not have joined the crew until a few days later. We were having a look around and probably getting to know one another a bit better too. Bill took the first one so he is not in the photograph. I'm on the left, then there's Harry, Sandy, Charlie and Don. In the second photo Bill has moved into the middle while Don took the photo. We look so young. Our average age was just twenty.

Marston Moor was a very dispersed aerodrome. It was a mile between our sleeping quarters and our sergeants' mess. It was very muddy and a totally bad place to get posted to. Our billets were Nissan huts with two non-commissioned crews to a hut. It was the same on the squadron later. They were pretty standard. A Nissan hut was made out of corrugated iron. There were five or six beds on both sides. In the middle of the hut was a pot-belly stove and it and the beds were the only furniture. We hung our clothes on pegs attached to the walls. Our crew occupied the beds on one side and another crew was lined up on the other side. Bill was an officer so he had his own quarters.

If you wanted to have a leak or do a number-two there were latrines nearby. There'd be a cluster of these huts, maybe a dozen of them in the same area and there would be a latrine attached to that cluster. The ablution hut with hot and cold water was a mile away near the sergeants' mess. If you wanted to have a shower you had a long trek down the road.

Bill had much better accommodation than us but he was not impressed with it and wrote in his diary:

> "Left some snaps to be developed before going out to camp. Some mail for me but mainly papers which were very welcome. I am in Silo 6. The facilities are P.P. (Piss Poor) but the meals are excellent and the mess very genial. The camp is pretty well dispersed, but the bike will be pretty handy."

Merv Simpson

While I was at Marston Moor, I learned about the death of my best friend, Mervyn Simpson. It was very sad. I found out about his death on the grapevine. When he died he was still one month shy of his twentieth birthday.

Merv was a trainee wireless operator when it happened. At 2017 hours on the 22nd of February 1944, he was in an Avro Anson that took off from RAF Dumfries, in south-west Scotland, on a night time practice bombing exercise. There was a staff wireless operator on board so Merv would have been under instruction.

Apparently visibility was poor so they called the exercise off. When they were heading back to base they got caught in a severe downdraft and their Anson crashed into the summit of a mountain called Cairnsmore of Fleet, about fifty kilometres west of Dumfries. The pilot and navigator were injured and Merv and two others were killed. Merv is buried in the Troqueer New Burial Ground, at Dumfries.

I knew his mother, Heather, really well too. She and Merv moved from Darwin, in the Northern Territory, when Merv's father died. They lived at Redhill, a suburb of Brisbane. Merv and I worked at Burns Philp together. I played tennis with him every weekend. My father had a romance with his mother. They met through Merv and me.

Flying exercises, cross countries and circuits and bumps

While we were waiting for our first flight we were going to lectures, instruction in our specialized areas and doing drills. I was being introduced to H2S and the API and continuing to work with GEE.

My log says that our first flight with our full crew of seven was on the 19th of March. This was a familiarization flight that lasted an hour. Then we began a series of twenty daytime flying exercises that went until the 20th of April.

The first flying we did was the usual circuits and bumps so that Bill could become acclimatized to our new plane. The last aircraft he had flown was a Wellington with two engines and he was converting to a Halifax with four so naturally he had to get used to it. That was what circuits and bumps were all about. Although the pilot was the only one in training, the full crew had to assume their positions in the aircraft, so we lived through all of Bill's takeoff and landing exercises. There is a whole page full of them in my log. We would take off and land, do a circuit and return with a bumpy landing and do it again and again. You can see from the times of each flight that most of them were short flights, twenty-five minutes, fifty-five minutes, thirty-five minutes, fifteen minutes. But the last two were long ones – three hours forty-five and five hours twenty. They were cross-country exercises to test my navigational ability.

There were twenty-one different flying exercises. Deliberately stalling an engine would have been one for John to be involved in and practice bombing was one for Don. Sandy and Charlie did air firing and there were navigational exercises using GEE. When I learned something new about GEE in the navigators' section, I practised it in the plane. I remember taking local GEE fixes and another time I was taking GEE fixes while Bill did a steep climb. On another exercise we shut down two engines and flew only on two. We had to cut out two motors to convince ourselves that a Halifax would fly even if we lost half of our motors. It was pretty hairy! Bill wasn't alone when we did this. He had a "second dickie" training pilot alongside him. We could hear the instructions from the bloke who was examining Bill over the intercom. The plane flew differently with two motors. It was sluggish and Bill would have been struggling to control it.

On one exercise, or maybe it was the same one, Bill and the training pilot took us right up to twenty thousand feet and put us in a deliberate stall. When you stall an aircraft, you cut the throttles back until she just hangs in the air because it has no more lift. The engines are throttled back 'til they can't withstand the pull of gravity and the nose comes down and you go into a screaming dive. They did it deliberately because various aircraft behave differently in a stall and the pilot has to know what his plane is likely to do. The instructing pilot wanted to show Bill how a Halifax behaved and what to do to get out of it.

The crew had no idea about it until it happened. Bill and the other chap must have planned it beforehand. We were twitchy because the aircraft was just hanging in the air and then we felt the nose come down and the Halifax started to dive. As soon as Bill increased the throttle speed the engines picked up revs and we got back to normal flying conditions and they pulled it out straight and level. Bill could fly all right! That's why we were so high - to allow room for us to go into a dive without diving into the ground. That was the only time we did a four engine stall. It was pretty scary!

At twenty thousand feet it was often very quiet and very still, depending on the weather I suppose. It was okay. I got used to it. At twenty thousand feet we were flying on oxygen. Harry Brabin, in his book, talks about Sandy getting blood in his oxygen mask from a nose bleed which he occasionally suffered from. We finally began night flying exercises on the 21st of April, starting with three sessions of circuits and bumps before we did a longer night flying exercise.

H2S

At Marston Moor we were introduced to H2S, sometimes referred to as "Y", and from then on our cross-countries were often just navigational exercises in its operation. H2S was a very valuable navigational aid for night flying or when the weather was bad. On a little round screen there were radar images like a ground map of the cities and coastlines and estuaries of the countryside we were flying over. If you look at a side on photograph of a Halifax you can see a "radome", the dome shaped structure under the fuselage behind the bomb bays. Inside was an antenna that sent back 360° radar signals to the H2S receiver in my nav position. The signals would bounce off the roofs of cities and different terrain. They didn't bounce back from water so you would be able to see the coastline clearly, just like a map. The reflection from cities and towns was a highly illuminated round circle of light, the larger the city, the broader the signal, the larger the circle. We had to become efficient in its operation and be confident that we could read it because we would be using it right through operations. Because the Germans blocked GEE over Europe it left navigators with only H2S. The Germans could home in on H2S signals but they could not block it because it was a self-contained system.

The centre of the Planned Position Indicator (PPI) tube, the H2S screen, was the aircraft's position. H2S worked in the following way: Imagine a PPI tube about nine inches in diameter. On the front of the screen is a moveable circular dial, just like those old fashioned radiograms we used to have. It was calibrated to 360°. As you rotated the dial, a line on the face, called a lubber line, moved with it. You placed the lubber line over the city you wanted to take a bearing from. Then you could read the bearing from the dial. The distance to the city was the next thing. There was a knurled knob on the set which you turned. A circle of light appeared on the screen. It increased in size as the knob was turned. When the line of the circle was over the city you could read off the distance from a scale in nautical miles. You had to map read correctly of course so that you didn't select the wrong city. That was most important. Coastlines and water provided a sharp contrast. As well, the Air Position Indicator and the last fix you took were always there to guide you. The more I used it, the more experienced and proficient I became. Coastlines and islands stood out brightly against the black water, so did the line of larger rivers but sometimes you had to rely on your other instruments and your experience to identify the towns that appeared in the circle of light on the PPI tube.

My first introduction to H2S was on the "H2S trainer" which was set up in a room down in the Nav section. It was highly secret. All the navigators trained on it. Don McLean used to come down and use the H2S trainer with me. Because of the navigation training he had done in the past, he was happy to do it, but it was rare to have such a multi-skilled crew member. The bomb-aimer on our second tour couldn't do any navigation.

More clapped out ex-operational aircraft

The Halifaxes that we flew at Marston Moor were clapped out ex-operational aircraft, the same situation as at Lichfield, because at any one time there was a serious shortage of serviceable planes. The HCU Halifaxes had old Merlin inline motors which had all done operational tours. When we were there the decision had already been made for the Halifax Mk 2 to be phased out of operations. 4 Group, of which we were part, and the Canadian 6 Group were converting to Halifax Mark III's.

Things were different. Charlie Hood was in his mid-upper gun turret and John Allen was in the flight engineer's position behind Bill, with a bank of instruments to keep the engines running. Don was still in the nose of the plane to do his bomb aiming. In Wellingtons, Harry and I used to sit behind the main spar, in the bowels of the plane, miles away from anyone else. We were stuck back there and if we turned our lamps off we were in the dark. We never got to see what was going on outside, even in training. It wasn't a very good place to be. In Halifaxes, Harry and I had moved to a much better position in the nose near Don. We had little windows in the walls of the fuselage and an excellent view through the perspex nose of the plane. On a good day, from my position, I could see for a hundred miles in front of me. Having Don so close was very beneficial for us because he could assist me with my navigation. The pilot and the engineer were just above us.

Then there was the Handley Page Halifax Mark II itself, a bigger, more powerful aircraft. Obviously, the Halifax was a bigger plane and with its four motors to the Wellington's two it had more power and speed but the Halifax was roomier and more comfortable as well. The Mark II Halifaxes at Marston Moor had a gun turret in the nose but the Mark III's that we flew on the squadron had done away with the front turret altogether. They were considered redundant because it was rare for planes to be attacked from front on. The closing speed of the two aircraft was too fast.

The elsan horse collar

Whenever we had the chance we left the base and headed off to a pub for a few beers and a game of snooker or if there was a dance on we'd go there hoping to meet a girl. From Marston Moor it was only ten miles to York so we'd go there if we had a few hours to fill in. Leeds was about twenty miles south. It was a big city so there were more pubs and clubs and entertainments, and good accommodation like the Griffin and Victoria Hotels where we liked to stay. When we had a forty-eight hour pass we'd head for Leeds. As time went on we were well known in the bars of both places. At the Victoria we had two favourite maids who always looked after us really well.

On the 17th of April 1944, our whole crew headed off together on a forty-eight hour pass to Leeds. Charlie Hood came with us which was good. He was like an innocent country boy lost in a big city. He was a raw kid. We were all young but Charlie somehow seemed a lot younger than us. We checked into the Victoria and then headed off for a session at a pub called the Prince Edward. Charlie was not a good drinker and got pretty blind after a few drinks. Later in the night we discovered that he was missing so we set out to search for him. We found him down in the Elsan - that's what we called the toilet on a plane. He was kneeling over the toilet bowl and the toilet seat had fallen back down over his head. It looked like he was wearing a horse's collar. Charlie was worried because he had lost his plate with one or two false teeth on it. Someone asked if he had searched in the toilet bowl. With that Charlie started fishing around in it and triumphantly held the missing denture up. He walked over to the wash basin, rinsed it off for a few seconds and put it back in his mouth. Our eyes just about popped out of our heads.

Later he went missing again and off we went to look for him again. He wasn't in the pub so we spread out and found him in a Salvation Army hostel. They had found an airman outside asleep and put him to bed. We told them to hang on to him and we'd get him in the morning but Charlie somehow made it back to the hotel. In his diary Don McLean wrote that when we went to the pub the next day, Charlie was too frightened to touch anything stronger than water. Charlie never went out with us again. We may have been too loud and rowdy for him but perhaps he just didn't like doing the things that we did.

Crash landing

On the 28th of April 1944, we were on an H2S cross-country exercise – Exercise 21 in my flying log – which was to take us from base to London before returning to base via Reading and Sheffield. It was the same route as the day before. In his diary, Don Mclean says that we were not going too well on the H2S. Just as we reached Reading things started to go wrong. We lost our port inner motor!

It went to full revs and locked there. We were petrified when it happened. The aircraft went into a screaming dive with the motor roaring its guts out, so much so that we couldn't hear Bill tell us on the intercom to bail out. We didn't need to be told! With great difficulty, I stood up and my seat collapsed against the fuselage. I managed to open up the Halifax's nose escape hatch which was immediately under the seat. Don and I clipped on our parachutes and we were ready to jump. Then I realized that my ripcord was on the wrong side. In my haste I had put it on upside down. I was panic-stricken. That would have been the first time I had jumped with a parachute and it was going to be in a Halifax that was out of control in a steep dive. When something goes wrong in the air all you want to do is get out and we were going! Luckily, before we could bail out Bill had the aircraft under control.

We settled down and we were flying straight and level even though we were flying on only three engines! John Allen, our flight engineer, had cut the fuel to the malfunctioning engine and it stopped but he and Bill couldn't control the wind-milling of the propeller. When you feather a propeller, instead of being at an angle to the airflow, the blades are supposed to turn and lock parallel to the slipstream to decrease the drag on the aircraft. If you fail to lock the blades into the correct position the propeller is no longer making any forward thrust and it continues to wind-mill which increases the drag on the aircraft and can cause it to stall. It was clear that we had to do an emergency landing, so Don moved from the navigational section to the second pilot seat to assist Bill with the landing. So there we were under control and flying along on three motors with one wind-milling propeller. Suddenly the same thing happened to the starboard inner motor! It went to full revs and locked there!

Bill was prepared for it this time. John quickly cut its fuel. Luckily for us the two outer motors continued to operate normally but both inner engines kept wind-milling with the propeller blades refusing to lock into position. This increased our drag so much that we were unable to maintain our height and we were in a slow glide downhill. We had to get down somewhere otherwise we were going to crash. Luckily we recognized the country below us. We knew it so well! It was a relief! We were very close to Lichfield which we had flown in and out of many times before.

When we lost power from the inner engines we also lost most of our contact with the ground because the engines powered my GEE box and Harry's wireless. Luckily, Bill's radio was independent of Harry's and he was able to contact ground control at Lichfield and tell them that we were in trouble and they gave us permission to land. By then we were at a thousand feet and going down rapidly.

Bill deliberately dipped his wing to decrease lift, trying to line up with the runway and he side-slipped in like that from a thousand feet with Bill fighting to keep control. In his diary Don McLean, who was sitting in the co-pilot's seat next to Bill, says that Bill "turned to line up with the runway" and "the plane just dived for the deck". Before we hit the ground Bill was skilful enough to right the aircraft and do a perfect three-point landing. But we were still doing 180 miles an hour, probably double the normal landing speed, and we were already halfway down the runway when we landed because Bill and Don had no control over the aircraft when it side-slipped in like that. By then all of us except Bill and Don were in crash positions with our feet behind the main spar, leaning back with our hands behind our heads and bracing ourselves for anything that might happen. Bill realized straight away that he was going too fast and he knew there was a canal at the end of the runway, so he pulled the wheels up. If he hadn't done that we would have careered into the canal and been killed. We shot off the runway and went on our belly through the grass and whatever else was growing on the side of the landing strip, bumping along as if we were on a corrugated road. The escape hatch near us was just forward of the mid-upper turret. It had a permanent ladder and I did a foolish thing then. I moved from my crash position and I climbed up the ladder, opened the escape hatch and looked out. There we were, going through everything, mowing down small trees with the ambulance and fire truck racing along beside us. Our petrol tanks had been pierced and we were leaving a trail of petrol along our pathway over the grass. I should have waited 'til the aircraft came to a halt. I wasn't trying to get out. I just wanted to see what was going on. I was curious because we were bumping around all over the place and being thrown all around the floor because of the uneven ground that we were tearing over. We didn't have seatbelts like in a plane or a car today.

Eventually the plane ground to a halt. All the bomb bays were torn out and the fuselage was full of twigs and soil and whatever. We'd lost the bottom out of the plane! As luck would have it, when we went off the runway no sparks flew up to ignite the petrol in the track behind us. Five of us, me, John, Charlie, Sandy and Harry, climbed up the ladder and pissed off as fast as we could go. After about thirty yards we all stopped and thought, "What about Bill and Don?" They were still in the cockpit of the plane. We started to run back towards the plane when we saw the canopy open up. They climbed out and ran back along the fuselage and jumped over the rear turret and joined us.

There were a lot people talking about the incident at Lichfield but we were too preoccupied with our own miseries to be concerned about it. Six of us were sergeants at that time so we headed for the sergeants' mess. I think Bill came with us even though he was an officer. We all needed a drink! It was just about lunchtime. I can remember that we all got the shakes when we tried to eat some soup. Our hands were shaking like leaves. Delayed reaction! In Harry Brabin's memoir, his account of the crash mentions that later when we were in the sergeants' mess we were laughing about some funny things we said to the rescue team. Harry remembered that when we were on top of the plane trying to get away before it exploded, I yelled out to the rescue team, "Is there a dance on here tonight?" It was wishful thinking. We were all looking forward to a dance in the sergeants' mess at Marston Moor that night but it was very clear to us that we were going to miss it. It's a good story but I don't know if it was really me who said it.

Bill rang through to base at Marston Moor and told them that we had pranged, and they sent a crew down to Lichfield immediately. We were expecting to spend the night there but they packed us off back to base on a train. Meanwhile Bill was ferried back in an Airspeed Oxford, a small training plane. They would have been anxious to talk to him because he was an officer and captain of the aircraft when it crashed.

We all survived. We were lucky. It was pretty hairy! We all owed our lives to Bill. The authorities thought he had done an exceptional job. In November, at the end of our first operational tour Bill received a "Green Endorsement" in his log book. They were not given lightly by the RAF. It was the highest commendation for the "avoidance of damage or loss of aircraft and crew by exceptional flying skill". The way he handled this crash landing would have gone on his record and been a big part of the recommendation. Bill describes the landing and aftermath in his diary:

".... Arrived at Lichfield at 1,500 ft and attempted a landing. The kite once more became nearly uncontrollable and caused me to land half-way down a short runway. The brakes could not stop the kite so to prevent us being killed in the Trent River, I ripped up the undercarriage and made a belly landing. Everybody by this time was in their crash-landing positions and she hit and the crash commenced. Don (who stuck by me at the front to help) and myself hung on for grim death. Eventually she stopped and everybody was out of that plane in terrific time. Bang on! So that is my first aircraft accident or major one. The plane is a complete wipe-off and £70,000 is lost to the Air Force. Good show. The preliminary investigation has so far shown maintenance trouble and I do not expect to have any trouble from my part in it, as the heads seem to think we were all fortunate to be alive. As it is, not one member of the crew received a scratch, so I think it was a fair effort, although I would have liked to have brought off a wizard show...."

They pulled the engines apart during a full investigation into the crash and found that a vital part of the Constant Speed Unit in both inner engines had been left on the workbench by the mechanic who had just completed the five hundred hour inspection of the plane. An inspection is like taking your car down for a twenty thousand kilometre service but the difference is that they pulled aircraft engines right down and rebuilt them. The mechanic was court martialled, but that was no consolation to us. We could have been killed.

The Willis Cup

We only did two more cross countries after that. The next day they sent us up on the same trip. You know the old story about falling off a horse. You get straight back and try again. That's what they did to us. If you look at my log book it says: "Forced landing! Pranged!" That was on the 28th of April, and on the 29th they sent us up on Exercise 21 again, the identical exercise, another cross-country that lasted five and three quarter hours. In his diary Don McLean described this flight as a "wizard trip" and remarked that we "had the set sewn up", by which he meant that he and I had mastered the use of H2S.

Our final flight at Marston Moor was a cross-country on the 30th using H2S. We did the same exercise again, except this was a night-time flight. It was a progression. An operational length training exercise successfully completed first during the day and then again at night. Being able to complete such an exercise at night to the satisfaction of our instructors was most important. Bomber Command operations at this stage of the war were all done at night and we showed that we were ready to be moved to a bomber squadron. Don's diary entry for this flight says:

> "We did a night cross-country with H2S and it was 'bang on'. We clung to track all the way – used Gee on the climb and we then got cracking on Y. Bas did a log and a half and we should get a good ass. for the trip."

Don was obviously very excited when he wrote this. We had used H2S to make enough accurate fixes to fill up one and a half flight logs. When we returned to base I handed them in to be examined as usual and they were considered good enough to be entered in the Willis Cup, a trophy awarded each year in 4 Group for the best navigational exercise. We didn't win the cup but it was good to know that our logs were considered to be up to that quality. We were a good navigational team, Don and I.

On the 2nd of May we received our clearances and were posted to No. 102 Squadron near the Yorkshire village of Pocklington. It had a reputation as a first class squadron.

RAF No. 102 Squadron, 1917 – 1939

No. 102 Squadron of the Royal Air Corps was formed at Hingham in Norfolk on the 17th of August 1917, late in the First World War. It relocated to St. Andre-aux-Bois in the war zone in France on the 24th of September.

The squadron flew the ungainly, two-man, Royal Aircraft Factory FE2b bomber as a night bomber until November 1918 when the war ended. The squadron flew with distinction during these fourteen months, attacking German airfields, ammunition dumps, railway stations, trenches and troop and supply trains, flying 295 operations and dropping over 823,000 pounds of bombs. This weight may seem large but, in comparison, Basil Spiller's 102 Squadron Halifaxes, fully bombed up, could drop over 300,000 pounds of bombs in one night. During the eighteen months the squadron remained in France it relocated ten times. In March 1919, its aircraft were broken up and burned at Cernay and 102 Squadron returned to England and was stationed at Lympne, in Kent, before being disbanded in July.

After the rise to power of Adolf Hitler in the 1930's, Germany's army, navy and airforce were rebuilt. Alarmed at the rise of Nazi militarism, Britain also began to rebuild its armed forces. The prospect of war was on everyone's lips. The Luftwaffe grew rapidly, becoming the most formidable airforce in the world. As part of RAF expansion and modernisation, 102 Squadron was reformed at Worthy Down, Hampshire, on the 1st of October 1935, flying four-man, Handley Page Heyfords. The squadron moved three times before the Second World War began, relocating to Finningley in 1936, Honington in 1937, and finally on the 11th of July 1938 it moved to Driffield and was based there when the war started. Three months after the Driffield move, the squadron began converting from the slow and vulnerable Heyfords to more advanced Armstrong Whitworth Whitley bombers, which carried a crew of five - pilot, co-pilot, wireless operator/navigator, nose-gunner/bombardier and rear-gunner. In the four years between its reformation and the outbreak of the war, the squadron lost six Heyfords and two Whitleys on training exercises.

As war approached, the pace of training increased and dummy nocturnal raids, referred to as Command Bulls-eyes, were undertaken. When war was declared, 4 Group squadrons, including 102 Squadron, were the first to begin RAF operations.

The Royal Aircraft Factory FE2b

With a maximum speed of 91 miles per hour and low service ceiling, the FE2b was considered vastly inferior to the German fighter planes of 1916 during daytime operations, but they found a niche as light bombers on night raids until the end of the war.

A Royal Aircraft Factory FE2b over northern France First World War.

The Fe2B was armed with two mounted 7.7mm Lewis guns, one facing forward and the second firing rearward, both operated from the observer's position in front of the pilot. A typical bomb load was four 25 pounders beneath each wing and one 230 pounder racked behind the undercarriage. The Fe2b was a potent WW1, night time, war machine.

The Armstrong Whitworth Whitley

The Armstrong Whitworth Whitley was a major improvement on the Handley Page Heyfords they replaced at 102 Squadron in October 1938. With a speed of 230 miles per hour, they were 88 mph faster than the Heyford, their range was 1650 miles compared to the Heyford's 920 miles and bomb load was increased from 2,000 to 7,000 pounds. However, when the Second World War started, the Whitley was already obsolete and no match for German fighters such as the Me Bf109E, with their powerful cannons and speeds approaching 350 miles per hour.

No. 102 Squadron Armstrong Whitworth Whitley aircraft during a press open day at RAF Driffield in March 1940.

Whitleys were finally withdrawn from operational service in July 1942. In the photograph above, the aircraft in the foreground is Whitley, C-Charlie N1241. On the 19th of April 1940 it was shot down by flak during a raid on Fornebu airfield near Oslo. The Whitley in the background is A-Able N1385. It was shot down by flak when attacking Augsburg on the 17th of August 1940, and it crashed near Voralburg in Austria.

Part 4

First Tour of Duty
No. 102 (Ceylon) Squadron
RAF Pocklington

Handley Page Halifax Mark III

Chapter 17: Operation 1 - Orleans

Orleans: 128 aircraft - 108 Halifaxes, 12 Lancasters, 8 Mosquitos - of Nos 4 and 8 Groups. 1 Halifax lost. Most of the bombs fell on the passenger station and the railway-repair workshops. *Total effort for the night:* 1,023 sorties, 34 aircraft (3.3 per cent) lost.
The Bomber Command War Diaries, 22/23 May 1944.

No. 102 Squadron Pocklington was a Royal Air Force squadron but its aircrew came from all over the British Empire. There were a lot of Royal Air Force Volunteers, mainly English, as well as Canadians, Scots, New Zealanders, Australian and some South Africans. It was pretty multicultural.

Before our first bombing mission the squadron had begun re-equipping with brand new Halifax 'B' Mark III's. These were much more powerful aircraft than the old Halifax 'B' Mark II's which we had been training on at Marston Moor. They had the latest Bristol Hercules XVI engines, each one giving 1,675 horsepower compared to the 1,480 horsepower of the Rolls Royce Merlin XX engines of the Hali 2. That's a lot. It's thirteen percent more! There was more acceleration and more power when we climbed and the takeoff weight increased from 60,000 pounds to 65,000 pounds.

Another big change was the shape of the fins. They were called "billiard table" fins because they were rectangular. They replaced the old triangular shaped fins that were found to be dangerous because they made the plane unstable and could cause Halifaxes to become uncontrollable and stall. So we had brand new planes when we started operations. The same thing was to happen to us on our second tour when the squadron was converting from the Halifax 3 to the Halifax 6. We were lucky!

We left Marston Moor on the 3rd of May and went straight over to get ourselves organised at RAF Pocklington which was about fifteen miles east of York. It was Sandy Concannon's twenty-first birthday so we all went down to the pub to help him celebrate. Then we were given twelve day leave passes.

The Australians in the crew went to our Lady Ryder scheme billets – Bill and Don to Minehead, Sandy and Harry to the Jean's farm at Currypool, and me to Rednal. The two Englishmen went home – John Allen to Bristol and Charlie Hood to Plymouth. The Australians in the crew had said goodbye to their families and friends and had gone off to war when they left Australia long before. John and Charlie were saying their goodbyes to their families and friends just before they headed back to begin operations on the squadron.

We returned to 102 Squadron on the 15th of May. This was the real thing for the seven of us. The training was over. The future would be dangerous and uncertain. Bill and Don's flying logs show that on the 17th and 18th of May the crew did three circuit and landing flights around the 'drome but I didn't have my first flight until the 20th when we headed off on a five hour night time cross-country. They did not need me for circuits and bumps. The pilot and bomb aimer did the takeoffs and landings. So while Bill and the others were getting the feel of the Hali 3 I was somewhere else. I may have been hard at work in the Nav. section. I would have been where I was ordered to be.

The cross-country was a different matter. It was my first flight in a Halifax Mark III and my only one before we went on our first bombing mission. We flew to Belfast and back to base and then down to London and back. It was the last chance to get all the bugs sorted out. As it turned out we had trouble with the Dead Reckoning Compass, the main compass on the aircraft. The Air Position Indicator and Bill's compass on his dashboard both ran off it. We got a bit off track but made it safely back to base.

Don and Bill's diaries for this time are very interesting. Both of them are full of praise for the Hali 3. On the 17th after a couple of hours of circuits and bumps, Don wrote:

> "We started our circuits and bumps and after two dual circuits Bill went solo on Hali. Three. They're wizard kites and they climb like a rocket ...."

Bill was just as enthusiastic when he wrote:

> "Flew my first Halifax III today and they are marvellous kites. They climb like a Spitfire and are very fast. I had no bother with them ...."

The disappointment that Bill felt at Lichfield when he found out that we were going to be flying Halifaxes and not Lancasters was well behind him.

Orleans

On the 22nd/23rd of May, we did our first bombing operation over enemy territory. We flew P-Peter on a night raid. The target was the marshalling yards at Orleans in central France. At that stage the favourite targets were railway yards because Bomber Command and the Americans were trying to restrict the movements of German reinforcements prior to the D Day landings. The Orléans Fleury-les-Aubrais railway station was a very important target because it was one of the centres of the German's railway network. Everything went through there - troops, weapons, munitions, supplies. Everything!

We took off at 2350 hours with 8,500 pounds of bombs and we were gone for five and a half hours. Nine Halifaxes from 102 Squadron took off on this raid. Six others went on a "gardening" operation, which was what we called our minelaying operations, and laid their mines at La Rochelle, a French seaport on the Bay of Biscay, where the Germans had built a big submarine base. With D-Day approaching the last thing the Allies wanted was strong U-boat activity in the English Channel, so they were laying down a ring of mines around the harbour to stop the U-boats from getting out. A garrison of twenty-two thousand Germans was under siege in La Rochelle from September 1944 until Germany surrendered in May 1945. It was the last French city to be liberated.

On night operations it was important that no light leaked out from the aircraft but navigators needed a lamp on their desks so they could work, so they painted our windows black and put blackout curtains between the navigator's table and the bomb aimer in the nose.

We taxied from our dispersal site around to take-off and the Wing Commander and Air Commodore were out watching us take off. They gave us the thumbs up and so did our ground crew. I didn't see anything of the flight until we got to the target. Then I switched off my lamp, parted the blackout curtains and poked my head out. It was my first operation and I was curious. I saw the target illuminated like the day by a ring of parachute flares that hung in the sky. The Pathfinders had released them. I never saw this manoeuvre repeated so successfully again. We bombed from eighteen thousand feet and couldn't miss. We clobbered the target very accurately and headed for home.

Don was an exceptional bomb aimer and Bill was an exceptional pilot, so they made a great bombing team. On a bombing run Bill responded to all of Don's instructions without hesitation. Don would be conveying his instructions saying, "Left, left. Steady! Right, steady! Hold it there! A bit more left. Left, left, steady! That's bang on! Bombs gone!"

While Don was saying these things, Bill was concentrating on holding the exact course that Don was asking him to. When Don said, "Left. Left. Steady!" Bill would make a minute correction to port. All the time Don was endeavouring to keep the target in his bombsight. Bill was making those little corrections by applications to the rudder and joystick. The joystick was like a wheel – a half wheel - about a third of a segment of a circle, divided into two. He had it about chest high and he had both his feet in the pedals making adjustments as pilots do. Bill always did his utmost to fly as Don instructed. If Don said "left" he would instinctively go left just like that. A minute correction. Not a big one.

We are on our bombing run. The plane is straight and level. Bill is holding the plane as steady as he can. He is listening to Don's instructions over the intercom and making slight adjustments to keep P-Peter heading for the target. Don is over his bombsight. The target is drifting down the bombsight. It gets to the crosshairs. Don releases the bombs by pressing the teat he is holding. He calls out, "Bombs going!" Then Don says, "Bombs gone. Bomb doors closed. Camera exposing!" Bill holds the plane on the bombing run track for thirty seconds longer while the P4 camera turns over and takes a succession of line overlap photographs. It doubles the danger! I am instructing Bill about the course to take, and the height and the speed we need for the next leg. The last photograph is taken. We turn on track for home.

It was important to hold the same course and speed until after the photographs had been taken. They were used to determine whether or not you got what they called an "aiming point". The last frame of the photograph denoted the target. While all this was going on I was preparing the course for Bill to turn onto once the bombing run was completed and that was only when all the photographs had been taken. I'd have to make all of the necessary calculations and corrections and be ready to tell Bill to alter course to so and so degrees, and fly at such and such an airspeed, at such and such a height, according to the flight plan. If we had strayed away from it on the bombing run, I had to get us back on track straight away. We certainly didn't want to be flying straight on at night, in the middle of hundreds of heavy bombers that were all turning away from the target and heading for home.

I didn't know what was going on outside the plane but Bill wrote in his dairy: "I was trying to concentrate like mad to fly well for (Don) with things banging on both sides of us." There must have been a bit of flak. I can't remember any of that. I was inside the aircraft and had a job to do. I couldn't afford to gawk around. If there were nearby flak bursts I would have heard and felt them but if I did I can't remember. I had to block them out. The close ones were the ones that you heard explode.

The Mark III Halifax was a noisy plane. We had leather flying helmets with our earphones tucked into the earpieces of the helmet and an oxygen mask adjacent to our mouth and an intercom switch under our chin. All this was part of the flying helmet. We wore battledress on every operation. It was too cold up there just in battledress so we had thermal underwear on and fur lined flying boots that came up both legs to just under our knees. We were quite warm. There were heating pipes from the exhausts of the engine running under the navigator's table and heat would be going through them so we were quite snug in the navigator's cabin. Sandy wasn't so snug though. He wore special electrically heated flying gear with wires running through it and he wore electrically heated gloves right up to mid arm below his elbow.

This was a successful night for 102 Squadron. Our bombing of the marshalling yards at Orlean was very accurate and so was the minelaying at La Rochelle.

It was about 0520 in morning when we returned. Everything had gone well until then. I looked over to starboard through the nose and on the right hand side and I could see a bunch of airfields. My navigation was about a mile out. I panicked! I couldn't distinguish one from the other and we overshot by a long way. In the end I said to Bill, "I don't know where I am. We'd better get a QDM." A QDM was when the wireless operator held down a key so the staff at Pocklington could get a bearing from it and issue us with instructions in Morse Code to fly such and such a course. So that's what our wireless operator Harry Brabin did.

I didn't know then that GEE could be used for homing because the Nav instructors had neglected to train me in it. I had been using GEE for three or four months with Don assisting me but we only used it to obtain fixes. There had been another use for GEE all along! You could use it to home onto a specific place. Nobody told us! We were as close as damn it to the 'drome and I didn't recognize where we were supposed to land. It was a combination of errors by all three of the navigation team - Bill, Don and me. Bill or Don should have seen the letters 'PO' for Pocklington in the Drem lights of our base, and I should have remained calm. We could have landed at any one of the other airfields but no-one thought of that either!

When we landed all I felt was shame because I had fallen from my high standards and got lost. Even though I wasn't trained in that aspect of GEE and you could say that it wasn't my fault, it was no excuse. I panicked at the point when I thought: "I don't know where we are!" My not having been trained to home on GEE would have come out straight after we landed and went to interrogation.

When I went down to the Nav section later that day, the Nav leader wanted to know what had happened. He straight away gave me lessons. It was an easy thing to learn and I quickly made sure that I was proficient in homing on GEE from then on. A couple of operations later I had to put it into full effect.

In his diary the day after Orleans Don McLean wrote:

".... I saw my photo of the Orleans do and I got an aiming point. We had a wizard trip except that we overshot base on the way back.... When we did our bombing run I got a beautiful sight on the railway yards and heard the Master Bomber in action...."

So we had done our first trip over enemy territory. I was relieved that we got back safely. Part of Bill's diary entry of the 22nd of May 1944 says:
".... Arrived back over the English coast and decided it wasn't such a bad little island after all. Then as dawn was breaking we arrived back at base tired but happy. Landed and went to interrogation."

Bill was very excited writing about the mission and calm about coming home. He didn't mention anything about me getting lost. Bill was a good bloke!

I am still annoyed after all these years when I think about our first raid. When we saw that flock of airfields, we should have gone over and investigated. The initials of our drome would've told us that we were landing at the right airfield. Instead we flew straight on because I was a mile off track. I reckon after it had happened to me they made double sure that every navigator from then on was trained to home in on GEE.

RAF No. 102 (Ceylon) Squadron, 1939 - 1946

On the night of the 4th/5th of September 1939, the day after Britain declared war on Germany, three 102 Squadron Armstrong Whitworth Whitleys were sent on the squadron's first wartime mission, a night time "nickel", dropping propaganda leaflets onto cities in the Ruhr Valley. Four nights later on the 8th/9th of September, three aircraft again went on a "nickel" to the Ruhr. Two of them K8950 (M-Mother) and K8985 (J-Jig), became the first 102 Squadron aircraft losses of the war. Badly off course, M-Mother ran out of fuel and landed at Itzehoe in Germany. Its crew became POWs for the rest of the war. J-Jig, after straying into the airspace of then neutral Belgium, was forced to land by Belgian fighter planes. The crew was eventually repatriated.

The squadron's first bombing mission occurred on the 12th/13th of December 1939 when one Whitley, on a security patrol near Sylt, a North Sea seaplane base, bombed "lights in the sea" which may have been a German boat. On the 19th of March 1940, the squadron is credited with leading the first, "real" Bomber Command operation of the war, when fifty aircraft attacked Sylt. From then on, the air war changed dramatically from security flights and "nickel" raids, and instantly became more menacing.

The "phoney war" was finally over when Germany invaded the Netherlands on the 10th of May 1940. Within days, 102 Squadron bombed industrial and railway targets in the Ruhr, and after Italy declared war on the 10th of June, the squadron attacked Turin. Reprisals were inevitable. At lunchtime on the 15th of August, a force of fifty Junkers 88 bombers attacked the Driffield aerodrome and scored 171 direct hits. Fourteen people were killed, including nineteen year-old, Marguerite Hudson, the first WAAF killed in the war. Five Whitleys from 102

Squadron and seven from 77 Squadron, which shared the airfield, were destroyed and several others were damaged. The airfield was in ruins. The destruction was so extensive that both squadrons were suddenly in search of new homes.

From the 25th of August until the 15th of November 1940, 102 Squadron moved four times before eventually being stationed at RAF Topcliffe in North Yorkshire, and for a short period, at its nearby satellite aerodrome, RAF Dalton. In early December 1941, several Handley Page Halifax B.1 and the more powerful B.2 aircraft began arriving at Topcliffe. While operational duties on Whitleys continued, the aircrew began conversion training.

During a night operation on the 26th/27th of January 1942 the last Whitley was lost by the squadron. After bombing Emden, it was shot down by a night fighter. During February and March 1942, no bombing operations were undertaken while conversion training on Halifaxes continued. When operations resumed, the squadron was flying brand new Halifax B.2's. On the 7th of August 1942, the squadron replaced Canadian 405 Squadron at RAF Pocklington, named after the small market town nearby, twenty kilometres east of York, and it remained there until the end of the war.

102 (Ceylon) Squadron
Tenate et Perficite
(Attempt and Achieve

During 1943, the bombing war intensified with Bomber Command losing some 702 Halifaxes at a rate of 4.62 percent per operation, compared to Lancaster losses of 919 aircraft at a rate of 3.3 percent. The Halifax loss rate was therefore 28 percent greater and only marginally less than that of the Short Stirling which by the end of 1943 had been relieved from bombing operations into Germany. In 1943, 102 Squadron lost 73 aircraft during operations. In January 1944, 102 Squadron, alone, lost 13 of the 48 Halifax 2's sent on operational sorties, a loss rate of 27 percent. It is little wonder that Basil Spiller's crew, and many like them, were disappointed to discover that, after finishing heavy conversion unit training, they were destined for squadrons flying Halifaxes.

At the end of February 1944, the losses of Halifax Mark II's were deemed unacceptably high, and Bomber Command stopped Halifax squadrons attacking targets in Germany until they were converted to the new, more stable and more powerful Halifax Mark III. While the conversion to newer Halifaxes took place, 102 Squadron remained fully operational. This period coincided with Allied preparations for the D-Day landings on the 6th of June. 102 Squadron continued minelaying operations. The two prime focuses at this stage of the war were the waters of the Heligoland Bight, Kattegat Strait and Kiel Bay, to prevent German battleships and submarines moving between the North Sea and the Baltic Sea, and secondly, laying mines in the French coast harbours where the Germans had established a large U-boat force with which they were attacking the Atlantic supply convoys from Canada and the USA, and which could be used to attack the D-Day armada.

On the 16th of June 1944, 102 Squadron re-equipped with its new Halifax 3's resumed bombing raids into Germany when it attacked Sterkrade in the Ruhr Valley. In the intervening four months it had flown 51 gardening operations, and to further support the Allied invasion force, conducted 28 bombing operations against strategic targets such as Orlean, Maisy and St. Lô in France.

Like all bomber squadrons, running 102 Squadron was a big logistical operation. On the 31st of December 1944, soon after Basil Spiller had completed his first tour of duty, "station strength" was 2,047 personnel. Their responsibility was to ensure that the squadron's Halifax bombers, were repaired, re-armed, bombed-up and refuelled, and that their seven-man crews were prepared, fit and ready to fly on bombing operations. Although most 102 Squadron aircrews were British, many airmen, sent to Britain as part of the Empire Training Scheme, were posted to Pocklington. In late December 1944, the squadron's aircrews consisted of 153 officers and 202 airmen, amongst whom were 32 Australians, 13 Canadians, 8 New Zealanders and 3 South Africans. The ground-staff was made up of 69 male officers, 1,272 airmen, 9 WAAF officers and 342 WAAF airwomen.

The number of aircraft lost by the squadron in the Second World War was amongst the highest suffered by Bomber Command squadrons. 102 Squadron lost 320 aircraft, ninety on non-operational duties such as training, ferrying and conversion flights, but 230 planes were lost on bombing raids (63 Whitleys and 169 Halifaxes). Of these, German night fighters are known to have shot down seventy (19 Whitleys and 51 Halifaxes). Forty-two were shot down by flak (19 Whitleys and 23 Halifaxes). Seventy-seven planes crashed over Europe or into the sea. Some of these were undoubtedly the result of flak damage but most would have crashed after being shot up by night fighters, which were responsible for almost sixty-five percent of known combat losses. Swelling these grave numbers are thirty badly damaged aircraft which returned from operations but crashed in England, and the eleven aircraft which are still listed as missing.

These sobering statistics demonstrate that 102 Squadron was in the thick of action during the war. From RAF Pocklington, the squadron participated in 298 bombing raids and 101 minelaying operations. Its Halifaxes attacked targets in the Ruhr Valley and the Rhein-Ruhr region, the most heavily defended part of Germany, more than eighty times. Over twenty of the region's key industrial cities were attacked, the largest ones repeatedly, including: Essen (15 times), Cologne (12), Duisburg (9), Dusseldorf (7), Gelsenkirchen (5), Bochum (5), Dortmund (4), Sterkrade (4), Wuppertal (3), and Wanne-Eickel (3). As well, the squadron flew deep into eastern and south-eastern Germany, attacking heavily defended cities such as Berlin (12 times) and Nuremburg (5).

102 Squadron's last bombing operation of the Second World War was a raid on the small East Frisian Island of Wangerooge on the 25th of April 1945, Anzac Day. Nineteen of its Halifaxes joined a force of 466 heavy bombers to destroy the island.

When the war ended on the 8th of May, things moved rapidly. The squadron was transferred into Transport Command, and on the 9th of May, aircrew began leaving. Australian and Canadian personnel left for Driffied and Warrington respectively to await repatriation.

102 squadron was officially disbanded on the 28th of February 1946.

A Halifax Beat-up

A low level "beat-up". Halifax Mk. II, JB911 X-Xray of No. 77 Squadron flown low over an audience of appreciative 'erks' (the common name for ground crew) during air tests at Elvington, Yorkshire, July 1943. After being replaced at Full Sutton in early 1945, this aircraft flew with HCU 1658 at RAF Riccall, also in Yorkshire. It survived the war and was struck off charge on the 1st of November 1946.

Chapter 18: Operation 2 – Colline Beaumont

106 Halifaxes, 102 Lancasters and 16 Mosquitos, split into small forces, attacked coastal gun positions at Boulogne, Colline Beaumont, Le Clipon and Trouville without loss. *Total effort for the night:* 888 sorties, 26 aircraft (2.9 per cent) lost.
The Bomber Command War Diaries, 24/25 May 1944

At the end of my first operation I had lost a bit of composure but I had regained it completely by this mission. After my instruction in homing on GEE I was quietly confident.

On the night of the 24th/25th of May, we were one of nine Halifaxes sent from 102 Squadron on a night raid to attack a German coastal gun battery near the small French village of Colline Beaumont preparatory to the Normandy advance landings. The target was in the Pas de Calais area about ten kilometres in from the coast. Colline Beaumont was probably a 4 Group do, and there would have been upwards of a hundred planes split up to attack several gun batteries. There were five "groups" in Bomber Command. Our Group, Number 4, and Canadian Number 6 group were equipped with Halifaxes and 1, 3 and 5 Groups were equipped with Lancasters.

Often on a small target like this, one Group would lay on the target and only their aircraft would bomb it. When I started operations, 4 Group operated from eleven airfields and it had twelve squadrons. RAF Elvington, had two Free French squadrons run from 42 Base at Pocklington. At full strength 4 Group could have upwards of 250 aircraft in the air. 102 Squadron had twenty-six planes but there were usually twenty-four planes in a squadron.

Allowing for serviceability, seldom would our squadron be able to fly at full strength. There were usually eighteen... twenty... twenty-two... sometimes twenty-four but very seldom would all of them be available. Only once while I was on the squadron did we have all twenty-six on an operation.

This was a completely uneventful mission. We took off at 2245 hours and carried eleven thousand pounds of bombs and it lasted three hours and thirty minutes. Don McLean's diary entry gives a good description of the mission. He wrote:

"We did a bombing trip to N. France (Beaumont) last night and it was a very quiet affair. We clung to track all the way down the south and lost a minute and a half and reached concentration point right on time. We bombed on the minute and I got a good run-up and sight on a nice cluster of green markers. We stuck well to track on the way home and landed about 2 am. A small amount of flak at the target.... I got another aiming point on the photo and the Intelligence Officer thinks I might have got a direct hit."

I don't have a lot to say about this mission. Bill and Don always saw everything. While I was cocooned in my little blacked-out space, Bill was in the cockpit with full perspex around him and as we approached our bombing run, Don moved down in the nose and stayed there until the bombs had been dropped and the line overlap photographs were taken. He had an uninterrupted view of everything that was unfolding in front of us.

On this night, six of our Halifaxes were also sent on a gardening trip to Brest, a seaport on the westernmost part of France where the Germans had built a large U-boat bunker that could hold fifteen U-boats. We had no losses from our squadron on either target.

Bill says in his diary that on the evening of the 25th we were briefed to bomb Ludwigshaven and Mannheim, two German cities located on opposite sides of the Rhine River. He thought it was going to be a "pretty grim show" which meant the pilots had been told that it would be an exceedingly dangerous mission or even that heavy losses could be expected. He started the motors and got ready for take-off but luckily for us the weather was so bad that the mission was called off. The weather was bad again on the 26th and then on the 27th we were given ten days leave and headed off for our Lady Ryder Scheme billets.

For part of their leave, Bill and John had to go to the Bristol Aeroplane Company engine school to do a four day course on the Bristol-Hercules Mark XVI radial engines which we had on our planes. Engines on a plane were the responsibility of the pilot and the engineer so they would have had lectures and workshops on keeping the motors running at their peak to get the maximum performance out of them on bombing operations – maybe emergency procedures too. I don't really know what they did but I do know that Bill found the lectures "full of interest." Bristol was a convenient location for John because it was his home town.

The Battle for Brest

In this chapter, Basil Spiller mentions that while his crew were sent on the bombing raid to Colline Beaumont, six Halifaxes from his squadron were also sent on a gardening trip to Brest.

Beginning on the 10th of May 1940, the German invasion of France was resolute, efficient and decisive. By the 23rd of May the Germans had trapped the British Expeditionary Force in Dunkirk and routed the French army and by mid-June the Cherbourg and Breton Peninsulas had also fallen to German forces.

After the surrender of Paris on the 22 of June, a string of French harbour cities on the Bay of Biscay, Brest, Lorient, St Nazaire, and La Rochelle immediately became locations for the German Kriegsmarine U-boat fleet and the inland port city of Bordeaux, 150 kilometres further south, became the base for the Italian submarine flotilla. A sixth U-boat base was built at Toulon, on the Mediterranean Sea in 1943.

From these bases the Kriegsmarine had unimpeded access to the Atlantic Ocean convoys. U-boats putting to sea from their French harbours were a mighty force menacing Allied shipping along the vital Atlantic supply lines from Canada and the United States. Of 3,584 U-boat patrols conducted during the war, some 1,707 (48%) left from their bases in France.

Control of the harbour at Brest was a significant victory for Germany. The French naval academy, the Academie de Marine, founded at Brest in 1752 was located there. In early 1941 construction began on the largest U-boat bunker built during the war. It was able to accommodate twenty-two submarines.

As the D-Day landings approached, the U-boat wolf-pack posed a direct threat to the D-Day invasion fleet of 6939 vessels that were to sail across the English Channel on the 6th of June 1944. To stop the U-boats from putting to sea, from May to September 1944, the RAF laid mines across French harbour entrances.

Reconnaissance photograph showing damage to the concrete U-boat shelters at Brest, following RAF raids on the 12th and 13th of August 1944. Two large puncture holes from 12,000 pound 'Tallboy' deep penetration bombs can be seen in the roof.

Brest was bombed over eighty times by the RAF and the USAAF. From May to September 1944, the RAF attacked Brest twenty-six times. There were fifteen minelaying raids to close the harbour and submarine pens, while fortifications and gun battery positions were bombed eleven times.

US airforce bombing raids on the city, harbour and hinterland prepared the way for the arrival of the American army which had finally broken through the German lines in Normandy and after capturing the Cherbourg peninsula had moved rapidly westwards towards Brest, first attacking the city in early August 1944. When the Germans surrendered on the 21st of September, Brest was in ruins. The US army had suffered over ten thousand casualties.

After ferocious house to house fighting, the city had gradually fallen to the Americans street by street. Because of the unacceptable loss of life and the fact that the invasion force in western France was brought to a halt for six weeks, it was decided in future to lay siege to French ports like La Rochelle rather than conduct full scale battles like the Battle of Brest.

Chapter 19: Number 2 Eachway Lane, Rednal

In between the mission to Colline Beaumont and our third mission, a raid on Maisy, a village on the French coast, we had about ten days leave. I went down to Rednal. The address of Mrs Reid's house was 2 Eachway Lane. I was welcome back there all the time. I didn't notify Mrs Reid when I was coming. She told me not to so I used to just drop in. Sometimes she would have another Australian or Canadian airman there. It was a double storey house and the whole of the upper storey was bedrooms. There might have been four. She had two spare bedrooms for airmen. Her son Adrian was there. He was a teenager going to school. There seemed to always be plenty of spare room. I got on pretty well with the other airmen who were there. I didn't do anything with them though. I was usually there on my own but I had palled up with a few girls by visiting the local pubs and dances. Naturally I used to go out with the local girls. Let's just say I had female acquaintances at Rednal. Perhaps I wasn't such a shy young man by then! Mrs Reid wasn't impressed. I can't remember all of the girls but I can remember one of them well. She was sweet on me and took me home to meet her parents but I was determined not to get entangled with any British girls. A lot of them wanted to marry Australians. I don't know if she had ulterior motives for taking me home or not but I was a bit suspicious.

    The first time I stayed with Mrs Reid, I could see a golf course straight over the road from her house. I had some experience with golf, caddying in northern Queensland, so I knew a bit about it. I took the trouble to buy a set of clubs while I was there and a friend of Mrs Reid who worked at the Austin Motor Works at Longbridge, made me a canvas bag to carry the clubs in. I used to climb over the stile on the fence and hit off at the sixth tee. The course was empty on weekdays so I usually had it to myself. Nobody at the club minded that I was not a member or that I had hopped the fence to have a hit. I was allowed to play whenever I wanted without paying green fees. Anybody in uniform was quite welcome. I used to play quite a lot and I'd buy second hand balls from the green-keepers. I didn't have a handicap and I didn't play in competitions. I headed off for a game on my own because there was nobody to play with. I didn't mind being on my own too much. I was brought up at boarding school back in Australia, so I was pretty self-sufficient. I didn't choose to get away from everything on my own. It just happened. I'd just hit the ball, wander around and try to improve my score. I don't know if I was any good at golf or not. I was quite a good tennis player and I suppose I was a reasonable sportsman. On a par four hole I could get a par every now and then so I suppose I was a reasonable golfer. I didn't just scrub it along the fairway, getting ten or twelve a hole. The golf club used to be called the Lickey Hills Golf Club but now it is called the Rose Hill Golf Club. I would not be able to draw the layout now. They wouldn't let me bring my clubs back to Australia and confiscated them. I never took it up when I came home. Tennis was my game.

The rest of my crew had other places to go to on leave. Sandy and Harry used to go to Jeans' dairy farm in Somerset near a village called Currypool just outside Bridgewater. Don and Bill used to go to a place in Somerset called Minehead. Their hosts, the Joneses, were in the timber industry. These places were all chosen for them by the Lady Ryder scheme. All of us were very happy with the host families we were allocated to.

Rose Hill Golf Club, Lickey Hill Country Park, Rednal

The Ninth Green. Rose Hill Golf Club

The Rose Hill Golf Club is a beautifully prepared, picturesque, 18-hole golf course situated on the slopes of the Lickey Hills near Rednal, in the UK. Lined by banks of forest pines, its undulating fairways offer excellent views over the surrounding countryside. The golf course is part of the Lickey Hills Country Park which covers some 524 acres, filled with a rich diversity of flora and fauna for ramblers and picnickers to enjoy. The highest point of the hills is Beacon Hill which is approximately 300 metres high. As well as the golf course, the park has picnic facilities, tennis courts, bowling green and visitor centre. The "Lickeys", as these parklands are locally known, have for centuries been a popular destination for people from throughout the Birmingham region.

Chapter 20: Operation 3 - Maisy

1,012 aircraft - 551 Lancasters, 412 Halifaxes, 49 Mosquitos - to bomb coastal batteries at Fontenay, Houlgate, La Pernelle, Longues, Maisy, Merville, Mont Fleury, Pointe du Hoc, Ouisterham and St Martin de Varreville. 946 aircraft carried out their bombing tasks. 3 aircraft were lost - 2 Halifaxes of No. 4 Group on the Mont Fleury raid and 1 Lancaster of No. 6 Group on the Longues raid. At least 5,000 tons of bombs were dropped, the greatest tonnage in one night so far in the war. Bomber Command effort for the night: 1,211 sorties, 8 aircraft (0.7 per cent) lost.

The Bomber Command War Diaries, 5/6 June 1944

After our leave we went on our third mission to bomb Maisy, in the Pas de Calais area of France. There were twenty-six Halifaxes from 102 Squadron on this raid. It was one of the few times that all of our planes were serviceable. We took off at 0115 hours and the flight took four hours and fifteen minutes. We carried 10,750 pounds of bombs. Technically the raid was conducted during the early hours of morning on the 6th of June but our preparations started well before midnight.

There was a lot that had to be done beforehand. We all went to our sectional meetings. At my Nav. meeting I copied down the flight plan and prepared my charts taking meticulous care to copy down the track exactly as it was shown. Then came general briefing. Next, the crew had a meal of eggs together and then we went to the parachute locker room to pick up our parachute and harness. Finally, we were driven out to the plane by a WAAF in plenty of time. We would be hanging around for half an hour at least. And of course we had to have a last pee!

Father Seary, a Catholic priest, always came out to give communion and say a prayer with our three catholics, Bill, Don and Sandy. When we got on board Bill would run the engines to warm them up. Then he and John Allen did a "mag-drop" on each engine in turn. They would flick a switch between the two magnetos in an engine and check to see if there was a drop in revs. If the revs were down, the engine would be declared unserviceable and the mission was scrubbed. It was a common thing for this to happen but it only happened to us the once, later in October after we had been briefed to bomb Essen the first time.

In his diary Bill wrote:

"….We were briefed to bomb "Maisy" a French place. It was Panzer divisions we were after and to block the roads for Jerry.... We bombed from 2,000 feet and went all the way to and from the target at 1,500 ft. It was a very low level attack and very exacting for me physically as we had a tremendous amount of cloud with severe icing to go through…."

Bill reckoned that we were after Panzer tank divisions but I remember clearly that we were after coastal guns. Don McLean in his diary agrees with me:

> "Back on 'ops' again and we were in N.Nuts. Spent most of the day getting everything ready. Our target was a gun battery at Maisy and as it is D-Day it was the biggest concentration of aircraft ever to bomb ...."

In *The RAF Pocklington War Diaries*, a book written by Mike Underwood, it says the target was "coastal batteries" as well. At Maisy the Germans had positioned a big battery between Omaha and Utah beaches where the Americans were going to land on D-Day, which was only hours away. It was not damaged on this raid and US soldiers eventually captured it on the 9th of June.

We bombed through three-tenths cloud on PFF (Pathfinder Force) flares. Squadron records say that we bombed from five thousand feet but Bill says we bombed from two thousand feet. He was correct. We were low into and out of that target and we were well out of the way of the Americans who were coming out to take over from us. The weather was foul and so was the night after when we flew again at two thousand feet, trying to stay out of the weather below broken cloud.

D-Day

Our Maisy operation was early on the morning of the D-Day landings. We didn't know it when we took off because the security was so tight. We realized something big was happening only when we were on the way back because I was picking up a lot of signals on the H2S set from hundreds of ships in the Channel that were going over as part of the invasion fleet.

I didn't see any of what was going on down below in the English Channel because I was in my navigator's blackout room. I wish I had now. On the way home Harry and I were glued to our seats near each other. The rest of the crew were having a real good look. In his diary, Bill says that there were "tremendous happenings" with "thousands of ships in the Channel". Don McLean was looking at what was going on down below through N-Nan's perspex nose. In his diary he wrote:

> ".... On our way home we saw hundreds of planes and gliders. The trip was easy and we picked up the Invasion Fleet on the H2S. I thought it was a moving island at first."

On the H2S screen, Don and I saw numerous blips of light from the reflection of the radar waves that were bouncing back from the steel hulls of the ships. I saw them and deduced that something big was going on. It was a shame that I didn't have a look out because it would have been a spectacle and a half with all those ships down there. We didn't know that it was the D-Day landing taking place until we got back to the drome. It was just ships down in the Channel as far as we were concerned - but there were hundreds of them.

As we came back dawn was breaking. While we were flying through broken cloud we could see British and American planes and gliders, all heading towards France. There were hundreds of Flying Fortresses in formation. They were probably at ten thousand feet and way up above us. And up above them, out of sight, were the fighter planes.

All of the American airforce and the RAF fighter force were out in support of the landings that morning. There would have been swarms of British fighters - Spitfires and Tempests. The Americans did all of their bombing in the daylight and they needed fighter escorts. They had Mustangs, Lightnings and Thunderbolts and whatever. It is estimated that over 170 squadrons of Allied planes supported the D-Day landings as cover for the armada crossing the English Channel, by attacking German troop positions on the coast and by bombing strategic targets.

We had been part of a one thousand bomber force sent out by Bomber Command in the early hours of D-Day! The next night we did it again. And we were on standby night after night.

The RAF bombing stream

The Americans nearly always flew in daylight raids on a more direct course to the target than us. If their bombing height was supposed to be thirty thousand feet, they would formate on takeoff and set course at thirty thousand feet.

They always flew in very highly organized formations. We heard that it used to take them two to three hours to formate into "box" formations at different heights. They carried a smaller bomb load than the RAF bombers because they had to take a much larger fuel load. We wouldn't take off, gather with the squadron and set off together like they did. Instead we had "takeoff" and "set course" times. After takeoff we circled the drome which we could see lit up below us and when the set time came off we went.

We all navigated individually following our flight plan which was designed to fly at certain heights on certain courses at certain times. We altered course continually to fool the German night fighter defences. Only on the last leg of the run in to the target would we be at operational bombing height – usually twenty thousand, nineteen thousand or twenty-one thousand feet. After we bombed and after the photographic run, we would occasionally lose height from, say, twenty thousand feet down to two thousand feet on the next leg, and change course repeatedly. That was the reason the RAF navigator was such an important part of the crew. He had to direct his pilot on changes of course, changes of height and changes of speed on each leg according to the flight plan to keep the plane away from flak and night fighters and get the crew home safely.

Upon takeoff, RAF planes would all have their wingtip lights on so they could see where the next plane was at night time, but when we crossed the English coast we turned them out. Because we were flying at night, we could not formate for protection in the same way that the Americans did. How could you?

RAF formations were more like a "gaggle" than the nice lines of rows of planes that people see on newsreel footage of the Second World War.

The theory was that when we were bombing at night time, or in daylight as it were, we stuck to five miles to port or starboard of track. In that way the German anti-aircraft batteries couldn't "predict" flak onto just us (isolate a single plane) because they would have upwards of two hundred bombers on their radar screens at any time. If you strayed more than five miles port or starboard of track you were out on your own and in danger of being subjected to predicted flak because they could predict your height, speed, direction and location. They would only have a single target to concentrate on. You!

Predicted flak was very accurate. German gunners could shoot us down very easily if we continued on the same track, whereas in the bombing stream there were hundreds of signals. It was impossible to single one out. Instead, they would put up a barrage right into the middle of it. That was all they could do. You might get hit. You might not. That was what they called "barrage flak". If our force was bombing at twenty thousand feet, they could predict our height all right, and they would put up a barrage from nineteen thousand to twenty-one thousand feet and the whole of the bomb stream would have to fly through it. It was like being one fish in a school of fish. You might get taken but the chances were that you wouldn't be.

In 1944, Bomber Command was prepared for a loss of two to three percent each night. Every now and then disaster would strike and we would lose eight percent or twelve percent but the odds of survival were in your favour. If say, eight percent was shot down, you still had a ninety-two percent chance of not being shot down. The odds of surviving the night were in your favour.

The flight radio alphabet

Every plane in a squadron was given a letter from the alphabet and they were known by that letter. In 102 Squadron we had twenty-six planes and there were twenty-six letters in the alphabet so we used them all. Most squadrons had twenty-four planes so they would have to drop off two. When we were in flight it helped make identification by radio easier.

The flight radio alphabet was composed of: A-Abel, B-Beer, C-Charlie, D-Dog, E-Easy, F-Freddie, G-George, H-Harry, I-Isaac, J-Jig, K-Kate. L-Love, M-Mother, N-Nan, O-Oboe, P-Peter, Q-Queenie, R-Roger, S-Sugar, T-Tommy, U-Uncle, V-Victor, W-William, X-Xray, Y-Yolk and Z-Zebra. That was the alphabetical names of the planes. You can understand why they had this. The names were clear and easy to enunciate because they used short words of one or two syllables. Some things you never forget - like the latitude and longitude of our base at Pocklington – 00.48° West, 53.56° North.

Briefing, debriefing and interrogation

An hour before the main briefing time, all of the navigators had to assemble in the briefing room to prepare their logs and charts, so I had to do a lot of work before the main briefing began. Then the rest of the crews going on a mission would file in. The room could seat about two hundred people. Each crew sat together facing a huge map of France and Germany which had the flight plan on it, represented by red string. It was always the main feature of the briefing room. The string ran from home base down through England, across France or into Germany showing us the target and denoting the track that we were being briefed to take going in and coming home. We were addressed by the wing commander and the chief intelligence officer on the defences we might encounter over the target area. Then we were addressed by the "met" officer about the weather we might encounter on our track.

When we got back from missions we went to the debriefing room. A feature of it was a huge blackboard on the wall. It listed alphabetically the planes that had taken part in that operation. The pilot was named and the time of landing was noted. You could always tell when a crew was missing because the space where it said "landed" was vacant. You could always see how many went missing that night. Some might limp back or some might have landed at other airfields but it was a pretty grim thing to witness.

When we filed into the interrogation room, each crew was allotted a separate table and an intelligence officer. We had to tell him exactly what had happened on the trip - how many attacks we'd had, whether we bombed at the right height, what the flak was like, what the searchlights were like – all general information – and he'd note it down. While this was going on, the padre would be hovering around with tin pannikins of coffee and a tot of rum if we wanted it. That was his job. I had had a bit of a bad history with rum in the past in Edmonton, so I always accepted my rum and I gave it to Sandy, our rear gunner, who liked it.

After leaving debriefing, aircrew went to their respective messes. All of us sergeants were picked up on a transport and taken back to the sergeants' mess and there we had a meal. It didn't matter whether it was half-past one in the morning, or five o'clock in the morning, it was always fried Spam and a fried egg. No bacon, only Spam in the war - tinned spam - but it was all right if it was fried.

The Briefing Room

30th March 1944. Squadron Leader Peter Hill, briefing Halifax crews from No. 51 Squadron, RAF Snaith, 4 Group, prior to their night time raid to Nuremberg. Station Commander, Group Captain Fresson, is sitting in the front row at right. The squadron lost six Halifaxes on this operation. Thirty-five men were killed, including Squadron Leader Hill, and seven became prisoners of war.

Night Bombing

The German Luftwaffe's domination of European skies in the four months from July to November 1941, resulted in the loss of over 520 aircraft from the British bomber force, roughly the number that were in service at any one time. Without sufficient fighter numbers for escort duties, during daytime operations, RAF bombers were at the mercy of German fighters.

Adding to the problem was the fact that the RAF bombing policy of attacking strategic targets had proven to be a woeful failure, with less than ten percent of bombs striking targets. As 1941 drew to a close it was obvious that the situation could not continue.

Air Ministry intervention in November 1941 saw Bomber Command's operations and tactics re-evaluated and a new direction was determined. From the start of 1942, German cities were to become targets for Bomber Command and bombing operations were to be conducted predominantly at night time when air escorts were unnecessary.

Chapter 21: Operation 4 – St. Lô

1,065 aircraft - 589 Lancasters, 418 Halifaxes, 58 Mosquitos - to bomb railway and road centres on the lines of communication behind the Normandy battle area. All of the targets were in or near French towns. 3,488 tons of bombs were dropped on targets at Achères, Argentan, Caen, Châteaudun, Conde sur Noireau, Coutances, St. Lô, Lisieux and Vire. .... Important bridges at Coutances were badly damaged and the town centres of Caen, Conde sur Noireau, St-Lô and Vire were all badly bombed and most of the roads through those towns were blocked. Total effort for the night: 1,160 sorties, 11 aircraft (0.9 per cent) lost.
The Bomber Command War Diaries, 6/7 June 1944

Mission number four was a night time mission on the 6th/7th of June to St. Lô a small town about fifty kilometres from Caen. We took off at 2230 hours and the mission took five hours and ten minutes. We carried six thousand five hundred pounds of bombs. Fifteen aircraft from our squadron participated in this raid and six others were sent laying mines - three went to Lorient and three went to St Nazaire.

The soldiers on the coast in France were doing it very tough. The weather was foul and we had to give them the utmost support. So we went on D-Day support again - two nights in a row. This was another large "one thousand bomber" operation against multiple targets. Bomber Command attacked nine French towns where the Germans were entrenched. We were trying to disrupt German supply lines. Our target, St. Lô, was an important road junction through which the Germans were able to reinforce and supply their troop positions.

Our pilot, Bill Rabbitt, wrote in his diary:

> "On again tonight and another tough trip done at very low level 2,000 ft. The cloud really takes the strength out of you and I was thoroughly browned off with instrument flying. The target was St Lô so we are certainly giving our support to the troops on the beach-head. We saw fighters tonight and took evasive action into cloud from one."

I can't remember being attacked by the German fighter but I do remember that we flew at two thousand feet from base right to the target and back again. We were flying in low cloud and stayed low because the weather was so bad. It rained non stop. Bill mentions that he was flying on instruments the whole time. It was hard work. In his diary for the 6th of June, Don McLean wrote:

> "On 'ops' again in X.Xray and the target is a road junction in St. Lô, a small town in France where the Germans were bringing Panzer divisions up against our troops. A low-level job ...."

Don's next entry was for the 7th of June:
> "We flew down England at 1,500' and climbed to 3,000' over the Channel. We had a very good trip and the squadrons all bombed between 2,000-3,000' on orders from the Master Bomber. There was a pretty decent fire going and the bombs exploding underneath rocked the kite. It was a very good trip and I got a good photo. I saw my stick of bombs knock over a whole street of houses."

So we bombed straight up the main street of St. Lô from a low level in pouring rain. I could feel the bombs exploding on the ground below us. It was like driving a car over a corrugated road because we were so low that I could feel the impact of the stick of bombs we released. Our squadron record says that St. Lô was "completely wiped out".

The plane leaked and the water got all over my log and chart much to my disgust. We were in heavy rain on our last mission to Maisy on the 5th of June, D-Day eve as well but there were no leaks because we were in N-Nan that night. On this flight we were in X-Xray MZ648. We didn't pick up N-Nan as our regular plane for a few more trips because on the next two we were in Q-Queenie. Then it looks like N-Nan became our regular plane from the 15th of June on, except when it was being serviced. I'm glad that we didn't inherit X-Xray. I was very particular about my charts!

Flak and the German 88 mm Flak Gun

The word "Flak" is a contraction of the German word for anti-aircraft cannon - "Flugabwehrkanone" – and is synonymous with the 88 millimetre Flak gun, one of the best known and most feared weapons of the Second World War. It was developed at the Krupp's Essen steelworks, and entered serious production as the "Flak 18" in the mid 1930's, after Adolph Hitler assumed power.

It was mounted on a cross shaped, mobile carriage which could be pivoted through 360 degrees, and elevated to a maximum angle of 85 degrees. The cannon was very manoeuvrable. Wheel bogies for the front and rear of the mount could be attached in a few minutes, the canon moved on this "trailer" to a new site, where it could be demounted and rapidly readied for action once again.

The Flak 18 was first used in war by the Germans in the Spanish Civil War. During the Second World War newer models, the famous Flak 36, and later, the Flak 37 with a more effective firing system, entered service. Over 20,000 Flak 18/36/37's were produced, some 11,000 of which were built in 1943/44 as the bombing war in Europe escalated and German cities became the targets of USAAF and Bomber Command.

It is estimated that 15,000 Flak 18/36/37 cannons, over three quarters of the total production, were employed in flak batteries near cities and in flak belts placed strategically from Holland to Germany, straddling Allied bombing routes. Flak belts with searchlight installations nearby were usually directed by radar controllers who found bombing streams, determined their height and direction and accurately predicted cannon fire and searchlights towards them.

Europe 1945. An RAF Lancaster explodes after being directly hit by flak.

When used as an anti-aircraft weapon, the effective range of the 88 millimetre flak gun was 25,000 feet, well above the height of Handley Page Halifaxes and Avro Lancasters on their bombing runs. The gun's ceiling height was over 40,000 feet.

Another feature of the 88 mm cannon was its rapid rate of fire of twenty rounds per minute which was achieved through the efficiency of the semi-automatic firing mechanism. A shell would fire automatically once it had been loaded from a tray which the loaders kept supplied with live ammunition. The barrel's recoil ejected the spent shell while the shell from the tray moved into the firing mechanism. The gun would automatically fire on the return stroke and the cycle would start again. Thus, each flak battery, usually with two or three groups of four cannons, could fire up to two hundred and forty shells every minute, creating a wall of exploding shrapnel through which aircraft on their bombing runs had to pass.

After suffering a direct hit, an aircraft would stagger and begin falling with a wing shorn off, or disintegrate in a ball of flame if bomb-bays suffered a direct hit while a plane was on its way to the target. Should a shell explode close to a plane, a withering fusillade of splintered metal would slice through wings and fuselage, cutting fuel lines, igniting petrol tanks and shattering control systems, while pilots fought for control of their craft and terrified crews frantically attempted to extinguish fires, tend wounded crewmates or don parachutes and bale out.

Co-ordinated fire from German 88 millimetre four cannon flak battery.

There has been much debate about the use of 88 millimetre cannons in their anti-aircraft role. Although they offered some protection against bombing raids and shot down thousands of heavy bombers, they did not prevent German cities from being destroyed, but their use as flak guns denied their greater deployment by the German army which was desperate to obtain them. They were used to great effect in European military campaigns such as the Battle of the Bulge when the war had decisively turned against Germany, and throughout the entire North African campaign, earlier in the war, when Germany was on the offensive. A direct hit from an 88 millimetre cannon could destroy a tank in the battlefield three to four miles away. So effective were they as "tank killers" that during Operation Battleaxe, during which British forces failed to rout the German army and break the siege of Tobruk, Flak 36/37 cannons destroyed ninety-eight British tanks, and almost one thousand British soldiers were either killed or wounded.

While discussing the power of the German 88 millimetre cannon, one young Australian soldier, fighting in North Africa, was overheard saying: "Anti-tank? They're anti-everything!"

Chapter 22: Operation 5 - Alençon

483 aircraft - 286 Lancasters, 169 Halifaxes, 28 Mosquitos - attacked railways at Alençon, Fougères, Mayenne, Pontabault and Rennes to prevent German reinforcements from the south reaching Normandy. All of the raids appear to have been successful. 4 aircraft were lost, 2 Lancasters from the Pontabault raid and 1 Lancaster and 1 Mosquito from the Rennes raid. *Total effort for the night:* 585 sorties, 4 aircraft (0.7 per cent) lost.

The Bomber Command War Diaries, 8/9 June 1944

Our fifth mission was a real shaky do. Ten of the squadron's Halifaxes were again sent on a gardening trip to Brest but we were one of fifteen crews who were briefed to bomb railway marshalling yards at Alençon a city in Normandy about one hundred and forty miles west of Paris. We took off in Q-Queenie at 2250 hours and carried 6,500 pounds of bombs. Once again marshalling yards were our target because we were trying to prevent German troops and supplies being transported by train. We had to bomb through the cloud. Although it was very difficult to see the target, there must have been a break in the cloud because we bombed it successfully.

This mission took us six hours and ten minutes, forty minutes longer than the raid on Orleans, although Orleans is one hundred and forty miles deeper into France. It should have been about an hour shorter, but when we headed back to base trouble started!

Near our 'drome at Pocklington there was a hill in our circuit area that was, I think, eight hundred feet high. In really bad weather we always had to be diverted to another drome because it was too hazardous to land if we couldn't see the top of the hill when it was in cloud. When we got back over the coast, Harry received a message from base to say that we were being diverted and we were given a latitude and longitude only. It turned out to be a fighter drome just inside the coast called Catfoss, with no runways and no Drem System to assist planes landing at night. Each airfield was surrounded by a unique series of lights. Pilots could see them and know that an aerodrome was there, and aircraft returning would be able to identify their squadron's airfield.

This was when the value of being able to home on GEE came into its own. I set the co-ordinates of the Catfoss latitude and longitude and homed onto it. There were two horseshoe shapes on the oscilloscope. As the plane got closer and closer to its destination the bottom horseshoe shape gradually drifted across the screen until it was eventually vertical with the top one and they formed an oval shape. Then you were over your home base! I put Bill on the course that brought the two horseshoe shapes together. This was putting my training after our first operation to the test only four trips after Orleans. Homing on GEE may have got us directly over Catfoss but we couldn't see anything below us.

When the oscilloscope told me that I was over the drome, I said to Bill, "There it is below us!" All we could see was fog and low cloud with a glow on the end of the landing field where they had built a bonfire to guide us - and we were supposed to land on that!

So we had a bonfire on a fighter drome with no Drem system, no lights or funnel, and no formed runways. It was purely a grass strip. This may have been typical of fighters who took off on the grass but not heavy bombers. Why they chose it I don't know. It was totally unsuitable for four engine bombers.

When we first saw the glow on the bonfire, I said to Bill, "Let's do it again." We did a circuit and came through again. When I told Bill we were over Catfoss again the same thing happened. Low cloud, fog and just a glow in the sky! We did that at least half a dozen times. We'd been on a bombing mission and by then we had been half an hour at least trying to get into this lousy drome and our petrol was getting low.

I had used GEE to find Catfoss but at two hundred feet we were still flying around in low cloud and fog. And there were a lot of other planes doing that too! We weren't going to break cloud after the experience that we'd had at the balloon barrages at Derby. Anyway, the cloud went all the way down to the ground!

Just at that time water got into my intercom and I couldn't talk to Bill, so I went up and stood behind his seat and stayed the rest of the flight there. Don McLean, our bomb aimer, was already sitting in the second pilot's seat alongside him. Don's previous pilot training was always a bonus for us. He always acted as second pilot on takeoff and landing and, as in this case, emergencies. Bill didn't ask him to go up and help him. It was something they had worked out previously. Bill had the side window open and he had his head stuck out into the slipstream trying to see where he was. There was no break in the cloud and we decided to go out to sea to break cloud and approach the aerodrome from out there, where there were no high tension wires and no hills. We were ready to ditch in the sea or bail out if we had to.

Suddenly a break in the cloud appeared and we could see the ground underneath. Bill went for it! He put the nose down and dived. We hopped through the cloud and BINGO! Below us was another bomber drome – Lisset – packed with aircraft. We had nearly touched down when up appeared this row of planes in front of us so Bill had to accelerate again. He pushed the throttles up and hopped over them and landed on the other side. It all happened very quickly. He was a good pilot! He was a terrific pilot!

Halifax Navigator

Bill explained what happened in his diary entry:

"....I saw a light and went to it. It was an aerodrome. I did a terrific turn on the deck and came around hoping to land. We lost sight of it almost immediately but kept turning until we were almost over it. Then I put the u/c (undercarriage) down, cut the motors and put my trust in the Lord. We were nearly on the ground when up loomed a row of planes on the ground. I gave the engines everything and we just jumped over them. I again cut everything and landed in a field on the drome...."

Just imagine the scene!

We are only flying at TWO HUNDRED FEET! Low cloud and fog are mixed in together. A hole appears. The drome's below! Bill drives the plane through the hole and it closes. Somehow we have lined up with the runway. It is pure chance! Two hundred feet! No margin for error. It doesn't give him anything! A second of flying. Sixty or seventy yards. There are planes IN FRONT! Bill pushes the throttles forward. We jump over the line of planes. We are down. Pure relief washes over me! It's just luck that we are down. We were fated to find this drome. It's been a real shaky do!

Half of 4 Group were on Lisset that morning. They all went looking for it because it was the only drome that they could get into. It was chaos! Pilots had to get down and get their plane off the runway as quickly as possible. All of the airfield was lined with planes. There were probably a hundred there.

Initially all of the squadron was diverted to Catfoss but only four aircraft landed there. Our planes landed all over the place – Catfoss, Lissett, Carnaby, Driffield and Dunholme Lodge. RAF Carnaby was a specialist crash landing drome, inside the coast about two miles south-west of Bridlington. No squadron was based there. It had an extra-long runway, about a mile and three quarters long and at each end it was cleared for about another quarter of a mile. It was five times as wide as a normal runway and divided into three "lanes" so several planes could land at the same time. For one of them, the southern one I think, a pilot did not need permission to land so he could go straight in. It was a good place to head if you had been shot up or were running out of fuel. There were two other crash landing airfields on the east coast. The other two were RAF Manston on the south coast in Kent, and RAF Woodbridge in

Suffolk on the coast of East Anglia.

In a situation like we were in, it is very disorderly. When you are bombing a target you come in and you do your bombing run with planes lined up in front of you or behind you. Everyone's going in and bombing in order but here at home trying to find a place to land is a bit of a free-for-all. We had been diverted to a strange drome and when we got there we couldn't see anything. That's why I did those half a dozen homing runs to convince myself that it was the place.

> *Everyone's coming back. We've all been out for six or seven hours. We have to land! They have to land! We're all converging on the same spot. It's getting desperate. It's dangerous. You don't know what's coming at you from out of the clouds!*

Two planes from our squadron weren't so lucky. Halifax T-Tommy, MZ659, had also been on the Alençon raid but it ran out of petrol. The record says that Pilot Officer Sambell pointed the plane out to sea near Carnaby, about ten miles north of Catfoss. The crew safely baled out but the plane crashed at Wass, a little village sixty kilometres inland. It must have done a U-turn, but I wouldn't have thought that a plane would do that! Tragically, Halifax M-Mother, LW 140, which was returning from the gardening trip to Brest, hit trees and disintegrated at Seaton while trying to land at Catfoss, about three kilometres away. The pilot, W/O Jekyll and his crew were all killed. Apparently they had dived to avoid colliding with another Halifax. The cloud base was just two hundred feet and all mixed up with fog. It was chaos and you had to take an opportunity like we did and go for it. Planes were running out of petrol. It was desperate and dangerous - a last resort. We heard a few days later that M-Mother cut out of petrol at 6 am before it crashed. We were due to be back at base at about 0500 so before they crashed they must have been going around and around for at least an hour looking for a safe place to land.

Sandy had a rough time in his rear turret on this mission .
His nose bled and he had trouble getting his oxygen mask off to wipe the blood away. His gloves were too thick.

The Drem Lighting System

The Drem Lighting System can be explained by drawing a large circle made up of dots. This represents the airfield perimeter. Each dot represents a light. One part of the perimeter lights formed the letters

"PO" for Pocklington. At the bottom of the circle the two ends don't join but go up towards the centre of the circle in two parallel lines. This represents the landing strip. So the Drem system was made up of three things.

First there were lights which identified the home airfield of the squadron. Second there was a wide circle of bright lights, miles out in the countryside. After home base was identified, the pilot would use this circle of lights as a flight path around his aerodrome while he waited to land. Thirdly, on both sides of the runway there were parallel landing strip lights which were turned so that they could only be seen from one direction – the direction that the air controllers wanted the planes to land from. We called this the "funnel" because it funnelled us towards the lights of the runway which was to be used.

The lights in the big circle were miles out in the country and sometimes they overlapped with neighbouring airfields. Every square inch of territory was part of the system. When you came home you were told to circle the drome always in a clockwise direction. In the first instance you called up base and told them that you were back. Our call sign was "Bedcoe, B-E-D-C-O-E." Bill would press his air-to-ground button and he would say, "Bedcoe this is N-Nan calling back to base." They would reply, "Stay on the Drem System at fifteen hundred feet" or maybe two thousand feet.

There might be twelve or so aircraft circling at the same time in different parts of the circuit and at different heights. We would have our wingtip lights on - port and starboard – and we kept a close eye on other aircraft which were in various stages of height from five hundred to two thousand feet.

Each drome had three intersecting runways going at different angles. The funnel would light it up according to the way the wind was blowing. The control tower had a system of switches whereby they could change the runway lights at a flick of a switch. They were powerful lights.

When your turn came you were told to "pancake", that was the term – not "land". It was always pancake. Bill would follow the Drem System lights 'round and fly over them until he saw the runway lights of the funnel, clearly. There was our landing strip. When he pancaked, he approached the start of the runway and he could see three lights on a pole, one above the other. which would appear in turn as he approached the runway - red for too high, green for medium height and orange for landing height. They were angled in such a way you could only see them in the funnel. In bad weather you could come in and still see these lights as you descended.

First of all you would see a red light. You were too high so it was telling you that you had to get down a bit. Then as you got lower it would change to a green light and you knew that you had to go down further. And when you saw the orange light you were just right. So the idea was to hop over the fence - by then you would have had your flaps and wheels down - and you would cut the motors when you saw the orange light and Bingo! You were down.

I always used to stand behind Bill and Don to land. I remember clearly seeing the red light change to green and change to orange and the next thing I knew we were safely down. And I would feel relief.

The "Drem" Lighting System

The *Drem* Lighting System was a lighting system laid out around all RAF airfields during the Second World War. It assisted pilots, returning at night, to identify the correct airfield and to position the plane for a safe landing.

In 1940, Wing Commander "Batchy" Atcherly, the commander of RAF Drem station, solved the night time landing problem encountered by his Spitfire pilots whenever they returned to base. Because of the Spitfire's long nose, the pilot's vision was hampered when taxiing and landing. Weaving slightly from side to side as the pilot moved into the takeoff position eased the taxiing problem but as the Spitfire approached the runway to land its nose had to be kept high to prevent stalling. This partly obscured the pilot's view of the runway. Landing at night made visibility poorer and if the weather was foul the risk to pilot and aircraft dramatically increased.

Atcherly had the idea of mounting lights on poles and placing them in the surrounding countryside to make a large ring of lights that encircled the airfield. Returning pilots would see the lights and fly their planes in a clockwise direction from light to light. As the lighted path on the runway came into view, each pilot positioned his plane and prepared his landing in confidence with the well lit path ahead.

Chapter 23: Operation 6 - Massy-Palaiseau

329 aircraft - 225 Lancasters, 86 Halifaxes, 18 Mosquitos - of Nos 1, 3, 4 and 8 Groups attacked railway targets at Évreux, Massey Palaiseau, Nantes and Tours. All of the raids appeared to be successful. 3 Lancasters and 1 Halifax - 1 aircraft from each raid - were lost. 33 Mosquitos to Berlin, 30 Serrate patrols, 13 Halifaxes minelaying on the flanks of the invasion coast. 2 Mosquitos lost from the Berlin raid. *Total effort for the night:* 405 sorties, 6 aircraft (1.5 per cent) lost.
The Bomber Command War Diaries, 11/12 June 1944

We had arrived at No. 102 Squadron at Pocklington in early summer. The weather leading up to Operation Overlord, the D-day landings in France, was foul. After that we had beautiful weather for a while and the Australians on the base started thinking it would be good to have a game of cricket. On inquiry we ascertained that the station had a cricket team representing RAF Pocklington that played against other airfields and munition factories and aircraft factories in Hull and various establishments in the area, but we had no hope of getting a game. The squadron team was captained by Curley Ambler, a squadron leader in charge of the engineering section. We called him "Curley" because he didn't have a hair on his head. He was in his forties and he was a permanent RAF officer. He was not a flying man. We got nowhere with him.

Although we had not seen his team play we decided to make it impossible for him to refuse us. We challenged the Poms to a test match against Australia. He accepted. He had to. No Englishman worth his salt could refuse a challenge like that. There was no doubt about the seriousness of the occasion. In his diary that day, Don McLean says that they "all went down to College Oval to see Australia v England".

The match took place on the 11th of June 1944. We spent the morning getting Q-Queenie ready for a bombing mission that night and in the afternoon played the cricket match. The squadron team was a crack team. There were over fifteen hundred pommy aircrew and ground crew to choose a cricket team from. There were only nineteen Australians on the squadron at the time and out of those we had to pick a team of eleven. We did not know of the ability of many of them.

Bill Rabbitt, Bob Selth, a mid-upper gunner from South Australia, and I had played cricket back in Australia. Bob was a wicketkeeper and a very stylish batsman. After the war he played A grade cricket at home in Adelaide. Bob's crew shared our hut with us. (A few weeks after this match, on the 24th of July, Bob was the only survivor when his plane was shot down over the English Channel.) The rest of the Australians made up the team.

Curley Ambler arranged for us to use the local Grammar School playing field and cricket pitch. It was a grass pitch and they provided all the equipment.

We fielded first and got them out for 163 which was a reasonable total so we had something to chase. I did some bowling. I was a slow right hand leg break bowler and I took 4/35. I can't remember my bowling very well but I can remember my batting prowess. When it came our turn to bat I opened up the innings for the Australian team with Bill Rabbitt. He was out LBW for 21. Bob Selth came in at number three. I was dead lucky in that two catches were dropped in slips off my batting and I made them pay for it because I ended up making 97. I was clean bowled trying to straight drive a fast bowler. Fast bowlers love being straight-driven, don't they!

We won and they rued the day they accepted the challenge. They were wondering what had happened. The Poms were good sports about it and Curley Ambler congratulated us. Bill was quite jubilant in his diary entry about the match:

> "The Aussies on the station picked a team and played the station crack team at cricket. They batted first and made 163. Bas took 4/35 and I caught one chap out. Bas and I opened and I was out LBW for 21. The next wicket fell at 90 and we really belted the ears off them. Bas carried on and made 97. He was very tired and we were all disappointed that he missed his century. Still we won the match very easily and shook the station rigid as they were expecting us to be heavily defeated. They have asked for a return match and we agreed. Bang on!"

Later that night we took off in Q-Queenie at 2205 hours to bomb the railway yards at Massy-Palaiseau.

Massy-Palaiseau

Massy is a town that over time has become a southern suburb of Paris and Massy-Palaiseau railway station is now part of Paris's regional express network.

The weather turned bad and Bill was hoping that the operation would be cancelled. There were twelve aircraft from the squadron on this mission. As well, nine planes went on gardening trips - three to Brest, where they encountered heavy ack-ack fire, and six to Le Havre.

This was a four hour twenty-five minute trip with six and a half thousand pound of bombs. They were a mixture of five hundred and one thousand pound bombs. The maximum sized bomb that we would carry was a two thousand pounder.

We stuck to track and time but it was too cloudy to find the target. Even after we were instructed by the Master Bomber to reduce height to three thousand feet we still couldn't see any target indicators. It was always scary dropping down near a target in ten-tenths cloud because there were always a lot of planes all doing the same thing.

The raid went ahead but it was not successful. Five aircraft, including us, were not able to drop our bombs because we could not find the target. One of our Halifaxes fought off a night fighter attack by either an Me 109 or a Focke Wulf 190. Sadly the crew of another Halifax Z-Zebra MZ651 were all killed. The pilot was an Australian, Flight Sergeant Russell Singleton. There were two more Australians in the crew – Pilot Officer Michael McNamara, the bomb aimer, and the wireless operator, Flight Sergeant Phillip Robson. They are all buried at Autheuil cemetery in the Haute-Normandie region of France.

Don McLean jettisoned two twelve hour delay bombs off the English coast to lighten the load and to make the plane more manoeuvrable when we came in to land, and we took the rest home. Landing with bombs on board was always very dangerous. If you had to make a crash landing you were dead because the bombs would explode. As it turned out, Bill made a lousy landing and frightened the hell out of us. In his diary he wrote that it "shook the crew a bit" which was a bit of an understatement.

Master Bomber

The Master Bomber controlled the bombing of Massey Palaiseau. When we started operations, Master Bombers would arrive at the target area a few minutes earlier than us. They flew low level to identify the target and then dropped the first flare on it – probably red or green. The Pathfinders would then come in and back up the initial flare with more flares. We would bomb on the flares. We usually didn't see the target at all. Don would have had a flare or a group of flares in his bombsight when he released the bombs.

Master Bombers started off in Pathfinder Force Lancasters but as the war continued things changed a lot. To improve the accuracy of marking targets with flares as well as to reduce the time that Master Bombers were at a low level over the target, pilots like Wing-Commander Leonard Cheshire flew the faster and more aerodynamic Mosquitos. Before Cheshire retired he was given an American P-51 Mustang to do his target marking in. Mustangs at that stage of the war were very fast, superior planes. It was supremely dangerous being a Master Bomber, flying in low to heavily defended targets. It was the most dangerous of the duties. Guy Gibson was killed on the Ruhr while being a Master Bomber and Leonard Cheshire got a VC acting as a Master Bomber.

Target Marking

The Master Bomber, as the term suggests, was the pilot who was in control of bombing raids. He marked the initial aiming point for the Pathfinder Force which then laid down a series of coloured target indicators and finally, by radio, he gave instructions to the approaching bombing stream about where they were to drop their bombs in relation to the target indicators.

8/9 February 1944, France. A still from a film taken from Avro Lancaster Mark I, DV380 'AJ-N', of No. 617 Squadron RAF, flown by the Squadron commander, Wing Commander G L Cheshire, the Master Bomber, during the low-level marking of the Gnome-Rhone aero-engine factory at Limoges.

This technique was first trialled on the night of 23rd/24th of June 1943 when four Pathfinder Lancasters led a force of fifty-six Lancasters to Friedrichshafen, near the German border with Switzerland and Liechtenstein, to bomb the Luftschiffbau Zeppelin factory where Wurzburg radar sets for night fighter interception boxes, and fuel tanks and fuselage sections for V2 rockets were being manufactured. With the Master Bomber directing part of the force, another group trialled an alternative technique bombing on a timed run with the nearby lake, The Bodensee, as its reference point. Reconnaissance photographs taken afterwards showed that only ten percent of bombs struck in the vicinity of the factory.

On the night of the 17th/18th of August 1943, the V1 and V2 rocket research site at Peenemünde was successfully attacked by 324 Lancasters, 218 Halifaxes and 54 Stirlings. This was then first full scale bombing operation conducted using the Master Bombing technique. Using a Master Bomber in this way became the standard procedure until early February 1944.

Above is a remarkable photograph of a successful raid led by a Master Bomber during the Second World War. It was taken by Wing Commander Leonard Cheshire after being given permission to demonstrate a low-level target marking technique which he was convinced would be much more accurate than methods the Pathfinder Force were using.

Cheshire, convinced that accuracy of marking depended upon a swift low level attack where visibility would be better and drift negligible, wished to "mark" the target flying a fast manoeuvrable Mosquito light bomber. This was denied but permission was given for him to demonstrate his technique with lumbering Lancasters which would be dangerously exposed at low height.

On the night of the 8th/9th of February 1944 he led a small force of Lancasters to bomb the Gnome-Rhone aero-engine factory at Limoges in France. After warning factory workers and correctly identifying the target with three runs across the factory, he dropped target markers directly onto the factory on his fourth run. Three Lancasters followed him dropping more target indicators. The photograph above shows that Cheshire's technique was very accurate. The buildings are brightly lit up in a shower of sparkling light from thirty pound incendiary bombs. With Cheshire now directing them from above, eight more Lancasters arrived and destroyed the factory with 12,000 pound HE bombs.

Following this raid Cheshire, now flying de Havilland Mosquitos, led a large bombing force to Munich and for the first time in the war, massive damage was caused in the centre of the city. A further improvement in the technique occurred later when Cheshire swapped his Mosquito for the very fast P-51 Mustang in which he would swoop down at the target to lay the first target indicators of the raid.

Cheshire had demonstrated that low level marking of targets in this manner dramatically improved the accuracy of bombing but inter-Group rivalry prevented this method from being universally adopted.

Chapter 24: Operation 7 - Evrecy

337 aircraft - 223 Lancasters, 100 Halifaxes, 14 Mosquitos - of Nos 4, 5 and 8 Groups attacked German troop and vehicle positions at Aunay-sur-Odon and Évrecy, near Caen. These raids were prepared and executed in great haste, in response to an army report giving details of the presence of major German units. The weather was clear and both targets were successfully bombed. No aircraft were lost. *Total effort for the night:* 769 sorties, 4 aircraft (0.5 per cent) lost.
The Bomber Command War Diaries, 14/15 June 1944

The target for our seventh operation was Evrecy, a small village southwest of Caen. Bomber Command was attacking several targets where there were large German troop concentrations preventing the advance of the D-Day forces. We were told that the object of our raid was to "smash" a German panzer division and attack the German headquarters. Twenty one aircraft from our squadron took off on this raid and we were carrying ten thousand pounds of bombs.

My log book says that we took off at 1220 hours on the 15th of June but we were in the plane well before midnight. This explains why Bill has the date for this operation in his diary as the 14th. We flew for five hours and five minutes and that put us back at the aerodrome at about 0525 as dawn was breaking. This operation took longer than our mission to Massy-Paliseau. The two towns are about the same distance away so we would have had a different track with more doglegs to trick the German radar and night fighters.

The Germans were defending the area desperately because the flak was pretty terrific and the fighter flares were going off everywhere. Bill's diary paints a very vivid picture of our raid:

"....what a prang! I have not seen such defences yet. They threw up flak, tracer, fighter flares, searchlights and everything possible at us. It looks a glorious sight if you could escape the reality behind it. We started getting fighter flares and searchlights off the Isle of Alderny and Guernsey and had it all the way into the target and back across the Channel. The fighter flares light up the sky like day and one feels as naked as a new born babe. We saw and experienced a tremendous barrage of flak. Le Havre was also putting on a terrific show. We bombed bang on the target, a real bulls-eye and came home flat out through the flames and flak...."

We bombed from 7,000 feet and "made a mess of the village" according to Don, our bomb aimer. In his diary he said that "we had to take evasive action from a fighter on the way in and hundreds of fighter flares were laid on the way out". He also mentions that "one crew on their first trip were hit by 'flak' and the navigator baled out".

This was Sergeant Roy Harris, the navigator on Pilot Officer Munroe's plane. They were damaged by flack, their turrets weren't working and the plane's intercom was playing up. He misunderstood the pilot's instructions and in the chaos he put his parachute on and jumped. After he landed, he hid in a hedge for two days and, after hearing some American soldiers talking, he surrendered and arrived back at the squadron a few days later. He was lucky that the Germans didn't get him.

It was pretty much touch and go for the army just after the D-Day landings. Raids like this one on Evrecy were to give them support because they were still having a hard time near the coast. They had lost territory and they were planning to make a counter attack. The Americans bombed the day after us and the whole of Bomber Command was on standby.

Dispersal and takeoff

After crews checked their motors we left our dispersal areas and taxied out on the perimeter track. Once aircraft started moving they followed each other out until all the aircraft were behind each other with all propellers going and all engines revving. It was very impressive. Exciting. My adrenaline was always pumping. There was no particular order in which we went. We just got on the perimeter track and followed the aircraft in front of us. There was no position that we preferred to be. It was just pure luck what position you were in. You might be in the first five or in the last five. When the takeoff time came, the first aircraft swung into position on the end of the runway and on the green signal from the control tower it would begin its takeoff run. Immediately it got halfway down the runway the second aircraft would swing into position and so it went on until up to twenty-six aircraft got the green light and took off. If the red light came on the op was scrubbed.

On takeoff, I was always standing behind Bill in the pilot seat and Don in the co-pilot seat on the flight deck, and looking over their shoulders at the runway bouncing up and down, and the end of the runway getting closer and feeling the aircraft leave the ground. Immediately we were airborne Bill would hold it close to the ground to build up speed and the plane would climb very slowly. It was more like crawling up rather than going up like a DC3. That's just what it was like. After he built up speed, he would pull the stick back and climb steeply. Generally it was a marvellous feeling and sight. The alternative was for me to adopt the crash position behind the main spar but with a full bomb load, if anything happened, we were curtains anyway. When we got airborne, Don vacated the second pilot's seat and headed down into the bomb aimer position. That made my way free to climb down the steps and go into my compartment. I figured that I might as well enjoy myself so I did it every time and saw more than most navigators.

Bill always used the last few yards of the runway. He would hold N-Nan down as far as he could to build up speed and then he would pull the stick back and we would commence to climb and hop over the fence. We seldom flew the first few legs at bombing height. Going up earlier was a waste of time and petrol. They might be at five thousand feet or ten thousand feet but as we got closer to the target we would climb to our bombing height on the approach legs of the flight plan, maybe from eighteen to twenty-one thousand. It was an exceptional circumstance when we bombed lower than that height. In every important target, like the Ruhr, we would bomb from our maximum height. Once we were airborne, especially if we took off early in the piece, we would circle around on what they called a "radius of action" to soak up time because we were timed to begin the operation by flying over base at a certain time to set course on our first leg. So we would takeoff with all the others from our squadron and circle 'round on a radius of action and at the same time I would navigate to be flying over our base at the exact departure time for our first leg. We had up to twenty-six planes all doing that with all of them coming back to the same point. They could go in any direction but they would all have to arrive back over base at a designated time. We were never above cloud doing this. It may seem dangerous that there we were all coming back to the same spot but we had clean air. In cloudy weather when we were completely closed in, we would circle the base below the cloud. We would then know where we were.

Bomb load

The ten thousand pounds of bombs that we dropped on Evrecy was not the largest bomb load a Halifax could carry. We flew with more but it was near our maximum bomb load. We carried 11,500 pounds of bombs to targets three times – to Venlo on the 3rd of September 1944, and then to both Heligoland and Wangerooge, my last two operations of the war. We were always at capacity with weight. They had what they called an "all-up weight". That was the weight of the aircraft, fully bombed and fully fuelled. It was probably about sixty-five thousand pounds and you couldn't exceed it because the plane wasn't built to take off with any load in excess of that. They varied the bomb load based on the distance to the target and back. It was always a compromise between bomb load and fuel load, but it never ever exceeded the all up weight. This was a war so we always took the maximum load of bombs but petrol weighs a lot too so naturally we could carry more bombs on shorter trips and vice versa. It was a ratio between the two.

N-Nan

We were in N-Nan for this raid on Evrecy. We had flown N-Nan once before on the D-Day operation to Maisy but this operation became the start of an almost permanent association with the plane. After Evrecy we were allocated N-Nan as our plane and we flew her exclusively from then on unless she was in for an inspection and maintenance or repairs. It was an exceptional plane and we had few problems with it. Bill handled it beautifully.

We thought she had a personality all of her own. The whole crew felt very strongly about N-Nan. She was our plane. We had a special affinity for her and we all came to love her. Eventually we had to say goodbye. It was a pretty hard thing to do!

Évrecy

16 July 1944, France. A British 5.5-inch gun crew firing at night during the offensive in the Odon valley near Evrecy,

In this chapter Basil Spiller describes his squadron's raid on Évrecy, a small town in the Basse-Normandie region in northwestern France. After the D-Day landings on the 6th of June 1944, the main thrust of the Allied forces was through the Normandy region where Evrecy is located.

This region juts out into the English Channel towards southern England. Because of its proximity to London it was of enormous strategic importance to the German forces who, after four years of occupation, had heavily manned and fortified the region.

The Battle of Normandy was fought from town to village. German fortifications, flying bomb sites, railway marshalling yards, armoured tank locations, troop positions and supply depots were located close to towns and villages in the region. Because of the relentless bombing by the RAF and USAAF, many civilians caught up in the war were killed and their towns and villages left in ruins.

Chapter 25: Operation 8 - Sterkrade

321 aircraft - 162 Halifaxes, 147 Lancasters, 12 Mosquitos - of Nos 1, 4, 6 and 8 Groups to attack the synthetic-oil plant at Sterkrade/Holten despite a poor weather forecast. The target was found to be covered by thick cloud and the Pathfinder markers quickly disappeared. The Main Force crews could do little but bomb on to the diminishing glow of the markers in the cloud. RAF photographic reconnaissance and German reports agree that most of the bombing was scattered, although some bombs did fall in the plant area, but with little effect upon production. Unfortunately, the route of the bomber stream passed near a German night-fighter beacon at Bocholt, only 30 miles from Sterkrade. The German controller had chosen this beacon as the holding point for his night fighters. Approximately 21 bombers were shot down by fighters and a further 10 by flak. 22 of the lost aircraft were Halifaxes, these losses being 13.6 percent of the 162 Halifaxes on the raid. No. 77 Squadron, from Full Sutton near York, lost 7 of its 23 Halifaxes taking part in the raid. *Total effort for the night:* 829 sorties, 32 aircraft (3.9 per cent) lost.

The Bomber Command War Diaries, 16/17 June 1944

On the 16th of June we went on our first trip over the German Reich and our squadron paid a terrible price. Bill in his diary describes it as a "very grim trip". Our target was a synthetic oil plant at Sterkrade, a city deep in the Ruhr Valley. The Ruhr was the most heavily defended area in Germany because it was the home of most of Germany's heavy industries, its armament factories and the site of the famous Krupp's steel works.

Twenty-three of our crews were briefed for this mission although two had engine trouble and they were forced to return. We took six and a half thousand pounds of bombs and we left at 2355 hours. The raid took four hours and fifty-five minutes and we landed back at base at roughly five o'clock in the morning.

As we flew towards Sterkrade the German air defences were waiting for us. There was a night fighter beacon at Bocholt, a town that was only twenty-five miles north of the target. The German night fighters were using it as a "holding point", so they were already airborne and buzzing around the beacon before we arrived. Sterkrade was only five minutes away and the night fighters had a picnic that night. German radar had been watching the bomber stream approach and once the controller was convinced that Sterkrade was the target, German planes flew above us – probably about five thousand feet above – and dropped "fighter flares" which drifted slowly down on parachutes to light up the sky and illuminate the bombers on their bombing run from above making us visible to any night fighters around the target, and the gun batteries on the ground.

As this was my first German target, I parted the blackout curtains and observed the German flak and searchlights for the first time. It was horrific! The sky was lit up. The night was filled with searchlights darting back and forth and flak exploding everywhere. Down below I could not see the ground but I could see bombs exploding and photo-flares going off continuously and glowing brilliantly as they hung in the sky. The light was blindingly bright. From below they were trying to catch our planes with their searchlights and shoot them down with their ack-ack guns. The Germans knew the height that we were bombing at. If it was twenty thousand feet, they would time their flak bursts to explode between, say, nineteen and twenty-one thousand feet. Anywhere we went within that band of two thousand feet anti-aircraft shells would be exploding all around us. I don't remember whether we had any close flak bursts. We had never experienced searchlight barrages and flak barrages like it. We flew into ten-tenths cloud over the target and the target indicators were bursting beneath the clouds so we bombed on our ETA (expected time of arrival).

The large number of night fighters tracked us successfully all the way to the target and back to the coast and made big use of the fighter flares,. Subsequently our losses were very heavy. Our squadron only had twenty-one planes in the raid and lost five to night fighters and flak. That's a loss rate of twenty-eight percent. Our satellite aerodrome at Full Sutton, 77 Squadron, sent twenty-three aircraft and lost seven. That's a loss rate of thirty percent. That means out of a possible forty-four planes we lost twelve altogether. Three or four nights at that rate and a squadron would have no more planes left. There were a total of 321 aircraft sent to bomb the oil plant at Sterkrade and thirty-one were shot down, ten by flak and twenty-one by night fighters. Whichever way you look at it, that's a pretty serious casualty rate. Amazingly, N-Nan didn't suffer any attacks. It was just pure luck.

The Halifaxes from 102 Squadron shot down were C-Charlie (MZ292), M-Mother (MZ301), O-Oboe (MZ642), R-Roger (LW192) and Z-Zebra (MZ652). Halifax M-Mother was piloted by Squadron Leader Fisher, our B Flight Commander. He was one of the youngest Flight Commanders in Bomber Command. He was awarded a DFM and a DFC in 1942 when he was a sergeant flying Whitleys at 77 Squadron which was then based at RAF Leeming, an airfield in North Yorkshire. Bill knew him. They were both pilots and had contact with him as our squadron leader and they no doubt had a drink together in the officers' mess. His plane crashed into the North Sea and the bodies were never recovered.

When I had finished watching the bombing run, I closed the curtains and went back to my compartment and began to follow the flight plan to get us back to base. It was always the same procedure as I had done from base to the target and the track was usually the reverse.

On the way home a lot of our crews had fighter attacks. It was just luck that we weren't attacked and Bill in his diary agrees. Luckily we encountered cloud cover and Bill, knowing the danger, ducked in and out of it as it occurred. He couldn't see anything in cloud so he was flying on instruments but it was a small price to pay because while we were in there no fighter could see us. There was always the possibility of collision in cloud but the chances were reduced because all aircraft in the flight stream were on the same track, doing the same things and all heading in the same direction.

After we had dropped our bombs and taken our photographs it was never a matter of "get home as quick as we can." I gave Bill the correct course, information about the height we were to fly away from the target and what speed to fly at. It was all predetermined. Our job was to go in and do our bombing and turn and head for home following the flight plan.

At night time we wouldn't see another plane. We all had our lights out and it was usually pitch black. That's why it was so important for all of us to stick to the flight plan. Then we would all be turning at the same time and following the same course at the same height.

According to Bill "it was almost daylight for the entire trip" and he mentions that the "Northern Lights seemed very bright". This was the Aurora Borealis and when it took over the sky would be quite bright - almost daylight. On our way back from the target Bill called us up to the cockpit to have a look at it. We had a quick glance outside and then went back to our jobs. A nice ending for us but it was a very shaky do.

Bill's diary entry for this raid is interesting:

> ".... We bombed at 20,000 feet and amidst terrific flak barrages. The raid in my opinion was a failure owing to Met and PFF "boobing". 33 planes were lost and there were 5 from here including my Flight Commander S/L Fisher. Full Sutton lost 7 kites. Most chaps had fighter attacks but we were more fortunate and I certainly hugged those clouds. Bas and Don did excellent work on their navigation. .... We took 6,500 lbs bombs and were on 5 tanks. The landing on return was O.K. Now to bed and rest a while."

Bill described the raid as a failure because of "Met and PFF boobing"! What he means is that the wind forecast that the meteorological bods had given to Don turned out to be unreliable. Don would have set that reading on his bombsight. The Pathfinder Force using the wind forecast must have placed their target indicators incorrectly, so the possibility of us bombing the wrong area were very high because we bombed on their target indicators which would have disappeared quickly under the thick cloud. Bill is saying that the PFF dropped their flares in the wrong place. The Master Bomber probably placed his initial flare incorrectly, and when Don set up his bombsight according to the met wind forecast it made matters worse.

Bill thought the mission was a failure but I was not worrying anything about that. I was always relieved to get 'em there and get 'em back. That was my job.

Navigator and bomb aimer

I have already mentioned that Don McLean also had some training as a pilot and a navigator. He always sat in the co-pilot seat alongside Bill for our takeoffs and landings. Then he would come down and sit at the table with me in the navigator's compartment. He was a most valuable crew member. On the way to and from the target Don helped me by operating the GEE set over England and assisted me with H2S fixes over Europe.

My chart table was probably about four feet long with a collapsible seat that could handle two people without any problem. We worked over the same chart. Over England and the Channel, while I was plotting the air position Don would determine our ground position from the GEE set and give it to me in latitude and longitude. I would plot it on the chart and join up the air position with the ground position and obtain a wind vector.

The Germans commenced jamming GEE as soon as we crossed the enemy coast into France. On the oscilloscope it looked just like green grass growing on the screen. It used to grow to an inch tall which was the height of our radar signal on the GEE oscilloscope so we couldn't read the signal through the grass. From that point on I had to rely on H2S fixes and the Air Position Indicator.

We were a team instead of a one man band. Don was more than an offsider. It was optional. I was happy to let him do it and he was happy because it gave him something to do otherwise he would've been twiddling his thumbs for three, four, five or sometimes six hours as we made our way to and from the target. Few planes operated like this because not all bomb aimers were trained as navigators. It depended on the relationship between the navigator and the bomb aimer in our case, and the skill mix of the crew. When the time came Don would get up and move into his bomb aimer's position. I often saw him there, looking into the bombsight lying down full length over it, prone, on the floor of the plane.

> *Don has dropped his bombs, He gets up, sits beside me and turns his attention to the H2S screen. We are on the first leg away from the target. We are looking at my flight plan and the chart. We are checking H2S all the time. GEE comes in as we head back across the French coast and the jamming subsides. We will stay on GEE all the way back to base.*

Weak bladder

Bill, our pilot, had a weak bladder and on every trip he had to pass water. Harry used to carry a milk bottle, and on Bill's instructions he used to pass it up to Bill and he would do the necessary. When he was finished, he would pass that back to Harry and Harry would dispose of it through the chute.

Window

"Window" was the code name for bundles of metallic strips about two feet long and about half an inch wide that every aircraft carried. When it was dropped from the plane, it would overwhelm the Germans' radar system with false echoes, reduce the accuracy of their directed flak and confuse their gunners. It was Harry's job to cut the bundles and free them up and stuff them down the chute as we approached the target. Then window would flutter down in millions of pieces. It was first used in operations in 1943 and we used it on every night time operation. It worked for a while but I don't know whether it worked all the time or whether the Germans counteracted it or not.

The elsan

The toilet in the Halifax was situated behind the main spar in the fuselage of the aircraft. In the airforce it is called an "elsan". If you wanted to empty your bowels you could utilise this contraption. Halifaxes had two or three oxygen stations along the fuselage to plug your mask into because it was quite a journey back to the elsan. You'd unplug your oxygen mask and carry your oxygen tube up the stairs, down the fuselage and over the main spar, plugging it in to the next oxygen station, taking a few gulps and going on to the next station. When you got to the elsan, there was a permanent oxygen plug there that you could plug into while you did your business.

Structures within structures

Things were very rudimentary in the airforce during the First World War in terms of the planes they used and the technical support and administrative structures that were in place. There had been a massive technical and structural leap by the time my story started. Not just the planes, armaments and the bombs but the advancements in radar navigation were enormous too. And then there was the organization of the airforce. The fact that these guys from intelligence arrived at my plane door and grabbed all my charts and logs to see if they were fair dinkum or not is a good example.

They had structures within structures by this time. It was massive! We'd get off the plane and be transported to debriefing where we would talk about the mission with an intelligence officer. Then we went to breakfast which was always waiting for us. Then after breakfast transport was waiting to take us to our sleeping quarters. That's why there was such a large number of ground staff on every station. The aircrew were only trained to do specific jobs when they were flying. There was a lot done around us to give us the support we needed.

In the First World War, when they started to use planes, the pilots on both sides would wave at one another as if they were part of a special club. Then when the war got nastier the first change was that they threw bricks at one another. Then it wasn't long before someone had a gun. They used to shoot at each other with revolvers. So things stepped up. It was evolution - more like a revolution. Mind you in the early stages of World War 2 parts of the RAF were pretty elementary as well. They learned fast. They had to.

Other crews

Your world was your crew. You didn't know very many other people as well as you knew your crewmates. You knew your crew intimately because you were thrown so close together so many times. Between operations all of us except Charlie, who was a bit of a loner, mixed with one another and went out together. We went down to the pub as a crew, unless one of us had something special on like a date with a particular girl. The other crew that shared our hut went out as a group as well, although their pilot, Harley Donald, never joined them.

Sometimes we simply hung around the mess and played billiards or darts or listened to somebody tinkling away at the piano. It depended on what we felt like. One person might have said, "I'm going down the pub at Pocklington tonight. Is anybody coming?" Two or three might pipe up, "I'm coming too." And the other two might stay in their quarters and write letters home. It was a fluid thing.

We didn't mix with the crew that we shared the hut with. We only shared the hut. Only three missions after Sterkrade, they were shot down and six of them were killed. It was very sad but we were somehow detached from them too. It was a shock because it brought death right into our hut. Don knew the bomb aimer and I knew the navigator, Sandy the gunners and so on because every morning after breakfast we had to report to our respective flights. The navigational flight was held in one building, the bombing flight would've been held in another. The gunnery flight was in another and the wireless operators would have been in a different building. The engineers had separate meeting too. We each mingled with our specialized groups and got to know them but our crew was the centre of our lives.

World War 1. Beginning of War in the Air

The Aviatik-Doppeldecker B1, an early German reconnaissance aircraft of the First World War.

At the start of the First World War, the British and German pilots and observers were unarmed, and often waved to one another if their paths crossed. It was not long before they began experimenting with ways of attacking one another. Pistols and rifles were ineffective, as were throwing bricks, and trailing bombs or grappling irons behind the plane.

By October 1914 aircraft manufacturers on both sides were experimenting with machine guns. Louis Strange (DSO, DFC) attached a safety strap to his

Avro 504, allowing his observer to stand up and fire a machine gun both forward and behind. On the 5th of October 1914 a French Voisin III two-seater biplane became the first plane to shoot down another plane when the observer stood up firing a machine gun and shot down a German Aviatik-Doppeldecker B1.

Halifax Mk 3, LW192, of No. 102 Squadron, Pocklington

Halifax R-Roger LW192 was delivered to 102 Squadron, Pocklington on either the 24th or the 25th of May 1944. On the 16th of June 1944, it was one of the aircraft sent to bomb Sterkrade in the Ruhr Valley. Basil Spiller's crew also participated in this raid.

In this chapter, Basil Spiller says that twenty-three Halifaxes left from Pocklington that night but two returned early with engine trouble. The flight was met by night fighter attacks and "terrific searchlight" and "flak barrages". During their bombing run, Basil parted the blackout curtains and stood behind Don McLean, the bomb aimer, to watch the "horrific" barrage. The sky was lit up by searchlights, fighter flares and flak exploding all around them.

Halifax LW192 , piloted by flight-sergeant E.F. Braddock, was attacked on its homeward journey at 0201 by a German night fighter, over the Netherlands, 130 kilometres west of Sterkrade. Under cannon fire, the Halifax exploded and debris was scattered between the towns of Buurmalsen and Buren, five kilometres apart.

The seven crew members of Halifax LW192 were killed. They are all buried in Buren General Cemetery. They are pilot, flight-sergeant Braddock, and sergeants E.W. Zaccheo, the flight engineer, W.A.C. Reid, the navigator, R.L. Putt, the bomb aimer, J.O. Booker, the wireless operator, and E.A. Finch and G. Hadfield the two gunners.

No. 102 Squadron lost five of the twenty-one Halifaxes that took part in this mission. In one night the squadron lost thirty-five men. Thirty-three were killed and two became prisoners of war. It was a terrible blow for the squadron.

Squadron Leader David Fisher, DFM, DFC, RAFVR

Flight Sergeant David Roy Fisher was just nineteen years old when he was posted to 77 Squadron at RAF Leeming in North Yorkshire to begin his first tour of duty. The squadron was equipped with Armstrong Whitworth Whitley bombers. Flight Sergeant Fisher was awarded the Distinguished Flying Medal and the Distinguished Flying Cross for bravery in April 1942 while on a bombing operation to Rostock, a coastal town on the Baltic Sea, in north-east Germany.

Rostock was the target of four consecutive night bombing operations from the 23rd to the 27th of April 1942. Whitley bombers made up a small part of the force each night. The raids were concerted, incendiary, area-bombing attacks although on each night a group of planes from the bombing stream unsuccessfully attacked the Heinkel aircraft factory on the town's outskirts, causing only minor damage. The town itself suffered massive destruction. Over 2,200 buildings were either destroyed or seriously damaged. Some sixty percent of the town was left in ruins and 204 people were killed. After the Rostock operations the RAF's Armstrong Whitworth Whitleys were removed from front-line service

Because of the shortage of replacement aircraft, the squadron briefly joined Coastal Command, moving to RAF Chivenor on the north-west coast of Devon.

In October 1942, the squadron moved to RAF Elvington near Pocklington in Yorkshire, converting to four-engine Halifax bombers. In May 1944, 77 Squadron moved once again to nearby RAF Full Sutton making way for two Free French squadrons, Nos. 346 "Guyenne" and 347 "Tunisie".

David Fisher's DFC was gazetted by the Air Ministry on the 15 May 1942. His citation reads:

> "One night in April, 1942, this airman captained an aircraft which attacked Rostock. On the outward journey, shortly after crossing the North Sea, his aircraft was attacked by an enemy fighter. Although his aircraft was severely damaged, Sergeant Fisher succeeded in evading the attacker and, displaying great courage and resolution, flew the remaining 140 miles to his target which he both bombed and photographed. He finally flew the damaged aircraft 'back to base and made a safe landing. Throughout, this airman showed great determination and skilful airmanship."

David Fisher completed a full tour with 77 Squadron. In April 1944 he was posted to 102 Squadron at Pocklington as squadron leader. He was Flight Commander of B Flight, to which Basil Spiller's crew belonged.

At twenty-one years of age, Squadron Leader Fisher was the youngest squadron leader in Bomber Command. He was killed with his crew in the early hours of the morning on the 17th of June 1944 after they bombed the Ruhrchemie AG synthetic oil plant at Sterkrade, in the Ruhr Valley. Their plane crashed into the North Sea.

Chapter 26: The Austin 10 and the "Naughty Nineties"

Soon after the Sterkrade raid Bill came to the crew and told us that he had an opportunity to buy a car and asked us if we would be in it. It was a pretty cheap car and we had no hesitation in buying it. I handed over ten pounds sterling which was a lot because I found out later that the car only cost twenty-five. Someone got a pretty cheap share. I was only on sergeant's wages but I still had the hundred pounds I left Australia with. Bill wouldn't have known that. Anyway we bought the car. I don't know where Bill found it. It was an Austin Ten sedan. It was referred to as "Rabbitt's Crew's Car".

It was a dog of a car! We had all sorts of trouble with it. It had no universal joints. In the main drive it had a series of fibre pads that were bolted together. When we changed down at too high a speed they would strip and we were left with no main drive between the gearbox and the differential. We used to run it on 100 octane aviation fuel. We got that cheap because we got it from the ground crew so it didn't cost us anything. There were mechanics in the ground crew so we had no trouble with maintenance. It should have been the fastest car in Britain with that high octane fuel but we had to be very careful driving it because of the shortcomings of the main drive. I didn't have a licence so I never drove it.

Having the car changed our lives. Our local pub was at Pocklington only half a mile down the road. Normally we would still walk there and not take the car but having the car meant that when we wanted to go to the pub we could go further afield. We could drive into York, Driffield or even Bridlington when we got a forty-eight hour pass which we did from time to time. And it gave us freedom and a bigger radius of action to find girls.

We could go where we liked as a crew without taking a bus. Somehow we fitted all of us in there. We'd all cram in. I can remember one night when somebody sat astride the bonnet coming home from the pub. We were larrikins I suppose. All in all, it was a good investment.

Charlie might not have come but the other six of us would go off the station on a forty-eight hour pass together, usually from Friday night at five o'clock 'til midnight Sunday night. If we went to York, we always went to Betty's Bar, a favourite meeting place for aircrew.

York was the centre of Yorkshire. North of the city was the Canadian 6 Group and east was RAF 4 Group. We used to meet Canadian aircrew quite a bit in Betty's Bar. York was also the home of a notorious dance floor. On our way to the dance we went to the pub and drank gin and orange to give us a hit and fill us up with "Dutch courage" to ask the girls to dance with us. The girls would be at the dance floor waiting. On a typical night in York, we'd go to Betty's Bar first, have a skinful of gin and orange to give us a quick hit, and then we would go to the dance.

There was a big dance floor in every major city in the UK. It was usually called the "Mecca" - the Mecca Locano. There was one in Leeds and one in Edinburgh and one in London and one in Birmingham. I went to all of them at various times while I was over there. I was too shy to dance without my gin and orange for Dutch courage. Once I had that I would go and dance all night. I did the slow foxtrot, quickstep and jazz waltz. I learned by trial and error. I hadn't done any dancing before I left Australia. Bett was a very good dancer and she taught me more after the war.

After we finished our first tour of thirty-five operations we sold our car to the padre for ten pounds but no-one ever saw the money. Father Seary was a catholic!

He was an Australian and he happened to be in the United Kingdom at the start of the war so he stayed there. Every night before we took off on ops he used to come out to our dispersal and the three devout catholic members of our crew, Bill, Sandy and Don, would disappear with him into the small hut adjacent to our dispersal area. He would give them his blessing or the last rites or communion. I don't know, but I reckon that's what saved my bacon while I was in the war. I didn't go and get a blessing. I coasted along and hitched a ride on their shirt-tails.

Fighter affiliation

In his diary entry on the 18th of June, 1944, Bill says: "Flew this morning on fighter affiliation but fighters would not play on account of poor weather - so I tested "George" and H2S up and down the coast from Hull to Flamborough Head."

Fighter Affiliation was all arranged by the flight commander. We would take off and rendezvous with a Spitfire or a Hurricane and practise evasive action when he attacked us. He would attack from the rear or at an angle and we would go into a corkscrew dive to try and avoid the attack. It was valuable training for when we were attacked on operations.

The pilot on this fighter affiliation called it off probably because his drome was in danger of being clouded out. They were in no more danger than we were though. No-one wanted to land in cloudy weather but instead of heading back to base, we climbed through cloud and put our time up there to a useful purpose. That's why Bill says that we tested G-George and its H2S up and down the coast.

Domleger

In between the Sterkrade mission and the next operation to Noyelle we had a seven bombing raids scrubbed. One of these was on the 19th of June at 2350 hours. We had been briefed to bomb Domleger, a V1 site in northern France. In my log I have written: "Ops abandoned on route." We were only up for one hour and ten minutes. The account of this mission in Bill's diary is interesting. He says:

> ".... the operation was scrubbed on account of particularly bad weather approaching. We flew out into the North Sea and dropped some of our bombs and brought the rest back. I had the fastest time for landing after the call up. The landing was wizard and just as well as we had about 4,000 pounds of bombs on board. My approach was similar to a dive-bomber and I was lucky to make a good landing off such an approach...."

Pancakes

Bill mentions that he had the fastest time for landing "after the call up". On our return to base we were always staged at various intervals waiting to land using the Drem system. Approaching base, Bill would have called, "Bedcoe. This is N-Nan." They would have told us to circuit at say.... a thousand feet. Our next call would be: "Hello N-Nan. You are permitted to pancake." That was the "call up". It was our turn to land. It was good to have a fast time. You weren't up there circling madly waiting your call. Bill says he pancaked like "a dive-bomber". He must have put the nose down and just checked in time to put it down with a three pointer. I don't know why he did that because with the bombs on board why try something tricky? Perhaps he got the call to pancake late and didn't want to do another circuit in bad weather.

When Don Maclean and Harry Brabin wrote about this aborted operation both said that the Signals Leader, who was filling in as the wireless operator on the Wing Commander's plane, made a big mistake. Don wrote:

> "We were briefed for another P.plane site in France and just after setting course, when we got south of the Humber we got a recall. We took our delay bombs out to sea and jettisoned them and brought the rest home. The Winco. got his recall late and reached the French coast – he had the Signals Leader as W/Op and was last home."

Halifax Navigator

Somehow he failed to receive the call and they flew on a long way before they realized they were out there on their own. They couldn't have been far from the target because Domleger is only about 140 miles from London and just twenty miles inside the French coast. The Signals Leader would have been mortified at his mistake. Receiving radio messages and sending distress signals were two of the most important jobs in the plane. It could have been bad for them because they were out there on their own without the protection of numbers in the bombing stream.

On the 20th of June we took Halifax O-Oboe up to test the repairs that the ground crew had done on it and to do a photographic exercise. In my log I wrote simply: "Air test." It took one hour. That night Bill wrote in his diary:

> "Ops on tonight and there seems to be something in the wind. Everybody must get as much sleep as possible. There is maximum petrol in the kite. The rumours are that it was Berlin in daylight (rather grim) ...."

The ground crew were responsible for getting the aircraft ready. Minor maintenance had to be done and any flak or fighter damage had to be repaired. The plane had to get bombed up and fully fuelled, the instruments checked and the ammunition put on board and it would be waiting for us on its dispersal site. They had put "maximum petrol in the kite" which meant that we were going on a long flight.

None of us knew what a target was going to be until briefing. There were always rumours about this or that target. It would have probably been the first RAF daylight raid on Berlin. I can remember this time well. Rumours that we were about to bomb Berlin in daylight were all around the squadron. To get to there you had to fly over Germany for a long time and it was always very well defended. It is almost four hundred miles heading due east to Berlin after crossing the Dutch coast into Europe. That's eight hundred miles across German controlled territory, shot at by flak and fighters all the way. It would have been "grim" all right.

Bill had also heard that there were going to be "5,000 aircraft on the target." That is a lot of aircraft. I don't know how they would be able to get that many because the maximum effort from Bomber Command would be a thousand and possibly twelve hundred from the Yanks. The number must've included fighters.

We were supposed to be called early in the morning at 0230 but the mission was scrubbed. Bill found being prepared for operations only to have them cancelled frustrating. On the 21st he wrote that we "went out to the kites to fly and they have flamin' well scrubbed it again". This may have been a mission to Renescure, another V1 site, between Calais and Lille. Bill goes on to explain why he is frustrated:

> "Here we are for six days and nights in succession standing by, all keyed up to top pitch, and this is what happens. Just as you are ready to take off – scrubbo! Just as you are airborne – scrubbo!"

If a mission was scrubbed while we were out in the planes, they would fire a flare from a Very pistol into the air from the control tower. You could hear a cheer ring out from the crews all around the drome when they saw that flare burst into colour. So, I don't know why Bill was so anxious to get out there. The rest of the crew wasn't so eager, that's for sure. We were alive. I didn't mind the missions being abandoned. By the sound of it Bill wouldn't have been one of those cheering.

Anyway he didn't seem to worry about it too much because on the 21st of June he went straight in and bought the car. He drove it back to base really excited and described it as "a wizard job". But as I have already said, it was a dog of a car! He writes that we "all popped in and off to York flat out - drove up the wrong streets and parked it outside of a pub tied by a cord to a lamp post." I remember that vividly. It was at Betty's Bar! We tied it up like a horse to a hitching post and when we came back a policeman was standing there and he told us that someone had tied up the car. We never told him that it was us.

On the next day, the 22nd of June, we were told that we were not going to be on ops as Bill and John Allen had to go as witnesses to the court martial about our prang at Lichfield when our two inner engines malfunctioned. Only the engineer and pilot were needed. The mechanic was court marshalled.

That night we headed off to the pictures in York. Bill says that the car "went like a bird". With the mechanics doing all the work on it and high octane fuel no wonder she went like a bird. When we came back from the pictures we watched our squadron taking off. Bill says that we were "envious of them" and that we wished we were with them. He might have wished to be with them but I didn't want to go any time I didn't have to. I am sure I am speaking for the rest of the crew when I say that too.

Bill goes on about it again the following day. There were all sorts of rumours that we were going to bomb Berlin and continue on to Russia and probably get bombed up again and do the same thing on the way back but no squadrons ever did this. There would be a few hundred planes. Where would they bomb us up and refuel us in Russia? At an airfield in Russia? Hardly! They would need a lot of gear – ammunition and bombs and fuel, so I doubt it. Bill was really hoping that it would "soon come off" but I think it was doomed to failure before it started. It would be such a big logistical exercise just to get everything to Russia. Impossible! It might have been at the time when Russia was clamouring for us, the allies, to open a second front and give them the assistance they required. Perhaps it was only a gesture of support that Bomber Command never really intended to carry out.

N-Nan's Nose art

When we took over N-Nan as our plane, "nose-art" appeared all of a sudden at the squadron. Crews began painting designs near the nose of their Halifaxes on the port side between the nose and the cockpit. Because we were flying in N-Nan, we chose the phrase "Naughty Nineties" and our emblem was a painting of Merle Oberon doing the can-can. I didn't have anything to do with it. Bill probably chose it in conjunction with Trevor who was in charge of the ground staff.

Our Naughty Nineties painting of Merle Oberon was beautifully done. It looked very professional and we all loved it. She was front on kicking up her legs, lifting up her skirt in the typical can-can pose. One of the ground staff did it. He was very artistic. It was not surprising. You met all sorts in the ground staff with many different talents. Some had good voices. Some were good artists. Some had good musical skills.

N-Nan's nose art only lasted a couple of weeks. I don't know whether it was the decision of Wing Commander Wilson or Group Captain Russell but there were orders from above and all No. 102 Squadron nose-art was painted over. A lot of squadrons had nose-art right through the war which led me to believe that it was a personal decision of the wing commander or group captain in charge of the squadron.

The only thing we were allowed to paint on N-Nan was a symbol on the port side near the cockpit of a little bomb for every mission that was flown in it. The twenty-first mission was represented as a key, just like when you celebrate your twenty-first birthday. It was customary to do this. It's in the photos of N-Nan that were taken at the time. There are other photos of the plane that show where Naughty Nineties and the Merle Oberon painting have been painted over.

Merle Oberon and N-Nan's Nose Art

In this chapter Basil Spiller discusses the nose art that was painted on N-Nan, his crew's Halifax heavy bomber. Their choice of subject was inspired by Merle Oberon's portrayal of Kitty Langley, a beautiful young variety belle, who is stalked by the strange Mr Slade, a fellow "lodger" in a London apartment house. Slade in reality is Jack the Ripper.

Released in January 1944, "The Lodger" was a gripping thriller, and red blooded servicemen in their thousands lined up to see Merle Oberon do the can-can although one Australian critic wrote of her performance: "It is a novelty to find Merle Oberon in the role of a can-can dancer; she has too much native dignity to fit the part more than nominally."

The "key" symbol in the photograph below, represents N-Nan's "coming of age", N-Nan's twenty-first combat operation. There are also twenty small bomb symbols, in groups of ten, one for each previous raid.

Halifax LW142 N-Nan's "Naughty Nineties" nose art.

The Austin 10

The Austin 10 first appeared on British roads in 1932 and it continued to be improved and modified.

It had a four speed gear box and was powered by a 10 horsepower, OHV in-line four cylinder engine, giving it a top speed of between 55 and 65 miles per hour (88 and 104 kilometres per hour).

Over the years many different types were built. It was initially released in two versions, a basic saloon model and a deluxe version which were priced at 155 and 168 pounds sterling respectively.

Other versions appeared soon after, including Tourer 2 and four-seaters and 6-8 hundredweight vans which became known as "Tillies".

Production continued through the war years and from 1939 until 1945 some 53.000 Austin 10s were produced.

When production ended in 1947, 283,092 Austin 10s of all varieties had been built.

An Austin 10, similar to one purchased by Basil Spiller's crew, June 1944. Basil Spiller cannot identify the flying officer in the photograph but believes he was a friend of his pilot, Bill Rabbitt.

Chapter 27: Operation 9 - Noyelles-en-Chaussée

321 aircraft - 200 Halifaxes, 106 Lancasters, 15 Mosquitos - of Nos 1, 4, 6 and 8 Groups attacked 3 flying bomb sites in clear weather conditions. All targets were accurately bombed; no aircraft lost.
The Bomber Command War Diaries, 24 June 1944

After Sterkrade, we finally took off on a daylight raid to bomb the V1 flying bomb launching site near Noyelles-en-Chaussée, near a small town in northern France. The region we flew over was the location of many First World War battles including the Battle of the Somme. Once again, being close to the English Channel made it an ideal location from which the Germans could fire V1 rockets at London. I remember writing this operation in my log book because "Noyelles" is such a strange name. In between the two raids the squadron was briefed for operations six days in a row and seven raids were cancelled because the weather was lousy.

This was our first daylight operation and the first daylight raid from Pocklington since an attack on Hamburg in August 1942, almost two years earlier. We had a Spitfire escort for this raid. We had them on all daylight raids. It was too dangerous without them. The Messerschmitt Bf109s and Focke Wulf 190s would easily cut us to pieces.

On this mission twenty aircraft left from 102 Squadron. We took off at 1535 hours, carrying 6,500 pounds of bombs, and the flight took three hours and forty five minutes.

In his diary for this raid, Bill says:

"Today was my first daylight operation. The take-off was really wizard and for a time my kite N-Nan was the leader of the entire force until we divided to lose some time."

We were not briefed to lead this flight. It just happened probably because of the prevailing winds pushing us faster. We did not want to get to the target ahead of time so our plane had to lose time by doing a dogleg which made us drop back. The planes behind us should have done the same thing if they were ahead of time.

The only time our crew was briefed to lead the formation was on our nineteenth operation, a daylight mission to the Forêt de Nieppe when I was wounded. You get the feeling from his diary entry that Bill is thrilled to be leading the force. After all, it's a beautiful day. You can see for miles. You're flying past London and you can see the French coast. Planes are stacking up behind you. They're formating on you! That's the pilot club at work!

On the bombing run flak burst in front of us and a piece of spent shell punctured the windscreen and hit Bill on the forehead. Luckily it had no momentum. It didn't even draw blood. Bill says that it shook him up a bit but it didn't stop him flying the plane. It just fell in his lap and he showed us when we landed. When the windscreen was broken it would get very draughty. It was uncomfortable and noisy because the noise from the engines was accentuated and the wind rushed in. We didn't try to fix the hole. How would you do that? The ground staff would patch the plane up as they did after every bombing raid. They would put patches on the holes in the duralium skin and new panels of perspex in the windscreen.

Bill mentioned in his diary that bombs went whizzing past us during the bombing run. This happened quite often because even though planes were told to drop their bombs at a certain height, they would be staggered at slightly different heights because the altimeter wasn't a precise instrument. Even so you wouldn't bomb a plane that was visible in the bombsight ever. There was never an excuse for that. Bombing at night was so dangerous because you did not know what was below you. This was why every crew had instructions to bomb from the same height. There should never be a plane below you. After our bombing run we turned right which took us over Abbeville where there was heavy predicted flak. Three of our planes were damaged and some aircrew were wounded.

We were not on operations the next day, the 25th of June but the squadron sent eighteen planes on a daylight raid to a V1 site at Montorgueil which was in the same area as Noyelles-en-Chaussée. N-Nan had been refuelled and bombed up and went to Montorgueil with a different crew. This was normal practice. We had been given a break but the planes were on operations every day unless they were damaged or needed maintenance. Another crew may have used N-Nan but we had first call on her.

Two hundred and two Halifaxes and one hundred and six Lancasters bombed Montorgueil that day. They were met by heavy flak over the target and two 4 Group Halifaxes were shot down – one from our squadron and one from 77 Squadron, our satellite squadron at Full Sutton. There is some doubt about what happened to them but it appears that the two Halifaxes collided with one another and crashed near the French town of Fontaine L'Etalon. The fourteen men from the two planes are buried in the town's churchyard. The Halifax from 77 Squadron, L-Love LL549, was piloted by Flight Sergeant Donald Steven. The Halifax from our squadron was Squadron Leader Guy Treasure's plane, M-Mother, MZ753. When David Fisher was killed on the Sterkrade operation, Guy Treasure became the new 'B' Flight Commander, so he was the second 'B' Flight Commander killed in eight days.

When the squadron was returning that morning, we watched Squadron Leader Kercher prang his plane, K-Kate. Don McLean wrote about the incident and in his diary:

> "There was an early morning trip to a P.plane site and F/Sgt. Campbell took our kite and landed away at Elvington. Sq/Ldr. Kercher pranged K,King in the potato paddock and he overshot pretty badly but nobody was hurt. In the evening we went over with Trev. and P/O Donald and crew and flew our two kites back to base."

I remember the crash well. Kercher misjudged the landing altogether and wiped off the undercarriage and reduced the plane to a mangled mess but they all got out safely. He underestimated the position of the end of the runway, landed too far down and ran off the end, through the fence and into the next field and wrote her off! Squadron Leader Kersher would have been in his late thirties or early forties. That was pretty old for doing that job. He was past it! They grounded him from then on and he never flew again. We got a new Flight Commander. The squadron record says that the plane overshot the runway because of the bad weather but although the weather was poor, that wasn't the real reason. Bill Rabbitt wasn't very impressed with Kercher's landing either. That's why he wrote in his diary: "The weather was a bit duff but ...." He doesn't finish the sentence and leaves it hanging like that because there was no excuse.

At 2250 that night we drove over to RAF Elvington with Pilot Officer Donald and his crew, the crew that shared our hut, and flew N-Nan and their plane back to base. They had both been diverted there after returning from the Montorgueil raid.

Duralumin and the Junkers J1

In the chapter above, Basil Spiller mentions that one of the jobs of their ground staff was to repair the damage to N-Nan with panels of perspex for windscreens and patches of "duralium" for holes in the plane's skin.

Duralumin (or Duraluminium) was the name given to the lightweight aluminium alloy sheeting invented by German metallurgist Alfred Wilm in 1903. He discovered the way to alloy copper, magnesium, manganese and aluminium. Its composition and the heating process to tamper (strengthen) it remained German wartime secrets.

The potential of corrugated duralumin as a strong, lightweight and tear resistant "skin" in aircraft manufacture was first recognized by the brilliant German aircraft engineer, Professor Hugo Junkers. His company Junkers and Co. pioneered some of the greatest innovations in aviation design and materials technology. Junkers' earlier aircraft were derided as "tin donkeys" and largely dismissed by German aviation officials. They were built from heavy sheet steel, the weight of which adversely affected their maneuverability and climbing ability -

even though their airspeed at the time was a respectable 110 miles per hour. Junkers persisted in his belief that all metal aircraft would prove to be superior to planes built with fabric stretched over a wooden framework and braced by reinforced wire. He simply replaced the sheet steel with duralumin and much lighter craft were produced.

Junkers J1 biplane

In 1917 the first all-metal aircraft, the Junkers J1, entered service with the Deutsche Luftstreitkräfte (the German Air Force). It was a biplane made primarily of duralumin. Its lower wings were cantilevered. Although steel struts were used to support the upper wing, there was no need for a "maze" of wire to hold the aircraft together, eliminating much of the drag that greatly reduced the speed of aircraft at that time. The J1 had a powerful 200 horsepower motor, steel plating protecting the crew, fuel tanks and engine, two forward firing guns, and a gunner to protect the plane against attack from the rear. This was a strong aircraft and one which by the war's end Allied forces had still not managed to shoot down.

In 1918, the first all metal monoplane fighter plane, the Junkers D1 began war service. Both the Junkers J1 and D1 appeared after the tide of war had turned against Germany.

Without doubt, Hugo Junkers' aircraft, based on lightweight duralumin, were amongst the greatest advances in aircraft manufacture and technology. His pioneering work has had an enormous impact on aircraft design from the 1920s through to the present day.

Chapter 28: Operation 10 - Mont Candon

721 aircraft - 477 Lancasters, 207 Halifaxes, 37 Mosquitos - attacked 6 flying bomb sites. All raids were believed to have been successful. 3 Lancasters lost. *Total effort for the night:* 1,049 sorties, 9 aircraft {0.9 per cent) lost.
The Bomber Command War Diaries, 27/28 June 1944

Our tenth operation on the 27th of June was a night time raid to Mont Candon, a flying bomb site inside the French coast, about twelve kilometres south-west of Dieppe. There were seventeen Halifaxes from our squadron. We left at 2230 hours and the mission took three hours and fifty-five minutes. We carried 6,500 pounds of bombs. We got back at about half past two in the morning.

The target was well marked and we suffered no opposition at all. Don scored another bulls-eye but according to photographs taken after the raid the main area bombed was to the east of the target. There was nothing to report. Nothing happened. No opposition at all. End of story.

Don's diary entry tells a similar story:
"We did a night trip to another P.plane site called Mont Candon and it was a pretty quiet affair but a good prang."

All of our crew were assessed after this mission. In his diary, Bill mentions that Don, John and I received "Ab. A" reports. That means that my log and chart scored ten out of ten and Don's bomb aiming was a series of direct hits. I don't know what they looked at for John's flight engineer report but it must have been pretty good as well.

The Junkers JU88

In 1936 the German Ministry of Aviation was impressed with Junkers and Co's initial designs for a high speed light bomber with a bomb carrying capacity of over two thousand pounds, and asked for two prototypes to be built.

The aircraft that grew out of this was the legendary Junkers 88, arguably the most versatile combat aircraft of the Second World War, but certainly the most flexible and adaptable plane used by the German Luftwaffe. It was used primarily as a medium bomber, heavy fighter and night fighter, and among other things, was used for reconnaissance and as a torpedo bomber against Allied shipping.

The JU88 first flew in 1936 at an impressive 360 miles per hour (580kph) which was faster than the fighter planes of that time. The addition of dive bombing capabilities, anti-barrage balloon cable cutting equipment, nose cannons, plus a bomb load of 2,200 pounds, reduced its speed to approximately 280 miles per hour (450kph)

The JU88 entered service with the Luftwaffe in September 1939 at the outbreak of World War 2. Manufacturing problems meant that early production was very slow but by the end of the war over 15,000 JU 88s had been built.

Junkers 88 G Series Night Fighter

In July 1940 the first night fighter versions of the JU88 appeared. They were heavily armed with a 20mm cannon and three machine guns in the nose.

In 1942 the JU88 G series appeared. They were aerodynamically improved with a reshaped fuselage and equipped with accurate intercept radar which made them deadly night-time predators. Four powerful forward-firing 20mm cannons fitted into a pod below the former bomb doors, enlarged fuel tanks, and Schräge Musik (upward firing) cannons were installed over time further extending the JU88's lethal night fighting capabilities.

Chapter 29: Operation 11 - Blainville-sur-l'Eau

202 Halifaxes of 4 and No. 6 Groups with 28 Pathfinder Lancasters attacked railway yards at Blainville and Metz. Both targets were hit. 20 aircraft were lost, 11 Halifaxes of No. 4 Group and 1 Lancaster from the Blainville raid and 7 Halifaxes of No. 6 Group and 1 Lancaster from Metz. The combined loss rate was 8.7 per cent.

The Bomber Command War Diaries, 28/29 June 1944

My eleventh operation was a night time raid on the 28th/29th of June to marshalling yards at Blainville-sur-l'Eau in the north-east corner of France, close to the Swiss-German-French border. Blainville was near the French city of Nancy. N-Nan had seven and a half thousand pounds of bombs on board. It was a long way to the target so we were fuelled right up. Although we took off at 2205 hours it was still quite light. The evenings were long because right through the war they had "double British Summer Time" where they advanced the clock two hours. It was also the start of summer. Even at 11 o'clock at night we would have been taking off in evening light.

It was a long flight which took six hours and fifty-five minutes so we landed at about 5 o'clock in the morning of the 29th. Luftwaffe night fighter squadrons had their airfields in France, which was occupied territory, so they would scramble and be waiting for us even before we crossed the coast. To make things worse on this mission we were flying over France for a long time – probably five of the seven hours. When he wrote about this operation Sandy Concannon, our rear gunner, said that at briefing everyone groaned when they saw how far our track was to the target. They were right because it turned out to be a very dangerous mission and another terrible one for our squadron. Numerous German night fighters were waiting for us as the flight approached the target and again as we headed home. We were lucky to survive the night!

Twenty aircraft left from 102 Squadron but two turned back. One had engine and compass trouble but the other one was late taking off. They may have turned back because it was a long trip and the petrol consumption would have blown out if the pilot had gone flat out to catch us. Being alone heading deep into occupied France was extremely dangerous and asking for trouble. It was a legitimate reason for turning back but if it was our plane, knowing Bill, he would probably have tried to catch up with the bombing stream.

After taking off from Pocklington we flew our usual course south over Reading, west of London, across the Channel over to Caen and St. Lô. We then flew a dogleg course north of Paris attempting to evade the German night-fighters, and then eastwards to Blainville. Charlie Hood in the mid-upper turret and Sandy Concannon in the rear turret would have been alert, constantly scanning the sky, on the lookout for an attack that could erupt at any second.

Bill's diary describes how we were attacked several times by night-fighters. The first attack was made by a "twin engine job". It was probably a JU 88. I can remember it. I knew immediately what was happening. Sandy had seen a night fighter from his rear turret. He warned Bill by calling "Corkscrew!" Bill's response was instantaneous.

> *Sandy yells 'CORKSCREW!' A stream of shells whizz past our port wing. Bill dives. He throws N-Nan all 'round the sky. It's violent! Evasive! A descending corkscrew! He goes hard left rudder! Stick full forward! Corkscrews to port! Then starboard! In a flash we drop two thousand feet. G-forces pin me down n the floor. I'm helpless. Hanging on for grim death! This is our eleventh mission. The first time we've been attacked! We've been lucky. Now it's our turn!" We begin to level off. I can move. We've shaken him off. I'm back at my desk. Get everything in order. Check Lat. and Long from the API. Get an H2S fix. Rule my lines. Calculate our drift. We're back on track.*

I don't know how Bill controlled the plane in that situation. You had to be strong. Bill was a short man but he was very strong in the upper body. There was nobody sitting beside him, helping him. Don was down with me in the navigational section. Sandy gave Bill good instructions and Bill mentions that in his diary. Sandy would have been talking to him all the time the evasive action was going on. Eventually the fighter gave us away and we resumed our track, height and airspeed.

We had two more attacks by single engine aircraft - Messerschmitt Bf109s – on the way in. I didn't know until then that the Luftwaffe employed their single-engine fighters as night fighters. We did corkscrews each time. Sandy, alone down at the back of the plane, watched "eight of nine bombers go down in flames or explode" on our port side. He was interviewed for the book *Flyers Far Away*, and he described the Messerschmitts attacking us:

> "I saw a fighter getting into position to have a go at us. I have two things to do; open fire and give the skipper the signal for evasive action. The fighters have twenty millimetre cannons. They can chew a bomber up with a few rounds. All this happens in four or five seconds. That's all it takes between being dead or alive. A minute later, another

fighter, the same procedure. Then another Bf109, going for someone else, goes underneath my turret, missing us by a few yards. It frightens hell out of me."

The target was very distinct and Bill could see the rivers and railway yards. The Master Bomber gave clear instructions and the Pathfinders lit up the target with flares. Don got another direct hit.

Heading back to base we ran into more trouble when a German plane opened fire on us. We took immediate, panic, evasive action and went into a corkscrew again while Sandy returned fire. Luckily the pilot's aim was astray and we survived. Bill says this in his diary:

"On the way out of France North of Le Havre a Jerry pounced on us at 9,000 ft and a stream of bullets whizzed past the port wing. Sandy gave him a long burst of fire while I endeavoured to turn the kite inside out. We eventually lost him and came home after 7hrs in the air. Good show."

On the 29th, Don wrote in his diary:

".... It was a 7 hr. trip and 1200 odd miles so you can imagine we were pretty weary when we arrived back..... The target was very well lit up and there were bags of fighter flares all the way. I saw one kite shot down and it was rather a bad night for the squadron as we lost five including one chap (Rogers) who only had three trips to finish his tour. We had Y all the way even though 9,000 was the highest we went ...."

We were part of a force of 200 planes that attacked two railway targets in north-east France that night. The other target was the marshalling yards at Metz. All up twenty planes were lost. That was 8.6 percent of the force, eighteen Halifaxes and two Pathfinder Lancasters.

Our squadron was really hard hit again. We suffered five losses - five of the eighteen that participated in the raid. That's twenty-eight percent – the second time in the month that we had lost five on a single operation. The previous one was on the Sterkrade mission in the Ruhr. The Halifaxes that failed to return were O-Oboe LW143, S-Sugar NA502, Q-Queenie LW159, V-Victor MZ644 and W-William MZ2646.

Of the thirty-five crewmen, eight became prisoners of war, seven evaded capture and twenty were killed. The five planes came down in a line following the flight plan which took the bombing stream north of Paris.

The line shows that the flight crossed the Normandy coast somewhere between Le Havre and Calais. Four came down north of

Paris. One was seventy-eight kilometres north-east of Paris and three were about eighty kilometres north-west. The fifth one crashed 190 kilometres east of Paris.

The pilot of Q-Queenie was Pilot Officer Henry Rogers, a good friend of ours. We used to call him "Harry". His Halifax was shot down by a night fighter in the early hours of the morning and it crashed near Coeuvres-et-Valsery. Henry is buried in the town cemetery with five of his crewmates. His navigator was Pilot Officer, Leslie Potter, from Melbourne. One of the crew members, Flight Sergeant Williams, managed to bale out and became a prisoner of war.

I knew Harry Rogers really well. He was a married man. Harry was older and more experienced than us. He was thirty-one years old when he died and he had done thirty-two operations - three to go to finish his "tour". He and his wife, Mary, used to come down to the pub in Pocklington with the boys and go out dancing with us. They were part of our group. She and Harry had rooms in Pocklington so that they could be together when Harry was not on the squadron. That type of thing happened now and then but it was not common. Not many of the aircrew were married because we were mostly only young men. After Harry was killed, I saw Mary for the last time at the village pub. She attended the wake and then she left to go back home to her family. It was very sad.

There is no mention of Charlie in either Bill Rabbitt's or Don McLean's diary for this mission when our gunners probably saved our lives. Mid-upper gunners did not get involved in attacks as much as the rear gunners because night fighters mostly pounced on bombers from behind or from below. But they were very important nonetheless. If we did not have the mid-upper gunner it would have been a different story because then we would have been attacked from above or side on all the time. As it was, the attacking night fighters had to be wary because they could easily find themselves straying into the mid-upper gunner's sights.

The Blainville mission was pretty horrific. I was either down over my charts all night and unable to get out to have a look around or unable to move because of the G-forces while we corkscrewed out of those fighter attacks. And of course when we got to the target we were always met by a nice warm welcoming party. We had to go through the searchlights and flak on every target which got heavier as the importance of the target increased.

This was probably the most dangerous time of the war to be flying at 102 Squadron. In June 1944 our losses were terrible. Five planes were lost on two occasions and all up we lost thirteen on operations. The German radar early detection system kept getting better at locating us and directing night fighters straight to us. Night fighters were everywhere and more and more of them were equipped with upward firing guns that the Germans called Schrage Musik. A crew wouldn't even know a night-fighter had moved in underneath them until it was too late.

Sandy Concannon

This operation to Blainville-sur-l'Eau showed what a good rear gunner Sandy was and also why the rear gunner position was of such importance. Most night fighter attacks came from behind to catch the gunners by surprise. It was hard for the gunner to pick up the fighter. They had to be on the lookout for hour after hour and be vigilant no matter how tired they were. If they got complacent, that could be the end of them and their crew. I do not remember Sandy ever claiming any "probables" – which meant shooting down a plane. There is no doubt that on this mission Sandy's quick thinking and Bill's brilliant flying saved our lives four times. What are the odds of that!

We were attacked three times going in and one time coming out. Sandy's reactions were instantaneous. He called "corkscrew" and at the same moment was firing at our attacker. Bill's response was instantaneous too. That was the difference between a good crew and a bad crew. In a good crew the pilot reacted instantly, without question, to what his crew members were telling him. Good crews had complete trust in one another's ability. Bill didn't say: "Are you sure about that, Sandy?" before he dived. He just did it. It was second nature. As we corkscrewed away from our attacker, Sandy and Charlie Hood, in his mid-upper turret, would have been trying to get the night fighter in their sights but it would have been impossible with the G-forces on them. Can you imagine what it would have been like in their gun turrets during a corkscrew, in the steepest of dives, lurching this way, then that? They had to know where the attacker was before we twisted and dived the other way. And when we finally leveled out, they had to stay on the alert.

Edinburgh and Leeds

After we returned from the Blainville-sur-l'Eau operation we slept until about midday. We went out to have a good look at N-Nan and then drove to Betty's Bar in York. We thought that we did not have an op on so we didn't get back to the base until midnight. We were stunned to discover that we were supposed to be heading off on a raid to St Martin L'Hortier, another flying bomb site, at 0200 hours on the 30th of June. They must have laid on the raid at the last minute. We would have had quite a few beers. Luckily the weather was bad and the mission kept getting delayed until finally at 0600 they postponed it until early the next day, the 1st of July. We were awoken by the tannoy and headed off to briefing at 0700. We were briefed for a daylight operation to St Martin L'Hortier but when the weather didn't improve it was postponed until 1330. That morning we received eight days leave and another crew took our place on the raid. Bill went to visit his grandmother in Aberdeen, the Englishmen went home, Harry and Sandy went to Currypool and Don and I wasted no time. We left camp at about 1pm and were in Edinburgh by 6.30pm.

We caught the Flying Scotsman in York and travelled to Edinburgh with "some very nice Scotch lassies". It was a popular destination for servicemen on leave. We stayed six nights at the Victoria League Club. It was a good break from the squadron.

We did the usual things. Naturally we headed for the RAF Club and other pubs that we discovered and had a few drinks or a game of snooker. We would chat with other airmen that we met, like the Australian wireless operator who had trained with Don's brother, John, at Parkes. John was killed on the 21st of June 1942. He was a rear gunner on a Short Sunderland flying boat which was shot down over the Bay of Biscay by a German Arado 196. In the evenings we went dancing whenever we could. We loved dancing and it was always a good way to meet girls. It rained a fair bit but the weather cleared and we got out and did a fair bit of sightseeing. Don was really impressed with Edinburgh. On the 5th of July, during our stay, he wrote in his diary:

> "The sun out today and Princes Street really looks lovely. I think it must be one of the prettiest streets in the world with the Castle and the Parks along one side – what a pity there isn't more sun. The people are very friendly and I don't think the war has made the same change up here as in Southern England. Went to a show in the evening and met an Aussie who bailed out near Paris and got back here O.K."

The next day it was raining again but it didn't dampen Don's spirits:

> "A real Scottish day – bags of rain and fog. Bas and I spent most of the day looking about plus our usual game of snooker and in the afternoon saw "The Phantom of the Opera" – a really wizard show. Went dancing in the evening and I've come to the conclusion that the Scotch girls are very nice."

On the 7th we left Edinburgh and headed for Leeds and booked rooms for three nights at the Victoria Hotel. That night we went dancing. Don wrote in his diary:

"We left Edinburgh on "The Flying Scotsman" and had a really comfortable trip to York. We each got a seat – miracles never cease!! We came from York to Leeds per train and booked in at Victoria Hotel per usual. Went dancing to the Mecca at night and quite enjoyed myself. Bas left rather early."

We liked to go to the pictures and while we were in Leeds this time we went to see "For Whom the Bell Tolls" a new movie. The next evening we headed out again, this time to the Odeon Theatre where Tommy Handley, a famous British comedian, and the "Squadronaires", the RAF dance band, put on a show for the RAF Benevolent Fund. Tommy Handley's char lady always used to open up his morning radio show on the BBC with the line: "Can I do you now, Sir?" The show was called "ITMA" which stood for "It's That Man Again". Other famous big bands in England at the time were the Jo Loss Orchestra and Geraldo & His Orchestra. Later the next day, the 10th of July, we headed back to Pocklington and caught up with the boys and what they had been doing on their leave.

Mimoyecques

During our leave the squadron was briefed for ten operations but five were cancelled because the bad weather continued. From the 17th of June until the 17th of July aircrews were prepared for thirty-two operations and nineteen were abandoned. It was summer so you would expect the weather to be good. On the 6th of July fourteen of our Halifaxes were part of a force of 551 aircraft that attacked five flying bomb sites in the Pas de Calais area. Our Halifaxes were briefed to attack Mimoyecques, reportedly a V3 cannon site. Wing Commander Cheshire was the Master Bomber for the raid. At the start of the war he was a member of 102 Squadron. He became a legendary figure in the RAF. This was his last mission. After this he was awarded the Victoria Cross but they banned him from further operations. He had done enough. He had completed four tours of duty and would have kept putting his life on the line.

Corkscrewing

On a raid whenever they were attacked pilots were trained to begin an evasive manoeuvre called a "corkscrew". Bill was pretty good at it. It was usually Sandy, in the rear gunner's position, who first saw an attacking night fighter. Suddenly we would hear him call out "Corkscrew!" Bill would immediately apply hard-left rudder and push the stick fully forward and from straight and level we would go into a sideways dive to the left. When we got to the bottom he would straighten out and then we'd go into a dive to the starboard side. He would keep throwing the aircraft around in a violent corkscrew until he had shaken off the attacking night fighter. He had to make it as difficult as he could for any fighter pilot to follow us. It had to be as violent as possible.

When we were in a corkscrew it was impossible for any of the crew to do anything because we were subject to tremendous G forces and we would be jammed into our positions. We didn't get tossed around because the G forces pressed us down hard. Even when the plane lurched one way and slewed this way then that, the G forces would transfer from one side of our bodies to the other. We were helpless to do anything while a corkscrew was in motion. Bill would endeavour to stay on the same course but we could have been heading in a completely different direction, anywhere, by the time we lost the fighter.

As soon as the Bill and Sandy were satisfied that the fighter had been shaken off, the corkscrew was terminated and everything got back to normal. As navigator I endeavoured, as quickly as possible, to get an accurate fix with H2S, and start the air plot all over again.

Wing Commander Geoffrey Leonard Cheshire

During the Second World War, Leonard Cheshire's exploits elevated him to legendary status in the RAF and his deeds captured the imagination of the population at a desperate time when heroes were needed. After the Mimoyecques raid on the 6th of July 1944, he was ordered to rest by the commander of 5 Group, a decision which effectively brought Cheshire's operational career to an end - although he was destined to fly one more operation, as the prime minister's official observer of the nuclear bombing of Nagasaki in Japan on the 9th of August 1945.

The scale of Wing Commander Cheshire's achievement must be considered extraordinary when one considers that he completed four tours of duty at a time when the RAF aircrew death rate was so high. By 1943 less than twenty percent of bomber crews survived one tour and less than three percent survived two tours. Cheshire was awarded the Victoria Cross for bravery sustained over four years of operational service (the only recipient to do so in this way) and for his contribution to the development of low level target marking which greatly increased bombing accuracy and hastened the end of the war.

At the outbreak of war Pilot Officer Cheshire joined the RAF and was posted to 102 Squadron, Basil Spiller's squadron, then located at Driffield where he flew Armstrong Whitworth Whitley bombers. In a 1940 raid, flak damage inside his plane ignited a photo-flare and blew out part of the fuselage. The crew doused the flames and Cheshire still in control of the plane bombed the target and then nursed the badly damaged aircraft back to base. For this he was awarded his first DSO

Geoffrey Leonard Cheshire, Bomber Command RAF.
Victoria Cross portrait.

He immediately began a second tour after being posted to 35 Squadron at Linton-on-Ouse flying Handley Page Halifaxes. He was promoted to Squadron Leader and in March 1942 his DFC was gazetted. In August 1942 Cheshire returned to operational service beginning a third tour as Commanding Officer of 76 Squadron which had moved to RAF Linton-on-Ouse, an airfield he knew well. At that time he was the youngest commanding officer in the RAF. After his third tour, Cheshire was appointed Station Commander at Marston Moor but he yearned for a return to operational life.

In September 1943, he was appointed Wing Commander of the legendary 617 "Dam Buster" Squadron. Here Cheshire made his most spectacular contribution to the war effort. He strongly believed that the Pathfinder Force (PFF) practice of dropping target indicators from high altitudes was too inaccurate, as occurred on the 5 Group raid to Munich on the 2nd of October 1943, when bombs were dropped along the approach route up to fifteen miles from the target. Cheshire was convinced that a rapid initial marking of the target from a low altitude in a faster plane, backed up by Pathfinder Force ground marking, would provide a significantly more accurate target for the bomber stream. This idea met with resistance from the leaders of the PFF but Cheshire was given permission to demonstrate his technique by leading a small force of Lancasters to bomb an aero-engine factory at Limoges. Because of the success of the raid he was able to convince Air Chief Marshal Arthur Harris, to allow him to lead a raid to Munich using the new method.

On the 24th/25th of April, his small group marked the target with pinpoint accuracy, in fast, manoeuvrable de Havilland Mosquito light bombers, leading a force of 244 Avro Lancasters which accurately bombed the Munich railway marshalling yards and devastated the centre of the city.

Cheshire ended his operational career as a 5 Group Master Bomber, having replaced his Mosquito with the faster, more manoeuvrable, American P-51 Mustang. For his bravery and service Leonard Cheshire was awarded the Victoria Cross, the Order of Merit, the Distinguished Service Order and Two Bars and the Distinguished Flying Cross.

Mimoyecques Raid – 6 July 1944

6 July 1944. Pas de Calais, France. A Halifax bomber (top left) attacks the Mimoyecques V3 canon site, near the English Channel, thirteen kilometres south-west of Calais.

On the 6th of July 1944, Basil Spiller and his crew were on leave from 102 Squadron when Wing Commander Leonard Cheshire flew his 102nd, and last, operation. Cheshire, flying a "borrowed" American P-51 Mustang was the Master Bomber on the mission to bomb the German V3 canon site at Mimoyecques. The V3 cannon was concealed in a tunnel system built into the hills. V3 cannons could fire shells with deadly accuracy at targets as far away as London.

On this day, 551 aircraft attacked five separate German flying bomb sites in the Pas de Calais. Fourteen Handley Page Halifaxes from 102 Squadron participated in the Mimoyecques raid.

Chapter 30: Operation 12 - Les Hauts-Buissons

230 aircraft - 196 Halifaxes, 17 Lancasters, 17 Mosquitos - of Nos 4, 6 and 8 Groups attacked 4 flying bomb launch sites. All targets were hit, the raid on the Bremont les Hautes site being particularly accurate. No aircraft were lost. *Total effort for the night:* 881 sorties, 12 aircraft (1.4 per cent) lost.
The Bomber Command War Diaries, 12/13 July 1944

After we returned from Edinburgh, the weather was bad and a lot of missions were either delayed or scrubbed. Our twelfth mission, a night time operation on the 12th/13th of July 1944, was to a flying bomb site at Les Hauts-Buissons about seventy kilometres to the south-west of Paris. Nineteen aircraft from the squadron took part in this raid. It was intended to be a daylight mission but it was postponed until later that night when the weather cleared. The flight took four hours and ten minutes and we carried seven and a half thousand pounds of bombs. We took off at 2225 hours. It was a four hour flight so we arrived back at Pocklington at about 2.35 in the morning.

There were no night fighters and very little flak over the target so it was a straightforward operation. Although we had to bomb through thick cloud, the markers were placed correctly and the raid was a success. The crews didn't know how accurately they had bombed until later that day when their photographs from the bombing run were developed. Then we would find out if Don had scored another aiming point.

Photo reconnaissance

PRU (Photo Reconnaissance Unit) planes were always sent to photograph the target of the previous night's raid but those photographs would go to Bomber Command not us. A specially adapted PRU Mosquito or Spitfire would fly over the target site at a great height and take photographs of the damage that was done to it. The photo recce bods would then know what state the target was in. That was the practice. On deeper raids into German occupied territory they might send a high flying Mosquito because Spitfires generally did not have the range of the Mosquito but then again specially adapted Spitfires easily flew to Berlin and back. The photo recce people were equipped with both types of aircraft.

Don McLean

Don McLean was a very skilled bomb aimer. Bill's diary entries on the 19th and 20th of November when our crew got their assessments after our first tour of duty say all that needs to be said about how good Don was. On the 19th he wrote:

> "Went down to the intelligence section today and was shown and told of our efforts throughout our tour. It is very gratifying to know that our efforts have proved to be the best ever in the history of 102 (Ceylon) Squadron. We secured more bulls-eyes on targets than anyone before our time and I have only the brilliance of my crew to thank for such a fine record."

And on the next day he wrote:

> "Squadron Leader Ward said we had twenty-six aiming points out of twenty-nine possibles. So that is a big credit mainly to Don and self, as it is judged on photographs returned."

The results of Don's individual efforts were determined from the photographs that we took on line-overlap the previous night. After all, there were hundreds of planes on the target and one individual bomb aimer's accuracy wouldn't stand out in a photograph taken by the PRU. Each station processed the photographs from all of its planes on the previous night's operation. As soon as our planes returned, the photographs from our bombing run were taken away to be developed on site in the photographic section.

Setting a course

The object of the navigator was always to set a course to the next turning point so that we would be back on track again. The course I set was always a straight line on a compass course for Bill to hold the plane on. If it was, say, one-sixty-five magnetic and the track was one-fifty-seven I would have been allowing for eight degrees of drift because wind is pushing on the plane all the time. It is like trying to drive a car with a flat tyre. You aim a little bit one way and drive straight on that line but the effect of the flat tyre keeps the car going straight up the road. A navigator is always dealing with the triangle of velocities - the wind speed, the air speed and the ground speed. It's all about finding the correct wind speed and direction and offsetting the course of the plane to track over the line that the navigator wants the plane to travel.

Our flight plans were designed to take us to the target and to minimize attacks from the German defences along the way. We normally began an operation by flying south over Reading, west of London, and then changing direction through a series of turning points that made a curving track into France. Germany sits on the north east corner of France. To attack cities like Stuttgart or Karlsruhe the flight plan might curve further south of Paris. To attack the cities in the Ruhr Valley, the curving track might take us across northern France and then Belgium. We started to fly more direct routes towards the end of the war to targets like Heligoland and Wangerooge and on gardening trips too, but they were straight across the North Sea and by then the Luftwaffe was on its knees.

There was a lot to do as a navigator. While I was obtaining a fix I was also checking the wind speed and direction and the difference between the track I required and the course that I'd take to get from point A to point B, and then on to point C. You draw it all up on the chart. The course the pilot steered had one arrow. The track I was trying to keep was shown by two arrows and the wind vector was shown by three arrows. At the same time as I was checking the wind speed and direction I'd be checking the groundspeed because the flight plan was also about getting to each turning point and the target at a predetermined time.

The time a flight took did not depend on the distance from base to the target. Most of our flight plans were on an indirect route because they were designed to confuse the German air defences. The time depended on the track of the flight plan and how many doglegs we had to do to stay on time. A difference in the time of one mission compared to another one in the same general area was usually caused by how directly you flew.

Wing Commander Wilson

On the 15th of July, two days after the Les Hauts-Buissons mission, the squadron had a new commander when Wing Commander Louis Wilson took over. He had joined the RAF in 1936 and had a varied career before he joined us. When the war started he was in 40 Squadron flying Fairey Battles in France, He then moved into the Photographic Development Unit as a reconnaissance pilot. For six months he was loaned to Vickers Armstrong as a test pilot. I'll have a bit more to say about him later.

RAF Reconnaissance Aircraft

At the start of the Second World War, the RAF's reconnaissance aircraft were the obsolete Westland Lysander and Bristol Blenheim both easy prey for German aircraft such as the Messerschmitt Bf109 and the Junkers Ju88.

The revolutionary idea of using fighter planes for long range reconnaissance had been proposed in 1939 but fighters were in short supply during the Battle of Britain and could not be spared from the task of protecting British cities from German bombing raids. As the war progressed, the Supermarine Spitfire and the De Haviland Mosquito were both adapted for photo-reconnaissance.

Supermarine Spitfire PR (Photo Reconnaissance) Mk XI.

The Spitfire was a fighter plane of exceptional quality. Stripped of its cannons and ammunition to reduce weight, and fitted with extra fuel tanks, the Spitfire could maintain cruising speeds of 360 mph (580 kph) at altitudes over 20,000 feet reaching targets as far away as Berlin with ease, returning with precious, strategically important data. Typical of photo reconnaissance Spitfires is the PR Mk XI, in the photograph above with its pointed tailplane. The traditional Spitfire tailplane was more rounded.

The Mosquito was a fast, versatile, light bomber. The first operational photo reconnaissance Mosquito, the PR Mk I, had a maximum speed of over 380 mph (610 kph) and could reach heights of 35,000 feet.

Photo-reconnaissance aircraft were painted in air camouflage colours, and were equipped with special cameras which were heated to stop them from freezing at altitudes of up to 40,000 feet.

Mosquito B Mark IV Series 2, DK338, test flight April 1942.

Chapter 31: Operation 13 - Bois de la Haye

132 aircraft - 72 Halifaxes, 28 Stirlings, 20 Lancasters, 11 Mosquitos, 1 Mustang - attacked 3 V-weapons sites without loss. Few details of bombing results were recorded.

The Bomber Command War Diaries, 17 July 1944

"Operation Crossbow" was the name given to the Allied raids on German flying bomb sites in northern France. At this stage of the war, it was a high priority for Bomber Command and the Americans because of the threat to the lives of civilians and the damage being done when the bombs exploded in London and other English cities. "Doodlebugs" as they were commonly called, also had a huge affect on the morale of the population.

During the war V1's destroyed or damaged thousands of buildings. In his diary for the 17th, Don wrote that "some of the chaps in our hut had their homes knocked over".

After the Les Hauts-Buissons raid, the bad weather continued and several missions were cancelled. We were briefed to bomb a V1 flying bomb site at Bois de la Haye in Western Normandy on the 16th of July. It was postponed until the next evening.

We finally left at 1905 hours in daylight and carried 7,500 pounds of bombs. Twenty-one of our Halifaxes took off on the operation but one returned with engine trouble. The trip took four hours so we would've come back just after 11 o'clock. We had a fighter escort and it was classed as a daylight raid because landed just after dark. It was a fairly straightforward mission.

I remember that as we were flying over the English Channel we did an orbit to lose time. The Pathfinders were due to drop their target indicators at a given time, usually one minute before we were due to bomb. We were given a time for N-Nan to be over the target and that was the time I always aimed for. I never wanted to be early or late.

We were obviously well before time because the met winds that were forecast were stronger than anticipated and really pushed us along. The way to lose time was to either do a dogleg or an orbit where we would go around in a long circle to lose two or three minutes. We decided to do an orbit. I calculated accurately and we arrived at the target on time. There was some cloud over the target but the markers were accurately placed and Don scored another aiming point.

On this operation flying was again hard work for Bill because we hit so many slipstreams. There were other aircraft in the vicinity and we were flying into the turbulence caused by their propellers. It was always a bumpy ride when you got into somebody's slipstream.

Wakey-wakey pills

On a flight we were given "wakey-wakey" pills to keep us awake. Sandy Concannon said that he took some only the once and that was on the Blainville-sur-l'Eau raid, two missions before this one. As we neared the French coast on the way home Sandy was getting spots before his eyes. He popped two pills and asked Bill to try to find some cloud cover so that he could shut his eyes and rest them for a few minutes. My other crewmates may have taken them but it was not something I remember talking about. They were carried in the emergency hospital rations. If anybody wanted them they were available. Our gunners may have been issued with them but that would have been up to the gunnery section leaders. I never took them. They were Benzedrine. Back then no-one would have known that they were so addictive.

"Sleepy-sleepy" pills are sometimes mentioned as well but we were not given sleeping pills to help us sleep when we got back. That would have been a matter for the individual crewman and the MO (medical officer). He would have to request them. I never knew of anyone who took sleeping pills.

The V1 "Flying Bomb"

August 1944. A German V1 flying bomb photographed heading across the English Channel towards London.

France, September 1944. Allied soldiers looking over a V1 "Flying Bomb" ramp near Amiens. French forces reported that up to ten V1's were launched daily from this ramp.

The V1 flying bomb was the world's first cruise missile. Its official name was the Fieseler Fi 103, named after the Fieseler Company that manufactured them. To the British it was known colloquially as a Buzz Bomb or a Doodlebug.

The V1 weighed 2,150 kilograms. It was 32 metres long, had a wingspan of 5.4 metres from wingtip to wingtip and was 1.4 metres high. It had an air speed of approximately 400 mph (640kph) and flew at a height of between 600 and 1000 metres. The platform from which they were launched resembled a ski jump. They were guided to their targets by a simple autopilot which was very advanced technology for its time.

The first V1 was fired at London on the 13th of June 1944, just one week after the D-day landings. On average, one hundred V1's were fired into south-east England cities every day. There were approximately 30,000 V1's manufactured and almost 10,000 were fired at Britain. Over two thousand four hundred were fired at London killing more than six thousand people and injuring an estimated eighteen thousand more. V1 launch sites throughout north western France became key targets of RAF and USAAF heavy bomber raids in a major operation called "Operation Crossbow". The last launch site was captured by ground forces in March 1945.

Chapter 32: Operation 14 - Vaires

110 aircraft - 99 Halifaxes, 6 Lancasters, 5 Mosquitos - of 4,6 and 8 Groups attacked the railway yards at Vaires but no report on the bombing results was filed. 2 Halifaxes lost. *Total effort for the day:* 1,052 sorties, 8 aircraft (0.8 per cent) lost.

The Bomber Command War Diaries, 18 July 1944

On the 18th of July, the day after we attacked Bois de la Haye, 102 Squadron attacked two targets. In an early morning raid, four of our aircraft were part of a very large force of almost 950 planes sent to attack villages near the French coastal city of Caen in Normandy, where British and Canadian troops were being held up by the German army which was well dug in. D-Day troops were still near the French coast. That afternoon we were one of twelve planes that joined the force to bomb railway marshalling yards at Vaires, twelve miles south-east of Paris. It was our fourteenth mission. Takeoff was at 1525 hours. It was a daylight operation that took five hours and we dropped seven and a half thousand pounds of bombs. The weather was perfect. It was a beautiful French summer's day and we could see for hundreds of miles. We had a Spitfire escort covering us.

At briefing for daylight raids, the intelligence officers always said that we would have fighter escorts but we never saw the fighters. They were anything up to fifteen thousand feet above us, watching and waiting for German Messerschmitts or Focke Wulfs to appear. We knew they were there protecting us all the time.

I anticipated that we were going to arrive at the target ahead of time so I allowed for a dogleg. I had the autonomy to do that. We did it over the Channel and it put our aircraft back on time. As we made our run towards Vaires we came upon the rest of the flight, over a hundred planes, orbiting short of a wall of flak that was coming up just in front of the target. Their orbit was a wide circular path, probably about five to ten miles around. It was a very dangerous thing to be doing because up there in that situation aircraft are like sitting ducks and it could have been avoided if they had done what we did. The Pathfinders were being directed straight to the aiming point by Oboe and they were going to arrive on time. Meanwhile the flight was waiting for the Pathfinders to lead them into the target and set the scene with target indicator flares.

While the others were circling, we were coming in on time right behind the Pathfinders. Bill was able to take all this in and then "nip through the flak belt on the heels of the Pathfinders" as he says in his diary. Before smoke obscured the target, Bill saw our bombs land in the target area "smack in the centre of the (railway) yards". He describes it as a "wizard prang". I can remember Bill saying that one Spitfire from our escort was shot down by flak and he saw it go all the way down to the ground and explode.

Wall of flak

A wall of flak was an incredible spectacle. It was always frightening to fly through but you've got to remember that the wall of flak comprised explosions that had already occurred so it always looked worse than it really was because the smoke of the explosion hung in the sky for several minutes and the smoke was added to by fresh explosions. You can imagine explosions going off but looking worse because of previous explosions still hanging in the air and making it look twice as bad even though all of the shrapnel from the earlier explosions has already dropped back to the ground.

Flak was really only dangerous to one specific aircraft that it exploded near. If you didn't hear it, it was far enough away not to cause you any damage. The ones that you could hear were very close and they were the ones that got you.

Dogleg

While I was obtaining fixes I would also be checking our groundspeed because the flight plan not only required me to navigate the plane towards a turning point but we also had to make that change in direction at a specific time. If we were late we had to make up time. If we were early we had to lose time. Every six minutes I would obtain a fix so I knew where we were and how quickly we had got there. The turning point might be miles ahead of us and I would be able to calculate the time we were going to get there at the speed we were going. We do that sort of thing all the time when we are travelling in our cars.

In N-Nan we could of course speed up or slow down but sometimes we would be so far ahead of time that we had to do something more substantial to lose time. In this situation we would either do a wide circular orbit as we did during the attack on the Bois de la Haye, or we would do a dogleg.

If by any chance you discovered that you were, say, three minutes ahead of time you could do a "dogleg". It is really an equilateral triangle. You would alter course 120 degrees and fly three minutes in that direction, alter course 60 degrees and fly for three minutes in that direction. Then you turned back onto the track. Each line of the equilateral triangle would equal three minutes. So it has taken you six minutes to advance three minutes along the track and you have lost three minutes. And that is what a dogleg comprised.

On our way to Vaires, I realized that if we held our current course and speed we were going to arrive at the target four minutes early. By flying eight minutes in a dogleg – four minutes one way and then four minutes back to the course – we lost four minutes actual time on our track. When we rejoined our flight after our dogleg the others were still orbiting just short of the target. In the meantime we were nipping along right on time. We flew past the orbiting planes and we bombed straight away with the Pathfinders. One hundred and ten planes attacked the Vaires marshalling yards that day. We sailed right through the middle of the wall of flak with all these planes around us, in an orbit of five to ten miles. You cannot orbit in a tight circle with so many planes. They were at the same height as us. These navigators were slack because they allowed it to happen. They all should have done what we did. It makes sense not being in a dangerous area like that any longer than you have to be. It was always preferable to get to the target on time rather than being up in the air hanging around. Why would anyone in their right mind choose to do that! This could only have happened in daylight. At night time there would have been multiple collisions in mid air. The fact that it was a daylight raid led many of these navigators to ignore the dogleg completely. Two Halifaxes were shot down over Vaires. The orbit could have been the reason.

On this day Bomber Command send 1052 bombers into northern France. There were no attacks by German fighters. It was clear that by mid July 1944, the Allied airforce had control over French skies by day.

Oboe

In 1940 and 1941, RAF bombing was very inaccurate. Reconnaissance flights proved that here had been successes but they also showed that there were many more failures. Meanwhile German wartime production continued unabated. Facing increasing pressure, Bomber Command, in mid 1941, commissioned a report into the effectiveness of its bombing operations. The investigation that followed was called the "Butt Report", named after David Bensusan-Butt, a public servant from the War Cabinet. After comparing the aerial photographs of over 600 bombing operations with the claims of bomber crews about the success of their raids, his major conclusion shocked many. From 1940 until early 1941, two thirds of the crews who claimed to have bombed their targets were mistaken. Aircraft which for one reason or another had failed to drop their bombs were not included in the report. Had they been included, the report would have shown that only five percent of bombers leaving England actually reached the target.

Fortunately for Bomber Command, British scientists at the time were making crucial advances in the field of aerial navigation and four complimentary navigation systems were invented. Three of these, Gee (August, 1942), H2S (January, 1943), and the Air Position Indicator (March, 1943) became standard equipment in RAF bombers, and they greatly improved the ability to direct aircraft to the target. The fourth was code named "Oboe".

Oboe was first used in December 1942. Its operation was straightforward for bomber pilots and navigators. A ground station, called the Cat, directed a plane onto the circumference of a predetermined, circular track which eventually led the plane over the target. With the Cat at the centre of the circle, the radius of the circle to the plane was carefully monitored with rapid pulses transmitted from the Cat to the plane's transponder being reflected back to the station. The time this took enabled the base station to determine whether the plane was following the circular track or straying from it. When the plane was on track, the pulse was sent with a continuous tone. The pulse was received as a series of continuous dashes if the plane moved too far from track or as a series of dots if it was too close. The pilot would then make corrections to regain track. A second station, the Mouse, some distance from the first, also defined a circle with its circumference also passing through the target. When the plane reached the point at which the two circles intersected, it was above the target.

Oboe was an accurate method of directing aircraft onto targets but it had several limitations. Oboe could position only one aircraft at a time which meant other planes had to follow that plane. This restricted Oboe to daylight operations because heavy bombers had to make their own way to and from targets at night when most Bomber Command operations were flown. Another important limitation was due to the curvature of the earth. Oboe being a line of sight system could operate only over a distance of about 300 miles. Targets over the Ruhr Valley were accessible but those deeper into Germany such as Berlin and Munich were not.

The introduction of Oboe coincided with the creation of the Pathfinder Force and on daylight operations Oboe complemented the way the PFF operated. PFF aircraft marked the aiming point for the approaching bomber stream with target indicator flares, on top of which bomb aimers would drop their bombs. During daylight raids, Oboe being restricted to one plane at a time was not a problem because Oboe operators in the Cat station would direct the leading PFF plane. Bombing streams rendezvoused with PFF aircraft, followed them to the target and dropped their bombs on the PFF marker flares. If anything happened to the leading PFF plane, the next one took its place. The number of Oboe led daylight bombing missions gradually increased after the D-Day landings in June 1944 and as the RAF and USAAF gained the ascendancy over the Luftwaffe. One by one German airfields in occupied Europe were attacked and destroyed and Luftwaffe squadrons were pushed back into Germany. The German retreat enabled Oboe stations to be erected in mainland Europe, which then overcame the problem of the range of the Oboe system and enabled the Pathfinders to use Oboe on raids deeper into eastern Germany.

On the 1st of November 1943, Bomber Command performed the first full-scale test of another navigational device code named "Gee-H" when thirty-eight Lancasters attacked Düsseldorf. Gee-H operated on the same basic principal as Oboe with pilots keeping their planes on an arc at a constant radius from a master radio station. Like Oboe, it was also a line of sight system, its range restricted by the curvature of the earth, but being a self contained system it could be used by up to eighty planes at once. It was believed at the time that Gee-H would replace Oboe, but because Oboe could be used to lead bombing streams of hundreds of aircraft, it continued to be used for the remainder of the war.

Chapter 33: Operation 15 - Chapelle Notre Dame

369 aircraft - 174 Lancasters, 165 Halifaxes, 30 Mosquitos - attacked 6 Flying-Bomb launching sites and the V-weapon site at Wizemes. All raids were successful except the small raid by 20 aircraft on the Forêt de Croc site where the Oboe leader, Lancaster, was shot down on the bombing run and the bombs of this force all missed the target. This was the only aircraft lost. Eight Mosquitos flew uneventful Ranger patrols.

The Bomber Command War Diaries, 20 July 1944

On the 20th of July we attacked Chapelle Notre Dame. We had an early morning call but the operation was postponed until later that day. We eventually took off at 1410 hours, carrying seven and a half thousand pounds of bombs.

There and back took three hours twenty-five minutes so it was a short flight to the Pas de Calais region of northern France. It was a flying bomb site. Fourteen Halifaxes from 102 Squadron were part of a bombing force of 369 aircraft on this operation.

We were the first aircraft on the target and according to Bill, ".... had a wizard run up," and Don got another aiming point. On the way back we had to evade the Calais-Boulogne air defences. Bill says that they "pumped up an appreciable amount of flak". Otherwise it was an uneventful trip. Not that going through the flak could ever be uneventful!

A lot of people don't realize that although we may have flown through the German defences getting in, they'd still be waiting for us on the way back. We would have evaded the Calais-Boulogne defences because we could see them and Bill went around them. Hopefully the flight plan had been designed to avoid flak barrages as much as possible.

Harry, our wireless operator, says that we attacked railway marshalling yards on this raid but I remember that it was a flying bomb site even though it was a long time ago. I also know because of the time that elapsed on the trip.

My log book says that the flight was just under three and a half hours long so it could only have been in the Pas de Calais area where the bulk of the Flying Bomb sites were. The target had to be just inside France. After all, the Vaires raid was ten miles south-east of Paris and that one took five hours.

Gremlins

There were a lot of things that could go wrong during a mission. Not just the obviously dangerous things. In the squadron record one of the crews on this raid reported: "Haze and smoke over the target. 'Y' unserviceable. Fishpond unserviceable. Port inner cutting out periodically. No oxygen in the rear turret. Windscreen broken by bird. Lousy trip." They had a bad day all right.

Halifax v Lancaster

I never flew in a Lancaster but over the years I have heard a lot of discussion about which was the better plane - Halifaxes or Lancasters. In my opinion, the Halifax Mark III was equal in quality to the Lancaster and the Halifax Mark VI was probably better. They might not have had the longer range of the Lancaster and they might not have been able to take the big bombs but as far as Halifax crews were concerned the Halifax Mark III and Mark VI were first class aircraft.

Statistics prove that they were more robust and easier to bail out of because the Lancaster had a narrower fuselage and bulkheads cluttering the way. The Halifax in contrast had a fuselage like a big tube that you could stand up in. It made movement inside the aircraft easier and if a crew had to bail out they could all get to the escape hatch more easily. This was a big problem for Lancaster crews.

My escape hatch was in the forward compartment which housed three of our seven man crew. It was under the navigation table for the bomb aimer, navigator and wireless operator to use if the worst happened. Bill and John could escape through a hinged section of the flight deck roof which opened outwards. Charlie would endeavour to escape through the main entrance door on the port side of the fuselage adjacent to his turret.

Sandy would have to reverse his turret. The back of it consisted of two self sealing doors which would spring open when he turned the turret and he could then tumble out. He had his parachute stowed in the main fuselage just outside the back doors of his turret. He had to reach out for it and clip it on before trying to escape. It was hard for rear gunners to get ready. That is why so few rear gunners survived when they had to bail out.

I've recently read about research that Bomber Command had done in January 1944 where they examined the survival rates of Lancaster and Halifax crews that had been shot down over Germany during 1943. The survival rate from Lancasters was only eleven percent but Halifaxes had a survival rate of twenty-nine percent. Air Marshal Harris, who ran Bomber Command, preferred Lancasters and kept the report secret. That was good of him wasn't it? If Bomber Harris had released the report there would have been a mad scramble of men wanting get out of Lancasters to join Halifax squadrons, that's for sure!

The Halifax was a very rugged aircraft and had the added advantage of seven self-sealing petrol tanks in each wing, whereas the Lancaster had three larger ones in each. This made Lancasters more vulnerable to being set on fire when they were attacked by a night fighter or flak. It also increased the risk that they would lose appreciable amounts of petrol if they were holed. The chance of this happening was correspondingly slimmer in a Halifax.

If one of the fuel tanks in the Halifax or Lancaster was breeched the chances were that it was not leaking all over the place because it was a self-sealing tank. The engineer could immediately switch the fuel supply to another tank. It was our engineer's job to bleed every one dry before he switched the 'cocks over and use another tank. John would empty one, then another and another in sequence. He had fuel gauges for every tank in each wing and he would know the average fuel consumption of the aircraft at various speeds and heights. I don't know how the tanks were made to be self-sealing. The engineering behind that would be interesting. I understand that rubberized material was used. If you got a severe enough rupture it wouldn't self-seal though.

There were more Lancasters than Halifaxes only because "Butch" Harris, was a big supporter of Lancasters. He was more interested in the bomb load that could be dropped on a target and the size of the bombs than the survival rate. As a result, in 1945, with the war winding down aircraft production was being cut back and the Halifax squadrons of Canadian 6 Group were slowly being re-equipped with the Lancasters that they were building in Canada and ferrying across the Atlantic.

When I was on operations the survival rate in Halifax crews was superior to those who flew in Lancasters. All the Halifax crews knew that. If you were trusting your life to an aircraft which one would you prefer? There is no doubt that the Lancaster was a safer plane for crews prior to 1944. Before that they were flying Halifax Mk2's which could be unstable when they had to dive or corkscrew. A lot of testing was done and the design of the tail planes was changed from the triangular shape to a squarer shape and that fixed the problem. The Halifax 2 was also given more powerful Bristol Hercules XVI engines and it became known as the Halifax Mk 3 which was more than a match for any Lancaster.

In 1944 and '45, when I was flying operations, there was a big turn around in the loss rate of Lancasters and Halifaxes. Halifaxes were at least a twenty-five percent safer plane.

You had no choice about where you were sent. War was a deadly game of chance and you needed whatever you could get to shift the odds in your favour.

Bombing V1 Sites in the Pas de Calais

Evening sunlight shines on a Handley Page Halifax Mk 3, during an attack on a flying-bomb site in the Pas-de-Calais, France, as smoke from target indicators rises from the target.

Self-sealing Fuel Tanks

Leaking or burning fuel put aircraft and crews at grave risk. During the Second World War, protecting fuel tanks from enemy bullets and flak with steel plating was not a satisfactory solution to the problem because it added considerable weight to aircraft thus restricting their range, armament and bomb carrying capacity. Self-sealing fuel tanks were developed to prevent fuel tanks from leaking and exploding when they were breeched by enemy fire. As the war progressed, aircraft were fitted with fuel tanks that contained two layers of rubber, one vulcanized and the other untreated. When the fuel tank was punctured, fuel would spill out and wet the untreated rubber layer causing it to swell and seal the breach.

    The self-sealing fuel tank was invented by the Goodyear company in the United States and in 1941 Corsair fighters were the first aircraft to be fitted with them.

    Handley-Page Halifax bombers were fitted with seven self-sealing fuel tanks in each wing, between the main wing spars and in the leading edges in front of the front spar. Avro Lancaster bombers were fitted with three larger self-sealing fuel tanks in each wing. Engines were normally fed from fuel tanks on the same side but fuel could be moved from one wing to the other through a system of transfer pipes, to feed engines and stabilize the plane if necessary.

Chapter 34: Operation 16 - Les Hauts-Buissons

116 aircraft - 102 Halifaxes, 12 Mosquitos, 2 Lancasters - of Nos 4 and 8 Groups attacked 2 flying bomb sites with accurate bombing. 1 Halifax lost from the raid on the Les Hauts-Buissons site.
The Bomber Command War Diaries, 23/24 July 1944

On the night of the 23rd of July we went back to Les Hauts-Buissons to have another go at the V1 flying bomb site. Sixteen planes from our squadron took off at 2140 hours. On board we had seven and a half thousand pounds of bombs and the trip lasted only three hours and twenty-five minutes, so we arrived back at base at about 1.05 am. We were in support of the army that had attempted to break out from the bridgehead in Normandy near the French coast. They were still having a hard time and had not progressed very far in the seven weeks.

On the way back, over the Channel, when we were only about thirty miles short of Beachy Head, we were attacked suddenly by a Junkers 88 night fighter which opened up before we even saw him. Suddenly Sandy screamed into the intercom, "Corkscrew! Corkscrew!" and immediately Bill Rabbitt went into the corkscrew manoeuvre and threw the plane all around the sky. The JU88 came at us on the starboard side from a little bit higher up on a "curve of pursuit" which means that he flew down at us on our right hand side and opened up before curving away. Its twenty millimetre tracers just missed our starboard wingtip.

There were a lot of aircraft in the bombing stream heading home around us but we could not see where they were at night. There was a lot of confusion. Bill thought that immediately the Ju88 pilot broke off from us he peeled away and shot down a Halifax away to starboard but Sandy Concannon, our rear gunner, remembers it differently. Sitting in his turret, Sandy had seen the night-fighter shoot down a Halifax off to starboard and then turn its attention towards us. Sandy said:

"I remember that night when we were attacked by a German night-fighter on the Les Hauts-Buissons raid. Looking out from my rear turret I saw a plane way off on our starboard side get attacked by a night fighter. I saw the flash of tracer shells which hit the plane from underneath and its two port engines burst into flames. Then the German pilot turned and attacked us. I didn't see his plane but suddenly a stream of tracer shells was coming towards us on our starboard side. Luckily for us they missed our starboard wing. I called out to Bill to corkscrew and I opened fire at the tracer shells which was what we were trained to do. When a bullet ever hits anything it has a sparking effect and that's what I saw so I knew I had hit the night fighter. At the same time I was calling out to Charlie Hood in his mid-upper turret: "Watch him Charlie! He's diving to port." Then I heard John Allen, our engineer, say: "Charlie can't do anything. He's not in his turret. He's lying on the floor. He's been sick." I saw an explosion way down beneath us and I believed that I had shot down the plane that attacked us, but there were other things exploding in the distance too. I didn't report it as a probable. My job wasn't to shoot them down. My job was to make sure they didn't get us."

Crews returning to the squadron that morning reported that they had seen a Halifax "on fire in a spiral dive over the Channel". When we got back to base we found out that it was F-Freddie MZ298, the plane belonging to the crew who shared our hut with us. We felt pretty bad about it. Of all the crews on the squadron, they were closest to us. We were sitting at debriefing looking at the names of the planes being filled in on the board when they landed back at base. There was just a blank space next to F for Freddie. The next day, Sandy and Bill were chatting to the squadron leader's adjutant about the mission. He told them that there a young WAAF on the squadron who was pregnant with the child of F-Freddie's pilot, Harley Donald. She was heart broken as you would expect. It was very sad.

There was one survivor from F-Freddie - Bob Selth, the mid-upper. His survival was miraculous. There is no other way to explain it. Bob told me that he saw the flashes of tracer shells along their port wing and a few seconds later both port engines caught fire. Harley Donald, the pilot, told them to prepare to bail out. Bob climbed out of his turret and put his parachute on. He remembered standing in the fuselage looking down towards the front of the plane and seeing Wilfred Cook, the flight engineer, fighting a fire in the cockpit. His battledress was on fire and he was spraying a fire extinguisher into the pilot's compartment "trying to do something to help his skipper". The plane suddenly dived and went into a spin. Bob was thrown onto the fuselage floor and was pinned there by the G-forces. He said he was "waiting to die". Then the plane exploded and broke up. Bob's flying boots were torn off and somehow the explosion threw him out of the plane. He pulled his ripcord and luckily the parachute opened first go. Bob said he was only about a thousand feet up when he pulled the cord because the next thing he knew he dropped into the water. He was worried about getting tangled up in the cords but he didn't panic and let the parachute float away from him before he released his harness. Rex Lathlean, the bomb aimer, had also parachuted from the plane but unfortunately he may have struggled with his parachute and got tangled up, and drowned. Bob floated around in the dark for five hours, wondering if it was going to be the end of him or not.

The crew on a destroyer had watched the plane coming down in flames. Warships would never stop at night time because they might be sitting ducks if there was a U-boat nearby. They knew where the plane had come down and at dawn they sailed into the crash site and found Bob in the water. The sailors threw down a rope with a triangle shaped harness on the end but Bob didn't bother about the harness and used the rope to climb straight up the side of the ship and then he flopped onto the deck. They also fished out the bodies of Rex Lathlean and David Rogers, the rear gunner. Bob was taken to hospital in Newhaven and stayed there for about six weeks. He was knocked about and had a deep gash in his buttock from when he fell out of the plane.

When he returned to the squadron, Bill Rabbitt was Bob's CO because he was the acting commanding officer of B Flight. Bob asked him, "What happens now?" and Bill said that he could fly as a spare gunner if he wanted to. Bob didn't think it was right to use him as a spare bod just because his crew had been killed and said that if they wanted him to go back on operations, the right thing was to send him back to an OTU and bring him through with a crew of his own. That was fair enough too. As it turned out, this was Bob's last operation. Out of the blue, he was invalided back home to Australia.

Bob Selth thought that his pilot, Harley Donald, was a strange fellow in some ways because he kept to himself. Unlike most pilots, Donald didn't mix socially with any of the six sergeants in his crew. But Bob said he was a brilliant pilot.

On the 8th of June, they were on the Alençon raid that we went on. When they returned the weather was so bad at Pocklington that they were diverted to Carnaby too and couldn't get down just like us because the weather at Carnaby was no better. Bob said that Harley Donald was flying on instruments and took the plane down to a hundred feet but still couldn't see the runway through the cloud. He told his crew to put their parachutes on because the plane had hardly any fuel left. Then he told them that he would "head it out to sea" and they would have to jump out. Just then a hole in the cloud appeared directly behind Bob in his mid-upper turret and he "picked up a couple of flares from the runway". "I've got it!" he called into the intercom. "It's directly beneath me!" Harley Donald in a flash turned the plane around, aimed it at the flares and "put it down so smoothly that it didn't even bounce".

Not long before he died, Norm Brand, the navigator, confided in me that he was worried about Donald because he always questioned the advice his crew gave him. Norm thought that it was dangerous for a pilot to hesitate when split seconds could mean the difference between life and death. If a gunner said corkscrew you had to go. There was no time to ask the gunner if he was sure. Norm thought we were lucky because Bill Rabbitt always reacted instantly to what we said and it saved our lives more than once.

Sandy knew Bob Selth and the rear gunner, David Rogers, quite well. They used to call David Rogers "Buck". The three of them were in the gunnery section together. The wireless operator, Reg Skeates, was a good friend of Harry Brabin. I knew the navigator really well too - Norm Brand. We arrived at the squadron together and he was in the Nav section with me. He was a short, chubby, Jewish boy. He was born in Warsaw in Poland and had originally served in the Field Ambulance Corps in the army. He was made an instructor but he wanted to be fighting the Germans so he remustered with the RAAF and became a navigator. Rex Lathlean was a special mate of Don's. They were both bomb aimers. Rex's nickname was "Chicken". I used to hear Don talk about Chicken Lathlean quite a bit. He was an excellent sportsman. In 1940, Chick was a rover for Sturt when they beat South Adelaide in the South Australian grand final. He was a good bloke. They all were. Five of the crew were Australians, so they were basically an Australian crew the same as us. They never found the bodies of Harley Donald and Norman Brand, and the two Englishmen, Reg Skeates and Wilfred Cook.

Even though our two crews shared the same hut, we operated separately. We often flew on different nights, took leave on different days and were coming and going at different times. We went out to pubs and dances with our own crew and so did the other crews. You knew the blokes in your own section and had lectures and briefings with them. You might strike up a conversation at the pub or in the sergeants' mess or you might have trained with someone and got to know them that way. That's just how it was. I knew very little about the bomb aimers and wireless operators and gunners from other crews. I was acquainted with the navigators of other crews because we shared the Nav section together but I spent most of my spare time with my own crew, not with other ones. After the war, Bob Selth and his wife came with us on a crew reunion trip to the Barossa Valley and we spent a couple of great days with them.

In 2004, on the 60th anniversary of the raid, Bob Selth, Sandy Concannon, Buck Rogers' two brothers and Norm Brand's sister had dinner together in Melbourne to mark the event. Round about that time, out of the blue, Harley Donald's son, Tony Webster, managed to track Bob down. Bob told Sandy Concannon and they both exchanged letters with Tony and told him everything they could remember about his father.

I understand that Tony had found the little hamlet of Les Hauts-Buissons and had laid one wreath there and another one in the English Channel for the 60th anniversary too.

Schrage Musik

Sandy Concannon's story about the shooting down of Bob Selth's Halifax F-Freddie MZ298 recounted in the chapter above suggests that it may have been shot down by "Schrage Musik", the upwards, firing cannons that were installed in German night fighters during the Second World War. The German word "schrage" means "slanted" or "at an angle". The term "schrage musik" in some circles was used as an informal name for jazz music.

Upward firing guns had previously been used in the First World War. The British mounted Lewis Guns on the upper wings of biplanes such as the Sopwith Camel and the SE5a. At the time of his death in May 1917, British air ace Albert Ball, had developed the technique of moving in behind and beneath unsuspecting enemy planes and shooting them down with his upper wing mounted machine gun. At the time of his death in May 1917 he was Britain's leading air ace with forty-four enemy aircraft destroyed.

Credit for the introduction of schrage musik cannons in German night fighters is attributed to Oberleutnant Rudolf Schoenert. As a night fighter pilot he recognized the shortcomings of directly attacking heavy bombers from the rear. The closing speed relative to two aircraft made frontal attacks unsuitable, and when attacking with the advantages of speed and surprise, a heavy bomber in the distance presented a relatively small target, and there was always the problem of closing in and being in grave danger from the RAF gunners - the rear gunner in particular.

Despite skepticism from among his own ranks, Schonert had a powerful sponsor in General Josef Kammhuber, who was then in charge of the German night fighter defense system. In July 1942, Kammhuber gave Schoenert the responsibility for overseeing the development of schrage musik, and ordered the delivery of three specially modified Dornier 217 J-1 aircraft, with upward firing guns installed, to be sent to Shoenert's squadron for operational testing. Further experimentation at the Luftwaffe's weapons testing centre at Tarnewitz determined that the best results were obtained when upward firing guns were mounted at an angle between sixty and seventy degrees. Too low an angle could bring the night fighter into a rear gunner's line of fire and too high an angle could result in the exploding plane above destroying its attacker below. The guns were placed behind the cockpit in aircraft such as the Junkers 88 and Dornier 217. They were fired by the pilot, who manoeuvred his plane into position, and sighted the target through two mirrors, one placed above his head with a second one, parallel to the first, placed behind the gun sight.

Directed to bomber streams by increasingly sophisticated radar systems, German night fighters were successful predators in their nightly stalking of RAF heavy bombers. From beneath, the target loomed large in silhouette. Tactics employed by night fighter pilots were critical to the success of schrage musik. The confident, fast and furious, full on attack, employed early in the war, was replaced by stealth and cunning. Night fighters were first directed into bombing streams by radar controllers. There they would select a target and gradually overtake it, taking care not to alert its radio operator to their presence below. The radio operator's attention would be fixed on his Fishpond screen, ever alert for a blip on the display moving rapidly across the bombing stream – the sign that a night fighter was approaching. The German pilot, now holding formation, would bring his plane up beneath his prey. Because of the risk of exploding bombs, the pilot would not aim his schrage musik guns at the belly of the aircraft but instead would fire at the wings, to destroy the engines and cause the petrol tanks to burst into flame. Schrage musik conversion was undertaken for night fighters already in service, and the cannons were built into new aircraft during assembly. A typical installation was two 30mm Mark 108 cannons. German testing showed that five hits from their 30mm high explosive ammunition was enough to bring down a heavy bomber.

In May 1943, Rudolph Schoenert shot down the first RAF heavy bomber using schrage musik and by the end of the year his tally was eighteen. With the incorporation of upward firing guns into its night fighters, the Luftwaffe had another effective weapon and their night fighters took a terrible toll on the invading heavy bomber streams. RAF records show that night fighters were responsible for at least 65% of all losses. In the six months from October 1943 until March 1944, 1,252 heavy bombers were shot down, an unsustainable loss rate of 4.7 percent. In January 1944 alone, Bomber Command losses amounted to 315 aircraft (87 Halifaxes and 228 Lancasters), a loss rate of 6.5 percent.

From January 1944 until the end of the war in May 1945, 2,554 RAF bombers were destroyed on operations over occupied Europe and Germany. So demoralizing were these losses for Bomber Command aircrews, that RAF intelligence began spreading the rumour, that the unexplained explosions in the bombing stream were not aircraft being shot down, but were "scarecrows", a special type of shell developed by the Germans to mimic an exploding plane. The truth in fact was that each explosion was either a Halifax or Lancaster bomber that had been shot down by Schrage Music.

Chapter 35: Operation 17 - Stuttgart

461 Lancasters and 153 Halifaxes to Stuttgart. 17 Lancasters and 4 Halifaxes lost, 4.6 percent of the force. This was the first of 3 heavy raids on Stuttgart in 5 nights and the only report available is a composite one for the 3 raids. The 3 raids caused the most serious damage of the war in the central districts of Stuttgart which, being situated in a series of narrow valleys, had eluded Bomber Command for several years. They were now devastated and most of Stuttgart's public and cultural buildings were destroyed.
The Bomber Command War Diaries, 24/25 July 1944

A raid on Stuttgart was our seventeenth mission. Thirteen aircraft from our squadron were part of a bomber force of over six hundred aircraft that bombed the city on the night of the $24^{th}/25^{th}$ of July. One of our planes returned early with engine trouble. I still have the log and chart of this raid. It was the longest flight we ever did, eighteen hundred miles, and it took eight hours and twenty minutes. We got back at 5.45 am. We took off at 2125 hours and carried four thousand pounds of bombs which was one of our lightest bomb loads. We had to carry an overload fuel tank in our bomb bay and that took up room that would otherwise have been taken up by bombs. The Halifax had the capacity to do that.

We had no sooner taken off when I realised that the Air Position Indicator was u/s. It should have been showing $00.48°$ West, $53.56°$ North - the latitude and longitude of our base at Pocklington – but it was showing something else. I informed Bill and we continued on our way. Having an unserviceable API wasn't reason enough to abort a mission. We still had GEE to lead us south over Reading and across the Channel, and H2S for France and Germany.

After all these years, it is still good to go through the chart and look at the tactics that were involved. Prior to turning onto our bombing run, the last leg towards Stuttgart, we did a feint towards Manheim. It was all about tricking the German air defences. All the way we led the Germans to believe that we were attacking Mannheim and they were fooled into that because the searchlights and fighter flares were already in evidence in the sky, waiting for us as we approached. Then just twenty-five miles short of Manheim, we did a sharp right-hand turn to the south east straight onto our bombing run. The right hand turn is very evident from the air plot that I did on the map.

Our target that night was the Daimler-Benz aircraft engine factory whose engines powered Messerschmitt fighters. I was very busy over my charts and instruments and I didn't see any of the bombing run. When we arrived, Stuttgart was covered in ten-tenths cloud so we had to bomb on "Wanganui" flares which the Pathfinders had dropped. They would hang

Halifax Navigator

in the middle of the sky above the clouds. Don waited until he saw them in his bombsight before he dropped his bombs. There were no line overlap photographs taken on our bombing run when we bombed over clouds like this but after Don said, "Bombs gone!" we still had to stay on and do the camera run. It was standard procedure. I did not see any searchlights or fighter flares. Searchlights couldn't penetrate ten-tenths cloud so we weren't bothered by them.

After we dropped our bombs we stayed on the same course for a few minutes and then turned almost due south for another three or four minutes. In his book, Harry Brabin says that when we were turning, Charlie Hood, our mid-upper gunner, called out that another Halifax had turned at the same time and just missed us by a few feet. That was always on the cards. There were over six hundred bombers on the raid so there were a lot of aircraft in the sky that night, all doing ninety degree turns at the same time. Next we did a right hand ninety degree turn to starboard and headed on a course that took us westward between Karlsruhe, on our starboard side to the north, and Strasbourg to the south, to keep us away from the air defences. The flight plan also told us to dive from twenty thousand feet to six thousand feet at 240 miles an hour to shake off enemy night fighters and it was successful for us because even though we saw fighters about we were not attacked. Then we headed south west for home, flying westward below Paris before we turned northwards towards Le Havre and crossed the English Channel into England.

It was a long and exhausting flight for Bill as his diary entry for this trip says:

> " ....The distance was approximately 1,800 miles and we took 8 hours 40 minutes to do it. It seemed a tremendous time to be up. The defences were pretty hot and I saw a kite go down in flames. We approached Stuttgart by making a feint at Mannheim and Ludwigshafen, then down past Strasbourg on to Stuttgart.... We lost one crew. F/Lt Page Weaver was shot up a bit and claimed a fighter. Feeling very tired at present."

For our crew this was a fairly straightforward mission. It was long and demanding. I had a lot of extra pressure on me because the Air Position Indicator wasn't working and I had to do a manual plot the whole way there and back for what was a complicated flight plan. We got in, dropped our bombs and headed for home not knowing that terrible damage was being inflicted on the bombing stream by intensive flak over the target, and by night fighters which were very active.

Halifax X-Xray, LL552 from our squadron was shot down and six of the crew were killed. It was piloted by Flight Sergeant Page. Their plane crashed near Piencourt, a small French village about forty kilometres south of Le Havre. They are buried in the Piencourt Churchyard. A report says that they crashed at about 04.00. That would be about right because we arrived back at Pocklington at 05.45. Apparently their flight path took them over German anti aircraft guns near the village of Barville about six kilometres east of Piencourt. They appear to have been heading towards Le Havre and were only about ten minutes from the English Channel when they came down. Nearly there! The seventh crew member Sergeant Robert Brewer, the rear gunner, baled out and was taken prisoner.

Another one of our planes, Halifax Z-Zebra MZ745, Flight Lieutenant Weaver's plane, was badly damaged and they were lucky to make it back to base. They were attacked at 0220 hours by a Junkers 88 night fighter. That was roughly five hours into an eight and a half hour flight, so they would have been on their way home. The plane had a lot of damage on the port side. Its outer engine, the aileron, rudder and elevator were all damaged. On this raid twenty-one bombers were shot down – seventeen Lancasters and four Halifaxes. I can never find the words to explain why we were spared. We just were!

The Air Position Indicator

The Air Position Indicator was the third of the three important navigational aids that were available to a navigator in a heavy bomber. The GEE box and H2S were the other two.

The API was the most important navigational aid because when you operated it successfully you didn't have to keep a manual air plot. The beauty of the airspeed indicator was that it automatically compensated for sudden changes in height and direction when we were in combat with a night fighter. After a corkscrew action I would not have a hope of plotting our position without it. It just followed us through the corkscrew and when we leveled off it would have an accurate latitude and longitude reading waiting.

After combat I would immediately take a fix from the nearest town and get us back on track. It was connected to the gyro compass, the air speed indicator, the magnetic compass that the pilot used, and also to the altimeter. It gave me an accurate air position at any time regardless of what was happening outside, recording all of the changes in course, and height and speed and then giving an accurate air position whenever I chose to read it off the dial.

Every navigator knows that the art of aerial navigation is finding out what your drift is. Drift is the angle that you are deviating from the direction you are flying and the track you are supposed to be flying. When I took a fix, I automatically logged our air position from our API and placed the fix and air position on my chart. They were always different dependant upon wind speed and direction. I had to be able to tell Bill what he had to do to get back onto track. That is the object of navigation – to offset your aircraft direction to make good your track. I used the Air Position Indicator all the time in conjunction with GEE and H2S and every time I took a fix on GEE or H2S I took an air position, put them on the chart, joined them up and obtained a wind vector.

This was the only time that our Air Position Indicator didn't work. I had to employ a manual air plot all the way to Stuttgart and back. It was pretty hard work. Without the API to automatically calculate the information from the altimeter, the magnetic compass and the air speed indicator, I had to first get my fixes using H2S, and then find out my air position by plotting the course Bill was flying and calculating the true air speed by means of the formula - three nautical miles per hour for every thousand feet in altitude above sea level. Then I would tell him to fly at such and such a speed on such and such a course and at such and such a height to stay on the flight plan.

At the end of the war, I was given my flight plans from all of our operations and I brought them back to Australia with me. They were cluttering up the house and no-one ever looked at them so a few years ago, I took everything down to the incinerator in the back yard and burned them. All I kept was my navigator's log book and the flight plan of our mission over Stuttgart. This was the longest raid I ever did and the most difficult as far as I was concerned. Despite all the problems I had, we still dropped our bombs to the minute specified in the flight plan. That's why I kept the log and chart of this mission.

Upon my return, I handed my log and chart of the mission in at the Nav. section. The senior navigation officer was Flight Lieutenant Samson. We used to call him "Sammy". Sammy gave me ten out of ten for the effort of bombing on time with only a manual airplot. He wrote on my log: "Bit early at F. Air position at Δ. Wind velocity a bit high due probably to manual Air plot. Jolly good trip Cock. 10."

Sammy used to call everyone "Cock"! He picked up something to do with our air position near Karlsruhe when I used the triangle of velocities to bring us back onto track. He uses the Δ symbol to indicate the location on my chart that he is talking about. At 'F' on my chart he thought we were a bit early turning from our run down from Orlean, westward onto our next leg towards Neufchateau, a course change that brought us into line with Mannheim. I was happy with my ten out of ten.

Wanganui

Sometimes when we reached the target it was obscured by thick clouds. It would have been useless for the Master Bomber and the Pathfinders to go down and mark the target because the bomber force approaching at twenty thousand feet would not have seen the markers through the clouds anyway. Special markers called "Wanganui" were employed in this situation. We always had to bomb the flares that the Pathfinders laid down. That's what Don would always aim for, so over a target like Stuttgart that night we still bombed flares but they were Wanganui sky markers instead. They would hang in the air above the clouds by parachute. When the sky was clear the Master Bomber marked the first flare on the target and the Pathfinders put their flares down as backup to make a clearer target to aim for, but in cloud like this where they couldn't see the target, they would take into account the course that the main force was flying and the prevailing wind speed and direction and the height at which we were bombing before they released their sky markers. We would set the course that was given to Harry over the wireless from Base who would have been told by the Master Bomber that the first planes were arriving at the target. Then Bill, with Don directing him, manoeuvred the plane so that the flares were in the bombsight when Don released the bombs.

The Pathfinder Force laid down different types of flares and markers depending on what they encountered over the target. The Master Bomber never laid sky markers. The Pathfinder Lancasters would do that. I would imagine that on this raid to Stuttgart, the Master Bomber, arrived at the target, found that it was ten-tenths cloud, decided that it was useless to mark at ground level, and instructed the Pathfinder Lancasters to lay on Wanganui sky markers. Bombing on Wanganui didn't happen very often.

Diary Entry – Lancaster Bomber Pilot, Bruce Johnston (RCAF)
115 Squadron RAF Witchford
Operation 12, Stuttgart, Tuesday 25th July 1944.

"Took 2,000 gallons of petrol above bomb loads about fifty miles north of Paris through to Stuttgart. We took within ten minutes or so of eight hours; about six of them over enemy territory which is a bit of a bugger let me remark – it's far too long for my liking! We had a bit over an hour's petrol to spare for the trip but we did quite okay.

The same conditions as at Kiel over the target (which we reached early and had to orbit) so we unloaded at the Wanganui sky marker and I imagine made quite a mess of things. Unlike last night the sky was completely dark (aside from stars) which struck me as a bit odd - I hadn't realized how much further south we were!

Saw two definite chops – one just inside the French coast on the way in and the other over the target. There were bags of scarecrows and a few fighter flares – some combats and one of our boys claimed a Junkers 88. We all returned safely.

For the first seventy-five miles out of the target they kept throwing up fighter flares and scarecrows (mostly scarecrows) right in front of us about half a mile – made us feel naked they lit us up so! (I did lots of weaving about and dodging but luckily I wasn't bothered). The last legs of the trip over France were the most interminable periods of flying I think I've ever put in – Lord how the time crawled.

There was a great barrage at the beach head and I hear since (I'm writing this Tuesday of course) that they were staging an offensive, it was just past dawn. We took off at 9:40 and landed about 5:30 – almost eight hours.

Set course at 10:10 at 10,000 feet. Climbed to 18,000 feet when we left England. Flew at that height until the last 100 miles, then as high as we could get (about 21,800 ft in Willie). About fifty miles from Stuttgart we dropped to 12,000 feet at 230 mph and 1,200 feet per minute. Then after another 100 miles or so we dropped to 8,000 feet maintaining that back to Reading then down to base.

Got turn seven and landed so closely behind another bod that I got caught in his slipstream and nearly pranged! Tsk, tsk.

Track miles were about 1,480 miles. What a trip!! Looking good in the log book though. Got to bed about 7:00 or 7:30 a.m."

The Stuttgart Raid Flight Plan

The flight plan of the Stuttgart raid from the website of the *WW2 Diary of Lancaster Pilot Bruce Johnston* of the Royal Canadian Air Force. Basil Spiller was the navigator aboard Halifax LW142 N-Nan from 102 Squadron RAF Pocklington on the same operation.

Except for the fact that Halifax navigator Basil Spiller's raid on Stuttgart began at Pocklington in Yorkshire, more than 180 kilometres north-west of Witchford where Bruce Johnston's twelfth operation began, the flight plan for the Canadian pilot's raid is the basically the same as that plotted by Basil Spiller. Basil still has the original log and chart for this operation.

On the map above, note the sharp right hand turn as Bruce Johnston's Lancaster started its run towards Stuttgart. This was the "feint" towards Mannheim that Basil Spiller describes in this chapter.

Basil's track approaching and leaving the target differs in that the bombing run took them straight over Stuttgart. They stayed on this course beyond Stuttgart for three minutes, turning south for a further two minutes, before making a right angle turn to the west which took them between Strasbourg and Karlsruhe.

Chapter 36: Operation 18 - Wanne-Eickel

135 aircraft - 114 Halifaxes, 11 Lancasters, 10 Mosquitos - of Nos 1, 4 and 8 Groups attacked the Krupp oil refinery at Wanne-Eickel. No aircraft lost. Only a few bombs hit a corner of the oil refinery and production was not seriously affected. Other bombs hit the south-eastern part of Eickel, destroying 14 houses and killed 29 civilians, 4 foreign workers and 3 prisoners of war and causing production at the Hannibal coal mine to cease. *Total effort for the night:* 852 sorties, 13 aircraft (1.5 per cent) lost.

The Bomber Command War Diaries, 25/26 July 1944

Our next operation was a night time raid on the 25th/26th to Wanne-Eickel. It was our third operation in three days and we carried seven thousand pounds of bombs. On the 23rd of July we did Les Hauts-Buissons, on the 24th of July we did Stuttgart and on the 25th there we were off to Wanne-Eickel. It was pretty full on.

This was our eighteenth operation. Twenty aircraft from 102 Squadron took part in this mission but one returned with compass trouble and another one bombed another town because they had an electrical fault on their way in and decided to get rid of their bombs. We left at 2245 and the trip was four hours and fifty minutes long.

Wanne-Eickel was in the Ruhr Valley. We called the Ruhr "Happy Valley". The target was a synthetic oil plant. There was no dogleg and no parting the curtains to have a look around. Straight in and straight out! According to the station record, the ground was obscured by haze and the Pathfinders did not lay their markers close enough to the target. Although we could clearly see the ground markers and our bombs fell in a concentrated pattern around them, not many bombs hit the oil plant.

The Ruhr defences were very strong. Searchlights were darting all over the sky, flak was going off everywhere and night fighters were very much in evidence. I remember that after leaving the target the flight plan had us repeating the Stuttgart tactic to fool the night fighters and we dropped height rapidly. We came down like the clappers from sixteen thousand feet to two thousand feet and roared across Holland at one thousand feet. All of the returning bombing stream did the same. If yu didn't you were all on your own, out on a limb – not a very nice place to be. It was safety in numbers. With over a hundred bombers on target, it was always be nicer to be in amongst them.

We were coming across Holland after 3.00 in the morning. Bill could see the flooded areas quite plainly. Perhaps it was moonlight reflecting off the water.

The Wanne-Eickel raid was mainly a 4 Group effort. It was good that every aircraft returned home safely. To experience no casualties on a

Ruhr target was exceptional. One of our planes claimed a "probable" Junkers 88. This means that the gunner believed that he had hit it and thought it had subsequently crashed. It would be hard to know if there is no explosion or you don't see it hit the ground. It's night time. You think you have hit it but you are going one way and it is going the other and soon you have lost sight of it.

Don McLean's account of this raid in his diary gives a bit more information about our flight plan:

> "We were sent to an oil refinery near Bochum in the Ruhr last night and what a target! ....The cloud was very broken at the target and the flak was terrific. There were a lot of searchlights and quite a few fighter flares. We flew over the North Sea at 2,000 feet – bombed at 16,000 and then dived down at 240 m.p.h. to 1,500 feet. All our squadron returned O.K. although one was attacked six times. Heard that they've identified Chick Lathlean's and Norm Brand's bodies. (Killed on the Les Hauts-Buissons operation 23rd/24th July.) Wanne Eickel was the name of the target and it was hot."

While we went to Wanne-Eickel in our Halifaxes, the Lancasters went back to Stuttgart. I understand that they did it again the next night as well. So Stuttgart was bombed three nights in a row and they probably made a terrible mess of it.

Happy Valley – The Ruhr

"Happy Valley" was the ironical name given by aircrews on bombing raids to Germany's Ruhr Valley and nearby Rhineland cities such as Dusseldorf, Cologne and Albrecht during the Second World War.

RAAF pilot, Jack Thomas, who served in No. 102 Squadron, RAF at Pocklington in Yorkshire, the same squadron as Basil Spiller, said this about one mission to the Ruhr Valley:

> "The outward trip to Gelsenkirchen was a breeze, but suddenly everything changed. The bomb aimer and I sighted the flak. It was unbelievable. The sky was a close pattern of black patches. The white-faced bomb aimer went down into the nose to his bombsight. I looked at the flak pattern ahead and thought, 'This is it. We die here. Nobody can possibly survive this barrage!' Reluctantly, we flew into this maelstrom expecting the worst. Amazingly, we were not hit and gradually I realized we had a chance – it was a box barrage, not predictor flak. It looked worse than it actually was. Perhaps the first wave suffered more than us. We were on our bombing run. Bombs away! Bomb doors closed. Photo flash taken and then we were turning away from the target – alive!"

12 October 1944. A well camouflaged Handley Page Halifax Mk 3 of No. 6 Group flies over the smoke-obscured target during a daylight raid on the oil refinery at Wanne-Eickel in the Ruhr.

There is no doubt that the bombing of the industrial cities of the Ruhr and Rhineland retarded Germany's wartime materials production but the campaign was not as successful as planned. This heavily defended region was shrouded in a cloak of industrial haze which made accurate bombing difficult. Consequently the steel, synthetic oil and munitions industries continued production albeit at reduced levels through 1943 and 1944. The toll paid by aircrews running the gauntlet of searchlights, anti-aircraft guns, and menacing night fighters, directed into bombing streams by advanced radar systems, was very high. Heavy bomber losses in Happy Valley were in the order of 4.7 percent, the limit of what Bomber Command believed sustainable.

Chapter 37: Commission Interviews

We returned from Wanne-Eickel at about 0335 hours on the 26th of July and later that day Don, John and I had appointments with Wing Commander Marchbank about our commissions.

The first indication that we had been recommended for a commission would have come from our Section Commanders, so I was told by the Navigation Leader. Then we waited.

We had to attend three appointments - firstly with the Wing Commander of the squadron, secondly with the Group Captain in charge of the station and thirdly with the Air Commodore in charge of the base. Bear in mind that RAF Pocklington was a base aerodrome and had two satellite aerodromes under its jurisdiction.

It was a big organisation with over two thousand personnel on site. The aerodrome was the location of 42 Base RAF which directed the operations at three airfields – RAF Pocklington, RAF Elvington and RAF Full Sutton.

On the 26th of July, I would have been informed by the Nav Leader that at such and such a time I was to report to Wing Commander Marchbank so that he could satisfy himself that I was worthy of a King's Commission so that's what I did.

Wing Commander Marchbank was a flying man. He was only permitted to do one operation a month because experienced flyers were short on the ground and they didn't want to lose him which was, obviously, more likely the more often he flew. He would have been itching to get up. As a Wing Commander he had the power not to fly if he didn't want to so he must have wanted to go up.

I would have saluted him and he would have invited me to sit down and remove my cap. He would have talked generally about my schooling and upbringing to determine whether I was a gentleman and worthy of a commission or not. This was my first step towards obtaining a commission.

I didn't know what recommendation he'd made but the next thing I knew I was called before Group Captain Russell on a later date.

I remember being called before him for the interview. The same thing happened. He was an older guy who wasn't flying. His job was to administer the whole of the aerodrome. So I met Group Captain Russell and did the same thing as I had done with Wing Commander Marchbank.

Unfortunately on our next mission I was seriously wounded. That interrupted my promotion and I didn't have my third interview until after I had recovered.

Rose Brothers and the Air Position Indicator

The manufacturing company, Rose Brothers (Gainsborough) Ltd., had an interesting beginning. William Rose, the founder, was a mechanical genius. In the 1870's, while working as a barber's assistant, he was often irritated when he had to stop shaving a client, rinse and dry his lathered hands and then measure out and wrap small amounts of tobacco for waiting customers. At home, Rose began designing a tobacco packing machine by first educating himself in the basics of applied mechanics and mechanical drawing. In 1881 he patented the world's first tobacco packing machine. In 1885 he founded the Rose Company to manufacture and market the machines worldwide. The Rose Company grew rapidly and produced a wide range of machines which packed a wide variety of goods including chocolate, razor blades, powder, tea, coffee, cakes and biscuits. In the 1890's, William Rose designed the "National" automobile, which his company manufactured from 1900 until 1908. In 1905, William and his brother Walter formed Rose Brothers (Gainsborough) Ltd. It was a company built on traditional values, often accepting challenging projects for little profit, enabling it to maintain its team of highly skilled craftsmen and engineers. The company gained an unrivalled reputation for precision machine engineering and meticulous attention to detail which eventually attracted the attention of the British armed services.

The Rose Company Air Position Indicator

During the First World War, Rose Brothers became involved in war manufacturing, securing contracts for manufacturing gun sights and breech mechanisms for the Royal Navy and artillery shells for the British Army. The company then designed and built synchronisation mechanisms for machine guns on RAF planes, allowing the guns to be positioned forward of the pilot and fired through the propeller blades without damaging them. This began a long-standing relationship with the RAF. After William Rose's death in 1929, his son Alfred, who had inherited his father's genius, became manager of the company.

In the 30's, the company's association with the Royal Navy continued and when the Second World War began, its sophisticated Mark 3 High Angle Control

Systems, which accurately predicted anti-aircraft fire onto attacking aircraft, were installed on many RN warships. Throughout the war, a steady stream of high ranking RAF personnel, such as Air Marshall Harris and Leonard Cheshire, visited Alfred Rose asking if their ideas could become reality and seeking solutions to problems as they appeared. On one such visit, Rose was asked if he could build a machine to provide an aircrew with accurate air position readings throughout their flight. The result was the inspired creation of the analogue "air position indicator", which was one of the great inventions of the war. After March 1943, API was installed in all RAF heavy bombers. It received information from an aircraft's gyro compass, altimeter and air speed indicator and was able to calculate the latitude and longitude of the plane's air position, which the navigator was able to read from the front of the set.

The Rose Company made many other significant contributions to the war effort, designing and manufacturing such things as "pom-pom" gun directors, gun sights, the 2-inch Howitzer and the Stiffkey offset sight for Bofors guns. The company also resolved problems associated with the transfer of petrol between tanks in Lancaster bombers, improved the provision of oxygen to aircrew, played a major role in the building of the release mechanisms for the "bouncing bombs" on the famous Dambuster's raid, and designed and manufactured superior rear turrets for heavy bombers.

It is interesting to note that Cadbury's "Roses" chocolates were named after the company that manufactured the machines that wrapped them.

Chapter 38: Operation 19 - Forêt de Nieppe

199 aircraft - 159 Halifaxes, 20 Mosquitos, 20 Stirlings - of Nos 3, 4 and 8 Groups attacked two launching sites and made two further separate raids on the Forêt de Nieppe storage site. All bombing was through cloud but the various methods used were believed to have led to accurate results. 1 Halifax lost from one of the Forêt de Nieppe raids.
The Bomber Command War Diaries, 28 July 1944

Bill's diary entry for the 28th of July 1944 describes our next mission as a "very shaky do". On this day fifteen aircraft from our squadron were briefed to fly to the Forêt de Nieppe in northern France on what was to be a fateful trip for me because I nearly got killed.

The squadron record says that two Halifaxes returned early - one must have been having engine trouble because it could not keep up with the bombing stream and the other was having navigation problems. We were carrying seven thousand five hundred pounds of bombs and we got away at 1610, late in the afternoon. It was a daylight mission and we were briefed to lead a force of three 4 Group squadrons. Wing Commander Wilson, flying on his first mission, had decided that Bill's crew would lead the formation.

The plan was that we would fly to Flamborough Head, a prominent headland sticking out into the sea north of the Humber. Whenever we flew across the North Sea, that was our leaving point on the coast of Britain. Then we were to approach the Belgian coast and rendezvous with two Oboe Mosquitos from the Pathfinder Force who would lead us to the target. On arriving at the target they would each release a flare and immediately we sighted the flares in the bombsite we would drop our bombs and the whole of the formation would drop 'em in unison.

On daylight missions RAF aircraft flew as a gaggle just as we did on night missions. After takeoff we just circled around our base as the squadron got airborne and when it was time to go, away we went. Whether or not a pilot took a position near another plane was purely voluntary as each navigator was navigating individually. In his diary on several operations, Bill talks about formatting on the wing commander. It was his choice. I knew nothing about what he was doing on those occasions and navigated as normal according to the flight plan knowing he would put the plane where I told him. On a daylight mission where pilots could see one another, they would often fly in a loose formation but it was their choice.

We led the formation so I was the lead navigator. It was obvious right from the word go that the Met. winds were out and we were gaining time. When I say that, I mean that the wind forecast that was used to draw up our flight plan, and turning points, was wrong. It was our way of saying that the winds predicted by the meteorological unit were wrong and on this raid they were virtually behind us pushing us on. They were too strong because we were ahead of our time most of the way. They were more north westerly blowing us faster to the south east than the flight plan said they would. The actual winds that I calculated were stronger than the Met winds and we made up too much time. So I had to slow the formation down to rendezvous at the correct time with the two Mosquitos and be taken to the target. I did not want to get there too early or too late. I didn't want to dogleg because I had three squadrons, approximately seventy aircraft, all taking their lead from me as the lead navigator, and that would have been too much of a manoeuvre. I instructed Bill to fly at the slowest possible speed so that the whole force would lose time.

There was not a cloud in the sky. The weather was perfect and Bill could see for two hundred miles. We had no trouble sighting the PFF Mosquitos. We picked them up at the rendezvous point dead on time and tucked in behind them. They were flying on their great circle track determined by their Oboe instruments but in doing so they led the flight directly over Ostend. Our target at Forêt de Nieppe was about twenty-five miles inland from the coast and forty miles south west of Ostend. When we crossed the coast we were already on our bombing run and Don was over his bombsight. The German ack-ack defences must have tracked us for quite a considerable period because when we crossed the coast at Ostend we were immediately attacked by very accurate anti-aircraft fire.

I don't know much about Oboe. It was a navigation instrument only available to the Pathfinder Force and it was top secret. But I understand that they would fly in a great arc and stick to it. It would eventually bring us around to the target. Bringing us in over Ostend and all of the fortifications that were there was a huge mistake. I suspect that it was all part of the flight plan. It was a bad plan. We ran into an absolute hail of flak.

Immediately the first burst of anti-aircraft fire erupted, a piece of flak shattered the whole of the perspex nose right in front of Don. Don was lucky that his head hadn't been taken off. While he was lying down over the bombsight with his head out into the glass nose section, the flak crashed right up through the bottom of the perspex, through the nose, severing his intercom communication with Bill and it smashed out through the top making a gap about three feet across. Don was no longer able to give bombing instructions. If Don had been hit by that lump of flak I reckon he would have been dead because the piece that took out

Halifax Navigator

the nose was pretty big. Don just stayed in there. He was totally confused. He was looking around bewildered and remained there for the whole of the bombing run. He was disorientated. The nose of the plane had just disappeared in front of him. Imagine what that was like. The front of our plane was just a gaping hole!

Then a second burst hit us! It exploded right under the plane and I was hit by a fragment of flak high up in the inner left thigh while I was sitting forward on my seat. It entered the aircraft directly between my shoes. There was a neat hole in N-Nan's floor in the middle of where my feet had been. It felt like somebody had hit me with a baseball bat. I felt no searing pain. We had numerous small holes through the bottom of the fuselage.

Harry Brabin was always sitting with his radio equipment in his little compartment to my left at right angles to me. I swung to the left facing him. He immediately saw I was wounded. He punched both his thumbs into the hole in my left thigh and held them there all the way back to England. He didn't have time to take my trousers off. He just pushed both of his thumbs into my wound and kept them there. It was bleeding profusely. I didn't know then that the shrapnel had hit my femoral vein.

Harry was still doing his job listening for messages and instructions but on raids there was always a radio blackout and although he could receive messages he was not allowed to transmit anything.

When the two explosions shook the plane we still had bombs to be dropped. Bill was under real pressure, trying to concentrate on keeping the plane steady on its bombing run without a bomb aimer and with about seventy planes behind him. When I interrupted him on the intercom to tell him that I'd been hit, I got no answer so half a minute later I repeated the message and was told to "Shut up!" because he was busy on his bombing run. By then Bill would have known that Don had no communication with him because of the severed intercom cord.

On the bomb run, the idea was that the three leading bombers would release their bombs as soon as the Oboe Mosquitos fired their flares. In his diary, Bill says that quite a few of them bombed early because of a misunderstanding, which sounds as though he was following the Pathfinders' lead and did what he was supposed to do. The other members of our formation were supposed to bomb when they saw our bombs go down so if we were early, quite a few of them would have been early too. Whether the flares were fired early or Bill dropped the bombs early I don't know because it was all chaos in the navigation compartment. We were on the last stage of our bombing run at the time of the explosions and Bill carried on towards the target. There was a backup bomb release mechanism in the cabin that he had to use it to release the bombs. The squadron had to go back to Forêt de Nieppe two days in a row after this raid so our mission wasn't a success.

Somewhere in the middle of all this, Bill must have been told that Harry was working on my leg and that I was not just wounded but that I could die because there was such a large amount of blood everywhere. Then Bill said: "We're cutting off from this and making a run for home to try and save Basil's life!"

The flight plan for the operation had us flying on our normal semicircular path back to England but Bill decided that because I needed medical attention we would fly a direct route home. We immediately peeled off and left the formation and swung away to starboard.

All the time Harry was holding his thumbs in my wound and his hands were covered in blood. We had done two right hand turns, one after bombing and one to get us heading towards England but we were still flying over the enemy occupied territory of northern France. At one stage we failed to realize that we were headed for a large built up area. It was probably Calais. That's when I got my wits together and saw our track on the H2S Plan Position Indicator screen. I knew that we were heading for a heavily defended area and I told Bill to take evasive action and go around it.

> *I'm wounded. The shrapnel burst up through the floor. There's blood everywhere. I'm calm. I'm trying not to think about the damage that's been done to my groin. Harry's hands are in there, pressing his thumbs in hard to stop the blood. Don is disorientated. He nearly had his head ripped off. I've got my wits about me. I am navigating the plane. Bill is going flat out. He's taking the direct route back to England. I need medical attention. Don has recovered now. He is seated next to me. I've got my equilibrium back. I've got Don there. I've got Harry. We're navigating by H2S. It is broad daylight and we are heading towards England. My eyes are glued to the screen. There is a big town ahead of us. I yell down the intercom to Bill, "Get away from the built up area!" N-Nan lurches hard to port!*

In the meantime an American P38 Lightning had seen our predicament and formated on us the whole of the time, shepherding us right across northern France where we were alone and subject to predicted flak. By shepherding us I mean that he formatted on our starboard wing and was there protecting us against attack by German fighters, making sure that Jerry fighters didn't jump us.

We evaded the predicted flak by skilful flying and eventually crossed the coast without difficulty. The P38 Lightning pilot left us as soon as he saw that we were safe and we flew back across the English Channel towards East Anglia.

When we were halfway across the Channel, Bill who must have thought that we were safe from a fighter attack by then, said to Sandy: "I guess you should go to the nose and see what's happened to Bas." The next thing I know Sandy appeared in my compartment and the first thing he did was to pull out a big bladed knife from his flying boot. We had no idea that he carried the knife. He thought it would make a useful weapon if we were ever shot down and had to parachute into enemy territory. It was a fearsome thing! I can remember saying: "Don't touch me with that bastard knife". Then he knelt down and cut off my pants above the wound and immediately a pool of blood spilled all over the floor. He removed the leg of my pants and Harry kept his thumbs jammed into the wound.

We arrived off the English coast, somewhere south of The Wash, and stooged along parallel to the coast which was just visible under our port wingtip. Our IFF had been shot away in the nose so we fired off two flares - the colours of the day - another identification method of establishing whether we were a friendly aircraft or not. They were fired from a Very pistol through a small hatch in the top of the fuselage.

Then we turned in and crossed the coast somewhere in East Anglia. When we saw the first aerodrome we requested permission to land and asked for medical help. It was a B17 Flying Fortress 'drome at Great Ashfield, belonging to the 8th American Airforce. As luck would have it, the Americans had built a surgical field hospital there, which was mainly occupied by casualties from the Cherbourg Peninsula after D-Day.

When we came to rest, after landing and taxiing, an ambulance drove up. The ambulance crew came into my compartment and decided that the best way to get me out was through the front escape hatch which was under my seat. I stood up and immediately the blood drained from my upper body and I felt as if I was going to faint. They opened the escape hatch and put a ladder up and brought in a stretcher. They bandaged my leg up and then manoeuvred me down the ladder and onto the waiting ambulance.

I don't remember any of the journey to the hospital and I presume the crew said goodbye to me but I don't remember anything about it. The next thing I knew, I was in a hospital situated way out in the middle of the wheat fields of East Anglia. I can remember going into the operating theatre and an orderly or a nurse stuck a needle into my right arm and told me to count. I only got to three and the next thing I knew I was awake in a ward. I can remember waking in great pain but a nurse was sitting alongside me and she gave me a shot of morphine straight away and I went out like a light. It is vivid in my memory.

In his diary Bill Rabbitt wrote:

".... today we had a very shaky do. We were briefed to lead 3 squadrons on an attack on the flying bomb depot and launching base in the Forêt de Nieppe. We arrived at our rendezvous smack on time with the 3 Squadrons in lovely formation behind N-Nan. Here we gave up our leadership to two Mossies who were "oboe" planes using special equipment. They proceeded to take us on to the target but led us over Ostend where we were predicted to very accurate heavy flak, resulting in the first seven planes of our squadron being hit badly. My a/c suffered numerous holes and Bas my navigator was wounded in the thigh pretty badly. We carried on to bomb but through a misunderstanding quite a number of us bombed early. Bas kept on working but was losing a lot of blood, so Don took over the navigating while Harry & Sandy attended to Bas. I headed for home like a bat out of Hades and the Jerries shot at us all the way out of enemy territory. I landed at Great Ashfield and the Yanks being very efficient soon had Bas away to hospital. We flew back to base, Don acting as navigator. Definitely a poor show."

The next day the crew went down to dispersal to have a look at the damage to the plane. N-Nan had "collected a packet" according to Bill Rabbitt's diary. He also wrote that Don McLean was "extremely fortunate as most of the perspex nose had been smashed."

N-Nan suffered considerable damage. Harry says that upon inspection N-Nan had eighty holes in it. It was amazing that she could still fly with the nose taken out of it. The Halifax was a rugged aircraft. If the controls had been damaged we would have had to bail out and I would probably have bled to death.

In his diary Don McLean reflected on his lucky escape:

"Wonder how Bas is making out. We don't look as if we will be doing much flying for a while as I think he will be U.S. for quite a while. Looking over the kite today I realize how lucky I was as the nose had holes everywhere, and all the kites were holed and Q.Queen a write off."

The *RAF Pocklington War Diary* says this about the raid:

"Heavy flak over coast and at the target. No enemy aircraft.

> Fighter escort. One aircraft damaged by flak so jettisoned bombs on Ostend and landed at Great Ashfield with navigator F/S Spiller wounded."

There was heavy flak all right. You do not have to tell me about it! The PFF Mosquitos led us straight over the top of it! The war diary is wrong when it says we jettisoned the bombs over Ostend. We were on our bombing run heading for the target when we were hit by the flak. With the bomb aimer's compartment blown out and Don, our bomb aimer, dazed and out of action, Bill Rabbitt released the bombs from the cockpit. He was too busy to listen to me on the intercom. All he knew was that his plane was damaged, there was danger all around us and there was still a job to be done. He would not have known how badly we were hit or if he was even going to be able to keep N-Nan in the air. He was doing what we were all trained to do. He was going to drop our bombs and finish the mission. The only bombs we didn't drop on the target were a couple of "hang-ups" in the bomb bay. (A hang-up was when a bomb got stuck in the bomb bay over the target.)

In his diary, Don McLean is very clear about us continuing on to the target:

> We pushed on to the target and bombed, but got hang-ups which we got rid of over the Channel. We came straight out between Dunkirk and Calais with Yours Truly in charge of the navigation.

Forêt de Nieppe was our shortest bombing operation. It only lasted two and a half hours. It was almost an hour less than the raid on Les Hauts-Buissons on the 23rd of July, our shortest mission up 'til then, and the targets were roughly the same distance away. It was quicker because we hadn't landed at home base and Bill had taken a short cut and gone flat out back to England. Don assisted me with the navigation when he recovered his wits. After I had been dropped off, Bill and John Allen considered the plane safe enough to fly back home and Don navigated N-Nan to Pocklington, a trip that took an hour. It would have been very uncomfortable for him at the navigator's table with the nose shot out and blood everywhere.

Great Ashfield Airfield, 2012

Great Ashfield aerodrome is in Suffolk, located two kilometres south of Great Ashfield village and some four kilometres north of the village of Elmswell, which gave the airfield its original name, RAF Elmswell.

During World War I the aerodrome was a grass landing strip for the Royal Flying Corps. In World War II, RAF Great Ashfield was rebuilt for the United States Army Air Force (USAAF) and on the 19th of June 1943, the 8th Air Force, 385th Heavy Bombardment Group, occupied the airfield and B-17 Flying Fortress operations over Germany and occupied Europe began from its three runways. In full operation, the squadron operated thirty-six bombers, with four hundred aircrew and two thousand ground staff. Facilities at the airfield included a hospital, a mortuary, doctor and dentist surgeries, fire-stations, shops, mess-halls, canteens, a church, a chapel and a synagogue.

Patchwork farmlands have reclaimed the Great Ashfield aerodrome. The original location of the dispersal track and perimeter roads, and the three runways can still be seen.

From June 1943 until the end of the war, the Flying Fortresses of 385th Heavy Bombardment Group carried out many raids. Targets included heavy industrial areas, fortifications, supply depots, oil refineries, communications sites and storage facilities. The 385th also attacked strategic German coastal locations and troop concentrations in support of the D-Day landings.

The 385th twice received Distinguished Unit Citations for successful raids on heavily fortified targets in western Germany near the Czechoslovakian border. On the 28th of August 1945 after it returned to America, the 385th Heavy Bombardment Group was deactivated. RAF Great Ashfield was used as a storage site after the war and was sold in 1955. Today, patchwork farmlands have reclaimed the Great Ashfield aerodrome site. The location of perimeter roads and the three runways can still be clearly seen in the rural landscape.

The Very Pistol and the Colours of the Day

The "Very" pistol was invented in 1877 by Edward Very, a lieutenant in the United States navy. Typically, Very pistols in RAF Second World War aircraft had a one inch bore enabling them to fire large calibre flares into the air, characteristically leaving a brilliant coloured trail arcing across the sky and erupting in a ball of colour hovering in the air. Using a Very pistol is an effective method of attracting attention in emergency situations by illuminating the night sky.

Every RAF aircraft was equipped with a Very pistol. In Halifax bombers they were stored in a holster on the starboard side near the flight engineer's position. The pistol was fired through a hatch in the fuselage roof. Before each operation the engineer was given flare shells of the colour combination which was to be used by all squadrons that day. This combination of colours was called the "colours of the day". Colours changed each day to prevent German planes from using flares to deceive the British defences.

The RAF Second World War 'Very' Flare Pistol

Upon boarding the plane the flight engineer would place the Very pistol in its operating position in the hatch where it could be easily loaded. After each operation the engineer placed the gun in its holster and returned unused shells to the store.

Returning aircraft deviating from their flight plans might be lost, damaged or running out of fuel. Below, anti-aircraft batteries were ever vigilant, watching for aircraft not following authorized flight paths. Crossing the coast into Britain, aircraft were in danger of being attacked by ack-ack fire and flak. To prevent this, flares with the colours of the day would be fired from the plane indicating that it was a "friendly" aircraft and advising the itchy trigger fingers below to relax.

Chapter 39: USAAF Hospital and Recovery

I can remember the American nurse at Great Ashfield waiting for me to come out of the anaesthetic and giving me a shot of morphine. It put me out for twenty-four hours and when I came to I was free of pain and there was an American colonel, the surgeon who had operated on me, sitting on a chair alongside my bed. He told me that I was "a very lucky boy" and that a piece of flak had shattered my femoral vein. He said that it had just missed my femoral artery and if it had cut that I would have bled to death in two minutes. He explained that the femoral vein and the femoral artery were encased in a membrane, in the same way as a two core electrical flex. The shrapnel took the right one and not the wrong one. That's why I was lucky.

The colonel gave me the piece of shrapnel that he had dug out of me as a souvenir. It was about one inch long, half an inch wide and about half an inch deep. It was a pretty big piece of metal. I kept it for years but lost it when we were living in Moorooka.

They left my wound open for a week to drain off all the muck that was in there and on the seventh day I went back into the operating theatre and they sewed me up. I can remember vividly that that my body resisted the anaesthetic a little more. The first time I counted to three before I went out but for my second operation I got to twenty-one!

The anaesthetic I had for both my ops was sodium pentathol. I asked the nurse what type of anaesthetic they had given me and she said "pentathol". They found a vein and injected some in. I didn't have any sickness or nausea when I woke up. When I came back to Australia, Betty's sister, a trained theatre nurse, had never heard of sodium pentathol. They were still using the old ether and chloroform here in Australia. I was already well experienced in the use of more modern medicine! I have since found out that because it was such a new anaesthetic during the war, overdoses in USAAF hospitals were linked to the deaths of many American service personnel. Years later, at the Greenslopes Repatriation Hospital in Brisbane, I talked to a nurse there about pentathol too.

I remained at Great Ashfield for about ten days while the wound healed up a bit. I got used to American food. It was fine. They served it on big aluminium trays with compartments pressed into them. One for meat and one for vegetables, one for sweets and one for jam and one for butter. It wasn't any better than the food we were getting at Pocklington because RAF food was quite all right too.

I can remember one guy who had appendicitis. I can also remember that the fellow in the bed to my left was a young mid-upper gunner from a Liberator squadron. He'd had all the flesh ripped from the back of his left leg by a piece of flak and he was going to have plastic surgery and skin grafts. I gave him my battledress jacket. My battledress pants were no good. Sandy had used his knife and cut a leg off in the plane!

After I left Great Ashfield I spent eight days at Ely RAF hospital. I remember that when they transferred me there, I didn't have any clothes. The first thing the matron asked me was how long it had been since my bowels had moved. I told her seven days and she was horrified so gave me two pills and I filled the bedpan. It may have been the American food! I don't know!

Leaving Hospital

On the 12th of August, Bill and Don travelled down to Ely to take me back to Pocklington. Bill had arranged ten days' leave for the crew after they had flown three missions without me. Bill and Don both mention the visit it in their diaries. Bill wrote:

> "Travelled down to Ely today. Met Bas in hospital and he expects to get away by Tuesday. He had a rough time of it and narrowly missed losing his leg. Looks thin on it. Very bright."

Don had a bit more to say about the hospital and my injury:

> ".... In the afternoon we went out to the R.A.F. hospital to see Bas and it is certainly a very nice place with all the mod cons. Bas showed us the piece of flak they took out of his leg and also the stitches and slices from the operation. He nearly lost his leg and the Yank captain who operated on him did a very good job. Bill is waiting at Ely for Bas and then is going to make sure that he gets a seat on the train on the way back. We called in at an orchard on the way home and Bill looks like having a date tomorrow night. We had a good yarn to Paddy Heffernan (G./Capt.) at the hospital."

Earlier on, when I was telling the story of our training at the Lichfield OTU, I mentioned that Group Captain Paddy Heffernan had taken up a pretty young WAAF on a Command Bulls-eye from Lichfield and he'd suffered a mid air collision but he had a miraculous escape. She was killed with the rest of the crew. Paddy Heffernan got badly knocked about when he parachuted out. Popular belief was that he had died in the crash. He was still in hospital at Ely over nine months later. He came around to see me as soon as he knew there was an Aussie in the hospital. He was in a wheelchair and he wheeled it around to my ward and we had a long chat. I told Bill and Don that he was there and they made a point of looking him up.

Bill and Don probably expected to be down and back on the same day but they had to wait for two nights in Ely until the 15th before I could leave. These were the three days when they had to get me walking again. For over two weeks days my leg had been bent up and out because the wound was high up in the inside of my thigh. That was the way they told me to keep it but when the time came to be discharged I couldn't straighten it. Bill and Don organised accommodation nearby and waited. It took three days of physiotherapy before I got it straight. The doctors let me go back to the squadron but I was still in agony walking.

Don decided to leave for Minehead and Bill escorted me back to Pocklington on the train. I could hardly walk. Bill said it was a "good show" so he was happy to have me back. The Medical Officer gave me a week's sick-leave and I went to Rednal.

Mrs Reid was in Edinburgh when the next door neighbours rang her up to tell her that I was there. I hadn't notified her. She came back. She was very upset because I had been wounded. I had left my golf clubs at Mrs Reid's place and the golf course was just over the road. I remember the first day I went out onto the course. I could only do one hole and then my leg packed up, but by the end of the week I was doing eighteen holes so the exercise helped me walk again. Even so, my leg would seize up and it would ache like mad and I couldn't walk for a while.

I am not sure exactly when I returned to the squadron but it was probably with the rest of the crew on the 22nd. We were briefed for a couple of operations but they were scrubbed. On the 24th we were detailed for a bombing trip only to have it scrubbed because thirteen of our planes that had gone out earlier to bomb shipping in Brest harbour were coming back just as we were getting ready to take off. Three of our planes were shot up – one badly. That was N-Nan! In his diary Don wrote:

> "The squadron went to attack shipping at Brest. There was quite a good deal of cloud at the target and the results are very doubtful. N.Nan was shot up again as the chap made three runs to get his bombs away, and they are fitting a new starboard outer."

I must have recovered fairly quickly. In his diary Bill says that when we got back to Pocklington on the 15th of August I was limping badly. Two weeks later, on the 27th of August, he says that I played tennis with him and the next day we played squash. On the 31st I was back on ops!

Air Commodore Patrick (Paddy) Heffernan

In the chapter above Basil Spiller relates his story about his meeting at Ely hospital with Group Captain Paddy Heffernan who had been gravely injured in a two aircraft collision while on a Command Bull's-eye to London on the night of the 6th/7th November 1943.

Paddy Heffernan was born in New South Wales on the 16th of April 1907. He graduated from military college at Duntroon and enlisted in the RAAF at Laverton airbase near Melbourne, in February 1929. When war broke out he was Commanding Officer of 8 Squadron RAAF and in August 1940 moved with his squadron to Singapore.

England. c. February 1945. Air Vice Marshal Wrigley (right) and Group Captain P. G. Heffernan AFC, RAAF. Paddy Heffernan, still recovering from a mid-air collision is holding a walking stick.

In January 1941 Wing Commander Heffernan returned to Australia to a new posting as inaugural Commanding Officer of No. 4 Service Flying Training School at Geraldton, Western Australia. In January 1942 he was transferred as CO to RAAF Station Pearce, at Bullsbrook, a transfer he described as "a bit of a blow".

Because of his wide experience and his distinguished service as CO of two RAAF stations he was posted in June 1943 to RAF Lichfield in England, as Group Captain commanding the Australian 27 OTU located there. He held this position until he was seriously injured while piloting a Wellington bomber on a night time training exercise to London, when his plane collided with a Wellington from 26 OTU.

Australian airforce records show that on the evening of the 6th of November,

Group Captain Heffernan was flying Vickers Wellington LN295 in a south easterly direction towards Huntingdon from Lichfield on a "Command Bulls-eye", a simulated bombing raid on an English city, and he may have been about to turn due south to begin his approach to London. On board with him were his four Australian crew members and Paddy Heffernan's friend, WAAF Section Officer Karin Hughes, who, counter to airforce regulations, was a passenger on the plane. Flying towards them in a north easterly direction was Vickers Wellington X3924 from No. 26 OTU based at RAF Wing in Buckinghamshire. Both aircraft were flying at an altitude of 15/16,000 feet and at 2208 hours they were on a collision course.

The two aircraft closed rapidly and by the time the two pilots realised the looming danger it was too late. It is believed that the pilot of Wellington X3924 pushed his control column forward causing his plane to dive, its tail colliding with the starboard side of Group Captain Heffernan's plane near his cockpit.

Wellington X3924 spun out of control, careering towards the ground and breaking up, its pilot being thrown through the cockpit roof before the plane crashed. Fighting vainly to control his aircraft and being badly injured in the collision, Group Captain Heffernan ordered his crew to bale out. In the mayhem surrounding him, with the intercom and warning lights destroyed, and not knowing if his crew and passenger had parachuted from his stricken craft, Heffernan finally baled out. Both aircraft crashed near the small Hamlet of Abbots Ripton, near Alconbury Airdrome, then a USAAF airfield.

Paddy Heffernan's crew and his female passenger were all killed and they are buried at the Cambridge City Cemetery. Karin Lia Hughes was twenty four years of age when she died. She was married to Patrick Hughes, of Orpington, Kent.

On 14th August 1944, Paddy Heffernan, still a patient at Ely hospital more than nine months after the collision, paid a visit to Basil Spiller who was also convalescing at Ely hospital.

In May 1953, Paddy Heffernan was awarded an OBE. He served with the RAAF for 27 years and retired with the rank of Air Commodore in 1956. He died on the 30th January 1996 aged 88 years.

Chapter 40:   102 Squadron - August 1944

It was just over a month before I flew on my next mission but the war and 102 Squadron didn't stop when I did. I think my crewmates were expecting to be stood down from operations while I was recovering. On the day after I got wounded, Don wrote in his diary that it didn't look as if they would be "doing much flying" as he thought I would "be u/s. for quite a while". That was wishful thinking. They were still briefed for operations and on each one a spare navigator was slotted into the crew.

While I was recovering in hospital I missed three missions in early August. They would have done more but the weather was terrible. I don't think they minded the raids being scrubbed. Don's diary shows that they headed off in the car to Bridlington a couple of times, when it didn't break down, and "renewed all (their) old acquaintances and had lots of eggs as usual".

There were other days when they were not briefed for ops and watched the squadron head off to bomb targets in the Normandy battle area and go gardening in the harbour at Brest. Maybe there wasn't a spare navigator. I was given "credit" for the missed operations and they were added to my tour of duty tally.

My crew's first raid without me was on the 3rd of August. It was their twentieth mission. N-Nan was still being repaired so they flew in Halifax MZ798, M-Mike. Ten of our aircraft went back to Forêt de Nieppe and they carried 8,000 pounds of bombs. The sky was clear over France but when they approached the target area they had 8/10ths cloud. Don was able to "get a visual". Bill's diary says:

> ".... The Op was the familiar old Forêt de Nieppe. We proceeded with the Wing Commander's navigator, Harold Hammond, and Paddy Kirkpatrick as flight engineer. Our hydraulics were unserviceable but we coped okay and bombed the blasted place beautifully. Arrived back in time to see Mitchell prang L-Love."

Here Bill is referring to Flight Sergeant Mitchell crashing L-Love, one of our Halifaxes, which overshot the runway. No-one was hurt. John Allen, our flight engineer, wasn't on this raid either because he had been assigned to another crew on an earlier raid that day. It was probably the raid on Bois de Cassan, a flying bomb site in a forest north of Paris.

I knew Harold Hammond, the navigator who replaced me on the flight, really well. He was Wing Commander Wilson's navigator. We used to call him "Honk" because he had a big nose. He was a New Zealander. Honk was a tall, easy-going man. He had to be to put up with

Wilson. Harold was part of the crew that Wilson brought with him to Pocklington when he took over the wing commander position. I met Honk on the squadron and he was a special friend of mine. He was awarded a Distinguished Flying Cross for bravery later on too.

The second raid that I missed was on the 5th of August when they carried 8,000 pounds of bombs and went back to the Forêt de Nieppe for a third time. This time N-Nan had been repaired and they flew her. The full squadron of twenty-six Halifaxes took part in this operation. One aircraft returned with engine trouble and the bombs fell out of another when they opened the bomb bay doors while it was on its bombing run about six kilometres north of the target. Apparently the bombs fell onto railway lines at Hazebruck.

The weather was clear over the target and Don thought the mission was a "wizard prang". On this raid, Bill got another chance to do some formation flying. He would have loved that because he mentioned it in his diary. It was the pilots' club again. Bill wrote:

"Went to our old friend Forêt de Nieppe today with Flight Sergeant McCorkingdale as navigator. Had a good trip and did some very tight formation flying with P-Peter and L-Love."

The last operation I missed with my crew was on the 9th of August when five of our Halifaxes bombed an oil storage depot in the Forêt de Mormal near the France/Belgium border. They carried 11,000 pound of bombs.

Bill was not impressed with the navigator who had been assigned to the crew. He led Bill up the garden path so Bill took over and headed for the target in a straight line across occupied territory. Bill must have said to the navigator, "Don't worry. I'll do it on my own." I don't know what happened because Don would have volunteered to work with the new navigator. He must have got them lost soon after takeoff. They arrived at the target just as the other planes had finished their bombing runs. In his dairy Bill wrote:

"I had a spare navigator who led me up a wattle, so I went across the Channel on my own and went full bore across enemy territory on my own - arrived just as everybody was leaving, but we dropped our bombs smack in the centre of the storage and had the pleasure of seeing a colossal upheaval. Had a look at the result and the smoke was up over 8,000 feet. The Master Bomber was hit by flak, but got back okay. Came back up this country low level and the boys thoroughly enjoyed it as much as I did. Good show. No word from Bas yet."

The next day Don wrote: "The prang was a wizard effort and I think poor old Jerry will have to run his tanks on their reputations". The Master Bomber and his crew were lucky to get back safely because their rear turret was shot away.

After this raid the crew had a three week break before the next operation when I rejoined them. Their leave may have been extended during this time because I was on sick leave, but after the debacle with the navigator on the Forêt de Mormal raid, I reckon Bill would have made it known that he wanted to wait for me to come back.

When all of us had finished our leave and returned to base it was still another nine days before we bombed Lumbres, our next operation. Five operations were cancelled during this time, probably because of the weather, but three others went ahead without the services of Bill Rabbitt's crew.

During August '44, our Halifaxes were prepared for thirty-seven operations but fifteen of them were either cancelled or postponed because of persistent bad weather. On the 30th of July, fourteen of our aircraft were sent to bomb in the Normandy battle area where the D-Day army was still bottled up but the weather was so bad that the Master Bomber abandoned the raid.

When they came back they were diverted to other airfields because visibility at Pocklington was so poor. But bad weather had set in right across the country. This was always a very precarious time for returning crews.

One of our Halifaxes, U-Uncle NA503, crashed and burned after it hit the trees killing all the crew at Blockley in Gloucestershire, 230 kilometres away from Pocklington. The pilot was Flight Sergeant Hulme. He was a New Zealander and so were his bomb aimer and navigator. The other four were in the RAFVR – the Volunteer Reserve.

The targets that the squadron attacked during this time were a real mixture. We bombed flying bomb sites in northwest France eight times. After I was wounded the squadron went back to Forêt de Nieppe five more times so we must have kept missing it. Our planes were bombed up ten times to attack fuel dumps, railway marshalling yards and battle zone targets in Normandy but seven of these were cancelled because of the weather. We attacked shipping in Brest harbour and the shipyards at Kiel on the Baltic Sea. We also bombed the German cities of Russellheim and Braunschweig.

On the night of the 12th/13th of August we lost two aircraft. There was always a big risk but any mission that took you into Germany was always more dangerous and anywhere in the Ruhr Valley was even worse. The squadron was attacking two separate targets in Germany.

Nine of our Halifaxes were part of a force of 297 bombers that attacked the Opel engine factory at Russellheim south west of Frankfurt. As well, thirteen of our aircraft were part of a bigger force of 397 aircraft that attacked the city of Braunschweig in the north of Germany. Bomber Command losses on both targets were terrible because flak was heavy and night fighters were everywhere. Thirteen Lancasters and seven Halifaxes were lost on Russellheim and seventeen Lancasters and ten Halifaxes were lost on Braunschweig.

My squadron lost one aircraft on each raid. Halifax J-Jig LW195 was piloted by Flying Officer Stanley Sambell. He was an Australian. He was taken prisoner with four of his crew. They must have baled out before the plane crashed near Rinteln after they bombed Braunschweig. This was about a hundred kilometres west of the target so a night fighter probably shot them down when they were heading home to England. The navigator and engineer were both killed. This was the same crew who bailed out when their plane ran out of fuel on the 9th of June after the squadron was redirected to Catfoss.

Halifax R-Roger MZ647, piloted by Flight Lieutenant Phillip Young, was shot down over Russellheim. All of the crew are buried in the Rheinberg War Cemetery near Frankfurt. Four of the crew were Australians from New South Wales – Phillip Young, the pilot, George York, the bomb aimer, and the two gunners, Alfred Harvey and John Gordon.

On the 15th of August, fifteen Halifaxes from 102 Squadron took part in a "thousand bomber" raid on nine German night fighter bases in Holland and Belgium. Our squadron successfully bombed Eindhoven airfield in south east Holland.

After a raid on the Kiel shipyards on the 16th/17th August, Halifax Y-Yoke NA504 failed to return. Apparently the flak was heavy and a lot of night fighters were around. It was piloted by Pilot Officer Coghlan. Five of the crew were English, the navigator was from Northern Ireland and the engineer was a Canadian. They were all killed.

My crew found out that the three planes were missing when they returned from leave on the 22nd of August. Bill and Don had been to Minehead, in Somerset. They met Harry and Sandy at Bridgewater and travelled up to Pocklington together.

In his diary Don wrote:
"We got up about 6.30 am. and after a very uncomfortable trip arrived around 7 pm. It was good seeing all the boys on the squadron again even though we heard that P/O. Sambell, F/Lt. Young and F/Sgt. Coghlan have gone."

Bombing Up

Armourers catch a ride! Tractors towing trolleys loaded with 500 pound General Purpose and Medium Capacity bombs to the Halifax dispersal sites at RAF Snaith, home of No 51 Squadron, Yorkshire.

Chapter 41: Operation 20 - Lumbres

601 aircraft - 418 Lancasters, 147 Halifaxes, 36 Mosquitos - to attack 9 sites in Northern France where the Germans were believed to be storing V-2 rockets. 8 of the sites were found and bombed. 6 Lancasters lost.
The Bomber Command War Diaries 31 August 1944

My twentieth mission was on the 31st of August 1944. The target was Lumbres, a V2 rocket storage site in northern France. Seventeen aircraft from our squadron took part in this raid. We took off at 1350 hours and we carried eight thousand pounds of bombs. The operation lasted three hours and forty-five minutes.

It was a daylight mission and we were getting back roughly at about half past five in the afternoon. We had a fighter escort and we didn't see them as usual. This was my first mission after I had been wounded and I was very apprehensive. Prior to the Forêt de Nieppe raid I had the feeling that other poor bastards could cop it but I was invincible. After I had a taste of wounding, realization set in that I was vulnerable too. My mindset changed altogether and I was fearful on every mission from then on. It affected me in the navigation seat because I was scared the whole time that something would happen to me.

It did not affect the performance of my duties. Not at all. But I was more aware of what was happening around me both inside and outside of the plane. The realization that something could happen to me was sharper. It did not make me reassess my attitude to others who had been LMF'd. I never thought of that even though I was probably going through the same sort of fears that they were going through. It had a pretty profound affect on me though. Bill must have understood how I was feeling because he wrote in his diary:

> "Daylight operation today on Lumbres. Bas with us on his first since being hit. Seemed a bit uneasy, but we did not strike any trouble."

Lumbres was not a straightforward mission so when Bill says that we did not strike any trouble he must have been talking about flak or German fighter planes. Over six hundred aircraft were sent to bomb nine V2 rocket storage sites in northern France. There was heavy cloud over the target and we circled around and around to find the target indicators. It was not cut and dried like a usual raid on a flying bomb site because we never circled around unless something was wrong. It was supposed to be straight in and straight out. Not going around and around which was asking for trouble. At least sixty of the six hundred planes sent out that day were on Lumbres. That's a lot of planes hanging about.

The target indicators were hidden beneath the clouds. Three planes from 102 Squadron were unable to bomb because the cloud was too thick. The squadron record says that the Master Bomber gave the order to cease bombing when one aircraft made four runs at the target before finding it. That would have been us because when we finally found the indicators we bombed them okay. In his diary Don wrote:

> "Bas had his first trip today since he had been wounded and we attacked a combination V1-V2 site at Lumbres in N. France. When we got to the target we all had to orbit left as there was about 8/10 cloud. P.F.F. dropped their markers miles away and I don't think it was much of a prang. We got quite a good photo but I think it was more good luck than judgement."

Then the way home we ran into a heavy snow storm and icing in cumulo-nimbus clouds. Icing and snow was dangerous for the plane because it increased the weight as it built up on the wings. The aerodynamics of the wing could be altered producing less lift and making it harder for Bill to fly. In extreme cases the weight ice on the wings increasing all the time could cause the plane to drop out of the sky.

In my navigator's seat, I never knew about the plane icing over unless Bill mentioned it on the intercom. It was his problem. When he experienced icing on his windscreen he activated his de-icing equipment. It was installed on every plane to stop ice build-up. Heat from the engines and exhaust gasses were piped through the wings. It was usually very effective.

Sometimes Bill would come back to base exhausted after a difficult flight because his arms and feet were working constantly to keep the plane level and on course.

There is a sense of boyish fun in Bill's diary entry when he writes about the trip home:

> "Kite marvellous sight. Very pleasant trip up England. Did
> some cloud-bashing as well. Good show."

The big build up of high cloud that Bill was talking about was cumulo-nimbus cloud and Bill was weaving his way around them instead of going through them. That's what cloud bashing was.

Sometimes if the top of the cloud was flat, we would sit down over the top of it, half in and half out and leave five furrows behind us – one for the fuselage and one for each of the four engines. We'd be half in and half out! If you looked behind, you could see five furrows imprinted in the cloud just like a ploughed field. Bill was having a bit of fun.

Lack of Moral Fibre

In the chapter above Basil Spiller uses the term "LMF", which was the acronym for "Lack of Moral Fibre". This was the official classification given to RAF airmen who refused to participate in flying operations over occupied Europe or Germany. The term "LMF" was a derogatory label which gave no thought to the airmen who were suffering from post traumatic stress and filled with dread at the prospect of flying bombing raids into German occupied territory night after night.

LMF served two main purposes. Firstly, it was a disciplinary measure imposed upon aircrew for cowardice against the enemy. Secondly the harsh punishment and the shame attached to court-martial and imprisonment of a man who was LMF'd often proved an effective deterrent to others. There were no executions for cowardice in the RAF. Airforce records show that during World War 2 over four thousand aircrew members were found guilty of LMF.

In the First World War men who refused to continue flying were sent home but in the Second World War being convicted of Lack Of Moral Fibre was accompanied by imprisonment, dishonorable discharge and disgrace. As well the label carried the potential of a lifelong stigma of being branded a coward in combat. Men were banished from their friends and crews.

Often men convicted of LMF were well into their tours of duty and some had even been previously decorated for bravery. Many had again and again put their lives on the line with their crewmates.

Being a member of an aircrew on a bombing mission over targets heavily defended by night-fighter aircraft and fierce barrages of anti aircraft fire needed courage, determination and strength of character and participating in such raids has been compared to soldiers going over the top of the trenches in the First World War. Aircrew did this night after night.

The affect of prolonged stress and trauma were not only restricted to aircrews. They and their ground staff often formed tight knit groups. Each night ground staff saw the affects of bombing missions on their crews when they returned and often witnessed the affect of combat, particularly when they were given the terrible task of recovering bodies and body parts from crashed and shot up aircraft.

In chapter 56, the bond between aircrew and ground staff is mentioned when Basil Spiller describes how upset his ground crew were when N-Nan was brought back to dispersal after he had been wounded on the Forêt de Nieppe raid. They could see that Basil had "copped it pretty badly" and there was blood everywhere which they had to clean up. It was not uncommon for ground staff to be LMF'd.

Chapter 42: Operation 21, Venlo

675 aircraft - 348 Lancasters, 315 Halifaxes, 12 Mosquitos - carried out heavy raids on 6 airfields in Southern Holland. All raids were successful and only 1 Halifax was lost from the Venlo raid. 2 Mosquito Ranger patrols and 1 RCM (Radio Counter Measures) sortie were flown without loss.
The Bomber Command War Diaries, 3 September, 1944

My twenty-first mission was on the 3rd of September 1944. We took off at 1335 hours and we flew for four hours neat. This was another daylight mission and we landed at about 1735 so it was roughly the same duration as our last mission. We carried our maximum load of eleven and a half thousand pounds of bombs. There were twenty-two Halifaxes bombed up from our squadron but one got stuck in boggy ground and it swung off the runway as it was taking off. The crew were very lucky because if it had crashed the bombs aboard would have exploded. It had to be towed out of the way so the remaining aircraft could take off.

We bombed a German night fighter aerodrome near the German/Dutch border at Venlo not far from the Ruhr. This airfield was very dangerous during the war and its night fighters were credited with shooting down about six hundred or our planes. I don't know whether you would say that the airfield was actually in Germany or Holland but it was very near the border. It wasn't far from the Ruhr Valley and was right on the track that our bomber force took when we bombed the Ruhr. We could not avoid it. Venlo is only forty kilometres from Duisberg. We would sweep in across northern France into Germany, drop our bombs and then turn northwest. Then we put our nose down and headed home at low altitude over Holland.

I have mentioned a few times that like all pilots, Bill loved to get the chance to fly in formation with the other pilots. Pilots thought they were in a special club – the Pilot's Club. In his diary entry for this raid Bill laid it on a bit thick:

"The Wing Commander led the formation and I was No. 2 from the squadron. We ran into some very bad weather crossing the Channel but I managed to keep in formation with him all the way to the target. I had severe icing on my windscreen but had a certain feeling of pride to be the only one in formation with him to the target."

It was news to me that Bill had formated on the Wing Commander and flew like that all the way to the target. What did he need a navigator for? I didn't know that he was doing it at the time. There I was navigating like crazy at my little table and he was just following the Wing Commander anyway. I was redundant!

Formating on the Wing Commander like that would not have been by invitation. It would have been a natural thing for Bill to do. He would have decided that as it was a daylight operation he would attempt to formate on the Wing Commander and it just happened that he was close enough to do it. The bomber stream was permitted to be five miles to port or starboard of the track. "Formate" means to form a set formation like the Americans did, whereas we were usually more like a "gaggle" as I have called it before - a much looser organization, making our own way but within an area five miles either side of the track. That's what we were trained to do at night so that is what we usually did in the daytime too.

Don's diary says that the weather conditions were "pretty poor" but the ten-tenths cloud cleared over the target. Don watched a Free-French Halifax from 347 Squadron at Elvington, our satellite 'drome, get shot down right in front of us. The pilot, a captain Millet, baled out and was captured but the rest of his crew were killed. The aiming point for Venlo was the runway intersection and the target indicators were spot on. Our bombing was accurate. Two of our planes had flak damage and another one got back to base on three engines. Two had stopped working over the target but they got one going again.

In his diary Bill is very complimentary about Don's bombing. Don's bombsight was unserviceable but, as Bill says, he managed to plant his bombs right "smack on the runway". I don't know how the bomb sight became unserviceable. On a mission you haven't got time to change anything if it becomes unserviceable so you have to do without it. You didn't know whether one of the instruments was serviceable until you turned it on. Don would not have known that it was unserviceable until he moved down into the bomb aimer's position on our bombing run and started to use it. How could you check it before takeoff? He would have presumed that the ground staff had checked and maintained it. Even if they did, things went wrong because we were in a plane that at any moment could be bouncing and diving all over the sky.

When we got back to England the weather was so bad that we were diverted to a US aerodrome at Wendling in Norfolk, about 110 miles south east of Pocklington. It turned out to be a B-24 Liberator base and they put us up overnight.

I remember that in the mess there was the biggest poker game I had ever seen. Because the weather was too bad to fly, the American officers were playing poker. They had tables all over the place and they were playing for big pots of money. There was a pile of pound notes about six inches high in front of every officer and I was staggered by what they were betting on each round.

In the morning we had a good breakfast and afterwards we had a look through one of their Liberators. They had an improved version of H2S which they called "Mickey".

We flew back to base that afternoon. It was only a forty minute trip. I remember it well.

The Aldis

In their books both Bill and Harry mention that Jack Ross's plane, A-Able from our squadron, was in a bit of trouble and we helped them to land at Wendling with us. I don't know exactly what the trouble was but I presume their gyrocompass was u/s because they obviously didn't have the capacity to navigate accurately. We were able to communicate with other planes by using RTs (radio transmissions) and "Aldis" but we were forbidden to use radio over the continent, even if it was an emergency, as German fighters could use our transmissions to locate us.

The Aldis was a big hand held torch that the radio operator plugged into power on the plane. It was bulky and about seven or eight inches in diameter. It had a trigger action so Harry could tap out Morse Code on it. When he pulled the trigger a shutter would come down and interrupt the transmission of the light. He was an expert in Morse Code so he was the one doing the communications with A-Able through the perspex nose of the aircraft. Harry would have tapped out "follow us" or something like that and N-Nan's perspex nose was flashing it out like a big globe. This was a daylight mission so the light would have been either green or red. Green probably! A-Able would see it because the Aldis light was very powerful.

More on the pilots' club

According to Bill, when we landed, the Americans on the base "marvelled at our bomb load and the Halifax aircraft". A lot of the Americans came out to have a look at N-Nan. It was a good opportunity for them to have a look over a British plane. We carried eleven and a half thousand pound of bombs to Venlo but the average bomb load of a B-17 then was probably four to five thousand pounds, depending on the distance the target was away from base. That's about the same load as our old Wellingtons. Even the Mosquito, our fighter bomber, carried a four thousand pound bomb. Everyone thinks that B-17's were mighty big bomber planes but our bomb bays were a lot bigger than theirs. We carried two to three times the bomb load they did, and were faster and had a lot more power. They carried a lot of fuel instead of bombs because it took them so long to formate. The Americans at Wendling would not have given the Halifax a second look if they didn't think it was so impressive.

Over the years the Flying Fortress has had a lot of publicity, a lot of it well deserved but a lot of it over the top too.

They marvelled at the Halifax too because Bill put on a bit of a turn when we took off. He held it low and did a couple of sweeps of the airfield to show off his airmanship. He was a member of the pilot's club so they naturally did things like that. They lived in a world of their own. He was cutting it close but that was the attitude of pilots generally. Bill was guilty of low flying on several occasions but he was too good a pilot to have an accident. I loved standing behind him on all our takeoffs and landings.

Venlo and the Kammhuber Line

The Venlo airfield was one of the largest German airfields of the Second World War airfields. It was situated approximately four kilometres east of the Dutch city of Venlo straddling the Netherlands/German border.

A burnt out aircraft hangar in ruins on the Venlo aerodrome site.

After the invasion of Holland, the Germans built a newer and bigger airfield on the former First World War airfield site. It became home to the legendary Nachtjagdgeschader (Night Fighter) Group 1. Fighter aircraft taking off from

Venlo played a crucial role protecting Germany's industrial heartland, the Ruhr Valley, from Allied bombing raids.

The night fighters at Venlo were part of the German night air defence system known as the Kammhuber Line, named after Colonel Josef Kammhuber. Radar stations with overlapping coverage and searchlights were established in a line stretching from central France to as far north as Denmark. The "Line" began operating in mid 1940.

When the location of an approaching RAF bomber was detected by a radar station "cell", the operators would illuminate the plane with a master searchlight. Manual searchlights were then also trained on the bomber. Meanwhile a night fighter dedicated to the radar station cell would be guided to the plane to attack it.

Advancements in German radar technology eventually led to the use of searchlights being abandoned. Night fighters fitted with the new Lichtenstein radar, could accurately locate incoming bombers when radar controllers directed them into an area.

Throughout the war Venlo was an important target for Bomber Command. The successful attack on Venlo described by Basil Spiller in this chapter occurred on the 3rd of September, 1944. At this time the D-Day armies were moving towards the western borders of Germany and the airfield was abandoned by the Luftwaffe. The city of Venlo was finally liberated from German occupation in November 1944.

In just over four years of operation, night fighters from Nachtjagdgeschader Group 1 shot down approximately 600 RAF airplanes.

Chapter 43: Operation 22 - Le Havre

992 aircraft - 521 Lancasters, 426 Halifaxes, 45 Mosquitos - attacked 8 different German strong points around Le Havre. Each target was separately marked by the Pathfinders and then accurately bombed. No aircraft lost.
The Bomber Command War Diaries, 10 September, 1944

After returning from the Venlo raid, we waited a week for the weather to clear before our next operation. Don was getting more and more "browned off" as we waited and in his diary on the 6th of September he wrote:
> "It rained all day again and I think after the peace has been signed they ought to make the Germans live on this island for a couple of months. It cleared a little in the evening and we went to a dance in the village."

Don was from Queensland and he missed the sunshine, blue skies and warm weather. He must have thought that the weather was so awful that it would be punishment enough for the Germans to be sent there. The only operation for that week was a night op on the 6th/7th of September, gardening in the Frisian Islands. That's all. We weren't flying much anyway because Bill was made acting Flight Commander and he was required to remain on the base and direct operations. This meant that his crew did not fly either. It started to become a regular occurrence which suited us because life on the squadron was pretty good if you survived. But then again, it also meant that completing our tour of duty was taking longer and longer. In the seven days we flew only twice. The day after the Venlo raid we flew back to base from Wendling and on the 7th we went up to test out a new Halifax. Bill entered this flight in his flying log but I didn't write it up in mine. We were no sooner up when we were recalled because of the shocking weather and we had "some difficulty getting in". A lot of men find it hard when they are all keyed up and ready to go. They can't leave the base and just hang around and keep waiting and waiting.

My twenty-second mission was on the 10th of September. It was also Don's twenty-second birthday and twenty-two Halifaxes from our squadron joined in a daylight raid to bomb German gun emplacements north of Le Havre, a port city on the Normandy coast. We were in support of the army. I understood that the Germans had been surrounded at Le Havre and our troops were about to attack it. We carried eleven thousand pounds of bombs and took off at 1450 hours. The operation lasted four hours and fifteen minutes and we arrived safely back at Pocklington in the evening just after seven o'clock.

The operation was a complete success and our bombs found the target. Our bombing had to be very accurate as our troops were only a mile and a quarter away. There was a big explosion. Bill in his diary describes it very dramatically with rockets and explosions and everything going off so we must have hit an explosives storage site:

> "We were blasting enemy gun positions at Le Havre for the army. We went early to bomb and bombed from 10,000 feet. Don, John, and Sandy saw our bombs hit a gun position containing explosives and was the result terrific! Great spurts of flame and rockets shot out, so we are proud of our individual effort today."

Pocklington pubs

We spent some of our time in Pocklington at the pubs while we were waiting. Bill and Don both mention in their diaries that we went to a dance in the village on the 6th. We would have all been there for that.

The pubs at Pocklington were filled with tobacco smoke. Everybody smoked except me. All the English people smoked and wherever I went, in a pub, the pictures or dance floor the air was always thick with smoke. There was something about a British pub though. They were wonderful. I loved British pubs. They were welcoming and homely and intimate. The smaller the better and country pubs were the ultimate.

I have just finished reading a little book called *Pocklington at War*, published fairly recently by local Pocklington historians. It stirred up a few memories about the town when I was there. I used to take out a young lass from Pocklington. She was a young married woman with a small boy. Her husband was in the Middle East at the time. I met her at a pub in Pocklington and she took me around to introduce me to the members of her household.

Leeds and York

York was the centre of 4 Group, to which we belonged, and the Canadian 6 Group. There were probably twenty operational bomber fields scattered around the farmlands of Yorkshire. By contrast Leeds had no airfields around its perimeter. It was nestled closer to the Pennine Chain and it wasn't flat country like northern Yorkshire or East Riding where Pocklington was. York was a place that you went to for a night out in a pub and Leeds was a place where you spent your forty eight hour pass. They were very different. One was very much an airforce city. Everywhere you'd go you'd be running into aircrew, from all over the countryside, at places like Betty's Bar. That was York. Whereas in Leeds, you could get away from all that a little bit more. Leeds was full of girls who loved going out with Australian airmen. They liked Australians because we had more money. British airmen took their money home to their families but we were young and single and our families and friends were back in Australia. We always had plenty of money to spend so when the opportunity arose we were always out looking for a good time. So were the girls. Leeds had some famous hotels which we stayed at – the Victoria, the Robin Hood, the Yorkshire Hussars and the Griffin.

There was a bus stop outside the officers' mess at Pocklington and a direct bus route to the centre of Leeds so it was very convenient to go there on a forty eight hour pass and not take the car.

Griffin Hotel, Leeds

Griffin Hotel on Boar Lane, Leeds. The hotel closed in July 1999. To the left of it is the junction with Mill Hill, and the National Westminster Bank on the opposite corner.

Chapter 44: Operation 23 - Münster

119 Halifaxes of No. 4 Group and 5 Pathfinder Lancasters carried out the first raid by RAF heavies on Münster since June 1943. 2 Halifaxes were lost. Many fires were seen but smoke prevented an accurate assessment of the bombing results. A brief report from Münster describes a 'sea of fire' in the southern part of the town which could not be entered for several hours and tells of water mains destroyed by high-explosive bombs so that 'the firemen could only stand helpless in front of the flames'.
The Bomber Command War Diaries, 12 September, 1944

On the 11th of September we were briefed to attack Gelsenkirchen, an important coal mining and oil production centre, but it was scrubbed. My twenty-third mission instead was a daylight raid on Münster. It was the headquarters of the German's 6th Military District which controlled military operations in Westphalia and the Rhineland, and stretched across into Belgium. It was heavily fortified, and four Panzer divisions and over twenty infantry divisions were stationed there.

We flew in Halifax L-Love MZ797, a replacement aircraft, as N-Nan was undergoing maintenance. There were twenty-two Halifaxes from our squadron. Our target was nominally the railway station near the centre of the city, but when we set off at 1640 hours only two thousand pounds of our bomb load was high explosive bombs. The other six thousand pounds were incendiaries. It was the first time we had carried them. They were small bomblets, two feet long and two inches wide with an hexagonal shape which enabled them to be stacked tightly together into canisters which took up about the same amount of space in the bomb bay as a 750 pound bomb. Each bomblet weighed four pounds. We carried eight cans so there were about 190 of them in each can. The incendiaries were held in their containers by bars fixed across them. When they were released, the bars fell away and the incendiaries scattered over a wide area beneath the plane as it travelled on.

I will always remember our intelligence officer at the briefing saying: "Münster is an old town and it should burn beautifully!" It is a vivid memory. When Don McLean wrote about this mission in his diary, he noted that "even though we were given the railway yards as our aiming point we carried 2/3 of our load as incendiaries". We all knew that the object of the raid was not to bomb the railway yards, a strategic target, but to set fire to the city. And Münster burned all right just as the intelligence officer predicted. The squadron record says that our crews saw their bombs straddle the railway lines and they witnessed fires springing up in the Old City. Firemen had to watch it burn because our heavy explosive bombs had destroyed the city's water mains.

This was another fateful operation for our crew. Something went amiss with our wing commander's plane before takeoff so we were told to lead the 4 Group bombing force to the target. When we took off, Bill would have regarded this as an honour, but his diary shows that his attitude had soured afterwards because he wrote that he "had the doubtful privilege of leading the entire bombing force to the target". It was a doubtful privilege because we were lucky not to be killed!

It was a quiet trip over, but things went badly from the start of the bombing run. Looking out through his perspex window in the nose of the plane, Don McLean could see that the Germans had "filled the sky with flak" and as he settled down over his bombsight he "saw a kite shot down" and blow up "immediately on hitting the deck". Most of our crew watched the plane going down in a power dive. Bill gave a running commentary over the intercom. The pilot was awfully unlucky. He may have been momentarily concussed by the flak because it looked like he was starting to pull the Halifax out of the dive just before it ran out of air space. It's a terrible story! This plane was Halifax T-Tommy MZ699, from our squadron. It crashed at the Kinderhaus railway station just four kilometres north of Münster. Pilot Officer Philip Groves and one of the gunners, Sergeant L. Duncan, were killed. Five of the crew safely bailed out and became prisoners of war.

On our bombing run we noticed an aircraft a thousand feet above us. The pilot was disobeying instructions being up there. As we released our bombs we were showered with incendiaries. They had dropped their bombs right on top of the bombing stream! Incendiaries rained down everywhere. Two of them hit us. One went through our tail-plane not far from Sandy's rear turret. It was a wonder that we didn't lose the tail. The second one hit us about a metre behind Charlie Hood in his mid-upper gun turret and carved a big hole in roof of the fuselage. You could have put another turret in the hole! Then the debris crashed through the plane and punched another hole in the floor and the incendiary bomb rolled along the fuselage. Luckily it didn't explode. They were packed with white phosphorous which is flammable to the open air, and if it had broken apart we would have been in all sorts of trouble. John Allen, our flight engineer, had to push it out of the plane. I was worried that the rear section would drop off.

There was a Halifax on our starboard side that had been hit worse than us, and flames were leaping up along the trailing edge of one of its wings. When we finished our photographic run and turned for home, we could see that it hadn't turned. It probably couldn't, and just kept on flying deeper into Germany. The pilot was probably trying to hold the plane together long enough to give his crew time to bail out?

This was the second of the two Halifaxes that were shot down over Münster that day. It was Halifax Q-Queenie MZ935 from 77 Squadron at Full Sutton, one of our two satellite dromes. Flying Officer Raymond Cave was the pilot. He and two of his crew, Sergeant John Brining, the navigator, and Sergeant James Haywood, the engineer, were killed. The other four managed to bail out and became prisoners of war. Flying Officer Cave saved their lives. He was a married man. His wife's name was Betty, the same name as my wife's. Raymond Cave was only twenty-one years old when he was killed.

The pilot who dropped the incendiaries on us was a New Zealand squadron leader. Somebody took down his plane's details and he was cashiered. He had destroyed two planes and killed three men. He could have killed us too. We were bombing at twenty thousand feet so the German gunners had predicted their shells to explode at a height between nineteen and twenty-one thousand feet. He was safe up there and to hell with the crews below him!

Bill's diary doesn't say much about the incident. He just wrote:
> "…. a shower of incendiary bombs fell on top of me and the plane in formation with us. Fortunately in my case I was not set on fire although the aircraft was difficult to manage. The other chap was not as lucky."

L-Love was hard to fly with the damaged tail-plane and Bill nursed it home. Saying that he found it "difficult to manage" is an understatement because as soon as our engineers back at base saw the state it was in, they sent the plane to the scrap heap. Yet Bill had flown it home!

We had also flown through a storm of flak but Bill's diary downplays the ferocity of the barrage and the flak damage done to the plane. He described the flak defences as "rather grim" and said that we were only hit by flak "a few times and not in a vital spot". When we had a look over L-Love the next day it had obviously been hit by a lot of flak because it had gaping holes in the roof, the floor and the tail-plane.

The raid on Munster lasted four hours and forty minutes and we arrived back home at 2120. It was classed as a daylight operation because Britain had double British Summer Time, and the clock was advanced two hours for the duration of the war and it was still daylight when we landed. We were lucky to survive Münster!

Charlie Hood

Munster was a traumatic mission for Charlie Hood, our mid-upper gunner. The incendiary bomb that crashed through the fuselage near his turret really unnerved him. If the bomb had been a yard closer it would have landed square on his turret. The bomb was about two foot long for a start so it was going to make at least a two foot hole in the top of the fuselage and a bigger one with all the debris in the floor. Charlie was up there in his turret and he had the floor taken out almost directly beneath him. Just imagine being up in that turret, thousands of feet up in the air with nothing underneath you. He stayed there until we got back to base. It would have been very scary. It was a big hole!

The crew didn't see Charlie again after this mission and I often wonder what happened to him. I presumed that he had gone off sick. There was a rumour that Charlie had refused to fly and that he was LMF'd (charged with Lack of Moral Fibre) but if that happened, it would have been a shameful thing for the RAF authorities to do to him. Aircrew who went LMF were sent to prison and dishonourably discharged. The RAF had LMF but the RAAF didn't. When the squadron's losses were growing or when things were going badly around the place we sometimes joked that the LMF queues would be growing but it wasn't really a laughing matter.

This was Charlie's twenty-third mission so his bravery could not be questioned. Sandy Concannon knew Charlie better than any of us because they were in the gunnery section together. He thinks that although being showered with incendiaries on this raid might have been the last straw for Charlie, it was more likely that Charlie left the squadron because he suffered badly from airsickness, just like he did on the Les Hauts-Buissons raid.

It may seem strange that we didn't know why Charlie had left and he wasn't missed, even though he had been part of the crew for eight months. He had nearly been killed but no-one was asking where he had gone or what had happened to him. After this raid, I can remember photographs of our aircrew and ground crew being taken in front of N-Nan and wondering where Charlie was. We had a six day break before we flew again and during this time he left the squadron.

Bill would have known what had happened to him but I can't remember anything being said and it is not mentioned in Bill's diary. For all we knew, Charlie had gone home on leave. He had long before withdrawn socially from the crew. We invited him to go out with us all the time but he never came. Our engineer, John Allen, wasn't an Australian and he was one of the boys, so it wasn't the fact that Charlie was English and we were Australians. He was quiet and unassuming. We were boisterous and confident. We didn't hear any more about him and moved on. Men were always disappearing from the squadron. They would be there one minute and then they'd be gone. You just kept going and hoped you wouldn't be next. Still, we should have done something for Charlie.

Mick Starmer

When Charlie left, we were allocated a new mid-upper gunner. His name was Neil Starmer but everybody called him "Mick". His first bombing mission was to Kleve on the 7th of October with us. He was in our crew for the remainder of our first tour, and then chose to rejoin us as our tail gunner for our second tour after Sandy Concannon was posted to a training squadron.

Mick was considered to be a pretty good gunner. By the time of our second tour he was very experienced. He had done thirteen more operations by then and had shot down a Messerschmitt 410, a German night fighter during a night raid to Goch on the 7th/8th February 1945, which wasn't an easy thing to do. As a matter of interest, our Halifax, N-Nan, was shot down on that Goch operation.

Halifax LW142, N-Nan Crew, September 1944

Basil Spiller and his N-Nan crewmates, standing in front of N-Nan several days after their raid on Münster. The Naughty Nineties can-can girl motif has been painted over. Their mid-upper gunner, Charlie Hood had recently left the squadron. Left to right: Sandy Concannon, Harry Brabin, Bill Rabbitt, John Allen, Basil Spiller, Don McLean.

Halifax LW142, N-Nan Crew and Ground Staff, September 1944

Halifax LN142 N-Nan's air and ground crews at dispersal, RAF Pocklington, after their Münster raid on the 12th of September 1944. Seated astride rear turret: Sandy Concannon. Back row: (left to right) Aircraftman 1st Class (name unknown), John Allen, Don McLean, Basil Spiller, Aircraftman 1st Class (name unknown). Front row; (left to right) Corporal (name unknown), Lance Corporal (name unknown). Bill Rabbitt, Sergeant Trevor ____ (surname unknown), Harry Brabin. Absent: Charlie Hood.

Chapter 45: Sea Search, Rugby & Brussels Petrol Runs

After the Münster raid it was almost a month before we flew on another bombing operation. Bill was acting Flight Commander while Squadron Leader Ward was on leave so we were on a reduced operational footing.

On the 15th of July we were one of a small group of six aircraft picked to go gardening to Brunsbuttel in the Elbe estuary where the Kiel Canal, which links the North Sea to the Baltic Sea, starts. Minelaying the estuary effectively closed the canal so the German navy couldn't use it. Anyway we didn't go because John Allen, our flight engineer, received his commission and was in London on a forty-eight hour pass buying his new gear.

The next evening John was back and we all climbed into the car and headed to a dance at Pocklington. All of us had a fair bit to drink and no-one was fit to drive back to base so we tossed a coin to see who would drive home. I hadn't learned to drive at that stage so I wasn't in the ballot. John Allen won! The car's headlights were u/s so we had to use two bicycle lamps as lights.

In his diary Don McLean reckons that "if (John) nearly wrecked us once he nearly did it a dozen times". Don took over "after (John) got half way or we would never have made it".

Sea search

In the fortnight after the Münster raid we flew only once. It was a sea search on the 18th of September. We were airborne for five hours and forty minutes searching for Halifax MZ289 which had gone missing with South African pilot, Captain Ronald Thompson and his crew on board. The navigator was an Australian, Flight Sergeant Gordon Reader from Perth, Western Australia. Bill had sent them on a bombing exercise over the North Sea and they had failed to return. Three planes were involved in the search.

Bill as Acting Flight Commander felt responsible for ascertaining what had happened to Captain Thompson and his crew so he instituted a Square Sea Search and volunteered us to be one of three crews that went out. I don't know where the other two went but there was a big area to cover.

We proceeded off Flamborough Head to the area in the North Sea where Captain Thompson was ordered to conduct a practice bombing exercise.

I don't really know what their exercise entailed but I presume it was operated at low level and he had gone into the drink. We took off at 1120 hours in P-Peter and soon we had crossed the coast and were heading over the North Sea.

The square search comprised flying up and down on parallel courses one mile apart. When we arrived at the search area we started doing a straight run for ten minutes. Then we would do a ninety degree turn to starboard for one minute then commence another ten minute straight run at the end of which we did a ninety degree turn to port for one minute. After that we did another ten minute straight run and so on – over and over. You cover a lot of area in ten minutes.

We were fifty feet above the ocean. It was hard, hazardous flying because the ocean was like a mill pond that day and there were no white caps to differentiate the surface from the horizon. We were all looking out - gunners, bomb aimer, engineer, navigator - everybody except Bill. We were concentrating on looking for any signs of wreckage and any signs of an oil slick.

After five hours we hadn't sighted anything so we returned to base. Bill wrote in his dairy that we had discovered wreckage "that could have been parts of the plane" but we never saw anything positive. He wasn't too sure either - you can tell from the way he wrote about it.

Rugby – Australia v Free French

On the 19th of September, we played rugby against the Free French from Elvington. I had been quite a good rugby player at school but Bill was an Australian Rules player. So was a friend of ours, Allan Crabb, a pilot from South Australia like Bill. He was a champion Australian Rules player. He played in the match too. I can't remember whether Sandy, Don or Harry played. Some of them had to play because we only had nineteen Australians to pick from. We had a mixed team whereas the French were all rugby players. Gus Walker, the Air Commodore of 42 Base Pocklington, was a rugby representative of the UK before the war and he refereed the game.

The French tried to kill us! They tackled fiercely and we started wondering whether we were really at war with Germany or the Free French. We thought they were taking it a bit too seriously. We were glad when the game was over and we were all still in one piece. The Free French won. They really belted us!

When we had time, Bill and I played tennis and squash against one another. We also played table-tennis at the YMCA. Bill mentions playing tennis and squash against me and Sampson, the Navigation Leader, who was an "RAF type".

Brussels petrol run

On the 25th of September we went on the first of four petrol runs to Brussels. Gus Walker was in charge of 42 Base with its four squadrons – Pocklington, Full Sutton and the two Free French ones at Elvington. Apparently, Air Chief Marshal Butch Harris called Gus Walker to his office and told him that for the next week all four 42 Base squadrons would be detailed to fly replacement petrol in jerry cans to an aerodrome called Melsbroek, just outside Brussels, to assist the 2nd Army in Belgium.

Melsbroek was one of the nine German airfields that Bomber Command attacked on the 15th of August 1944, the same day I left the hospital in Ely and returned to base with Bill. Melsbroek was soon abandoned by the Luftwaffe and by the 3rd of September the Germans were driven out of Belgium. Three weeks later the runways were repaired and we were using it to deliver petrol for the army. The army was still doing it tough and the weather was pretty foul. The Battle of Arnhem was in full swing. The British 2nd Army led by Field Marshal Montgomery had taken France and Belgium and were moving into the Netherlands. They had launched Operation Market Garden on the 17th to secure key bridges and towns over the border, with British and Polish paratroopers. It was a disaster. The main army was trying desperately to link up with the paratroopers who had made it through to the Arnhem Road bridge but they were forced to make their front line south of Arnhem. The paratroopers were overwhelmed. Out of about 9,000 who were sent in, only about 2,400 escaped. Nine days after it began on the 26th of September it was all over. We started our petrol deliveries on the 25th.

Each of our Halifaxes could carry 165 four-gallon jerry cans strapped inside the fuselage, held in place by canvas straps. So that's what we did. The four squadrons of 42 Base spent the next seven days ferrying petrol to the aerodrome at Melsbroek. Seventy aircraft were involved. They would land back at base be reloaded and take off with a fresh crew. They worked around the clock. The weather was so bad that we were ordered not to fly above the cloud, yet despite this we made almost 500 sorties and delivered about 325,000 gallons of fuel without mishap.

These trips were fairly straightforward. I was navigating but I was able to have a good look around as well. They were daylight flights so there was no blackout curtain in place between me and the bomb aimer's compartment.

Our crew went four times to Brussels on these petrol runs. The first three times were in N-Nan on the 25th, 27th and 28th of September. On the first trip the cloud base was five hundred feet and we indulged in a bit of low flying. When we got to Melsbroek, there were about 200 RAF and American Dakota transport planes and a lot of Halifaxes mixed up in two overlapping circuits all wanting to land. My immediate impression was about how well the Germans had camouflaged the airfield. I was also amazed at the amount of damage that the rocket firing Hawker Typhoons had inflicted on the German planes that had been parked there. At this time, Typhoons were the low level ground attack aircraft of the RAF. They would have come in straight after the bombers and continued to attack every day after that. The German airforce had evacuated the aerodrome in haste. It was littered with German aircraft. There were Junkers 88s and Focke Wulf 190s and Messerschmitt Bf109s and Ju188s all over the ground. We were instructed not to approach them because they might have been booby-trapped. I can remember that on the way home the first time, we flew over Ostend and had a look at the pill boxes and defences that had fired on us when I was wounded. Ostend was in our hands by then.

On the 27th of September, we were able to sight the marshalling yards at Courtrai about fifty miles west of Brussels that had been bombed by Bomber Command. The devastation was enormous. I could see that the whole marshalling yard had been taken out. The only indication that there had been a marshalling yard there was a set of railway lines coming in one side and going out the other. In between them was complete devastation. It was a tribute to Bomber Commands' accuracy. Later we went down into the local village and had a beer in the pub. It was strange to stand in a bar that the Germans had frequented a few days earlier. We were down there drinking with the locals. The blokes in the pub didn't mind having a beer with us. We took over our chocolate rations and gave them to the local kids. They thought we were marvellous. On this trip, we were able to buy big baskets of grapes from the local farmers and we took a load of them back to England and gave them to our favourite WAAFs. On the way back we had a good look at Brussels. From the air it appeared to be surrounded by glasshouses.

On our third trip on the 28th, we smuggled Trevor, the NCO sergeant in charge of our ground crew, on board and took him down into the village to get some grapes. We also flew around and showed him Brussels, Courtrai and Ostend from the air.

We made our fourth and final trip to Brussels on the 30th of September. N-Nan was probably having maintenance done, so we flew in Halifax LW169. *The Halifax File*, a book that lists the history of every Halifax they built, says that this plane was shot down on a raid to Siracourt, a V1 bunker in France, on the 6th of July 1944 but that can't be right because both Bill and I have the same registration number written in our separate flying logs for this petrol run and that was in October.

The petrol runs to Brussels were a welcome distraction and it had been an enjoyable time for us. We had been to Brussels and had a look around, flown to Ostend and went down low for a good look at the vacant pill boxes and anti aircraft defences from where the flak barrage which wounded me would have come from and so on. We bought grapes, drank beer with the locals, smuggled Trev on board, took him sightseeing, and gave chocolates to the kids. However, we never had the feeling then that the war was being won or that we could be a little more relaxed as we flew around. We knew we were on a special mission and things would be very different when we got on heavily defended targets again.

I know that Harry, our wireless operator, wasn't very impressed with the petrol runs because he reckons they should have counted as operations because the Melsbroek airstrip in late September 1944 was still a dangerous places to be. Just two months later, on the 1st of January 1945, thirty-six German fighters hit the airfield hard and really shot it up. The Germans claimed over one hundred and twenty planes either destroyed or damaged on the ground. Perhaps Harry was right!

On the 29th we went on a practice bombing exercise in Halifax NP950 but it only lasted fifteen minutes. When we got airborne the countryside was closed in by bad weather so we abandoned it after one circuit of the base. Bill wrote in his diary that it was "very grim landing in the rain and low cloud" but he was able to land the plane "fairly smoothly." This plane was written off when it overshot the runway in poor visibility and crashed at Pocklington five months later.

The Raid on Courtrai – 20th/21st July 1944

In the chapter above, Basil Spiller describes flying towards Brussels on his crew's second petrol run on the 27th of September 1944. Their flight path took them over Courtrai (Kortfijk), a town some seventy five kilometres west of Brussels. It was the site of a devastating Bomber Command attack two months earlier. They "stooged" around above and saw the destruction below them. Basil Spiller's pilot, Flight Lieutenant W F (Bill) Rabbitt wrote in his diary:

> "We flew in today at 800 ft and went across to Courtrai to have a look at the marshalling yards that had been bombed by Bomber Command. Flew around it for a while and viewed a scene of absolute destruction - hardly a part of the yard had escaped the very successful and concentrated effort."

The raid on the marshalling yards at Courtrai was a night raid conducted on the 20th/21st of June 1944. 305 Lancasters and fifteen Mosquitos attacked the railway depot. Each Lancaster carried 13,000 pounds of bombs. They encountered little flak but there was strong night fighter opposition and nine Lancasters were shot down.

Fliegerhorst (Air Base) Melsbroek

Before the start of the Second World War, the main Belgium airfield at Haren was considered too small to satisfactorily accommodate existing aircraft and service increasing demand. After the German invasion on the 17th of May 1940, the Luftwaffe began constructing a new airfield with three concrete runways on farmland at Melsbroek, ten kilometres east of the centre of Brussels. This location made it an ideal base from which attacks could be launched against the United Kingdom and for its fighter planes to intercept incoming aircraft. Aircraft hangars, ammunition storage facilities, workshops and control towers on the airfield were elaborately camouflaged as large apartments and other domestic buildings.

Melsbroek, Belgium 1945. A Hawker Typhoon of 181 Squadron RAF is being serviced outside a hangar, camouflaged by the Germans as domestic buildings.

Melsbroek was one of nine German airfields targeted by Bomber Command in a daylight mission on the 15th of August 1944. Over one thousand planes took part. The destruction of these German airfields severely weakened the ability of the Luftwaffe to defend Germany against the daily bombing raids being mounted by the Allies.

Aerial reconnaissance photographs taken after the attack show the airfield pitted with deep craters. Melsbroek was then abandoned by the Luftwaffe.

Basil Spiller's crew walked around the airfield and Flight Lieutenant R N (Bill) Rabbitt, the pilot, described what he saw:
"We landed okay, unloaded our aircraft and then proceeded to have a look around at what was shortly ago a German

aerodrome. There I saw numerous Jerry kites such as Ju88, Ju188, Fw190, Me109 and others. We duly inspected them."

By the 3rd of September, German forces had withdrawn from Belgium, and Allied forces controlled the airfield. Repairs were quickly made to the runways and it was occupied by various squadrons including No. 440 Squadron of the Royal Canadian Air Force.

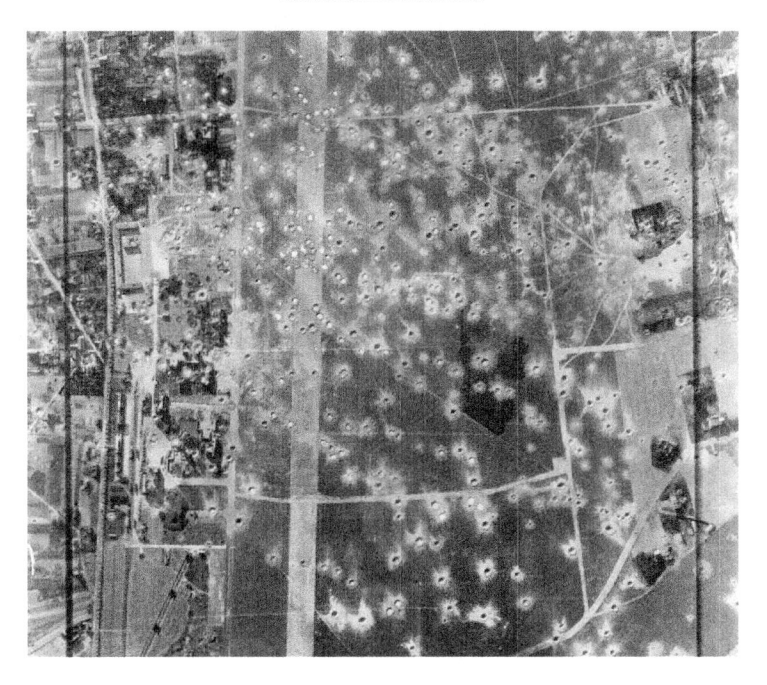

Melsbroek Airfield

RAF reconnaissance photograph of Melsbroek airfield in Belgium, after the Bomber Command daylight raid on the 15th of August 1944. The airfield can be seen pitted with craters. After this attack it was immediately abandoned by the Luftwaffe.

Although the allies had control of Belgium, the airfield was still vulnerable to attack from the air. On the 1st of January, 1945, German night fighters attacked Melsbroek causing severe damage to aircraft stationed there. The pilots of the thirty-five planes that attacked the airfield found a complacent scene before them – anti aircraft defences were unmanned and planes were lined up neatly and bunched together. Mayhem prevailed as the German pilots opened fire.

The numbers of planes lost or damaged vary but at least eleven Wellingtons, five Spitfires, seven Harrow transports, five B-52s, up to twenty other USAAF bombers, five Avro Ansons, at least one Dakota transport and all of No. 140 Squadron's Mosquitos were destroyed. The German pilots claimed eighty-five planes destroyed and forty damaged. Twenty German planes were shot down.

On the 20th of January 1945, Melsbroek became home base to a detachment of four Gloster Meteor Mark III jets from No. 616 Squadron, the first time British jets were flown on operations in mainland Europe. Although still experimental in many ways, Meteors had been used successfully in Britain against VI rockets and by January 1945 it was decided that Meteors were ready for combat although pilots were forbidden to fly over German territory because of concerns that a downed plane could fall into German or Soviet hands.

After the war two of the Melsbroek runways built by the Germans were extended and are still in use today. The modern Brussels airport, built on what was originally Fliegerhorst (Air Base) Melsbroek, is regarded as one of the best airports in the world.

Chapter 46: Pilot Officers Basil Spiller & Don McLean

On the 23rd of August, while I was recuperating from my injuries at Rednal, Don and John went to see Air Commodore Walker about their commissions. In his diary Don wrote:

> "I saw Gus Walker (the Air Commodore) and he is a great chap to talk to. He recommended me for my commission so it shouldn't be long now. Went into Pock. for a dance in the evening and had a few beers."

I returned to the squadron not long after that and had my third interview for my commission with Gus Walker as well. He was the last officer to interview me. Gus Walker was a thorough gentleman and straight away he recommended me for a commission as a Pilot Officer, and six months after that I was automatically promoted to Flying Officer. After the war Gus Walker became the Inspector-General of the RAF. In 1966 he was promoted to Deputy Commander-in-Chief of Allied Forces Central Europe and in 1967 he was appointed RAF Air Chief Marshal, the highest ranker in the RAF.

Years after the war, Don McLean phoned me to say that Gus Walker was going to be the guest of honour at an RAAF reunion at the Gaythorne RSL, in Brisbane. He had been flown out from England especially for the occasion. Gus was the Air Marshal of the RAF at that stage. We both went and took a large photo of our crew along.

The RSL was packed. After the formalities and speeches were over airmen who had served with him were invited to come up from their tables to talk to him. He was very popular and we queued up to meet him. When our turn came we shook his hand and reminisced. He was very pleased to see us and remembered our crew well, Bill Rabbitt in particular.

On the 30th of September 1944, the day of our last petrol run to Brussels, my commission came through with Don McLean's and it was backdated to the 12th of July when the first application was lodged and I was paid back-pay.

As soon as we landed we headed off to London on a 48 hour leave pass to get kitted out with our new uniforms. We were both given one hundred pounds sterling. When we arrived we booked in at the Strand Palace Hotel. In his diary on the 30th Don wrote:

> ".... My commission came through today so we came home early (from Brussels) and Bas and I went to London on a 48 to collect our gear. York-Brussells-York-London in one day – some traveller!"

The next day, Sunday the 1st of October was my twenty-first birthday. I can't remember when we went shopping but Don's diary suggests that it was on Monday morning. In his diary for Sunday he wrote:

"We stopped at the Strand Palace and after going to church we met young Wal Adams and spent the rest of the day with him. We had a walk down through Hyde Park in the afternoon and went to the Codgers in the evening."

Then on Monday the 2nd of October he wrote:

"A very quiet day and in the afternoon we went to see Miss Dexer down at the Whitehall. We caught the afternoon train to York and took our gear back to the squadron."

It is interesting that Don did not mention what was involved in buying our kit or even going shopping for that matter. You couldn't go into one place and purchase everything you wanted. You had to go to various establishments before you were fully kitted. I initially went to the Boomerang Club which was in Australia House in the Strand. It was the mecca for Australian airmen on leave in London. There was a tailor installed in the foyer where I was able to acquire a "whipcord" officer's uniform, with the correct insignia of a pilot officer, from the rack. It was originally tailored to suit a fellow who had been killed. That didn't bother me. It fitted me to a tee. The tailor had racks of uniforms available. He would have adjusted one to fit me anyway. I left his shop knowing that at the end of the trip I would at least go home with one uniform.

I also was told the address of a tailor in Saville Row and there I went to acquire a second uniform tailored to measure. The tailor's name was "Carr, Son and Warr". I remember that name vividly. I chose a beautiful barathea cloth with which to have my second uniform tailored. Barathea was a very expensive fabric and it was regarded as the best fabric for uniforms by officers' in the airforce. I was informed that it would take a couple of months and they would notify me when it was ready.

After that I took off down Regent Street and bought six "Van Heusen" officers' shirts at "Austin Reed" a firm that is still operating today. Then I went to the "Army & Navy Stores" – that was the department store's name - to acquire the necessary underwear and socks. Next I had to buy a greatcoat and cap. These I acquired at "Moss Brothers" in Piccadilly, which is still open today too.

When you bought a new hat it was stiffened by wire. The tradition was that you took the wire out immediately and bashed it into a shape that suited your personality. So that's what I did. I bashed it into a shape that I liked. It had to look mistreated a bit.

I don't know what would have happened if I had gone back to Pocklington without a uniform. I would have been an officer but I don't know if I could have gone into the officers' mess or not. I probably could have. I can't remember whether I retained my shoes or whether I bought new ones. I think I was able to keep the shoes I wore as a sergeant.

By then my money had almost run out and I headed back to Pocklington with Don. I didn't have to buy a new battledress. Aircrew wore the same type. When I was a patient at the hospital in Ely, I didn't have any clothes because my trousers had been cut up and I had given the top away. The hospital arranged for me to get a new battledress then. The only problem was that it was an RAF one. They were different from the ones the RAAF issued to us. Ours were a rich dark blue whereas theirs were a dull grey. Anyway I wore the RAF battledress right through to my last flight in England. When the war was over, I bought a new RAAF battledress while I was waiting at Brighton before I embarked for Australia, and I threw the RAF one away.

I was duly welcomed into a three bedroom hut, which I shared with Bill and Sandy. We had a WAAF batwoman who used to press our uniforms, wake us up and bring us hot shaving water every morning. I still have a laugh when I think about that. I was welcome in the officers' mess from the start. We had to dress in full officers' uniform at night and at other times we were permitted to wear battle dress. I was nervous about being welcomed into the officers' mess for the first time. There was no change in my relationship with our ground crew. It was very democratic. They didn't salute me or anything like that. There were no big differences to being an officer and being a sergeant. The only real change was that we had access to different facilities - the officers' mess, our own ablutions block and a bedroom rather than a bunk in a Nissan hut.

There were no other fringe benefits. No walking around in a uniform, or walking into a pub and having the girls look more kindly upon us. No upsurge in popularity by any means. It didn't put any limits on us that weren't there before either. We still got out in the car and we still toured around, girl hunting as we did. We still played up. Dancing! We still went to the pub. Life continued on as normal. It was just that we were officers instead of flight-sergeants.

Harry Brabin

Four of us received commissions - John, Don, Sandy and me. Harry was quite upset that he did not get a commission. There may have been a certain prestige about being commissioned and he obviously felt left out because he was the only one that dipped out. It would have been hard for him. Münster was Harry's twenty-sixth mission and other men had faded away long before that. A lot of people had been killed and then there were others that just couldn't take it any more. There was a real lot of steel and endeavour and courage in just doing what Harry had done. And then to see all of his mates getting rewarded with commissions he would have been thinking: "What have I done? What is it?" He may have done something. I don't know. It was a shame that Harry didn't get it.

Harry's initial recommendation had to come from the Wireless Operator section leader. There was a delay which wasn't good for Harry because the rest of us were interviewed by Wing Commander Marchbank but Harry was interviewed later by the new wing commander, Louis Wilson. Wilson was a different type of bloke and this is probably the reason that Harry didn't get a commission. There may have had a clash of personalities and it is here that the truth about Harry's promotion lies.

Wilson was a different kettle of fish to Marchbank. He was a much more difficult person. I only had one conversation with him and I wasn't impressed with him. It was when I was back on base after my first tour of duty. Wilson left 102 Squadron in January 1945 so this conversation happened just before then.

When I was wounded, I was entitled to wear a "wound stripe" on the left sleeve of my uniform. One night in the officers' mess, I looked across the room and saw Wing Commander Wilson in conversation with another high ranking officer. He looked at me, came over and asked why I was wearing a wound stripe. I explained to him that I had been wounded during the operation on Forêt de Nieppe which we had been asked to lead because it was his first operation with the squadron after being appointed wing commander. I said that I was Bill Rabbitt's navigator. He said, "Was that you?" and somewhat sarcastically I replied, "That was me all right!" He left me then and went back across the room to the officer he was drinking with.

After Forêt de Nieppe I had done thirteen more missions in his squadron before I finished my first tour and he didn't have a clue who I was. I thought he was rude and disrespectful. He didn't show any courtesy towards me and he had no real knowledge about one of the members of his squadron who had been seriously wounded in the course of duty. You would think that he would check first before querying my wearing of the wound stripe. I would only have been wearing it if I had a right to it. He was querying whether I was entitled to it or not. It was an insult. He did not appear to be a fellow with very much empathy for the men on his squadron and he was a stickler for the rules. What we all called "an RAF type". He probably did it to impress the other officer. Wilson thought he was above everyone else. I thought he was a prat!

My assessment about why Harry might ran foul of Wilson is probably right. He was the person ultimately responsible for Harry not getting a commission. Harry thought he didn't get one because he didn't go to the right school. That was not normally the case but it might well have been the way with a man like Wilson.

Wound Stripes in the News

No Wound Stripes
The War Office has decided, as a general principle, against the revival of the custom of wearing wound stripes or service chevrons on the sleeves of Army uniforms, as was done in World War 1.
Sunday Times (Perth, Western Australia). Sunday 2 March 1941

Wound Stripes for the RAAF
Wound stripes will be issued to the RAAF, Mr Drakeford, Air Minister, announced yesterday.

A red stripe will be worn vertically on the left sleeve for any number of wounds suffered in previous wars, and a gold stripe for each wound received in this war. Wound stripes for this war would be issued for wounds or injuries due to enemy action and sustained on duty, wherever serving; wounds due to enemy action, sustained in an operational command outside Australia, whether on duty or not; and wounds not due to enemy action, sustained while serving in a forward operational area and in contact with the enemy.
The Argus (Melbourne, Victoria). Saturday 27 May 1944

Chapter 47: Operation 24 - Kleve

351 aircraft - 251 Halifaxes, 90 Lancasters, 10 Mosquitos - of Nos 3, 4 and 8 Groups to bomb the small German town of Kleve which, together with Emmerich, stood on the approach routes by which German units could threaten the vulnerable Allied right flank near Nijmegen which had been left exposed by the failure of Operation Market Garden. Visibility was clear and the centre and north of the town were heavily bombed, although some crews bombed too early and their loads actually fell in Holland near Nijmegen. 2 Halifaxes lost. 340 Lancasters and 10 Mosquitos of Nos 1, 3 and 8 Groups carried out an even more accurate attack on Emmerich. 3 Lancasters were lost. *Total effort for the day:* 846 sorties, 7 aircraft (0.8 per cent) lost.

The Bomber Command War Diaries, 7 October, 1944

While Don McLean and I were in London getting our officers' uniforms, the rest of the crew had two flights, an air test in N-Nan on the 1st of October and on the 2nd Bill mentions that he "converted a chap to Halifax III's... and he coped particularly well. Begbie a Sth. African". Don and I were back for the crew's next flight, a fighter affiliation on the 4th. We were lucky to miss out on a daylight raid on a synthetic oil plant at Scholven in the Ruhr on the 6th. Twenty-two of our planes reached the target and it was a very shaky do. In his diary Don said:

> "The squadron did a daylight to the Ruhr today and did they get a bashing! All 'the kites bar one were holed by 'flak'. Looks as though that L/M.F. queue will be growing.... Two of the planes today were write-offs and Ray Dodd landed at Woodbridge pretty badly shot-up."

Our turn came the next day on our twenty-fourth mission to the town of Kleve on the 7th of October. Kleve is a town in northwestern Germany near the Rhine River and the border with Holland. It was a daylight mission. Another bomber force was hitting Emmerich which was just ten kilometres away on the other side of the Rhine. There were twenty-four planes from our squadron on the Kleve raid so we were almost at full strength. We took off at 1130 in the morning and the raid lasted four hours fifty minutes. This was the first raid for Mick Starmer, our new mid-upper gunner.

Kleve was being defended by the Germans and the Allied army was trying to take it. Bill's diary mentions that there were "Jerry troops and some oil stores" at Kleve. My understanding from briefing was that there was concern the German army holding Kleve would be able to outflank the allies and we were going in to support our troops. This was a five hour trip, longer than any we had been on for over two months. We were bombed right up with a load of eleven thousand pounds - all high explosives. Bomber Command would have given the order for us to be bombed up that way because they wanted as much of the German defences knocked down as possible.

It was a clear day with good visibility. While we were on our bombing run, Don McLean lying down in N-Nan's perspex nose had a bird's eye view of what was happening as we approached the aiming point. The flak was very accurate and he saw two "kites right in front of us blown out of the sky". In his diary he also wrote that he "saw three or four more spiralling earthwards and burning." These may have been planes from the nearby raid on Emmerich, which was a Lancaster operation. Only two planes were lost on the Kleve raid – both Halifaxes.

We were on our bombing run when we passed Nijmegan and after dropping our bombs turned south-west and headed past Antwerp on our way home. Don got another aiming point through the smoke that covered the target. Bombing was well concentrated and we wiped the town out completely. Our squadron records say that smoke was reported rising up to thirteen thousand feet in the air and a "large mushroom shaped cloud over a ten mile area (was) visible from the French coast, 150 miles away".

Bill's dairy gives a few more details about the Kleve and Emmerich raids. He says that there were about six thousand planes out on sorties that day. On our flight there were only about 350 planes but in the twenty-four hour period from the night of the $6^{th}/7^{th}$ of October, during daytime on the 7th and the night of the $7^{th}/8^{th}$, there were a total of 1839 sorties flown by Bomber Command. Bill's information may have been a bit out but then again on most days the Americans had a lot of planes in the sky as well – probably over a thousand - heading off to different destinations, so half of the planes Bill was talking about would have been American. In addition to heavy bombers there could have been a similar number of RAF and USAAF fighters above us giving us protection. There may have been six thousand planes up but regardless of the number, there were a lot of planes about. It was a difficult trip for Bill because the slipstreams of so many aircraft made flying difficult. He said it was "a lot of hard work" and it would have been.

Our plane

N-Nan was our plane. She had done a lot of work up until this point. She had been hit by flak and her duralium had been repaired almost a hundred times - some were big holes and some were small. She had done forty-five operations. Our crew had done twenty-seven, most of them in N-Nan, and I had been on twenty-four, eighteen in N-Nan.

We thought that she was a lucky plane for us. The more flights we had in her, the more experienced we became, the longer we were on the squadron, the more she became our plane. They would never have taken her away from us and we would never have let her go.

George Augustus "Gus" Walker GCB, CBE, DSO, DFC, AFC

In 1934 after completing his MA at St Catherine's College, Cambridge, George Augustus "Gus" Walker joined the RAF. When the Second World War began, he was a squadron leader. On the 5th of November 1940 he became the Commanding Officer of 50 Squadron at RAF Lindholme near Doncaster, flying Handley Page Hampden medium bombers. While stationed there he was awarded both the DSO and DFC for bravery.

Gus Walker, AOC, at his desk, 42 Base Pocklington.

On the 20th of April 1942, Walker was appointed Officer Commanding RAF Syerston in Nottinghamshire, where No. 61 Squadron, then being re-equipped with Avro Lancasters was based. It was here that he was involved in a terrible tragedy, which had a dramatic impact on the rest of his life.

On the 8th of December 1942, his squadron was briefed to bomb Turin in Italy. While supervising his aircraft taxiing for takeoff, Gus Walker noticed incendiary bombs drop from the open bomb bay of reserve Lancaster R5864. The incendiaries hit the ground and ignited. Gus Walker raced to the Lancaster in his car, followed by a fire truck. With a rake he began clearing the burning incendiaries but the 4000 pound "cookie" bomb in the plane exploded and he was hurled backwards some distance from the plane. In the explosion his right arm was severed above the elbow. Several months later after his recovery, he was given permission to return to duties with the RAF. He continued flying with the aid of a prosthetic arm with a hand that he clamped to the control column of his aircraft.

On the 24th of March 1943, Gus Walker was appointed Air Officer Commanding at 42 Base Pocklington, where 102 Squadron was based. He was the commander of the station when Basil Spiller's crew was posted there. It was Gus Walker who conducted the final interview for Basil's promotion to Pilot Officer. Basil Spiller regards Gus Walker as one of the finest men he has ever met, an opinion echoed by everyone who met him. On the 26th of August 1943 he was appointed Air Aide-de-Camp to George V1, the King of England and with the end of the war in sight, Walker was appointed Senior Air Staff Officer at No. 4 Group headquarters.

After the war, Gus Walker remained in the RAF as a career officer playing a key role in its development as a powerful jet age airforce. Through the 1950's and 60's he received a series of promotions leading finally to his appointment as RAF Air Chief Marshal on the 1st of March 1967. He retired from the RAF on the 7th of July 1970 after a career spanning thirty-six years. Gus Walker was a household name in the United Kingdom both during and after the Second World War. His bravery and self sacrifice were inspirational to the men and women of the armed forces and the wider community in Britain. He died aged seventy-four on the 11th of December 1986.

Gus Walker In The News

Airman Rugby International Loses Arm

Injured on active service when an explosion blew him over the top of a motor car, Group Captain G A Walker, DSO, DFC, the England rugby player has lost his right arm. Regardless of his own danger, he warned other people when an explosion seemed imminent, but one person was killed and another lost a foot.

Walker also received leg injuries but he came through an operation successfully.

Born at Garforth, near Leeds, he was educated at St Bees and St Catherine's college, Cambridge. He was commissioned in 1934 and his operational exploits during the war brought him rapid promotion. Walker was the RAF's youngest group captain.

The Glasgow Herald **(Scotland, UK). Friday December 11 1942**

Just Gus

Group Captain Shines on Rugger Field

LONDON, Dec 15, - On the playing field they just call him "Gus". At his Royal Air Force station he is "sir" because Gus Walker, the England rugby international, is a group captain who has won the D.S.O. and the D.F.C. and just doesn't know the meaning of the word "quit," be it on the playing field or just anywhere on the ground or in the air.

Walker left his bomber station to play for the R.A.F. against the army at Rugby. For 20 minutes he was virtually the whole air force team. Then he was carried off the field suffering a bad concussion. Right after half time he was back, arguing in vain to be allowed in the game. That was on Saturday.

On Monday – Group Capt. Walker was back with his boys in bomber command getting ready for the next trip out to the Axis target towns.

The Leader-Post **(Saskatchewan, Canada). Wednesday December 16 1942**

Chapter 48: Operation 25 - Bochum

Bochum: 435 aircraft - 375 Halifaxes, 40 Lancasters, 20 Mosquitos - of Nos 1, 4, 6 and 8 Groups. 4 Halifaxes and 1 Lancaster lost. This raid was not successful. The target area was covered by cloud and the bombing was scattered.
The Bomber Command War Diaries, 9 October, 1944

Mission twenty-five was on the 9th of October 1944. There were twenty aircraft from our squadron on this night trip to Bochum, a town deep in the heart of the Ruhr, about fifteen kilometres east of Essen. At briefing the intelligence officer made the point of emphasising that it was the site of the largest steelworks in Germany. Our primary target was the power works which supplied the steelworks with electricity. Naturally we expected heavy defences but we were agreeably surprised that flak wasn't as bad as usual.

We took off at 1700 hours and carried ten thousand pounds of bombs, no incendiaries. You can tell from this that we were almost fully bombed up and also that our intention was to knock out the steelworks and not to set fire to the town. The trip took five hours and fifty minutes, so we arrived back at about 10.50 pm. That was a pretty long trip to the Ruhr so we must have doglegged a lot. It was classed as a night op. because it was mid autumn and finished late. The days were getting shorter as we approached winter.

The trip was uneventful but there was a lot of work for me because it was quite a complicated flight plan with a lot of course changes and height variations coming out of the target.

After leaving base, we flew down across the south coast England at 1,500 feet, turning north-east over the English Channel and crossed France into Belgium. When we reached 05.00E longitude we commenced a fully rated climb to 20,000 feet which we held all the way to the target. A fully rated climb is at maximum boost, so it's a very steep climb – as steep as possible. We did not do that often. Generally it was a more gradual ascent. We always went into the Ruhr that way and came out over Holland. The curving route would take us into our bombing run straight up the valley of the Ruhr River.

When we changed altitude or direction, at each of those points, I was saying over the intercom to Bill something like: "Bill, do a fully rated climb to twenty thousand feet!" or "We're approaching Ostend. Get ready to dive to ten thousand feet!" I always gave him instructions about what to do on the next leg. It might seem like the raid had quite an eccentric flight plan but it was probably our best defence because the German radar defences were trying to plot our course and speed so that they would know where to direct their night fighters and cannons. If we were able to confuse them or if they made a mistake, we'd be on our bombing run facing only the permanent flak batteries at the target while their night fighters were buzzing around over another city miles away, which is exactly what happened during the Stuttgart operation back in July.

Even a few minutes were important. If they knew where we were going and had time to prepare a reception committee it was a different story. They would light up the night with photo flares and have searchlights dancing across the sky. Night fighters would be circling about waiting, and they'd be moving mobile 88 millimetre flak guns into position to augment those that were already there.

There was a lot of cloud over Bochum so the Pathfinders marked it with both Wanganui and ground markers. Seventeen of our planes bombed on ground markers but three of us bombed on Wanganui because the target was clouding over when we arrived.

It is not surprising that the attack was unsuccessful and the bombing was scattered. There was a lot of flak coming from Dortmund on our port side but our bombing run took us clear of it. In his diary Bill says that the "flak was pretty hot but nowhere near the usual Ruhr defences". Five aircraft from our squadron still received flak damage. It was always hot in the Ruhr!

We came away from Bochum and dropped to 10,000 feet in seven minutes. That was a steep dive. We all loved it. We were airmen after all. A modern day passenger in a plane would be apprehensive but we were quite blasé about it. It was also good to know that we were fooling the night fighter defences.

From Bochum we curved north-westward on our homeward journey and flew over Nijmegan and then south-west to Antwerp, climbing to 17,000 feet. We lost height to 10,000 feet over Ostend and then over the Channel turned north-west for home. The Bochum flight plan was a busy one but it was typical of night operations.

In daylight in good weather you could see where you were going but nights were different because you couldn't see anything so once again it was very important for me to follow the flight plan religiously.

As we returned to base, Bill noticed that there were a lot of planes with their lights on. He calls them "dumb clots." They were just inviting trouble. There could have been German night fighters about waiting for an opportunity to attack and the lights would show them just where our planes were.

We nearly had a collision on our return and our landing was rough. It shook all of us up. Bill's diary says that his poor landing happened because this was our first night landing since we attacked Wanne Eikel on the 25th/26th of July and he was a bit rusty.

Fighter affiliation

Earlier that same day we had a 1015 takeoff and we took N-Nan up for a "fighter affiliation" exercise. Bill mentions that we went up with a Hurricane for fifty-five minutes. We picked up the Hurricane fighter, from a nearby airfield, and the pilot indulged in practice mock attacks by "attacking" us. It would have involved us doing violent corkscrewing actions and steep banks and violent evasive actions. The Hurricane came at us from behind and from both quarters but not from in front. All of our attacks at night time were from behind and below. The Germans wouldn't attack from the front because the closing speed of two aircraft approaching one another head on would have been too great for the pilot to have a visual at night time. The closing speed was the important thing. There would be two planes coming at one another, a fighter at three hundred plus miles per hour and a bomber cartwheeling along at two hundred plus miles per hour and the closing speed would be more than five hundred miles per hour. That would be as fast as a modern day jet. Instead German pilots waited until they were directed onto us by ground controllers using radar until they had a visual. Then they would come at us with their cannons blazing away or travel in the same direction as us so that they didn't alert us on Fishpond, slip in below us and attack us from underneath. Affiliation exercises were designed to test our night flying responses, not daylight ones because we always had daylight fighter escorts. Interestingly, Don McLean's diary entry shows that he was not impressed with this particular fighter affiliation exercise. He thought that Hawker Hurricanes were now too slow for us in our fast and manoeuvrable Halifax. We had no trouble getting the better of the Hurricane. Bill was brilliant in adopting violent evasive action. He thought that there was no point in half-measures.

Real flying boys

So there we were doing corkscrews in our fighter affiliation in the morning before we headed off on an operation later that afternoon. We loved going up on bombing practice, cross countries and fighter affiliations and we would go up at the drop of a hat. We were real flying boys. Some people can't understand how we could go up and do practice corkscrews in the morning and all of that, having our bodies put through it all and then be back up flying an operation that night. We did it and we loved it. And we did as we were told. We would have had no choice but to do that anyway because the flight commander would have told us to but we didn't have to be told. We would have done it anyway!

At this time there wasn't a crew on the squadron who had done a tour. We were still the most experienced crew. We had been the most experienced crew back at the time of my wounding too and we had only done nineteen operations then. In December 1944 there were 355 aircrew personnel on the squadron, made up of 153 officers and 202 airmen. If you allow seven men to a plane it means that there were about fifty crews at 102 Squadron and we were the most experienced even though we had done only two-thirds of a tour. A lot of the others had been killed. Sobering isn't it?

The Ruhr Administration Area

Monica and Fishpond

In early 1942, the early warning, radar system "Monica" was installed in all RAF bombers. When planes were approaching them from behind, a series of audible beeps alerted crews to the potential danger. Monica had two major problems. Because RAF bombers usually flew to and from targets in large but relatively compact bombing streams it was difficult to determine which signals were "friendly" and which ones were coming from enemy planes that were joining the stream. As well, the Germans had salvaged Monica sets from downed RAF bombers and their scientists created "Flensburg Fu227", a radar detection system which allowed their night fighters to home in on Monica. In mid 1944, two years after its introduction, RAF investigators after examining a captured Junkers 88, realized that German aircraft had been using Flensburg to locate bombing streams. Monica was immediately withdrawn from service and replaced with "Fishpond" a more advanced early warning, radar system.

Fishpond was a derivative from the ground scanning radar system H2S. It was developed when British researchers realized that echoes at the centre of the navigator's H2S radar display were in fact reflections from aircraft in the bombing stream beneath the plane The echoes were separated and displayed on a screen in the radio operator's position. Monica provided him with the bearing and range of aircraft both below his plane and above it to an angle of approximately ten degrees. Echoes from planes in the bomber stream appeared almost stationary on the screen and those that moved at an angle to the general stream or moved faster than the stream were regarded as hostile and emanating from German night fighters. Upon receiving a warning, the pilot would make the necessary change in flight pattern. The gunners immediately commenced a concentrated visual search of the night sky and when they sensed immediate danger told the pilot to take evasive action.

Fishpond was effective up to a range of five miles. Approaching from the rear, the relative closing speed of a German Ju88 night fighter could be as much as one hundred miles an hour. When detected, a crew had at most two minutes to prepare for its attack. The German response to H2S was the development of the Naxos-Z system with which night fighters were directed to the general position of bombing streams. Bomber Command knew of the existence of the Naxos-Z system but its planes continued using H2S and Fishpond. 4 Group squadrons like 102 Squadron, to which Basil Spiller belonged, were not told that German planes had the ability to home in on them.

Chapter 49: Operation 26 - Duisburg

1,013 aircraft - 519 Lancasters, 474 Halifaxes and 20 Mosquitos - were dispatched to Duisburg with RAF fighters providing an escort. 957 bombers dropped 3,574 tons of high explosive and 820 tons of incendiaries on Duisburg. 14 aircraft were lost - 13 Lancasters and 1 Halifax; it is probable that the Lancasters provided the early waves of the raid and drew the attention of the German flak before the flak positions were overwhelmed by the bombing.
The Bomber Command War Diaries, 14 October, 1944

After Bochum we were on stand-by for two operations but they were cancelled - the Gelsenkirchen raid on the 12th was scrubbed at briefing. As soon as we knew that operations had been cancelled for the day we were off. If we had time we would travel into York to the pictures or the pub, if not we might go to a pub in the village. If there was an ENSA show we might stay on the squadron and watch that.

My twenty-sixth mission was on the 14th of October 1944. It was a big operation. We were briefed to go to the Ruhr Valley in daylight for the first time. Our target was Duisburg, one of the important manufacturing and rail centres in the Ruhr. Twenty-five aircraft from 102 Squadron took off but two returned, one with an oil leak and the crew was having trouble with their oxygen in the second one. We had an early start and got the call to get ready at 0145 hours and finally took off at 0600. We flew for five hours and ten minutes and took nine thousand eight hundred pounds of bombs. We bombed at twenty thousand feet and Don would have sighted on red or green flares just the same as at night time.

The Duisburg raid was the start of "Operation Hurricane". Bomber Command was ordered to demonstrate to the Germans the terrifying firepower that the Allies possessed. This raid was carried out by upwards of one thousand bombers. One thousand was the magic number. These "one thousand bomber" raids were a big thing. It was all about making the Germans feel shock and awe. It would have been a frightening thing to know that a thousand bombers were on their way to bomb you. This was a tactic to intimidate the civilians – the ordinary people.

By the time all of the bombers had dropped their bombs, the bombing time on the target would have been in the vicinity of half an hour's duration. There could not be a thousand bombers over the target at the same time. This meant that they had to split it up into at least five waves of say two hundred planes. There were waves on every Bomber Command target. The only exception was when 4 Group bombed a target on its own. The waves were five minutes apart. It worked like this. Say the first wave was due to bomb at 0100. The second wave would be due to bomb at 0105 and the third wave would have been due to bomb at 0110 and the fourth one would have been to bomb at 0115 and so on. Waves of bombers passing over the target at five minute intervals meant that the raid lasted almost half an hour and there were no more than two hundred bombers over the aiming point at one time. Can you imagine what it was like for the population down below?

Before the planes left their bases they were all given the same target but slightly different flight plans which stipulated what time they had to bomb. Five minutes doesn't sound like a lot in time between waves but it is really quite a distance when you are travelling along at over 250 miles an hour because we were always at maximum speed on a bombing run. Each wave approaching the target would be over twenty five miles apart.

As I have said, it was our first Bomber Command attack on the Ruhr in daylight and it was a full Bomber Command exercise with over a thousand bombers. The flak was intense. I can remember looking out and seeing the sky filled with puff marks of smoke from exploded flak shells. They were pretty frightening. Our Flight Commander, Squadron Leader Ward was shot up badly by flak but was able to return to base. Once again we escaped being damaged and got back to base safely.

On these daylight raids, we did not have to keep the black curtain between me and the bomb aimer closed so I always saw a lot more. Momentarily, I was able to look out and see flak and observe what was going on.

I didn't know that on the way over, Bill had formated on Squadron Leader Ford and was following him into the target. I kept giving Bill instructions to keep us on track but he wasn't taking directions from me. Ford's navigator mistakenly took us well to port of track. Looking through scattered cloud over the target, Don McLean realized the mistake and told Bill to make a "decent sized correction to starboard" and we bombed the target. Our photograph was the best photograph of the raid.

Except for the correction on the bombing run, the mission was straightforward for us but it was disastrous for other crews. We dropped our bombs and got out of there as quickly as we could but a lot of crews were not so lucky. The air defences were pretty intense and fourteen aircraft were shot down, thirteen Lancasters.

The Bomber Command War Diary makes the point that the Lancasters were in the early waves which destroyed the flak concentrations. This is part of the ongoing myth that Lancasters were given harder targets and more difficult roles than Halifaxes. It is not true. I know what I saw when I looked out through the perspex nose. It was frightening. Bill's diary contradicts the war diaries. He says that we were one of the first three planes going in to bomb the built up area and that there was so much flak we were lucky not to collect "a packet". As well Squadron Leader Ward, from our squadron, got badly shot up and it was just luck that he and his crew weren't killed. He wasn't in a "softer" wave was he? Everything about this mission was so dangerous. It is just an example of another ill informed person who thinks that Lancasters did the hard work. There were no "soft" raids, day or night.

After our daytime raid on Duisburg, Bomber Command sent another thousand bomber force to bomb the city again that night. In his diary entry the next day, Bill records that the pilots on the night raid said that they could see the glow of the fires from our raid in the morning still burning in the distance a hundred miles before they reached the city. Then when they were heading home the fires could be seen from 160 miles away. Over nine thousand tons of bombs had been dropped on Duisburg in less than twenty-four hours.

There was a chance that we were going back to the Ruhr on that night time raid too but luckily we were taken off the operation. Bill's diary entry is interesting. It sounds like he was looking forward to the possibility. At the thought of it he says, "Good show." That was Bill!

More on Master Bombers

The Master Bomber and Pathfinders operated in daylight as well. The Master Bomber could abort a raid but he did not have the power to hold up a wave of bombers. Once the planes took off it all went in accordance to the flight plan. Although he could not speed up or slow down a wave he could redirect it by telling the Pathfinders to drop TI's (target indicators) in a certain place and the main force to bomb those TI's. He might say: "Ignore the TI's to port and bomb the centre of the TI's to starboard." The Master Bomber hung around while the raid was going on, circling around observing the raid as it progressed. He would say for instance: "Bomb the centre of the green TI's!" Or he might say: "Don't creep back. Bomb the leading edge of the red TI's!" He might even change that later on and say to the next wave, "Now I want you to bomb the leading edge of the green TI's." In a raid lasting thirty minutes or more, smoke and wind could dramatically change the appearance and position of target indicators.

Some Pathfinders were in each wave and they would drop backup flares according to instructions from the Master Bomber. Thirty minutes was a long time to be hanging around the target. For every one else it was - bombing run – drop bombs – photographic run – and then get out of there as quickly as you could. For the Master Bomber it was much more dangerous. That's why Cheshire got his VC for master bombing.

True Air Speed

It was vital that I knew what our true air speed was as we approached the target. I had to get us there right on time. Never late. Never early. I would instruct Bill to fly at an Indicated Air Speed (IAS) according to the flight plan. IAS was measured on the airspeed indicator in the pilot's dashboard. Bill's airspeed indicator did not show our True Air Speed (TAS), which was the speed we were really travelling at. Airspeed increased about three knots for every 1,000 feet you bombed at. So if the airspeed indicator at 20,000 feet was showing 150 knots per hour, the TAS would be three knots per hour greater per 1000 feet in altitude. So our cruising speed at 20,000 feet would be 210 knots per hour – 240 miles per hour. I measured our True Air Speed with a purpose built hand held calculator. I would put the IAS into the calculator and then the temperature reading from outside the plane and then the altitude at 20,000 feet. Then I would read off the TAS. So arriving at the target on time was controlled by TAS and following the track laid down in the flight plan. On a raid our true air speed approaching the target at twenty thousand feet would be in the vicinity of 220 knots an hour with the bomb load. That's over 250 miles per hour.

Notes on our tour of duty

Including Duisburg, our crew, with the exception of Mick Starmer, had now completed twenty-nine missions. Six more and we would finish our tour of operations on 102 Squadron. Then we would be "screened", given leave, and unless we volunteered for another tour, we would most likely end up training crews in a heavy bomber conversion unit. I have already said that I had done three less ops than Bill, John, Don, Harry and Sandy but it didn't make any difference. I stopped when they did. I was screened when they were screened. The fact that I spent that time in hospital and they did three more didn't matter. I was still part of the crew as far as the tally was concerned. It would have been a bit rough if it wasn't - considering I nearly died! Thirty operations made a tour when we arrived at the squadron in June '44 but not long after it was increased to thirty-five. That was good of them wasn't it?

At the end of our first tour, Mick Starmer had completed only nine operations so he was a long way from being screened when the other six of us finished. He had to do thirty-five operations like everyone else. If he moved into a crew that was just starting its first tour and did his thirty-five he would leave them and they would get another gunner. On the internet there is an account of Mick's flying log, war medals and some photographs being auctioned in 2004. In the auction notes it said that he had done thirty operations when the war ended. He did eight more with us on our second tour so he must have done thirteen when Bill, Harry, John and I were between tours.

"Operation Hurricane", 14 October 1944

Duisburg was a key target for Allied bombing operations throughout the war. The city is located at the confluence of the Rhine and Ruhr Rivers. Then, as now, it was a major chemical, steel production and manufacturing centre and its large inland harbour was a major transport and logistical centre for the heavy industrial cities of the Ruhr Valley.

Military historians regard Duisburg as the most heavily bombed German city of the war. One estimate puts the number of attacks on the city at 299. It was also chosen as the target for a major upscaling of the bombing offensive and a redirection of bombing operations away from military and industrial targets to the city and its inhabitants.

Operation Hurricane was the name given to the intensive series of Bomber Command raids on Duisburg and USAAF raids on targets in the Cologne area, over the twenty-four hour period beginning in the early hours of the morning on the 14th of October 1944. The joint operation was intended to "demonstrate to the enemy, in Germany generally, the overwhelming superiority of the Allied Air Forces" and "cause mass panic and disorganization in the Ruhr, disrupt frontline communications and demonstrate the futility of resistance".

A huge amount of heavy explosive bombs and incendiaries were dropped on Duisburg that day. The first raid, a daytime attack with fighter escort, is described in this chapter by Basil Spiller. A force of 993 heavy bombers dropped some three thousand tons of high explosive bombs and over eight hundred tons of incendiaries. That night, Bomber Command launched two further night time assaults on Duisburg two hours apart. In these attacks a total of 966 heavy bombers dropped over four thousand tons of heavy explosive bombs and some five hundred tons of incendiaries on the city.

As part of Operation Hurricane, the USAAF sent over twelve hundred heavy bombers in daylight raids to Euskirchen and other targets close to Cologne.

Duisburg was bombed many times during the war but the Operation Hurricane attacks were the most devastating. The historic centre of the city and an estimated eighty percent of residential areas were destroyed. After the war virtually the entire city had to be rebuilt.

Flying Officer Greenhaig 158 Squadron

Flying Officer Greenhaig was the wireless operator on Halifax MZ928 S-Sugar on the Duisburg raid on the 14th of October 1944, the operation Basil Spiller descrices in this chapter. While on its bombing run, flak exploded near S-Sugar's inner port side motor and badly damaged it. Shrapnel also shot through the port side of the fuselage near the wireless operator's position tearing off two of Greenhalgh's toes.

Wireless operator F/O F. Greenhalgh of 158 Squadron, based at RAF Lissett, standing by his badly damaged Halifax MZ928 S-Sugar.

At the end of their bombing run, his pilot turned the Halifax sharply to begin the homeward journey, and the propeller sheared off, smashing into the fuselage near the wireless operator's position where Greenhalgh had been sitting just minutes before. He had luckily moved to bandage his wounded foot. The damaged aircraft was nursed back to Carnaby and two days later was struck off charge.

Flight Sergeant Neil (Mick) Starmer Medals Auction Details

"Flight Sergeant N. T. Starmer, Royal Air Force, an Air Gunner who completed a tour of operations in Halifaxes of No. 102 Squadron. He claimed a confirmed Me. 410 after a raid against Goch in February 1945.

E350-400 Starmer, who was from Kennington, enlisted in the Royal Air Force in July 1943. Having qualified as an Air Gunner in September of the same year, he gained experience in Wellingtons at No. 20 OTU. at Lossiemouth, and afterwards attended a conversion course for Halifaxes.

Posted to No. 102 Squadron at Pocklington in September 1944, Starmer commenced his operational tour with a strike against Kleve on 7 October. Targets visited in the remainder of his 30-sortie tour included Bochum (twice) Cologne (twice), Duisburg (thrice), Essen (twice), Hamburg, Munich, Saarbrucken and Wilhelmshaven, but it was in a raid against Goch on the night of 7-8 February 1945, that he gained his confirmed victory. The Halifax was on its way home when an Me410 came up from behind. Before it could open fire, Flight Sergeant Starmer gave it a long burst and saw a red glow in the fuselage as the enemy fighter broke away. The Me. dived vertically and was seen to explode on the ground.

"The enemy pilot must have been surprised because he never opened fire at all," said Flight Sergeant Starmer ...' (accompanying wartime newspaper cutting refers).

Starmer completed his final sortie, against Wangerooge, in late April 1944 and was demobbed in August 1946.

Medals/Orders/Decorations Three:- 1939-45 Star; Air Crew Europe Star : War Medal 1939-45, good very fine and better.

Sold with the recipient's original Flying Log Book, covering the period August 1943 to May 1945, together with three wartime photographs, one featuring his crew and the other two his Halifax's nose-art, 'The Naughty Nineties'."

Chapter 50: Operation 27 - Wilhelmshaven

506 aircraft - 257 Halifaxes, 241 Lancasters, 8 Mosquitos - from all groups except No. 5 Group on the last of 14 major Bomber Command raids on Wilhelmshaven that began in early 1941. Bomber Command claimed 'severe damage' to the business and residential areas.
The Bomber Command War Diaries, 15/16 October, 1944

On the 15th of October '44, fourteen crews from 102 Squadron were briefed to bomb the port city of Wilhelmshaven, a large naval base and shipbuilding centre on the north-west coast of Germany. This was a night time op. We took off at 1130 hours and carried two thousand pounds of high explosives plus eleven canisters of incendiaries, an all up weight of about 10,000 pounds. The trip took only four hours and ten minutes so we must have flown on a more direct flight plan with long legs across the North Sea arriving back at base at about 0340 hours on the 16th. As we headed off the weather was very rough and soon our wings iced up and we were travelling through an extensive electrical storm.

There was a lot of cloud and mist over Wilhelmshaven so the city's searchlights were ineffective. There would have been German naval ships in the harbour but in those conditions we did not know what was below us. I can remember this mission well because it was the first time I was able to look outside from my blacked-out window. I don't know how I was able to do that but I did. Perhaps the black paint had worn thin. I could see hundreds of winking lights, pinpricks of light, just like fireflies on a tropical night. I remember being momentarily taken by how beautiful they were but then commonsense returned and I realized they were exploding flak shells and just how deadly it was.

On our bombing run, we didn't experience any close shaves, no bangs, even though hundreds of shells were exploding all around us. We bombed from eighteen thousand feet and the attack caused massive damage. In his diary Bill mentions having a "good look at all the fires, flak and searchlights" as we flew away. The fires were still visible sixty miles behind us. *The Bomber Command War Diary* says that the raid caused "severe damage to the business and residential areas of the town". Don McLean's diary entry for this mission is very interesting:

"Last night we went to Wilhelmshaven and what weather. From the moment we took off we were in cloud and electric storms. The plane was leaking like a colander and there were sparks everywhere. On the run in to the target Jerry had some beaut dummy TI's and a beautiful dummy target. Some of the boys were sucked in but while I was down in the nose Bas stuck on the H2S and we bombed bang-on time. It was very hazy over the target but the ground markers could be seen O.K. The flak was very heavy and the fighters were there also...."

I cannot remember what the Wilhelmshaven aiming point was but the war diary suggests it was an attack on the city's "business and residential areas". I was monitoring the H2S screen to make sure that we stayed on track over the city. Using H2S we were not going to be distracted by the phoney target indicators and false target that the Germans had lit up. Don was obviously impressed by the German's attempts to fool us but I didn't know anything about what was going on down below.

A cat and a mouse

I can remember coming back across the North Sea on a long leg in stormy conditions. A night fighter with a red light chased us almost all the way back to the English coast playing a cat and mouse game. Sandy and Mick knew it was there and kept an eye out for it. Bill nipped into the clouds and stayed there as much as he could and we were lucky enough to evade being attacked. We'll never know why the plane didn't attack because it followed us for a long time. It had superior speed and could have closed on us whenever the pilot wanted to. He must have been waiting for an opportunity which never came.

When he lost us in the clouds, the night fighter pilot would have known the course we were following and, using his radar to track us, kept going on that heading hoping we would reappear. He knew that we had spotted him the first time we altered course to duck into some clouds. It is one thing to take a plane by surprise but he might have been reluctant to come straight at us from behind because Sandy and Mick were on the alert in their turrets and they could see him. The element of surprise was gone. Halifaxes and Lancasters were small moving targets in the distance when they were attacked from behind. Night fighters preferred to come in underneath and use their upward firing guns if they could. The clouds made it impossible for him. I don't know at what point he peeled off and left us alone. It was probably when his range blew out or he may have found a more likely target.

Slipstreams

It was quite a rough trip home. In his diary, Bill talks about how it was about "the toughest" trip he had flown "from a pilot's point of view". As well as icing on the wings and the storm, he was flying blind on instruments and with over five hundred planes on the operation, slipstreams were a big problem for him. Slipstreams were always with us. No matter where we were, turbulence from the propellers of hundreds of planes on the same track would hit us and make us wallow around in the sky. Hitting slipstreams was like going over a bumpy dirt road in a car and Bill had to fight the controls all the way.

Flying on instruments

Because this was such a dark and stormy mission Bill was in cloud for most of the time so he had to fly on his instruments. Flying in cloud is just like having a blanket thrown over you. You can't see anything. Bill had to rely entirely on his instrument panel - the turn and bank indicator, the altimeter, air speed indicator and the compass. They were the main ones. The turn and bank indicator indicated whether you were straight and level and didn't have one wing lower than the other. It showed up as little aircraft wings which had to be kept within two parallel lines. If you dropped a wing the indicator would show it immediately. If you straightened up it would come back between the parallel lines.

Brake pressure

Our brake pressure was u/s when we landed. This happened every now and then. As soon as we touched down and Bill applied the brakes he knew immediately that we had no brake pressure. The last thing we wanted was to go racing off the runway into the paddocks at the other end.

Coming in to land Bill always reduced our airspeed as much as possible and touched down at the start of the runway because of the possibility of overshooting if the brakes failed. When they did, Bill had to make a split second decision. Was there enough runway left on which N-Nan could come to a halt on without brakes, or should he boost up the engines, take off and make another landing attempt – approaching more slowly and touching down at the very start of the runway? Bill judged correctly and we gradually stopped. He then had to be very cautious about taxiing around the perimeter track back to our dispersal. He used the motors to turn the plane left or right. When he revved the starboard engine the aircraft would turn to port. If he revved a port engine the aircraft would turn to starboard.

RAF aerodromes were usually built with three runways that crossed each other like the sides of a triangle. That's what RAF Pocklington was like. One of our runways was shorter than the other two. The controllers in the tower would direct us to a particular runway depending on which way the wind was blowing but one of these was always the main runway that was used most of the time. The drome was on the outskirts of the town situated within a triangle formed by three roads – the main York Road to the south, the Barmby Road to the north-west, leading into the village, and Hodsow Lane/West Green road to the east which also led into Pocklington. There was farmland on every side, so if you overshot you went through a fence, across the road, through another fence and out onto a field. The plane would be a write off.

There were many planes that overshot and broke their backs as they continued over the main road. One night we came back from the pub and found three in the fields on the other side of the main road. They were all told to use the short runway. Three in one night! There is a lot of money involved in that. On the 2nd of January 1945 when Bill had to conduct an investigation into a plane overshooting the runway, he put the cost of the plane at seventy thousand pounds. That was 1945 wartime money!

Operational life

After we arrived back from the Wilhelmshaven raid, we went to debriefing and then to bed. Later that day Bill was told by the wing commander that he was going to be acting operations commander for the squadron and as such we were only allowed to fly one operation per week. It had to be someone of high rank and when the OC was on leave Bill was the next highest ranked officer on the squadron. If officers got killed, or left the squadron when they completed a tour of duty, officers moved up in seniority. That was Bill. Someone had to be in charge of each raid at the operation centre at the airfield. As OC, Bill was also acting Squadron Leader of our flight, "B" Flight. Being cut down to one operation a week meant it would take longer to complete our tour of duty. It meant we would be on the squadron longer and we loved the squadron life.

The downside was that after this mission the crew had completed thirty operations of our tour of thirty-five. Five more and we would be screened. That was something to look forward to as well. With scrubbed operations thrown in, being restricted to one operation a week meant we might not be finished until Christmas. We believed it would be a shame for it to be over too quickly. Two years non operational and then six months operational in a squadron and would be the end of it – the end of your tour! Life on the squadron was good as long as you survived. That was the criterion. There was no strict discipline and you could do what you liked as long as you turned up for operations. We all liked the free and easy attitude, no saluting unless it was the Wing Commander or the Group Captain or the Air Commodore. The other ranks didn't salute us either. Life on an operational station was different to any other.

It was ten days until our next flight. We were not on leave but we hung around enjoying life on the squadron, going over to the officers' mess, playing billiards, playing ping-pong, playing darts, drinking and heading off in the car chasing girls. That was life on the squadron!

H2S

The oddly named H2S was a terrain scanning radar system developed for RAF Bomber Command during the Second World War. It was first used on a combat mission on the 30th of January 1943. By May 1944, when Basil Spiller began operations, H2S was installed in every heavy bomber, and navigators used it as an aid to obtain fixes for accurate tracking and locating targets at night, during bad weather and when targets were covered in ten-tenths cloud. Because H2S was a self contained system it was always available to the navigator, unlike GEE which the Germans jammed after aircraft crossed into mainland Europe.

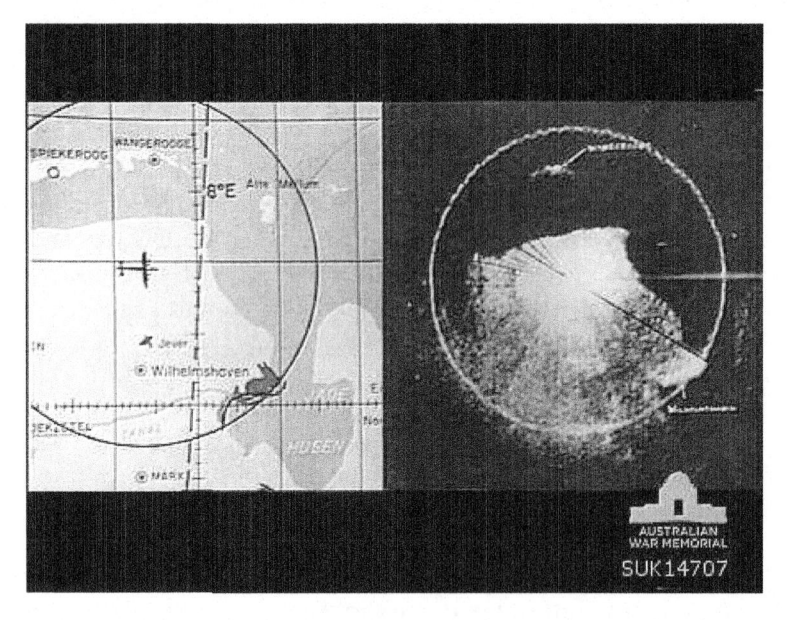

Map and H2S image of Wangerland, East Fresian Peninsula, 1944

H2S, sometimes referred to by aircrew as "Y", was based on the British discovery that pulses of microwave energy from the then highly secret CV64 Magnetron, when transmitted towards the ground, were immediately reflected back to the aircraft. The reflected beams were then "captured" and passed through a cathode ray tube onto a small oscilloscope screen where they appeared as a reasonably accurate image of the landscape below, with the aircraft at the centre.

Special rotating scanning aerials were installed under the fuselage of aircraft and enclosed within a radome which protected the antenna and hid it from view. The strongest echoes came from built up areas of cities and towns which appeared as brightly illuminated areas. Because water gave no echo and terrain reflected strong echoes, the shape of coastlines, estuaries, bays and larger rivers could also be identified on the screen. The photograph above is an excellent demonstration of this.

To the right is a map-like H2S image of Wangerland, on the north-eastern tip of the East Fresian Peninsula, taken during a raid on Wilhelmshaven in August 1944. When compared to the regional map on the left, it is clear that the shape of the coastline in the H2S image is a satisfactory representation of the same area on the map. Wilhelmshaven is seen as a patch of strong illumination, on the outer limit of the circle in the bottom right section. After turning a knob on his H2S set, the navigator has adjusted the perimeter circle to sit over Wilhelmshaven, and would know that his aircraft was approximately twenty kilometres from the city. The echo from the city would increase in intensity as the plane approached.

H2S was not a perfect system but it was a very reliable aid when operated by skilled navigators. It was most effective on coastal and inland targets which enabled clear distinction between topographical features.

Basil Spiller's log and chart of the Stuttgart operation on the 24th/25th of July 1944 demonstrates that he was a navigator of the highest order. With his air position indicator unserviceable, and flying to a complicated flight plan for eight and a half hours, over a landscape with few distinguishable features other than the bright glow from large towns and cities on his screen, he used H2S to stay on track and guide his plane unerringly to the target, bomb exactly on time and fly safely home.

Chapter 51: Cross-Country Test Flight

On the 22nd of October 1944 our crew tested a brand new Halifax, registration number MZ450. It was an improved version of the Halifax Mk 3. That plane only had a short stay at the squadron and was written off on the 6th of December after it had sustained a large amount of battle damage.

The test flight of a new aircraft entailed a cross-country to check all the navigation and radio equipment while the pilot and flight engineer had to satisfy themselves that it flew correctly. Don McLean's log says that this flight was a fuel "consumption test" for the engines. That may have been included as well. Bill decided that we would fly down to Somerset.

When he and Don took leave they were in the habit of visiting the folks at Minehead, on the Bristol Channel, where they were originally placed by the Lady Ryder scheme. They had become good friends with the family.

In the same way, Harry and Sandy continued to visit the farm at Currypool, near Bridgwater which was also in Somerset. The two towns were only about forty kilometres apart. As we had to go on the cross-country and plan our own route, why wouldn't we fly down there?

First, Bill put on a show for Harry and Sandy's hosts, the Jeans family. We did a bit of low flying over their farm at Currypool and then over the home of the Joneses, his and Don's hosts at Minehead. They all knew it was us because they came out and waved. They were quite excited about it. Bill had a good day. In his diary he wrote:

> "Decided to have a look over the country. Flew down to Reading across to Cheddar, my old stamping ground and country that I flew over at A.F.U. Shot up Currypool Farm where Sandy and Harry stay on leave. We dropped them a note. I then went down to Minehead and made a few runs at "Tries". It was good seeing Ed, Rene and Rosemary run out and wave to us all the time we were flying over the house. We could see them very distinctly as I went fairly low. Rosemary especially seemed excited. It will be something to tell them when I next see them. The visibility was filthy and this caused a restriction on manoeuvres that I could have done if the weather had been good. Still we all enjoyed our little jaunt."

Harry Brabin, our wireless operator, also had a good day. In his book he writes:

"We flew down to Somerset and over "Currypool", the farm where Sandy and I often spent our leave. And dropped a note by a parachute I made from a handkerchief. We dived down at low level several times, then we flew to the place where Don and Bill spent leave with the Jones family and did the same stunt. We could see quite clearly the family run out of the house. Even from the height we flew, we could see the excitement on their faces."

There were air observers all over the country and one of their jobs was to report low flying aircraft. They were like policemen. They would dob us in - no worries. They would not have liked pilots and crews having a bit of fun. I don't know how we got around it because low flying was strictly forbidden. Bill must have squared it off with somebody.

When we were doing a cross-country like that I was not stuck in my navigator's seat. I was looking out up in the nose with Don. You could stand fully upright in the nose of a Halifax which was one of the best things about the Halifax compared to the Lancaster.

While we were flying to Currypool and Minehead, N-Nan was one of ten planes being made ready for a night time gardening trip to the Kattegat off the east coast of Denmark. The next day, Don McLean noted in his diary: "Compton (the flak magnet) took our kite on a mining stooge".

When the planes returned, the Drem runway lights at Pocklington were unserviceable so they had to land at Full Sutton about ten minutes away. The next morning we drove over in the back of a truck and flew N-Nan back home.

Later that day, the 23rd of October 1944, we were briefed for a raid on Essen, another city in the heart of the Ruhr. We were out in the plane going though our pre-flight procedures and getting ready for takeoff. John and Bill were checking the engines when they discovered that N-Nan had a mag-drop. Two of our engines were unserviceable so our crew didn't go.

Don was sarcastic about it when he wrote in his diary:

"We were all set to take off when we got a mag. drop – it was the first time we had ever got one in Nan and we were a non-starter. A funny thing as it always happens when another crew takes our kite."

Don obviously thought that Compton, "the flak magnet", was to blame!

The Handley Page Halifax Mk. III's Engines

Pilot's starboard side view of the Bristol Hercules XVI engines of a Halifax bomber from No. 466 Squadron.

Chapter 52: Operation 28 - Essen

771 aircraft - 508 Lancasters, 251 Halifaxes, 12 Mosquitos - attacked Essen. 2 Halifaxes and 2 Lancasters lost. The bombing was aimed at skymarkers, because the target area was covered by cloud. The Bomber Command report states that the attack became scattered, but the local Essen report shows that more buildings were destroyed - 1,163 - than in the heavier night attack which had taken place 36 hours previously. The Krupps steelworks were particularly hard-hit by the two raids and there are references in the firm's archives to the 'almost complete breakdown of the electrical supply network' and to 'a complete paralysis'. Much of Essen's surviving industrial capacity was now dispersed and the city lost its role as one of Germany's most important centres of war production. *Total effort for the day:* 1,021 sorties, 4 aircraft (0.4 per cent) lost.
The Bomber Command War Diaries, 25 October, 1944

On the 24th of October the squadron was briefed for another raid on Essen but it was scrubbed because of bad weather. The next day, the 25th of October, the weather improved and we headed off. There were twenty-four aircraft from our squadron in a combined bomber force of 759 bombers and twelve PFF Mosquitoes. It was my twenty-eighth mission and the rest of the crew's thirty-first. Essen was the home of the Krupps Steelworks, a very important target. It was the biggest manufacturer of heavy weapons and other military equipment in Germany. This was the second time we had been to the Ruhr in daylight - the previous time was Duisburg. We took off at 0930 in really thick fog - a "filthy fog" according to Bill. The raid lasted five and a half hours and we carried ten thousand pounds of bombs.

The weather was fine until we approached the target. Don Mclean's diary says that he was able to "map read all the way until about four minutes off the target" when we entered ten-tenths cloud. The Pathfinder Force marked the target with Wanganui flares and we bombed above the clouds from an altitude of twenty thousand feet. Don thought it was an amazing sight to see all the "sticks of bombs dropping" and from his position in the nose "saw a few kites get direct hits over the target". A smaller bombing force, mainly Halifaxes, had earlier bombed an oil plant near Homberg about a hundred miles east of Essen. While we were on our bombing run they cut across our bombing stream at right angles on their way home. It could have been disastrous. As far as I can remember, other than that, it was a copybook attack. There was not much flak. I remember vividly the freezing conditions operating that day. It was bitterly cold and we had a job to get warm. Then when we arrived back at base, Bill had a hard job landing because the weather was really bad.

We had flown back above the clouds and it was particularly satisfying to see all the Halifaxes around us. It was a lovely clear day.

Bill mentions in his diary that we had a formation going in and a good formation coming home. The pilots' club would have formated at the drop of a hat, just like the RAAF Roulettes aerobatic team do today. That was the essence of good flying as far as they were concerned – being in a tighter formation than was strictly necessary, just to show how good they were and how they could keep it all together. That was the idea. Like a marching band. Bill thought it was "marvellous". He formated on the Squadron Leader as his "number three". He was so proud of his achievement that it was worth a big mention in his diary.

We heard that the Master Bomber's plane was shot down on this mission. Two Lancasters were shot down and one of them could have been a Pathfinder Force Lancaster. Bill and Don don't mention it in their diaries and it is not mentioned in the *Bomber Command War Diaries* either. Still it would not have been unusual for us not to know about something like that even though Bill had a senior position as Acting Flight Commander on the base. The Master Bomber was part of the Pathfinder Group and if Pathfinder planes were shot down, that was Pathfinder business. In the same way they wouldn't necessarily know who was getting shot down at the other squadrons. They wouldn't have a clue and probably wouldn't care. Everybody kept to themselves and knew their own business. We may have heard things that were being talked about but we would not know everything that was going on. We heard when Wing Commander Guy Gibson was killed as a Master Bomber though because he was renowned as the leader on the Dam Busters' raid. After the raid on Essen we were given eight days leave so we may have been a bit out of the loop.

Bill, Don and Sandy went to London on the 27th of October and I met up with them the next day at the Boomerang Club in Australia House. Bill left that night to visit his relatives in Glasgow. After a day or two I made my way to Mrs Reid's place in Rednal.

While we were on leave, the squadron bombed Cologne three times, then Dusseldorf and Bochum. The night raid on Dusseldorf on the 2nd/3rd of November was a bad one for us. On our return from leave we were told that the Dusseldorf raid was made in bright moonlight and there was a lot of night fighter activity including the new jet propelled types. We lost two aircraft. Halifax U-Uncle, LW141, was piloted by Flying Officer John Redmond. His plane crashed at Lammersdorf near the German/Belgian border, south-west of Cologne. They were probably shot down on their way home because after bombing in the Ruhr the flight plan would have taken them past Cologne. Nowhere was safe. All of the industrial centres and big cities had huge flak defences and there were night fighters everywhere. Six of the crew were killed and the navigator

Flying Officer Lemmon became a POW. There were three Australians in the crew. Pilot Officer Jack Binstead and Pilot Officer Henry Permain, the two air gunners, were from New South Wales. Don knew the airbomber. He was Pilot Officer Jacques Picken, from Annerley, near Brisbane, a Queenslander like Don.

The second aircraft, Halifax M-Mother MZ798, was piloted by Lieutenant James Begbie. We had previously had a bit to do with him. On the 3rd of October, while Don and I were buying our gear in London, Bill had taken him up for a familiarization flight. Bill had been quite impressed with him, and wrote in his diary that he had "coped particularly well". He was only in the squadron for about a month before he was killed. I can remember him well because South Africans were in a minority. There were only a handful of them on our squadron.

I also remember his name and the fact that he wore a different uniform. It was a brown army uniform because their airforce was a branch of the South African army as they weren't a separate entity. He was conspicuous as he moved around the base and we noticed him a lot. Don McLean remembered him well too. On the 17th of October, one f the officers, Ray Dodd had a "screening party", celebrating the completion his tour of duty. They headed off to the New Inn, a pub in the village where they no doubt had a fair bit to drink. Then they came back to the officers' mess and kicked on. In his diary Don wrote that "....Mess. Ronny Heiders and Jim Begbie (both S.A.A.F. pilots) put on a good turn on the floor with a couple of magazines". Poor fellow! James Begbie only lasted for a couple of weeks and may have done three or four missions – no more.

He and his crew had had some bad luck. On the way to Dusseldorf their Halifax was hit by machine gun fire from one of our own bombers, which must have mistaken it for a German night fighter. Then on the return journey, they were shot down by a night fighter at 1942 hours. The plane crashed at Leuven about twenty-five kilometres east of Brussels. They took off at 1612 hours and this attack came three and a half hours later, so it sounds right. Three crew members were killed. The other four were lucky because they parachuted into liberated territory in Belgium. Commonwealth War Graves Commission records show that James Begbie was from Johannesburg. He was twenty-six years old. It might be a bit of a coincidence but in the records there is another South African pilot, Lieutenant F. W. Begbie, who was killed on the 14th of June 1944. He was from 16 Squadron which flew reconnaissance Spitfires. He was twenty-six years old and came from Johannesburg too. I wonder if they were related!

The Krupp Steelworks, Essen

The Ruhr Valley city of Essen was a prime target for Allied bombing operations during the Second World War because it was one of Germany's major industrial and armaments manufacturing centres.

Essen was home to the powerful Krupp family which began steel production there in 1810. By the end of the nineteenth century Friedrich Krupp AG was one of Europe's largest companies. During the First World War it was a leading producer of armaments, its engineers designing and manufacturing the massive siege guns Big Bertha, Lange Max and the Paris Gun, which bombarded Paris with ninety-four kilogram shells from over 120 kilometres away.

Aerial reconnaissance photograph of the devastated Krupp steelworks at Essen, 25 October 1944.

In the 1930's Krupp enterprises was a massive conglomerate. The company had expanded to eighty-seven industrial sites in Germany and had controlling interests or huge investments in over 250 German companies. It had spread its interests overseas, had investments in over forty foreign companies and owned a hotel chain, banks, cement works and shipyards.

Krupp was Germany's biggest armaments manufacturer. As well the company built locomotives, trucks, warships and submarines. In 1936, the Friedrich Krupp Germaniawerft in Kiel built the legendary German battle cruiser Prinz Eugen and during the war built 131 U-boats for the Kriegsmarine. When war began, the Krupp business empire was a central part of the German war machine, its Essen factories producing a wide variety of armaments including Panzer tanks, naval guns, armour plating and munitions.

In 1944 the RAF alone launched twelve bombing raids against Essen, the principal target being the Krupp steelworks. Seven raids were made by small flights of Mosquito light bombers, but five were large scale Lancaster and Halifax heavy bomber raids, including the 1000 Bomber Raid on the night of the 23/24 October during which over 4,500 tons of high explosives were dropped. This and the raid on the 25 October, described by Basil Spiller in this chapter, devastated the steelworks and paralysed the city.

In the reconnaissance photograph above, taken soon after the 25 October operation, the destruction of the Krupp steelworks and its hinterland is clearly visible.

Limited and dispersed production continued around Essen after these raids. On the night of the 12th/13th December 1944, 540 heavy bombers again attacked the Krupp steelworks. This was the final heavy bomber raid on Essen.

Chapter 53: Operation 29 - Bochum

Bochum: 749 aircraft - 384 Halifaxes, 336 Lancasters, 29 Mosquitos - of Nos 1, 4, 6 and 8 Groups. 23 Halifaxes and 5 Lancasters were lost; German night fighters caused most of the casualties. No. 346 (Free French) Squadron, based at Elvington, lost 5 out of its 16 Halifaxes on the raid. This was a particularly successful attack based upon standard Pathfinder marking techniques. Severe damage was caused to the centre of Bochum. More than 4,000 buildings were destroyed or seriously damaged. Bochum's industrial areas were also severely damaged, particularly the important steelworks. This was the last major raid by Bomber Command on this target. *Total effort for the night:* 1,081 sorties, 31 aircraft (2.9 per cent) lost.

The Bomber Command War Diaries, 4 November 1944

On the 4th of November '44 we were briefed to attack Bochum which is north-east of Essen in the heart of the Ruhr Valley. This was the second time we had bombed Bochum. It was a major coal-producing centre with extensive coke, gas, synthetic oil, and iron and steel plants. The Bochumer Verein steelworks were there – one of the biggest in Germany. There were sixteen aircraft from my squadron. We took off at 1745 and the raid lasted four hours and thirty five minutes. It was a night raid which we started and finished before midnight. We carried one two thousand pound H.E. bomb plus eleven cans of incendiaries. Using incendiaries was the dominant thing in the industrial areas. They wanted to burn as much of the city as they could by just setting fire to it all. They weren't so much concentrating on blowing it up. They just wanted the city to burn. The industrial areas suffered a lot of damage too so it was a bit of both I suppose

Don's description of this raid in his dairy is very vivid:

"…. Our trip as far as The Hague was uneventful; although from a navigational viewpoint we were flat out as the met. winds were out quite a bit. We had quite a Guy Fawkes celebration as the target was the most brilliant I've ever seen. There must have been nearly 200 searchlights, red, green and yellow T.I.'s, V2's taking off on their way to England, jet-propelled fighters, scarecrows and acres and acres of incendiaries burning all over the target area. It was a scene that defies description …."

I remember the mission well. It was one of those times when I turned my light off and parted the blackout curtains. What a sight I beheld! The defences of the Ruhr were in full swing. Bags of searchlights, fighter flares, exploding flak, exploding photo flares. Bill said we were "coned" twice. This meant that a searchlight found us and it was immediately joined by other searchlights. The Germans co-ordinated their anti-aircraft guns and cones very effectively. Once a cone had locked onto you, the gunners locked onto you too and set about trying to destroy you. If the cone had you for twenty seconds you were in real trouble. Luckily for us the flak wasn't predicted at us and for some reason the searchlights moved away.

Photo flares and photographs

All our heavy bombers carried a photo flare, not to be confused with the "fighter flares" the Germans fired from planes high up above us, to drift down on parachutes and light up the night sky so their gunners, searchlights and night fighters could see us. The photo flare was carried in a chute in the bomb bay and was dropped with the bombs. Its job was to light up the target at night so our onboard camera could take line overlap photographs of it. When we returned to base, the photography section developed the prints and they could tell whether we had successfully bombed the target or not. Line overlap photos were a series of twenty-four photographs. When they printed them off they were about ten inches square. The last exposure of the target area would in theory be the best one because it was timed to be taken when the photo flare was at its maximum brightness and at the exact time the bombs landed. Photo flares were six or seven hundred million candle power so they were very bright. Every aircraft dropped one so that added to the spectacle. With photo flares mixed up with searchlights and fighter flares and flak bursts and bombs exploding and fires on the ground it was an awesome spectacle. I looked at it all through the bombing run, standing behind Don while he was lying on the floor over his bombsight. With just the full perspex nose in front of me I had a marvellous view.

In his diary Bill describes how a lot of "window" was lit up by the searchlights and floated towards us when we were over the target. It looked like winking lights falling all around us. The target was clear and the bombing was accurate and concentrated. Fires could be seen from eighty miles away. Two of our planes had hang-ups and had to jettison them later. Bomber Command didn't bomb Bochum again after this raid. They didn't have to. The city was wrecked and the steelworks were destroyed.

On the way out we saw a German jet plane. It was probably a Messerschmitt Me262. In his diary Bill wrote:

> "We saw a jet-propelled fighter and did about four corkscrews away from attacking aircraft - saw a rocket scare which is still an unknown quantity. It flashed from ground

level up to 12,000 ft in about 3 or 4 seconds and eventually hit the deck with a big explosion after careering through the sky at a phenomenal speed...."

When Bill wrote that we did four corkscrews away from attacking aircraft, it meant we had at least four attacks and he had to take immediate evasive action each time. I couldn't prepare for it. We dived and Bill rolled the plane from side to side. G forces grabbed me and held me until it was all over then I would reorganise my desk and get back to work. Then it all happened again. It was a torrid night in terms of the barrage of flak that was up and the night fighters that were out and about. We were all hanging on like grim death. Even Bill, who was always in control, was worried about what he saw in front of us as we headed into the Ruhr. He thought that "on the approach to the target it seemed almost impossible to expect to go through the searchlights and flak and survive."

The flight plan home was over Wuppertal, Dusseldorf and Cologne. We ran into accurate flak all the way out of Germany. It was impossible to avoid. The whole area was heavily defended so there was no other way for the flight to be organized. There was no easy way in or out.

When we were flying back home we saw a doodlebug heading for Brussels. The Germans were now firing on Brussels as well as the south of England. Because it was flying at night time we could see a trail of jet flames coming out the back of the engine. Bill says that in the distance he "saw the searchlights and flak attempt to shoot it down and the explosion after it landed".

Heading home Bill put George the automatic pilot on. Every plane was equipped with automatic pilot but I don't know whether Bill used it very often or not.

Losses on this raid were shocking. Twenty-three Halifaxes and five Lancasters were shot down, mainly by German night fighters. That's a lot of planes and a lot of men. Halifaxes were in the thick of the fighting just as much as the Lancasters were. Five of the Halifaxes came from No. 346 Squadron at Elvington, one of our satellite dromes.

RAF Elvington

RAF Elvington was converted to a Free French station in mid 1944. All of the crews were French. Two squadrons, No. 346 and No. 347 were based there at the same time. They were the only squadrons that the Free French flew in Bomber Command. I don't know how many crews each of these squadrons had but they were both smaller than 102 Squadron. The largest operational flight from No. 346 Squadron was eighteen aircraft and from No. 347 Squadron it was seventeen. Pocklington had one squadron and we had twenty-six planes. On this raid No. 346 Squadron sent sixteen crews to Bochum and five of them didn't come back. That was more than a thirty percent loss in just one night!

Our squadron lost one aircraft. Flying Officer Anthony Cameron's Halifax, Q-Queenie MZ772, was shot down at Laurensberg which is about 130 kilometres south of Bochum near the Germany/Belgium border so they were probably making their way home. Bill knew him. In his diary Bill says that "he was an Aussie with an excellent crew". The pilot, navigator, bomb aimer and wireless operator were all Flying Officers.

Allan Crabbe

After this raid, when we returned to base, some bod interviewed us all and said he was sending the story back to Australia, and true to his word some articles appeared in the newspapers back home a couple of days later. Sandy, Don and I are mentioned in one, and three South Australians who took part in the raid, Bill, Sandy and a pilot named Allan Crabb are in another.

Allan Crabb was on our squadron for most of the time we were there. He arrived after us and he was a member of the Australian contingent right up until the war ended. He played in the rugby match against the Free French at Elvington and he was goalie for the station soccer team. Back home in Australia he was a cricketer and a very good Australian Rules player. He was certainly versatile. At this time Allan was near the end of his Tour of Duty like us. On the 21st of November, a few days after we finished our tour Bill wrote in his diary: "Allan Crabb back from ops OK. Very Good show." For some reason they must have been worried about him. Perhaps his plane was late getting back. Allan completed his tour about a fortnight after us. We met up with him again in January '45 when we all headed back to the squadron at roughly the same time.

Bob Selth once told me a story about the day Allan Crabb arrived at 102 Squadron. (I have mentioned Bob before when he survived being shot down over the English Channel after the Les Hauts-Buissons raid in July 1944.) The names of the incoming crews were posted on the squadron notice-board. One day Bob was hanging around with his mate, Chick Lathlean, and they walked down to see if they knew any of the new arrivals on the list. Bob immediately recognised Allan Crabb's name. They used to play Australian Rules football against one another in the Under 19's in Adelaide. Apparently, one day Bob "dropped" Allan on the Glenelg oval. Bob reckoned that little blokes like him could get in and under a big bloke and, if you knew what to do, you could do a lot of damage if you hit them right. So that's what he did and Allan Crabb was carried off on a stretcher. A couple of years later, they were going to be on the same squadron in England! Bob decided to shoot through. Later that day, Chick and Bob were playing tennis when they saw Allan Crabb wandering down towards the court with a tennis racquet under his arm.

"Would you mind if I had a game?" he asked.

They stopped playing but when Bob Selth turned around Allan Crabb realised who it was and said, "But not with you. You dirty little bastard!" It's a good story.

Several years after the war finished I met up with Allan when he represented South Australia in the Australian Rules Football carnival that was held in Brisbane in the late 1940's. I visited him at the Gresham Hotel which was pulled down in the mid 1970's. One feature of the carnival was that it rained every day and the exhibition ground was a mud bath. Allan married one of the WAAF officers who was stationed at Pocklington. They came to live in Australia after the war.

The Bochum Raid – Newspaper Articles

3000 –Ton Raid On Bochum

London, November 6. - Australian Air Force Halifax crews participating in the Bomber Command 3000-ton raid on Bochum reported very concentrated bombing, heavy flak, and that numerous night fighters were encountered.

Pilot Officer A. J. Concannon, rear gunner, from Lucindale, South Australia, saw a jet-propelled fighter, which he described as "not seeming much faster than any other modern fighter."

Among the Australians participating were Pilot Officer D. B. McLean, bombardier, from Bowen, Queensland, and Pilot Officer B. G. Spiller, navigator, from Brisbane.

The Northern Miner **(Charters Towers, Queensland). Wednesday 8 November 1944**

Air Assault Kept Up

Great Day. Fleet Out Again, AAP, LONDON, November 6.

Following a concentrated 24-hour air offensive against Germany, during which over 5.000 Allied planes struck shattering blows at the enemy's war industries and communications, RAF Mosquitos last night launched a double attack against Stuttgart.

The great blitz was continued today, when over 1,100 US heavy bombers from Britain, escorted by more than 700 fighters, swept over Germany to attack oil plants near Hamburg and Harburg, factories in the Ruhr Valley, and other objectives in the Ruhr.

Stuttgart is one of the Reich's chief engineering centres and is an important communications city. The Mosquitos left large fires burning. All returned safely.

First reports on the attack on Solingen yesterday afternoon indicate that the bombing was well concentrated, says the Air Ministry. The escorting Spitfires and Mustangs flew supporting sweeps. One bomber is missing.

The attack by Lancasters and Halifaxes on Bochum on Saturday night was the heaviest attack yet launched against the city. Well over 3,000 tons of high-explosive and incendiary bombs were dropped. Bochum is one of the main centres of the steel industry in the Ruhr, and an important railway town.

The weather was clear, and when the smoke from the great circle of fires threatened to hide the target, a high wind quickly blew it away. The crews say that there were many explosions, from which black smoke rose to a height of several thousand feet. Experienced crews considered that the flak was as heavy and the searchlights as active as at any time during last year's battle of the Ruhr.

S.A. Men In Raid

Australian crews of the Halifaxes which took part in the raid on Bochum last night reported very concentrated bombing despite heavy flak and numerous night fighters.

PO A.J. Concannon, rear-gunner, of Lucindale (SA) saw a jet propelled fighter, which, he said, did not seem much faster than any other modern fighter.

Other South Australians who were over Bochum were Flt-Lt. W.P. Rabbitt, pilot, of Crystal Brook and Flt-Lt. A.J. Crabb, pilot of Adelaide.

Escorted Fortresses and Liberators bombed targets in Vienna through cloud yesterday, states a correspondent in Rome. Medium bombers hammered the Brenner Pass line and the railroad to Yugoslavia.

The Adelaide Advertiser **(South Australia). Tuesday 7 November 1944**

Newspaper Articles - Allan Crabb

Pilot Scores In Night Cricket
By Ray Barber

Allan Crabb, who cannot play regularly because of his duties as an air pilot, made 200 for Brighton in this week's RSL Electric Light Cricket Association matches.

Crabb is also a State and Glenelg footballer. Jim Edwards, State lacrosse player, hit 100.

The Mail **(Adelaide, South Australia). Saturday 4 December 1948**

Ron Phillips Best Again

Adelaide, Mon. - For the second year in succession Ron Phillips, half-forward in North Adelaide and South Australian National Football League teams, has been awarded the Magarey Medal as the fairest and most brilliant player in this season's club competition.

Allan Crabb, captain of Glenelg club and interstate ruckman, tied with Phillips in the final voting aggregate but Phillips received the greater number of first preference votes.

A sudden illness shortly after play began in the last match of the final round on Saturday undoubtedly cost Crabb the medal and two newspaper trophies.

He had opened brilliantly but had to leave the field for hospital.

The Mercury **(Hobart, Tasmania). Tuesday 6 September 1949**

Chapter 54: Operation 30 - Kattegat

41 Mosquitos to the Kamen oil refinery, 12 to Osnabrück, 9 to Wiesbaden, 6 to Gotha and 3 to Erfurt, 36 RCM sorties, 59 Mosquito patrols. 26 Lancasters and 24 Halifaxes minelaying off Oslo, in the Kattegat and in the River Elbe. No aircraft lost.
The Bomber Command War Diaries, 11 November, 1944

In between the Bochum raid on the 4th and our next one there had been little to do. We weren't on the raid when the squadron attacked Gelsenkirchen in the Ruhr Valley on the 6th, but we were briefed to lay mines in Oslo Fiord on the 8th and 10th but both missions were scrubbed.

My thirtieth mission was a gardening trip on the 11th of November. Twelve crews from 102 Squadron were briefed to lay mines in the Kattegat Strait. We carried four 2,000 pound mines - eight thousand pounds in all. We took off at 1615 in the evening and the trip lasted five hours and twenty-five minutes. We felt no more vulnerable laying mines in a small flight than we did on a big bombing operation. When planes were laying mines they were attacked and shot down just the same.

This was a very difficult trip. Things went wrong from the start. There was an electrical storm with hail sleet and snow and 'George', the auto pilot, was unserviceable so Bill had to fly on instruments for most of the way. We stuck to track really well but the winds changed and we had to make up time. The intelligence bods at briefing were concerned that the Germans would track our H2S because at briefing we were told not to turn it on until we reached 10°E, which runs through eastern Denmark. We were close to the target by then. On arriving at the Kattegat we turned on the H2S and discovered to out horror that it had frozen up and was unserviceable. Minelaying was done on a timed run at a certain bearing and distance from a prominent point on the H2S screen. Without H2S we were flying blind. We went down to the dropping zone and attempted a visual run but the cloud was right down to the sea, so we could not complete the operation. Instead we had to carry our mines back home because they were top secret magnetic mines and we were instructed that on no account were we to jettison them. Carrying mines or bombs back was dangerous enough in fine weather. In bad weather it was worse still. In the event of a crash… WOOSH! You'd all go up!

Another one of the crews from our squadron had to take their mines back as well. The other ten planes laid their mines successfully although one mine exploded when it hit the water. It must have hit something solid. It could have been anything - a boat, some debris or another mine.

When we got back to Pocklington, Bill did a very ropey landing and we were all packing it! A real ropey landing with mines on board! I can laugh now but I wasn't laughing then! I don't blame him. We were all scared. This was another near miss. We had a lot of them. But then again all of the crews that survived the war did. Didn't they?

The centre of the bombing stream

I always tried to position our plane right in the centre of the bombing stream. We were there because if I was navigating correctly we were right on track and I was usually able to put our plane dead on track. It was probably the safest place to be. I have heard it said that crews tried to get there for safety. We were there by virtue of my navigating - not taking shelter in the safest position. How would you know where you were in the stream at night time? The stream could be ten miles wide. The argument doesn't weigh up. Anyway nowhere was really safe. The only way navigators knew where they were at night time was when they checked their navigation chart and looked at the fixes that they had obtained.

Extra passengers

On the day after the Kattegat mission, N-Nan had its H2S and autopilot repaired so on the 13th we did a short fifty-five minute flight to test it out. We had three extra passengers. We smuggled Trevor, our NCO sergeant in charge of our ground crew, and a friend of Bill's onto the plane. Bill's friend was a pilot who flew either Lancasters or Mosquitos. He was visiting and we took him up to show him how the Halifax performed. We also smuggled a young WAAF on board. She really enjoyed herself. Our favourite WAAF's were frequent passengers. They liked going up. They must have because they were prepared to don parachute harness and carry a parachute before they got into the aircraft. We had to get parachutes and other gear for them. It was a bit of a logistical operation!

The Kattegat and Skagerrak Straits

The Kattegat Strait, the target of Basil Spiller's mine laying operation described in this chapter, is one of two large sea areas separating the North Sea from the Baltic Sea.

The Kattegat is bounded by the Skagerrak Strait to the north, the Jutland Peninsula to the west and Denmark's Kattegut Strait islands to the south. Denmark's capital city, Copenhagen, is situated on two of these islands, Zealand and Amager. To the east are the Swedish provinces of Västergötland, Scania, Halland and Bohuslän.

The Skagerrak is bounded by Norway to the north, Sweden to the east, the Kattegut Strait and the northern coast of Jutland to the south. To the west is the

North Sea and beyond that the Atlantic Ocean. In both the First and Second World Wars control of the Kattegat and Skagerrak was of immense strategic importance to both Germany and Britain.

Surrounded by Denmark, Sweden and Norway, the Kattegut and Skagerrak Straits, linking the North Sea and the Baltic Sea.

From the 31st May until the 1st June 1916, the largest naval battle of the First World War, the Battle of Jutland, was fought in the Skagerrak. This was the only battle of the 1914-18 war in which the battleships of Britain's Grand Fleet and Germany's High Seas Fleet met in action.

In the Second World War, German control of the Skagerrak and Kattegat Straits was critical to its access to the North Sea, and denied Britain a strategic location from which to launch attacks on Germany and open supply lines into the Soviet Union.

After leaving the Baltic Sea, German warships and U-boats had to move through the choke point of the Kattegat before heading through the Skagerrak and out into the open waters of the North Sea. Returning German warships had to do this in reverse, running the gauntlet of the Kattegat, before reaching the relatively safe harbours of their home ports. The longer German ships were kept at sea the more dangerous it became for them because they would inevitably become low on fuel, provisions and munitions and the likelihood of being detected would increase.

On the 8th April 1940, Operation Weserübung, the German campaign to invade Denmark and Norway and seize control of the Skagerrak and Kattegat began. With control of these waters ensured, Germany's fleet of mighty battleships and lethal U-boat packs were then able to roam the Atlantic Ocean harassing the Atlantic convoys sailing from North America to Britain, and disrupting to Allied supply lines.

In order to frustrate and even cripple Germany's access to and from the North Sea, more than fifty thousand mines were laid by the Royal Navy and the RAF during the Second World War.

Remnant mines are still being found today. In June 2009, the Swedish navy believed it had found mines belonging to Germany's Wartburg mine barrier. On the 11th February 2010, two intact mines were found in the Kattegat Strait by mine clearing boats. It is estimated that over three thousand potentially dangerous mines still remain in the northern waters of the strait.

Chapter 55: Operation 31 - Jülich

Bomber Command was asked to bomb 3 towns near the German lines which were about to be attacked by the American First and Ninth Armies in the area between Aachen and the Rhine. 1,188 Bomber Command aircraft attacked Düren, Jülich and Heinsburg in order to cut communications behind the German lines. Düren was attacked by 485 Lancasters and 13 Mosquitos of Nos 1, 5 and 8 Groups, Jülich by 413 Halifaxes, 78 Lancasters and 17 Mosquitos of Nos 4, 6 and 8 Groups and Heinsberg by 182 Lancasters of No. 3 Group. 3 Lancasters were lost on the Düren raid and 1 Lancaster on the Heinsberg raid.
The Bomber Command War Diaries, 16 November, 1944

The second last mission of our Tour of Duty, was on the 16th of November 1944 to Jülich. We had been briefed to go to Gelsenkirchen on the 15th but it was scrubbed just before midnight so the next day we were sent to Jülich instead. The town is on the Roer River, south-west of the Ruhr Valley about twenty kilometres inside Germany from the Netherlands border.

We attacked the town because we were in support of the American army which was trying to break through the German defences at Jülich which was being heavily defended by the German army. Bomber Command was attacking three towns close to one another – Heinsburg, Düren and Jülich. They were roughly in a north/south line. Düren is about ten miles south of Jülich, and Heinsberg is about fifteen miles north - not a long way.

The Americans were moving into Germany through the north-east of Belgium and had come to the three towns. They were in very strategic positions. Cologne and Dusseldorf, two of Germany's biggest cities, were only about forty kilometres away. Beyond Dusseldorf was the Ruhr Valley the heart of Germany's industrial power. That's why Jülich was a critical target.

This was a daytime operation with our usual daytime fighter escort. We took off at 1230 in the afternoon. Briefing went for a long time because we were going to be bombing close to the American forces and they didn't want any mistakes. It was a long trip that took six hours and thirty minutes. We carried two thousand pounds of heavy explosives plus eleven cans of incendiaries each of which weighed about 750 pounds, which gave us an all up bomb weight of about 10,500 pounds

In the thick of things, Bill and Don saw a Halifax from Full Sutton go down and its crew bail out. There is no mention of a Halifax being lost on this raid in the *Bomber Command War Diaries* which is inaccurate. The 77 Squadron record shows that on the 16th of November, Halifax J-Jig MZ750, was lost on the Jülich raid. It crashed in Allied occupied territory after all its crew bailed out just as Bill and Don had said. The pilot was Flying Officer Hilton Beadle, DFC. He and three of his crew evaded capture but the other five became POWs. Bill and Don were obviously close enough to see the crew bail out and close enough to read the identification letters on the plane. Three Lancasters were shot down on the Düren raid and one on the Heinsberg raid. Bill saw another plane go down so it would probably have been one of the these Lancasters.

The attack on Jülich was a great success. We took a really good photograph on our bombing run that showed our bombs exploding in the centre of the town – our aiming point. Our previous photographs were black and white but on this mission we started using colour film.

In his diary, Bill mentions that Ray Hogg finished his tour of duty on this mission. Ray Hogg was a pilot of another crew but I didn't know him. We had been the most experienced crew on the squadron for quite a while but his crew had caught up to us and were just finishing their tour before us. By this time we had only one more to go anyway.

After the mission, Bill made the comment in his diary that "Francis was shot up but I thought the defences fairly moderate".

This is interesting because all rests on your point of view. I wonder if Flying Officer Francis thought the flak was moderate when he got "shot up"! His Halifax was Q-Queenie NA165. One of the gunners was wounded but the rest were uninjured. Francis was able to land the plane at RAF Woodbridge, the "crash" aerodrome, in Suffolk, just inside the coast, about 120 miles south of Pocklington. With a stricken plane he would have been heading for it even before he crossed the Channel. The plane was repaired because it was not struck off charge until January 1947. In his diary, Bill also mentions that on this flight Wing Commander Wilson led the attack, with him at Number 2 position and Allan Crabb at Number 3. The pilot's club was showing off to see how close they could get to their leader.

The Bombing of Jülich, 16th November 1944

Jülich, the subject of this chapter, was a key target for several reasons. It is situated on the Roer River, which in late 1944 was an important natural barrier to the US Ninth Army's progress. The Americans believed that German engineers were preparing to blow up large dams on the river to sweep away the invading army should it attempt to cross.

On the 16th of November 1944, over eleven hundred RAF heavy bombers participated in three raids, attacking the towns of Düren, Jülich and Heinsburg in the Aachen district, where the German army had halted the American army's advance into Germany. The USAAF targeted the same area with a force of over twelve hundred heavy bombers.

The bombing raids caused hundreds of civilian casualties and the three towns were decimated. It is estimated that ninety-seven percent of Jülich was destroyed in this attack. The massive devastation wrought on the town can be clearly seen in the accompanying photograph. As destructive as the November 16th 1944 air-raids were, the German army held the city until the 23rd of February, 1945.

Jülich in ruins after bombing raids on the 16th of November 1944.

Chapter 56: Operation 32 - Münster

479 aircraft - 367 Halifaxes, 94 Lancasters, 18 Mosquitos - of Nos 4, 6 and 8 Groups to Münster. 1 Halifax crashed in Holland. The raid was not concentrated and bombs fell in all parts of Münster. 3 Halifaxes flew RCM sorties.
The Bomber Command War Diaries, 16 November, 1944

My thirty-second mission was the thirty-fifth for Bill, Don, Harry, John and Sandy. It was the last mission of our first tour for all of us except Mick Starmer our mid-upper gunner who had to keep flying with other crews to complete his tour.

On the 18th of November, 1944 we were briefed to bomb Münster again. Eighteen crews left from 102 Squadron but one had to return early when its port outer engine caught fire. The last time we had been to Münster all sorts of things happened - we were bombed and showered with incendiaries from our own planes above us and we had to consign L-Love to the scrapheap when we got back. Don described that raid as "10/10's flak!" With a certain amount of trepidation we set out on a daylight mission to Münster again. We took off at 1300 hours and the trip took exactly five hours. We carried eight thousand pounds of high explosives – no incendiaries. In his diary Don wrote:

> "We didn't get airborne until we had almost crossed the York Road and Bill flew tight formation all the way with the rest of the boys packed in. It was pretty quiet at the target as there was 10/10. (cloud) and P.F.F. were laying sky-markers all over the place. We had a quiet trip back although it was a bit 'dicey' getting in to base. Our last op. of our first tour over – what a thrill!"

There was moderate amount of flak but the target was unusually quiet. When we got there we had no trouble bombing and getting an aiming point. Altogether it was a most successful operation.

Bad weather made flying conditions difficult. We were well into a bitter winter. It was really bad weather. We had a lot of icing on our wings. It was so bad on our return that in the distance Bill could see RAF Melbourne airfield, the home of No. 10 Squadron, and they had FIDO going. FIDO was a landing device used in filthy weather. It consisted of pots filled with oil and placed at regular intervals on both sides of the runway. They were lit individually and the heat from the burning oil dispersed the fog somewhat and assisted the planes to land. Not every aerodrome was equipped with FIDO and I was surprised that Melbourne had it.

When we got back to base there was a welcoming committee waiting for us. I remember that Trevor and the ground crew were there to congratulate us. When you come to think about it, we were the first crew that had finished a tour of duty on N-Nan for quite some time, so they would have been pleased with themselves too. They were N-Nan's maintenance crew and they didn't work on any other plane. She was their plane through the whole campaign - all of the replacement N-Nan's that superseded the older models. Every aircraft had its own maintenance crew because then they were responsible for everything that went on in the plane. Trevor as the sergeant in charge would be ultimately responsible for everything connected to N-Nan's maintenance. They had seen us through thick and thin. We became good mates as we all went here and there about our business at our dispersal site on the 'drome. I was told that they were very upset when they saw the state of N-Nan the day I was wounded because there was blood everywhere. It was quite obvious that someone had copped it pretty badly. As well as that, the plane had holes all over it, and the front of it, the perspex, had been blown out! They would have had to clean N-Nan out and fix her with an aircraft frame rigger.

Later we celebrated in the officers' mess. We got back at 1800 hours and it was getting dark by then. First we had to go to our debriefing. By the time we had a meal and got debriefed it would be at least two hours later. After dinner we adjourned to the mess and had a few drinks and celebrations. Bill was very happy and in his diary wrote:

> "Trev and the boys were all waiting for us and gave us a great welcome back to dispersal. Everyone in the squadron have been marvellous to us and we have received dozens of congratulations. We were all invited to have drinks in the mess. The Group Captain (Russell) stood me a drink and complimented me on the job the crew have put up. Air Commodore Walker and the Wing Commander were both full of congratulations so we all feel very happy tonight. Good show. Very tired."

In his book, Harry Brabin mentions that we did a lot of celebrating but there was not much going on for him to enjoy alone in the sergeants' mess. I can't remember what happened there. Harry was the only member of the Australian contingent in our crew that didn't have a commission. He was a bit disappointed but he would not have been allowed in the officers' mess with us. A strict "RAF type" may have embarrassed him and us and asked him to leave and we couldn't have done anything about it. It would never happen though because we knew that going into other messes was banned. We wouldn't have been able to go into the sergeants' mess with him either. That's just the way it was. It was not a good situation at a time like that but everyone was tired anyway because it was a long flight. We had a celebratory dinner, two nights later at the local pub in Pocklington and we invited all the ground crew to be in attendance with us. So in the end, all of us were able to have a good time and celebrate our achievement together.

I had finished a tour of duty and I was just twenty-one!

Rear Gunner

A rear-gunner, isolated and alert scanning the night sky in Dennis Adams' painting "The Tail Gunner" (1946) from the Australian War Memorial collection, Canberra.

Part 5

Between Tours

An aerial photograph taken during the night raid on Hamburg on the 24th/25th July 1943 while flying eastwards over the city. At the top, sticks of incendiaries are burning in the Altona districts and lower left, a photoflash bomb glows brilliantly over the Binnen Alster and the Aussen Alster lakes.

Chapter 57: Indefinite Leave

After we finished our first tour we had a celebration at the local pub and Bill arranged our clearances from the squadron. We were then posted on what they called "indefinite leave", so there was no fixed time for us to report back to the squadron.

Bombing operations were effectively over for us unless we chose to start a second tour. This was a big thing because it obviously meant that we did not have to be putting our lives on the line in bombing missions over Germany any more. A lot of aircrew decided to volunteer for a second tour but most didn't. They were still in the RAF but generally became instructors in their specialised areas. That is what being screened was all about.

After we all took some leave, Sandy was screened as a rear gunner instructor and Don became a bomb aimer instructor but Harry, John, Bill and I elected to do a second tour.

Currypool

Bill, Don, Harry, John, Sandy and I left 102 Squadron on the 23rd of November, four days after the Münster raid. Don, Sandy and Bill decided to go to Ireland. They headed for Leeds first, then took a train to Stranraer and went across the Irish Sea in an "old tub". They spent ten days in Belfast and Dublin. I could have gone too but Harry had asked me, in Sandy's absence, to accompany him to the Jeans' dairy farm down at Currypool. He was smitten with their daughter, Ann. She was a very attractive young lady and she was sweet on Harry too. I agreed and we duly left the station and headed off.

Jeans' farm was owned by old Mr and Mrs Jeans. It had a six hundred year old brick and stone farmhouse that accommodated plenty of people. The farm was managed by their youngest son, Medford.

We settled into the daily routine of the farm, helping to muck out the cow bales in the morning, clean them up and sluice them out. Because it was winter time the cows were under shelter twenty-four hours a day. They slept where they were milked in cow bales, and the bales had to be cleaned out every morning and fresh straw laid. The feces and urine soaked straw was put into a stone farm building and distributed once a year at "Doong spreading time" as the locals referred to it. That was the way they fertilized their fields.

I can remember that the midday meal was the main meal of the day. The Jeans had apple trees growing on their farm. The apples were in cool storage all the time. Every day at midday we would have apple dumplings with custard for dessert. We ate very well because although it was primarily a dairy farm they also had pigs and sheep. Medford was permitted to kill stock every now and then. We ate bacon and lamb, eggs and vegetables.

Medford's elder brothers had farms in the surrounding districts. They used to brew their own cider. Every now and then we would visit them at night time after the evening meal and they would ply us with their homemade cider. It was pretty potent stuff. I can remember Harry and I riding back to Currypool on a tandem bike and falling off all the time. We were laughing and carrying on.

On the 8th Of December 1944, during our stay at Bridgewater, Harry and I went down to Minehead to visit Don and Bill. They had returned from Ireland on the 4th of December and made their way down to Minehead on the 7th. We spent the day with them. We talked about their experiences in Ireland. We were not making plans about another tour and what we were going to do then. There was no mention of it. It was good to catch up. That afternoon we all went out hunting for pigeons and pheasants. Harry and I didn't shoot anything but Bill and Don each shot a couple of pheasants.

Rednal

I stayed at Currypool for about a month until I felt I was outstaying my welcome. I decided that it was time to move on so I left Harry there and went to Rednal. Harry spent Christmas at Currypool. He and Anne were sweethearts but Mrs Jeans frowned on their relationship and it didn't blossom. It wasn't through want of trying on Harry's part. It was mutual. Anne was besotted with Harry too. I don't know whether they used to sneak off together or not. It may never have blossomed beyond forlorn looks at one another but I think it went further than that. So I spent the Christmas at Rednal and experienced a typical English Christmas with Mrs Reid and her son, Adrian, and some other airforce blokes. I can remember we had an enormous roast goose for Christmas dinner. All the festivities continued far into the night.

While I was there I played golf and went out to the pubs and dances. I used to take out a local girl that I met at a dance. I can't remember her name. She took me home to meet her parents, which was dangerous. I didn't want to get entangled with a girl because I knew Betty was waiting for me back in Australia.

I probably headed back to base to back out of the relationship because that's where I ended up.

Incendiary Bombs

13 September 1942. Armourers load a mixed bomb load of three 1,000-lb MC bombs and small bomb containers (SBCs) filled with 30-lb incendiary bombs, loaded into the bomb-bay and wing cells of a Handley-Page Halifax Mark II of No. 405 Squadron RCAF at Pocklington, Yorkshire. By 1944 heavy bombers carried the 4-lb incendiary packed in 1,000 pound containers. The 30-lb incendiary bomb was considered obsolete after the introduction of the 4-lb incendiary, which would scatter over a larger area and light more fires.

Chapter 58: 102 Squadron, November '44 – March '45

Our second Tour of Duty effectively started on the 25th of March 1945 with a raid to Osnabrück so I had a four month break between operations.

While we were away, the bombing war took on a different shape from what it was when we went on our first operation to Orlean on the 22nd of May 1944. There were fierce battles being waged on the ground in France, Belgium and the Netherlands by the British, Canadian and American armies and by mid December they had closed in on the German border from all sides and pushed the German army back into Germany.

The squadron records show some very interesting things about this time. Firstly they show that except for gardening trips mainly to Oslo Fiord and the Kattegat virtually one hundred percent of the bombing was now inside Germany.

Bombing operations were still dangerous but were conducted without the risk of being shot down in flak barrages over occupied France and Belgium, and German night fighter airfields that had been built in occupied countries had either been abandoned or destroyed. The Luftwaffe was still capable of launching attacks at incoming raids but it had been forced to pull back what was left of its night fighter force deep into Germany.

Secondly this was a real bad winter and I can remember the snow ploughs clearing the runways during these winter months. A lot of operations had to be cancelled and even when operations got under way and the bombing force reached the target they usually had to bomb through ten-tenths cloud on Wanganui sky markers. Then while the force was away the weather would sometimes turn foul and aircraft often had to be diverted from home base to other airfields.

Halifaxes from 102 Squadron were bombed up for seventy nine operations, while I was between Tours, and twenty-eight of them were cancelled. Two more were curtailed which meant that only some of the aircraft were able to take off and join the force, and our planes were diverted to other airfields six times. On at least eighteen missions the squadron had to bomb through ten-tenths cloud on sky markers or H2S.

On the 17th of February, the squadron was briefed to attack Wesel, a German town about thirty kilometres from the Dutch border. It had bridges that crossed the Rhine so the Germans were defending it and the Allies wanted to capture it. The weather was so bad that the Master Bomber brought the force down to ten thousand feet and when they still couldn't see anything he abandoned the mission. Only eight Halifaxes had managed to bomb out of a force of 247 Halifaxes and twenty-seven

Lancasters, all of which had to return home with their bombs. To make matters worse the weather was so filthy that a lot of them had to be diverted to other airfields around England. This was very dangerous. Imagine all those bombers, fully loaded, trying to land at strange airfields in terrible weather. Three Halifaxes crashed in England trying to land but they were not from our squadron.

A third thing that I noticed in the squadron records during this time was that a lot of the targets were now smaller ones. The big cities were in ruins and the railways and the big industrial centres of Germany had been destroyed. The squadron still went into the Ruhr, to places like Sterkrade, Dortmund, Duisburg and Essen but by February and March we were bombing towns like Soest, Bingen, Dulmen, Goch, Bohlen and Hemmingstedt. The squadron was still attacking specific targets like synthetic oil plants and marshalling yards and they still had orders like "block rail routes, destroy enemy troops and armour" but now often the order from above was for the "complete destruction of built up area, rail facilities and industry."

The last thing that struck me, in the squadron records, for the period from mid November 1944 to mid March 1945, was that for most of the fifty raids that the squadron took part in, the opposition is described as "slight" or "flak moderate" and small numbers of German fighters were sometimes seen but there were usually "no combats." This was because the German radar and flak barrage systems were largely destroyed and their night fighter force had been decimated. It still wasn't safe to fly anywhere though.

A good example of this was "Unternehmen Gisela" - Operation Gisela - which was a night time raid conducted by the Luftwaffe on the 3rd/4th of March 1945 when about two hundred German intruders mingled with about five hundred and fifty planes from one of the returning bombing streams. Almost eight hundred of our planes were coming back that night.

102 Squadron had just bombed a synthetic oil plant at Kamen and the other major target that night was an aqueduct at Ladbergen. The Germans flew low over the Channel to confuse the radar defences and were undetected so they were allowed into British airspace. They attacked when our aircraft were in the circuit area getting ready to land with their wheels and flaps down. In this situation the aircraft were most vulnerable.

The German night fighters could see the airfields all lit up anyway so they would have known where the planes were heading. Many of our boys were being careless and overconfident and had stupidly turned their lights on.

The Germans shot down twenty aircraft. Three of their own crashed. A Junkers 88 crashed near Elvington airfield. It was the last German plane to crash in England during the war. This was a terrible night for Bomber Command.

We were never followed back to base and attacked by German fighters but intruders had followed us on legs of our homeward journey. 102 Squadron was only attacked like this once and that was during Operation Gisela while I was between tours, stationed at Pocklington but posted to 42 Base.

I happened to be on leave at Leeds on a forty-eight hour pass. I heard the air-raid warden's siren operating. Leeds was thirty five miles away from Pocklington but when enemy aircraft were in British airspace the sirens would sound all over the British Isles, letting everyone know that enemy aircraft were invading British airspace. We were not interested in going to the air-raid shelter and stayed in bed.

102 Squadron lost ten Halifaxes in bombing raids while I was between tours. Two planes were shot down on the 24th of December 1944 when the squadron attacked the Luftwaffe airfield at Mulheim.

The squadron's worst operation was on the night of the 5th/6th of January 1945 when three planes were shot down after attacking Hannover. Another one was lost on a night time raid on Magdeburg on the 16th/17th of January.

On the night of the 7th/8th of February we lost two more planes when the squadron attacked Goch. One of these had a special significance for my crew. It was Halifax N-Nan LW142. Our plane! I will talk about this later.

On the 5th/6th of March 1945, Halifax Q-Queenie RG502, piloted by Flying Officer John Hurley, crashed in Czechoslovakia after attacking Chemnitz near the Czech border way out in the East of Germany. Three of the crew managed to bale out and were taken prisoner. This was the first Halifax Mark VI to be lost from the squadron.

The last plane from 102 Squadron lost in combat was A-Able, PP179, piloted by Flying Officer Royston Jeff. All the crew were killed. It was another Halifax 6. It was shot down on the 18th/19th of March during a raid on Witten in the Ruhr Valley. It's not that far from Bochum.

While we were away from the squadron, our Halifaxes were also sent on ten gardening trips intended to lock up Oslo Fiord and the Kattegat and stop German naval movements in and out of the Baltic Sea. The German navy really had nowhere to go at this stage of the war. Small numbers of Halifaxes, usually about six, were sent on these gardening trips. Bad weather also caused the cancellation of four gardening operations.

Grounded! Winter 1944/45

Handley Page Halifax B Mk III of No. 426 Squadron RCAF at Dishforth, Yorkshire, waits forlornly at its dispersal site, its engines covered in tendril-like strands of ice and its wheels sinking in slush and mud. This photograph was taken during the bitter 1944/45 winter and presents a grim picture of the conditions with which ground crews had to contend to get their aircraft ready for action when the weather broke. The plane's nose-art consists of a painting of "Honey Chile", a woman's head and shoulders, the names of the crews' wives and girlfriends, and thirty-nine bomb symbols indicating the thirty-nine bombing missions that had been completed in the plane.

Chapter 59: 42 Base Pocklington

On the 17th of January in the new year, out of boredom or because I decided that I had imposed enough on Mrs Reid, or because a young woman was too keen on me, or because I missed life on the squadron, I decided to go back to the 42 Base Pocklington and take it from there. Bill mentions my return to base in his diary when he says:
> "Have to go through London in a day or so, on further investigations. Don and Bas came back today. Otherwise quiet."

I arrived in York late in the afternoon. I was standing in the queue at the bus stop waiting for a bus to take me to Pocklington when I was approached by a young WAAF. She enquired if I knew an Australian airman who was supposed to meet her for a date in York but hadn't turned up. I told her that I'd been on extended leave but I would inquire about him from some aircrew who were also in the queue. When I quizzed them I ascertained that the man she was supposed to meet had gone missing on a raid the night before. She was extremely upset and I felt that I couldn't leave her on her own so I took her for a meal and to the pictures and later in the evening I took her on the bus back to Pocklington and said goodbye. I felt very bad about it. Her name was Rae. I can't remember her surname but I do remember that she worked in the intelligence department on the squadron. I saw a lot of Rae after that. I used to take her to the pictures and dances in Pocklington and I struck up a relationship with her.

I did not know the man who went missing. Subsequently I found out more about what had happened to the plane and its crew. Halifax Y-Yoke LW179 was shot down and all the crew were killed on a night raid to Magdeburg on the 16th of January, the night before I met Rae at the bus stop. It was a disastrous mission. Seventeen Halifaxes were shot down. Theirs was the only one from our squadron. The plane crashed near the villages of Langelsheim and Wolfshagen in the Harz Mountains in northern Germany about ninety kilometres from the target. It took off from RAF Pocklington at 1838 hours but nothing more was heard from the aircraft. A later investigation found that it was attacked by a night fighter. It must have been badly damaged but the pilot, Squadron Leader Arthur Jarand, kept it flying. The townspeople of Wolfshagen heard it circling their village at least twice but there was nowhere to land in the mountains and it crashed about a mile away. The crew are all buried in the Hanover War Cemetery. Two of the crew came from overseas. Pilot Officer James Carter, an Australian, was the wireless operator. He was from Yarrawonga in Victoria. Pilot Officer Ernest Davis, the bomb aimer, was a Canadian. Warrant Officer Daniel Galbraith was the navigator. Flight Sergeant George Telfor and Sergeant John Wilson were the two gunners and Sergeant Enoch Pope was the flight engineer. It is a sad story. Just a few months earlier, on the 31st of October, five of this crew were on their bombing run over Cologne in Y-Yoke NA599, a Halifax 3, when it was struck from above by incendiaries from another aircraft, just the same as happened to us. Two crewmen were injured. On that occasion, Squadron Leader Jarand was able to fly the stricken plane back to Pocklington. He must have been an excellent pilot. At the last, trying to keep his damaged plane airborne and searching for a place to land.

Bill had been back at the squadron since the 29th of December. When he was screened, Bill got a job investigating air crashes. He had to visit aircrew all over the country. Some of them were in hospital. One of the crashes he was investigating occurred on New Years Day 1945. In his diary he wrote:

> "Last night Max Langham pranged P-Peter and I have now been given the job of carrying out the investigation. So today I went out to the scene of the accident. It firstly hit a tree, then a house, and finally crashed in a field about 500 yards from the end of the runway. Have to go to Group Headquarters tomorrow to find out what is required."

Flying Officer Max Langham, the pilot, was an Australian. He came from the little seaside town of Penguin on the north-west coast of Tasmania. The bomb aimer, James Sheridan, was killed and the pilot, Max Langham, was badly injured while the rest of the crew sustained minor injuries. The Halifax was P-Peter LW158. It was a write-off. Photographs that Bill had taken of the crash show it lying in the field with its back broken and its nose crushed. If Flight Sergeant Sheridan was in there he never stood a chance. When it crashed, Flying Officer Langham was making his fourth attempt to land after returning from a raid on a Benzol plant in Dortmund. It undershot the runway and careered out of control crashed into a house at Riverhead, seven hundred yards from the runway and burst into flames.

Harry Brabin had arrived back on the 8th of January 1945 and John Allen arrived back at about the same time as me. We all got bored at the same time. We already knew that Sandy had been posted and wasn't coming back. Don came back to 42 Base but he was screened soon after to a training squadron. He was one of their "gun" bomb aimers and they were taking him out of the squadron. He didn't have a crew. We were there but we were not operational. We were finished. Our tour had been completed. We decided to ask for a job with 42 Base because we were sick of leave. We were just spare bods and because we were only doing some testing, training the French crews and ferrying Halifax 6's we didn't need a bomb aimer or a rear gunner like the training squadrons did.

Goch

I was back at the squadron when our beloved N-Nan LW142 was shot down by a German night fighter. It happened during the night raid to Goch on the 7/8th of February 1945. It was a terrible blow for all of us. Pilot Officer Smallwood and his crew all perished in the plane. We knew them all well because they often flew N-Nan, although we had first call on her. We were often backed up with them and both crews had a big interest in making sure N-Nan was going well.

They were a very experienced crew. They had three commissioned officers – Flying Officers Ronald Smallwood the pilot, Wilfred Russell the navigator, and the bomb aimer Bernard James. The others were sergeants – John Gallagher, the engineer, Peter Hewitt the wireless operator, and the two gunners, James Lennon and Walter Scott.

It was very sad. They crashed near Hamme-Mille, Belgium, in the early hours of the morning. The target that night was a town called Goch, a German town about ten kilometres inside the Dutch/German border. It was being bombed because it was in the way of the British XXX army corps' advance into Germany. The Master Bomber commenced the raid but then cancelled it because there was too much smoke over the target.

The records show that the entire crew died in the 10th British Field Hospital at Heverlee in Belgium, about ten kilometres south of where the plane crashed. What is more likely is that the crew all died in the crash and they were taken to the hospital where they were confirmed dead. They are all buried at the Heverlee War Cemetery. They did not have much warning and there was no time to bail out. Ironically this was the same raid in which Mick Starmer, who had replaced Charlie Hood as our mid-upper on our first tour, shot down a night fighter. When we left the squadron he became the rear gunner for another crew.

102 Squadron lost two planes on the Goch raid that night. The second one was Halifax Q-Queenie NA175. They had been turned back from the target and were heading home, carrying a full bomb load. When they were about twenty kilometres from Goch, the mid-upper gunner, Bill Ollerton, spotted a JU88 high up on their port beam and the pilot began a series of corkscrews to evade it. The engineer, Sergeant John Grist, reported seeing sparks shooting through the bomb bay and when

they levelled out to head for home they noticed that the starboard wing was on fire. Pilot Officer William Smith ordered the crew to bail out and he was able to hold it up long enough for his six crew members to bail out safely. Luckily for them they abandoned the aircraft in liberated territory near Eindhoven in the Netherlands. The bomb aimer and the rear gunner were injured but the other four made their way back to Pocklington. Sadly Bill Smith was killed when the plane crashed in Belgium, at Leopoldsburg, about ninety kilometres south-west of Goch. He is buried at the war cemetery there. By another twist of fate, their mid-upper gunner, Sergeant Bill Ollerton, became our mid-upper for our second tour.

The raid on Goch had a big impact on us. We lost some good friends and N-Nan, and picked up two crew members for our second tour of duty. That's war for you!

Conversion to Halifax 6's

In February 1945, No. 102 Squadron was in the process of converting to Halifax 6's. All of the 42 Base squadrons, 102 at Pocklington, 346 and 347 at Elvington and 77 at Full Sutton were replacing their Halifax 3's with the great plane. We were the only squadrons in 4 Group to be fully converted to Halifax 6's. This was partly because the "chop" rate (loss rate) was low for Halifax 3's and they were not being replaced as frequently as the Halifax 2's had been in the past. The casualty rate was lower and the planes were lasting longer so there was no need to equip other squadrons with Halifax 6's. Even so, other 4 Group squadrons received them when replacements were needed for their Halifax 3's as they were struck off charge. 158 Squadron received eighteen, 78 Squadron received nineteen, 76 Squadron received twenty-one, and 466 and 640 Squadrons received four each.

They gave us a job of air testing some of the new Halifax 6's before they were released to the squadrons. At that time, the Free French squadrons at Elvington had a lot of inexperienced crews because of their high loss rate, so we embarked on several cross-countries with them to develop their skills. They would come over to Pocklington and we'd take up a new Halifax Mk 6 and take them on a long cross-country.

Assimulated operations

In my log book the flights with Free French crews from Elvington are called "assimulated operations". I did three, one at night time on the 14th of February and the two others were daytime flights on the 19th and 25th.

They lasted approximately six and a half hours each so they were full on, big cross-countries. Six hours thirty. Six hours thirty-five. Six hours forty-five.

My log book shows that Bill was the pilot and I was the navigator on these flights but I didn't do any navigating. They would have chalked them up to me and credited me with the flying time in our Nav Section meeting the next day. The changes to the Halifax 6 mainly concerned the pilot and the engineer. Because the Hali 6's were more powerful aircraft than the Hali 3's the Free French were flying, their crews needed to go through the conversion process.

On these assimulated operations the aircraft was under the control of the French pilot. He would take off and Bill would act as second "dickie" instructor to see how the Frenchman was handling the plane. We would do a blind bombing somewhere like the one we did over York on the 3rd of May when we were waiting for the war to end. They had their own wireless operators, navigators and bomb aimers. I was not supervising or instructing the navigators but I may have been there as a standby navigator.

Instead I sat in the mid-upper's turret as a passenger for all of the cross-countries so I had an experience of what it was like in the mid-upper gunner's position. Life in that turret was interesting. It would be hard to fly through a flak barrage up there, perched on top of the plane. You could see everything. If I had experienced it earlier, it probably would have made me a bit more sympathetic with Charlie Hood.

I also had two flights in Airspeed Oxfords during this time. On the 5th of March I was the navigator for Flight Lieutenant Allan Crabb when we flew one of the commanders to RAF Bury-St-Edmonds, a USAAF Flying Fortress airfield in Suffolk, about 130 miles south of Pocklington. It was a two hours and forty minute return trip. Oxfords were aircrew training planes but the top brass also used them to travel around the country if they needed to. We would probably have taken Squadron Leader Barnard. He would have been important enough to have his own aerial taxi. I don't know why Bill didn't fly the plane. It might have been something that happened quickly and Allan Crabb and I just happened to be there and were told to do it. We were two spare bods around the base. Allan was between tours like the rest of us..

My second flight in an Oxford was on the 10th of March when Wing Commander Wilson was posted to RAF Madley in Herefordshire. Bill and I flew him to his new posting. Our new commanding officer was Wing Commander Hyland-Smith. The rest of our time flying at 42 Base Pocklington, was spent ferrying some new Halifax 6's to Full Sutton.

Air Crash Investigation

Handley Page Halifax, P-Peter LW158, after crashing on New Years Day 1945 at Pocklington. The photograph was taken on the 7th of January during Bill Rabbitt's investigation into the cause of the crash.

Chapter 60: Mosquitos

After my return to Pocklington, Bill asked me if I was interested in volunteering with him to fly Mosquitos on a second tour of duty. I was surprised because I thought he was satisfied with training the Free French and being on the squadron. I had been already thinking that if we were going to fly, we may as well be on ops. We were really only passengers of the Free French, not masters of our own destiny. It was interesting for a while but I was just flying around in the mid-upper gunner's turret! I agreed readily because I had a lot of respect for Bill and his capabilities.

He would have chosen me to go with him because he was convinced that I was a capable navigator. Mosquitos only had a two man crew – pilot and navigator. He never told me why he wanted to change but Bill loved operational life and wanted to go back into a squadron. I suppose he also wanted to fly the best machines, as any pilot would, and Mosquitos then were the best of the best.

They were fast and manoeuvrable. They operated in a variety of roles from night fighter, to intruder, to photo reconnaissance and the strategic bombing of key industrial sites and German cities. They could carry a four thousand pound bomb as far as Berlin. By the start of 1945 it was common practice to send Mosquitos night after night to bomb Berlin. Although they were a little faster than Messerschmitts and Focke Wulfs, they were less manoeuvrable than them in a dogfight so they would not engage in one. They were capable of great speed and great ceiling. That was their main defence.

At Pocklington once, I once saw a Mosquito pilot do a slow roll on takeoff using only one engine. After the plane was airborne, he cut the motor and climbed in a slow 360° roll. The pilot was showing off but it just goes to show how aerodynamic and strong Mosquitos were.

I had no previous desire to go over to Mosquitos so it never occurred to me to change.

Unfortunately, when Bill finally made the decision to switch to Mosquitos he had already missed his opportunity. Back on the 28th of October when I met up with him, Don and Sandy in London, I didn't know that he had been to see the RAAF liaison officer at Australia House in the Strand about changing over. He mentioned the meeting in his diary:

> "Interviewed liaison officer about a posting after completion of my tour. He said I would be able to give OTU instructional duties a miss. Could get Mossies okay now if I wished to do a second tour. May be able to get transport.

Could also fly Hurricanes on fighter affiliation. Also intruder work on Mossies. Cannot make up my mind whether to do a second tour immediately or stick in for Transport which means a change of command."

This is pretty clear isn't it! The liaison officer and Bill must have discussed all his choices. OTUs were out. Transport was only a possibility. He could get Hurricanes for fighter affiliation with bomber crews. But if he wanted to go to Mosquitos he would have to commit to a second Tour of Duty immediately and start straight after completing his first one. Bill says that he couldn't make up his mind and it appears that when he did it was too late. The diary entry shows that he had been thinking about it for at least four months when he asked me.

I cannot remember exactly when we went down to London and volunteered. We had a photograph of the two of us taken by the RAAF photographer at Australia House. It gives a clue about when we did it. It is clear that I am a flying officer in the photograph. Pilot Officers were automatically promoted to Flying Officer after six months. So six months after I became a pilot officer would have been on the 12th of January 1945. And it had to be before we agreed to do a second tour of duty.

My log book shows that our last flight for 42 Base Pocklington was on the 10th of March. We would have decided to volunteer for a second tour a couple of weeks before that. The photograph could not have been taken before I became a flying officer and had to have been taken before we decided to go on a second tour at 102 Squadron.

So it is likely that we popped down to London and applied for Mosquitos sometime in early to mid February because we would have had to wait a while to see if we were accepted or not before committing to a second tour on Halifaxes.

We went to the wartime headquarters of the RAAF in the UK, at Australia House in the Strand. Bill and I were paraded before a high ranking officer. He told us that he would put our names down on the list of volunteers but he also said that there was a queue a mile long all wanting to switch to Mosquitos. I am sure this convinced Bill to volunteer for a second tour when we got back to the squadron because he knew that there was not much chance of us doing a second tour on Mosquitos. The fellow didn't hold out much hope for us. Not many Mosquitos got knocked down. That was one of the reasons why there was such a long waiting list.

Although we were in an RAF Squadron, we went to the RAAF not the RAF because we were Australian aircrew and everything had to go through the Australian RAAF hierarchy. The RAAF had access to

Mosquito appointments. They would send the requests up the line. It never occurred to us to pursue volunteering to the RAF authorities. They probably would have told us to go back and do it through the RAAF anyway.

The photograph of Bill and me taken in Australia House when we volunteered for Mosquitos is in the Australian War Museum archives. The date accompanying it in the museum records says "circa May 1945". This is wrong. The war in Europe finished in early May, 1945.

Pilot and Navigator

London, England. February 1945. Portrait of Flight Lieutenant W. F. Rabbitt, DFC, of Crystal Brook, SA (left), and Flying Officer B. G. Spiller, DFC, of Samarai, New Guinea (right), taken at RAAF headquarters in Australia House, London when the two men applied unsuccessfully for a second tour of duty flying De Haviland Mosquitos.

Part 6

Second Tour of Duty
No. 102 Squadron
Pocklington

Handley Page Halifax Mk VI, C-Charlie, from No. 346 Squadron, RAF Elvington, flies over liberated Paris, with the Eiffel Tower in the background. No. 346 Squadron was one of two Free French squadrons that operated from RAF Elvington until the end of the war.

Chapter 61: Second Tour of Duty

In early March, after we had missed out on Mosquito and ferrying planes and doing odds and ends for a month and a half, Bill came to me and said: "Would you be interested in going on a second tour of duty at the squadron with me?" Naturally I said "Yes". It was not an emotional moment although looking back now I feel very emotional about my decision. I was on base and filling in time so I felt it might as well be on operations. It was a pragmatic decision. I realize now that it was a foolish decision because I was sticking my neck out when I didn't have to. Then again I had a lot of respect for Bill and if I didn't go with him he would have had to get another navigator. Then Bill asked Harry and John and they said the same as me, so all four of us volunteered for a second tour. We said that we wanted to fly the new Mark V1 N-Nan and it was agreed that we could.

Mick Starmer then rejoined our crew as a rear gunner. While we were away, he had proven his skills during a raid on Goch when he shot down a night fighter. It was lucky because it was very rare. He still hadn't finished his first tour so he had kept on flying while we were between tours. He had no qualms about leaving his crew and coming back to us. Bill would have arranged it. Perhaps Mick was a spare bod at the time without a permanent crew of his own. At the end of the war he had still had to do five ops to complete his tour.

Next came Bill Ollerton, our mid-upper. He hadn't finished a tour either. Bill's plane been shot down on the Goch raid that Mick had been on, and he baled out to safety. He would have been a spare bod around the squadron after that and luckily he was allocated to us. He had bags of experience.

The seventh member of our crew was Pilot Officer Doug Young. He was our bomb aimer. He had completed a tour on Wellingtons in the Middle East so he had bags of experience as well. We had a really experienced crew. Four of us had done a full tour together so the strong relationship between the four of us continued. The others fitted in very well. They did not go out to the pub with us in the car and things like that - not that I remember. They might have liked a beer but we didn't mix at all socially. Even in our free time the whole crew didn't head off as a group. Mick and Bill were non-commissioned officers and they probably had a relationship with Harry in the sergeants' mess. Bill, John, Doug and I were in a different mess as commissioned officers. The three of us headed off in the car. As far as I know, Doug didn't come and Harry pulled back on that too, even though he had been very involved in everything - the purchase of the car, the pubs, going on trips together. It was good that Harry didn't hesitate to rejoin us to do another tour. We were all good friends. He may have been bored stiff like Bill, John and me and yearned to return to squadron life.

DFCs

Just before we began our second tour, we were told that Bill's DFC was gazetted on the 23rd of March 1945. Five of us got them. Don, Sandy, John and I received them too. Our DFCs were gazetted on the 27th of March. By that time we were a well respected crew. We were very experienced. We'd done one tour and had just started another one when our DFCs were gazetted. It was hard for Harry Brabin to see the five of us get the medals, especially after he was knocked back for a commission. He could have got a DFM, the Distinguished Flying Medal, as a non-commissioned officer but that didn't eventuate either. I can understand why he was upset about it. I don't know the reason why he wasn't put up for it, particularly when we were a crew that had completed a tour together and signed up for a second one. He did what we did but we got the medals. It was not fair. By the end of the war he had done forty-three missions so his bravery was obvious.

Basil Spiller's Crew - Second Tour of Duty

Basil Spiller's crew for his second tour of duty. Back row (left to right): Bill Rabbitt, pilot; Doug Young, bomb aimer; Basil Spiller, navigator. Front Row (left to right): Harry Brabin, wireless operator; Mick Starmer, rear gunner; Bill Ollerton, mid-upper gunner; John Allen, flight engineer.

Chapter 62: The Halifax Mark III and Mark VI

When we joined 102nd Squadron, the Halifax Mark II was being replaced by the Halifax Mark III. On the 22nd of May 1944 we flew our first mission in P-Peter, a brand new Halifax Mark III. Then in mid February 1945, when we started our second tour, I was lucky enough to fly in the best Mark of all, the Halifax Mark VI. Our squadron had started to be equipped with them. So were the two Free French squadrons at Elvington and 77 Squadron at Full Sutton. Our new plane's registration number was RG532. It was another N-Nan.

The Halifax 6 was a vastly improved aircraft to the Halifax 3 – not to say that the Halifax 3 wasn't a very efficient and likeable aircraft. But the Hali 6 was vastly superior in many ways. For a start it was equipped with Hercules 100 engines and each one put out 1,800 horsepower compared with the old Hali 3's 1,675 horsepower. So there was an appreciable difference in power. It showed up in the rate of climb which was terrific in the Halifax 6. You could really feel the difference in a fully rated climb. The Halifax 6 had an increased speed by virtue of the increased horsepower of the motors. Where we'd cruise at 150 miles per hour with a full bomb load in the Halifax 3's, we would now cruise at 165 to 180 in the Halifax 6's. It made a big difference. This was Indicated Air Speed (IAS) at ground level. Our True Air Speed (TAS) was faster than that because as I have said before, it increases by three knots per hour for every one thousand feet of altitude. Temperature was a factor as well. If it was cold, air speed increased too. At twenty thousand feet, TAS could be as much as eighty knots per hour more than IAS.

In addition the designers had increased the wingspan by four feet and rounded them off. This gave us an extra one or two thousand feet increase in ceiling height. The larger wingspan had been included in the original design of the Halifax, but the Air Ministry insisted that the designers at Handley-Page were to shorten the wings because aircraft hangars at the time were too narrow to accommodate the proposed wingspan. Inside the plane there were no differences.

Although Halifax 3's were gradually being replaced with the Hali 6, they were still being kept on in other squadrons because they were not being lost on missions as much so there wasn't the need for them to be continually replaced. The Mark III's were still going strongly. If they'd suffered heavy losses they would have been quickly replaced with Mark VI's.

I believe that the Halifax 6 was the best heavy bomber in the war, although I accept it is difficult to compare the Halifax 6 with the Lancaster. I do know that it was superior to the Lancaster in speed because on one occasion, just after we had set off on a gardening trip to the Flensberg Fiord, when we were flying over the 6th Canadian Group territory, we caught up with their Lancs going out on a raid. We were fully bombed and we left them for dead. We went through them like a pack of salts.

Bill would be commenting over the intercom about how well she climbed and when we went into a steep climb you could feel the surge of power underneath your feet, just the same as when you go up in a fast lift. You are ascending fast. When the plane was cruising along there was a lovely purring noise from the motors but it was always a bit bumpy because we were continually being buffeted around by the vibration from the slipstreams from the other planes.

Because the Halifax 6 was such a wonderful plane, I do fire up whenever people talk about Lancasters being the best plane in the war. It is one of the few things that gets me going.

More on "tougher targets"

There has been a lot of misinformation, spread by historians and aircrew who were loyal to their Lancasters, that Lancasters were given the toughest targets and Halifaxes were given softer ones. This is clearly untrue and does not bear up to simple examination. For instance, Canadian Lancaster pilot, Bruce Johnston (RCAF) was in 115 Squadron based at Witchford in Cambridgeshire. His family have assembled a beautiful website as a tribute to him. He began his tour at roughly the same time as I did. My seventeenth mission on the 24th/25th of July 1944 was to Stuttgart. He was on that Stuttgart raid too. When you compare what we did on N-Nan, or what our squadron did with what Canadians like Bruce Johnston were doing in their Lancasters, you cannot say that Halifaxes were given easier targets. We went to some of the same places – Le Havre, Vaires, Kiel, and Stuttgart. They were bombing the V1 sites and railway marshalling yards too. They were also in support of the D-Day troops. All of that sort of thing.

In Bruce Johnston's thirty missions his squadron went into Germany eight times and once across the border into Poland. In our thirty-five missions we went into Germany twelve times. His crew only made one incursion into the Ruhr Valley but we went there six times. I am not saying that 115 Squadron's operations were not dangerous. They all were. But it didn't get worse than the Ruhr. It is simply not correct to say that Lancaster squadrons were given the hard targets.

The big issue as far as I am concerned is that it sounds like Bruce Johnston's Canadian crew only had to do thirty missions to complete their tour of duty. We had to do thirty-five! That is a big difference when you are up there putting your life on the line. Remember that our good friend Harry Rogers was killed on his thirty-second mission when our squadron attacked Blainville-sur-l'Eau on the 28th/29th June 1944. It would have been good for him and his wife Mary if his tour had finished at thirty!

Handley Page Halifax Mark VI

Halifax B Mark VI LV838, after conversion from a Halifax B Mark III, at the Aeroplane and Armament Experimental Establishment, Boscombe Down, Wiltshire. May 1944.

Chapter 63: Operation 33 – Osnabrück

The Bomber Command operations on this day were directed to towns on the main reinforcement routes into the Rhine battle area. Heavy attacks were made on the railway routes through these towns and on the surrounding built-up areas. Hannover attacked by 267 Lancasters and 8 Mosquitos of Nos 1, 6 and 8 Groups. The bombing was observed to fall in the target area. 1 Lancaster lost. 175 aircraft - 151 Halifaxes, 14 Lancasters, 10 Mosquitos - of Nos 4, 6 and 8 Groups raided Münster. 3 Halifaxes lost. Few results were seen by the bombers because the target area rapidly became smoke-covered. Münster reports a large number of bombs but only 2 people dead. 156 aircraft - 132 Halifaxes, 14 Lancasters, 10 Mosquitos - of Nos 4 and 8 Groups to Osnabrück. No aircraft lost. Osnabrück reports extensive property damage throughout the town. *Total effort for the day:* 606 sorties, 4 aircraft (0.7 per cent) lost.
The Bomber Command War Diaries, 25 March 1945

On the 25th of March 1945 I did the first operation on my second tour. We were not in N-Nan on this raid. Instead we flew in Halifax M-Mother RG505, another new Halifax Mark VI. It was a daylight raid with a fighter escort. Fifteen Halifaxes took part from our squadron. The target was the railway marshalling yards at Osnabrück in north-west Germany. We set course at 0710 in the morning. The raid lasted five hours and ten minutes. We carried two thousand pounds of high explosive plus eleven 750 pound clusters of incendiaries giving us an all up bomb load of 10,250 pounds.

Osnabrück was a major railway hub in central Germany. The main station near the middle of the town was the primary target but it was inevitable that the town was going to be hit.

The Bomber Command War Diary says that the raid caused "extensive property damage throughout the town". With nearly 150 heavy bombers on the target and each plane carrying upwards of ten thousand pounds of incendiaries we were obviously going to set as many fires as we could. That was the object of carrying incendiaries and that was exactly what happened.

In three separate raids on this day Bomber Command sent over six hundred bombers to attack three cities which were all in the same general battle area. Osnabrück was only thirty miles north-east of Münster and Hannover was sixty miles to the east. Three Halifaxes were shot down over Münster and one Lancaster was lost over Hannover.

This was a full on attack on Osnabrück after what had been a recent series of smaller raids against the city. Before we came in, there were three smaller night time raids with Mosquitoes. On the 8th/9th of March, five Mosquitos attacked Osnabrück. Then on the 9th/10th, sixteen Mosquitos were sent on "nuisance" flights over Bremen, Hannover,

Osnabrück and Wilhelmshaven. Finally on the 16th/17th of March, six more Mosquitos attacked the city.

Bomber Command was using Mosquitoes more and more for lightning raids and precision bombing but they had smaller bomb loads and could not do the enormous amount of damage that we could.

On our bombing run we could not see the target because there was so much smoke hiding the sky markers, so the Master Bomber instructed everyone to bomb the centre of the smoke.

This mission was entirely uneventful for us. It was interesting that the first operation of our second tour was a daylight raid. This would never have been attempted when we headed off on our first operation to Orlean just ten months earlier. It was a big contrast. We were now bombing deep into Germany and there was heavy, accurate flack but there were no fighter attacks because our fighters were well in evidence. The war had changed and the Germans were facing defeat. The cessation of hostilities in Europe was less than two months after this raid. The closer we came to the armistice the less opposition we encountered.

Chapter 64: Operation 34 - Hamburg

327 aircraft - 277 Halifaxes, 36 Lancasters, 14 Mosquitos - of Nos 4, 6 and 8 Groups attacked the Rhenania oil plant, Harburg. The target was easily identified and severe damage was caused to it. 2 Lancasters and 1 Halifax lost. *Total effort for the night:* 1,172 sorties, 16 aircraft (1.4 per cent) lost.

The Bomber Command War Diaries, 4/5 April 1945

On the night of the 4th/5th of April 1945 we were briefed to attack Hamburg. The target was the Rhenania (Shell) oil refinery in the Hamburg suburb of Harburg. At briefing we were told that the aim of the mission was "to complete the destruction of the repaired and partly active oil refinery at Rhenania".

We took off at 2005 in N-Nan RG532, a brand new Halifax Mark VI. We carried eight thousand pounds of high explosives as sixteen 500 pound bombs. Fifteen aircraft from our squadron took part in the trip which took five hours and thirty minutes.

On our bombing run Bill and Don Young had a clear target in sight. The Master Bomber and the pathfinders had laid down their sky markers accurately and when we arrived it was well lit up with photo flares and bomb blasts. There were large explosions and a lot of damage was caused.

It was uneventful for us even though there was a lot of flak and two Lancasters and one Halifax were lost during the raid. The 102 Squadron diary reported that two of our aircraft were attacked by night fighters and one claimed to have shot one down. Another one of our planes had been shot up by flak but returned safely.

For me nothing had changed. I did my job the same as before. I continued to follow the flight plan and kept Bill informed with accurate information so that he could get us to the target on time and then back home to base, regardless of what was going on outside. All I could control was around me at my desk in the navigator's compartment. I was in my own little world - trying to stay calm and to concentrate on my charts and instruments.

I can remember that in the Nav Section the day after this operation, they told us that the record should show that we had attacked the Rhenania oil refinery at Harburg. We were always told what to write and we copied it down into our log books. We always had to write down exactly what had happened on our previous raid. That is why I know that the details in my log book about our next operation to Flensburg Fiord on the 9th of April are accurate, even though the *Bomber Command War Diary* says otherwise.

Hamburg Shipyards and the Rhenania Ossag (Shell) Oil Refinery

Hamburg was one of the main targets for RAF and USAAF bombing during the Second World War.

The city was attacked at least ninety three times, seventy one times by the RAF and twenty two times by the USAAF. RAF Bomber Command sent de Haviland Mosquitos on over thirty small scale raids attacking strategic targets in the Hamburg area as well as carrying out nuisance and diversionary attacks, but the majority of raids were full scale heavy bomber operations which devastated the city.

Hamburg was a large port, shipbuilding, engineering, manufacturing and petro-chemical centre. In the shipyards of Blohm and Voss the heavy cruiser Admiral Hipper and the legendary pocket battleship Bismark were built.

As well, four of Hamburg's ship building companies built 394 (34%) of the 1153 U-boats commissioned by the Kriegsmarine. 224 (56%) of Hamburg's U-boats were manufactured in the Blohm and Voss shipyards making the company by far the largest of the Hamburg U-boat builders.

The Rhenania oil refinery, near Hamburg, in ruins after RAF and USAAF raids in July 1944. In the foreground can be seen a stretch of water, which is covered in oil from the devastated refinery. The refinery was capable of producing 46,000 tons of refined petroleum products monthly.

Hamburg was also one of the principle locations of the German petro-chemical industry. Its refineries were vital to Germany's ability to conduct the war. Before September 1939, Germany imported crude oil from Mexico and Venezuela but after war was declared imports ceased and Germany was forced to use lower grade crude oil from its own oilfields at Reitbrook, Heide and Neinhagen, as well as sourcing crude oil from Austrian fields.

Fifty seven percent of Germany's oil came from crude oil refineries. The remaining forty three percent was synthetic oil produced by both hydrogenation and the Fischer-Tropsch processes in cities such as Essen, Cologne and Leipzig.

The twelve oil refineries in the Hamburg area produced 212,600 tons of crude oil per month, forty one percent of Germany's total crude oil production. To put this another way, the Hamburg oil refineries produced almost a quarter of Germany's oil during the war.

Rhenania (Shell) operated three oil refineries in Hamburg. The company's largest was the Rhenania Ossag (Shell) refinery located in the Hamburg suburb of Harburg - the target of the attack that Basil Spiller describes in both this and the next chapter. This refinery processed 60,000 tons of crude oil per month while the company's other Hamburg refineries at Grasbrook and Wilhelmsberg processed 17,000 and 8,350 tons respectively. Rhenania (Shell) therefore processed forty percent of Hamburg's crude oil.

It is little wonder that Hamburg, with its U-boat and shipbuilding capabilities and its large petro-chemical industry, was a prime target for the RAF's Bomber Command and the USAAF.

As well, Hamburg was a target especially chosen by Britain's War Cabinet because war strategists at the highest level believed that as Germany's second largest city, its destruction, as well as demonstrating the awesome power of the Allied bomber force, would be a massive psychological blow to the confidence and morale of the German people.

During the war the Blohm and Voss shipyard was the specific target for eight large scale bombing raids, and large scale raids were directed at Hamburg's oil refineries on at least sixteen occasions.

In the final twelve months of the war, over 45,000 tons of bombs were dropped on Hamburg's refineries. Although the refineries were repaired each time, Germany's oil production was severely disrupted which is in contrast to the Operation Gomorrah raids in July 1943 which destroyed the city, caused massive loss of life and although they clearly demonstrated Allied air superiority, they did not damage the oil refineries and oil production continued unabated. The war in Europe may have ended earlier had Hamburg's refineries and those in other cities, been targeted instead of the of indiscriminate policy of carpet bombing the large cities, a strategy which failed to break the spirit and resolve of the German population.

Chapter 65: Operation 35 - Hamburg

440 aircraft - 263 Halifaxes, 160 Lancasters, 17 Mosquitos - of Nos 4,6 and 8 Groups dispatched to Hamburg. 3 Halifaxes and 3 Lancasters lost. This attack was intended for the shipyard areas but partial cloud caused the raid to become dispersed. Some damage was probably caused to the shipyards but, as an American raid on the yards had taken place a few hours earlier, damage seen in photographs could not be allocated between the two forces. *Total effort for the night:* 918 sorties, 12 aircraft (1.3 per cent) lost.

The Bomber Command War Diaries, 8/9 April 1945

My thirty-fifth mission was the third mission of my second tour. It was another night time raid on Hamburg.. It was almost an identical mission to the one on the 4th of April. This one went for five hours and forty minutes, only ten minutes longer. We again carried sixteen, 500 pound heavy explosive bombs. On this operation we left at 1945 hours, so they were very similar. We returned to base in the early hours of the morning at 0125 hours.

The target was the Blohm and Voss Shipyards. At briefing we were told that the aim of the mission was to "destroy dockyards and associated buildings". Fourteen Halifaxes left from our squadron. There was heavy, accurate flak over the target area. Three Halifaxes and three Lancasters were shot down by flak as no enemy night fighters were encountered, a big contrast to our night time missions in 1944 where they were buzzing around in all directions.

As far as I was concerned it was an uneventful raid only because nothing noteworthy happened to us. I was busy at my navigator's desk. I remember that there was a lot of flak on the way in to the target but we went in, dropped our bombs and headed home. The raid itself was a failure because the target started to cloud in and the bombing ended up all over the place. It was a little bit more eventful for one of our crews who after their bombing run discovered that they had a hang-up in the bomb bay. It was very dangerous because crews had to worry about a live bomb on board all the way back to the squadron. It would be a long and nervous trip. Sometimes they might not know. It could also be very tricky particularly if armed bombs did not release properly from their shackles or were threatening to come loose. They could even fall out when landing. A decision had to be made about what was to be done with it – carry it back to base or try to get rid of it. On this raid, the engineer noticed the hang-up and jettisoned the bomb manually on the way home. If it could not be done manually, the pilot would have to try and shake it loose - side to side. And up and down. We had a hang-up on the Forêt de Nieppe raid but we had occasions when we had to jettison bombs in the

Channel and then there were others when we had to land with bombs and mines on board as happened when we went gardening in the Kattegat and Bill did that bad landing with all our mines on board.

There were several other raids conducted by Bomber Command on this night, including a large force of over 230 Lancasters which attacked the Lützkendorf oil refinery right out in the east of Germany. It was about a hundred and forty miles further east than Stuttgart, which at eight hours and twenty minutes was our longest raid, but the flight probably took a more direct route because it was much further north. The Lancasters took off for Lützkendorf an hour and a half before we left for Hamburg and they would have been coming home a couple of hours after we got back. They were flying over enemy territory for a long time. They destroyed the refinery but six planes were shot down on this raid too. The *Bomber Command War Diary* says that the total losses for the night were twelve planes, or 1.3% of the bombing force. Twelve planes meant the loss of eighty-four crew members. That was a lot for one day at this stage of the war which only had four weeks to go. It highlights the fact that bombing over Germany was still a very dangerous thing to be doing.

After this raid Hamburg was in ruins and Bomber Command never attacked it again.

Dinner invitation

One day during my second tour, towards the end of my stay in Pocklington, Bill came up to me and said, "I've accepted an invitation to dinner on your behalf from Doctor Usherwood." He was the local doctor at Pocklington. Doctor Usherwood was a middle aged gentleman. He was not our doctor. We had our own medical officers on the base. At the dinner there were only the four of us - Doctor and Mrs Usherwood, Bill and me.

Doctor and Mrs Usherwood were very gracious. Apart from the nice wine, Mrs Usherwood cooked us a slap-up meal. It was the first time I'd been presented with a whole fish on a platter to be carved up for the guests. I don't know what sort of fish it was but it was a big fish on a big plate and it was delicious. Mrs Usherwood brought it out and then Dr Usherwood did the honours of serving it up. A feature of the visit was the lovely classical music that was playing on the gramophone. That was my first encounter with classical music and I was wrapped in it from then on.

I notice that one of the contributors to the booklet *Pocklington at War*, which was produced by the local Pocklington Historical Society, has the name Mike Usherwood as one of the contributors. I wonder whether he is the son or grandson of the good doctor and his wife. Mike

Usherwood is also the author of several books which I have been reading re4cently - *The War Diary of RAF Pocklington* and *The War Diary of RAF Elvington*. "Usherwood" is an unusual name and there seems to be a logical connection.

Operation Gomorrah – Bombing Hamburg

The RAF code name for the series of bomber raids on Hamburg during the Second World War was Operation Gomorrah. Cynically named after the biblical city of Gomorrah, destroyed with "hell fire and brimstone", Operation Gomorrah was a campaign of devastating attacks designed to destroy the city and its industrial infrastructure and kill its inhabitants. Four large scale RAF heavy bomber night time operations and a series of smaller strategic raids were conducted between the 24th of July and the 3rd of August 1943.

Aerial view of ruined residential and commercial buildings of Hamburg, Germany. These were among the 16,000 multi-storeyed apartment buildings destroyed by the firestorm which developed during the raid by Bomber Command on the night of 27/28 July.

On the night of the 24th/25th of July an RAF force of 347 Lancasters, 246 Halifaxes, 125 Stirlings and seventy-three Wellingtons bombed Hamburg. Although conditions were ideal, only half of the bomber force dropped their bombs near the centre of the city but because Hamburg was such a large city the carpet bombing did massive damage to civilian areas within the creep back area some distance from the aiming point and it is estimated that fifteen hundred people were killed. On this raid German night fighter activity was dramatically reduced due to the first wartime use of "window". Thousands of strips of thin aluminium backed paper strips were dropped by the approaching bomber force. German operators were totally confused by radar displays which were suddenly overwhelmed with false echoes and they were unable to accurately direct night fighters, searchlights and ack-ack barrages towards the bomber stream. Altogether twelve RAF aircraft were shot down, the 1.5 percent loss rate was considered small for such a well defended target.

The second heavy bomber operation as part of Operation Gomorrah was conducted on the night of the 26th/27th of July. The carpet bombing on this raid was so catastrophic for the citizens of Hamburg that the firestorm that developed is often talked about in the same terms as the infamous bombing attacks on Dresden, by RAF and USAAF forces between the 13th and 15th of February 1945, the bombing of Tokyo by the USAAF on the 9th/10th of March 1945 and the nuclear bombing of Hiroshima by the USAAF on the 6th of August 1945.

A force of 787 heavy bombers was sent to attack Hamburg. On this night several unusual weather events coincided to produce a firestorm in the city when the bombing began. Summer temperatures were high, there had been no rainfall for weeks and the humidity was low. Everything was dry. When the attack began, heavy explosive bombs smashed buildings and blocked roads preventing firemen, stretched to the limit and still dousing fires from the previous bombing raid, from moving into the bombing zone. Hamburg was ready to burn.

The heavy bombers were guided to the aiming point by clearly defined target indicators and began dropping their bombs on the densely populated suburbs of Hammerbrook, Hamm and Borgfeld. The bombing stream took almost an hour to pass in what was an unrelenting and concentrated attack. When the bombs smashed through roofs it allowed incendiary bombs to fall inside and burn wooden substructures. In the resulting inferno fires raging in these areas linked up and created a conflagration of such intensity that a firestorm described as a "tornado" of swirling fire some fifteen hundred feet high swept through the city at a speed of over 250 kilometres per hour, killing over forty thousand people.

On the night of 29th/30th of July, seven hundred and seventy aircraft bombed Hamburg in the third massed bomber raid of Operation Gomorrah. The target was intended to be the undamaged areas in the north of the city but misplaced markers resulted in many bombs falling in the firestorm area of the previous raid before the fires raged through the north eastern residential suburbs of Wandsbek Barmbek and Uhlenhorst. Twenty-eight RAF bombers were lost on this raid.

The final raid of Operation Gomorrah was conducted on the night of the 2nd/3rd of August 1943, when 740 aircraft attacked Hamburg. While approaching the target over northern Germany, the bombing stream ran into a terrible thunderstorm. Many planes abandoned the mission and dropped their bombs on German towns they flew over before returning to England. Few aircraft actually bombed Hamburg. Thirty aircraft were lost on this raid, many due to icing, air turbulence and lightning.

Losses for 102 Squadron were heavy during the period of Operation Gomorrah. The squadron participated in the four major bombing raids as well as a raid on Essen on the night of the 25th/26th of July, losing six planes in seven days, with forty men killed and three becoming prisoners of war.

Chapter 66: Operation 36 - Flensburg Fiord

591 Lancasters and 8 Mosquitos of Nos 1, 3 and 8 Groups to Kiel. 3 Lancasters lost. This was an accurate raid, made in good visibility on two aiming points in the harbour area. Photographic reconnaissance showed that the Deutsche Werke U-boat yard was severely damaged, the pocket battleship Admiral Scheer was hit and capsized, the Admiral Hipper and the Emden were badly damaged. The local diary says that all 3 shipyards in the port were hit and that the nearby residential areas were severely damaged. 22 Halifaxes in a diversionary raid to Stade, 44 Mosquitos to Berlin, 37 to Plauen and 24 to Hamburg, 45 RCM sorties, 37 Mosquito patrols, 70 Lancasters and 28 Halifaxes minelaying in Kiel Bay and the Little Belt. 1 Halifax from the diversion raid crashed in France.
The Bomber Command War Diaries, 9 April 1945

On the 9th of April we were briefed to lay mines in Flensburg Fiord. This was mission number four of my second tour, my thirty-sixth operation. The town of Flensburg is situated at the innermost part of the fiord. It has an interesting history. It is Germany's closest town to the border with Denmark. In 1920, after the First World War, the townspeople voted to stay in Germany when the League of Nations decided that the argument about the border would be settled by a plebiscite. After Hitler's death on the 30th of April, the last German government, led by Grand Admiral Donitz, was moved to Flensburg.

War records say that seventy Lancasters and twenty-eight Halifaxes laid mines in Kiel Bay and the Little Belt, a strait separating the Jutland Peninsula from Funen Island and Kiel Bay. Anyway, Flensburg Fiord is in the middle between the Little Belt and Kiel Fiord. Fourteen aircraft from our squadron took off for Flensburg Fiord that night, but one returned with engine trouble. That was where we were directed to go at briefing and that's what we did no matter what the official record says.

We set course in N-Nan at 1952 hours and the trip took five hours and twenty minutes, so we arrived back at base at 0112. We carried four eighteen hundred pound Mark VI mines. They were big mines. Bomber Command was putting a stranglehold on German warships by stopping them from sailing through the straits between a maze of islands. If the fiords were mined German ships couldn't shelter in them either. I have already explained that gardening was done using H2S, with the plane usually making a timed run from a coastal feature which was readily distinguishable on the H2S oscilloscope. We simply did a bearing and distance run from it, on a prescribed course and at a prescribed time. We didn't go through the typical bombing run process of "Hold it steady! Hold it steady! Left! Left! Right! Right!" and all that. Gardening was mainly a navigational exercise. I would set up H2S with the prescribed heading and distance and Bill would hold the plane on the correct heading at the right speed and altitude. When we were in the correct position on the screen I told Don and he would release the mines. We were always in contact with Bill. When he dropped the mines Don told him, "Bombs gone!"

I can't remember exactly what level we gardened at because that information was lost when I destroyed my flight plans and charts, but I think we were anything from ten to twelve thousand feet high. We didn't get low to the water because each mine had its own parachute, so they used to float down slowly and drop into the water. Because the mines had a soft landing they did not explode when they hit the water from way up there. Our four mines sat in the bomb bay close together. We released them in a stick - all at once. We didn't go back and repeat the exercise four times. Thirteen of our planes laid mines that night, so we planted fifty-two mines and didn't know if other squadrons had joined us. As it turned out there were almost a hundred planes gardening in that general area that night. Four mines would be released there. Four released there. Four released there and so on. It wasn't important for the mines to be in a line or in a pattern. They would be moved all over the fiord by the current anyway.

While we were stooging around dropping our mines, a Bomber Command attack on Kiel was taking place with almost six hundred Lancasters. Stooging was the term we used for hanging around, which was what we were doing compared to what the others were doing at Kiel. We had a bird's eye view of the whole operation. During our mining run, Mick in our rear turret, reported that a single engine German fighter was haring past us, going like a bat out of hell towards Kiel. He wasn't interested in us at all. We knew we were better off laying mines where we were than bombing Kiel. There was good visibility so we saw all the planes buzzing around and the explosions and everything else that was going on over to starboard. It was an amazing spectacle!

The Germans were desperate to defend Kiel that night. They had dropped fighter flares onto our bombing stream to illuminate the path of the bombers through to the target. The flares were hanging from parachutes and drifting down ever so slowly. As well, all of our planes had released their photo flares, and each time a bomb load hit the ground and exploded a photo flare lit up the sky with 700 million candlepower. Flak! Searchlights! Fighter flares! Photo flares! All going off! Imagine the scene! We saw the whole thing.

This was a big raid on a major target. There were almost six hundred planes bombing the city. They were after the submarine yards and no doubt reconnaissance planes had photographed the three German warships tied up in the harbour. We had been gardening consistently in the Kiel Fiord and there was a minefield blocking it, so the ships would have been unable to put to sea. At this stage of the war, where could they go? In the raid, three Lancasters were shot down. The famous pocket battleship Admiral Scheer was sunk. Another pocket-battleship the Admiral Hipper and the light cruiser Emden were both badly damaged. The Germans scuttled the Hipper and blew up the Emden on the 3rd of May to stop them from being captured by the Allied army.

It was a four hundred mile journey home, straight over the North Sea all the way.

Admiral Scheer Destroyed

The German pocket battleship Admiral Scheer capsized in the harbour at Kiel after being hit by five 12,000 pound Tallboy bombs during a raid by Avro Lancasters on the night of 9th/10th of April 1945.

British Minelaying in World War 2

Naval mines are self-contained bombs which are sown in both offensive and defensive positions in oceans, rivers, estuaries and harbours. Mines are employed for a variety of reasons, including the indirect destruction of ships and submarines, impeding the passage of enemy vessels and locking them into their own harbours, protecting one's own shipping and creating safe zones for their unimpeded movement. They can be laid from both sea and air and moored into position or float freely, ready to explode when approached by enemy vessels.

In this chapter Basil Spiller and his crew flew a minelaying operation to Flensburg Fiord. His pilot, Bill Rabbitt, wrote in his flying log that his plane was carrying four 1,800 pound Mark V1 mines. These mines were first employed by Bomber Command in 1944. They were very powerful bombs, charged by either

450 kilograms of amatol, made from a mixture of TNT and ammonium nitrate, or 500 kilograms of minol, typically a mixture of ammonium nitrate and powdered aluminium. When a mine was released from a plane's bomb bay, a parachute attached to the mine opened when a fixed line attached to the parachute pulled it out of its pack. The mine's descent was slowed down, and it had a smoother landing in the water. Mark V1 mines exploded when naval vessels approached causing the mine's acoustic-magnetic trigger to activate.

An acoustic mine is triggered when a microphone built into the mine detects sound waves from a ship's engines or the rotating screws of its propellers. A magnetic mine is equipped with built in sensors to detect changes in the magnetic field. As a metal hulled ship approaches, the magnetic field changes rapidly and when a predetermined level is reached, the firing circuit is closed and the mine explodes.

The effectiveness of defensive mining operations in World War 2 is the cause of much debate. Over 200,000 mines were laid to protect ships in their harbours, to restrict the passage of German ships between northern Scotland, the Faroe Islands and Iceland, and to protect the Atlantic convoys bringing troops and supplies to Britain. Despite being a deterrent, German battleships and U-boats took a heavy toll of Allied shipping. The large number of mines laid was responsible for the destruction of only one German U-boat, U-647.

Britain's offensive minelaying on the other hand was obviously very successful. Bomber Command sowed almost 50,000 mines in enemy waters. They were responsible for sinking 217 German warships of various types and 545 merchant ships, almost three quarters of a million tons of shipping. Ships of the Royal Navy sowed more than 20,000 mines in offensive situations. It is estimated that combined, British airforce and naval minelaying operations were responsible for destroying more than one thousand German ships and damaging some 550 more. Interestingly, during the war RAF minelaying operations sank more German shipping than the Royal Navy.

Chapter 67: Operation 37 – Nuremburg

129 Halifaxes of No. 4 Group and 14 Pathfinder Lancasters attacked the railway yards at Nuremburg with great accuracy. No aircraft lost.
The Bomber Command War Diaries, 11 April 1945

On the 11th of April '45 we flew N-Nan on a daylight operation to Nuremburg. This would have been unthinkable when I started operations. Bear in mind, the last time Bomber Command operated against Nuremburg was a bit over three weeks earlier, during a night raid on the 16th/17th of March, when they lost twenty-four Lancasters. Nuremburg had always been a difficult target. In March 1944, a record number of ninety-five aircraft – sixty-four Lancasters and thirty-one Halifaxes, that's 668 men - were shot down over Nuremburg - the heaviest losses that Bomber Command had ever suffered against a target. So, naturally, we were filled with some sense of trepidation when they told us what the target was.

I don't know what our bomb load was and I did not write it in my log book probably because we turned back and didn't drop any on the target. I've got a copy of Bill Rabbitt's flying log too and he didn't write it down either. After each raid we just wrote what we were told to. On the Stuttgart raid we could only carry four thousand pounds of bombs because we needed an overload fuel tank in the bomb bay. The Halifax Mark VI was more powerful and had a range of 2,500 miles compared to the Mark III's 1,800 miles, so we were probably carrying more on this raid.

Nuremburg is in the south east of Germany, about a thousand miles from Pocklington. It was going to be a long flight because our flight plan was taking us in an arc south of Paris and turning eastwards across southern Germany. Our longest operation up until then had been the Stuttgart raid on our first tour. That took us eight hours and twenty minutes, and Nuremburg is a hundred miles further east. This was going to be another eight hour plus operation. When crews bombed central Germany they took a more direct route over France and Belgium and it was straight in and out. But every crew was so uneasy about attacking Nuremburg. They were over German territory for such a long way. It was tempting fate.

We took off at 1145 in the morning but we only got half way to the target when we had to abort the mission. We had been routed to fly south of Paris and we were advancing into central France when the flight plan on the next leg required us to engage the superchargers on each engine and climb ten thousand feet to a higher altitude. Bill attempted to engage the superchargers but two of the engines backfired badly and threatened to blow apart. We lost height and speed rapidly. Bill regained control but in a short time the main force was miles ahead of us. He decided to abort the operation and return to base. At the lower height we didn't have to engage the superchargers. The trouble occurred only when we attempted to engage the superchargers, so it was obvious that the superchargers were faulty. We cruised back on four engines and left the superchargers alone. I can't remember what we did with our bomb load but we probably dropped them in the channel on the way back. This was the only time we aborted an operation. Our flying time was only four hours and ten minutes so we only got halfway to the target. In my log I've written: "Turned back. Two engines u/s."

The attacking force met moderate opposition over Nuremburg. No planes were lost, although one of our planes suffered flak damage. *The RAF Pocklington War Diary* says that sixteen Halifaxes took off on this operation escorted by Mustang fighters. One plane returned with engine trouble. That was us. The Master Bomber was able to direct the attack on the railway yards with accuracy. With good visibility and little flak the bombing was on target and a lot of damage was caused. There were large explosions and smoke clouds were seen rising 12,000 feet into the air.

Our two Free French sister squadrons, Nos. 346 and 347 based at RAF Elvington, each sent fifteen planes on this raid. It was interesting to discover that the pilot of Q-Queenie of No. 347 Squadron was trying to open the bomb doors incorrectly on their bombing run and by the time he realised what the problem was they had overshot the target. He wanted to go around and make another run but he was overruled by the navigator who was the captain of the aircraft. The navigator decided that by the time they had made a second run, the main force would be well on the way home while they were still deep inside Germany. It was too dangerous to be miles behind the bombing stream on the return journey.

This situation is interesting for several reasons. The highest ranked crew member on the Free French aircraft was the "captain" and he made the decisions – not the pilot. In this case it was the navigator. This was not the case in the airforce I served in – the RAAF or the RAF. I didn't know it was different for the French. In the RAAF and the RAF, the pilot was always captain of the aircraft no matter what his rank. I am sure that Bill would not have thought that the reason given for not having a second go at the target was good enough and we would have gone back to complete the job we were sent there to do. Anyway, it is a moot point because Bill would never have made the mistake with the bomb doors in the first place.

The story also shows the importance of staying in the bomber stream. The Free French navigator knew the importance of staying in the bombing stream and that being out there on your own was inviting trouble. At night there was the cover of darkness but you would always be vulnerable to predicted flak or night fighters which targeted you. But in the stream you were one of hundreds of planes. At night when flak was bursting all around you or if a night fighter attacked, there was always a good chance that it was not your plane that bought hit. Even a big loss of eight percent was good odds. It meant that you had a ninety-two percent chance of survival. In daylight, heading home alone, miles away from the bomber stream and without fighter protection, you were in peril. Every German radar controller and every Messerschmitt and every gunner would be looking just for you, while your daylight fighter protection was heading home covering the bombing stream.

Bombing Nuremburg

In this chapter, Basil Spiller says that the aircrews at 102 Squadron were filled with "some sense of trepidation" when they were told the name of the target. This was because bomber squadrons around Britain knew that in past operations, Nuremburg had been heavily defended and night fighters and flak had taken a heavy toll of the attacking force.

Nuremburg, April 1945. Photograph showing some of the destruction wrought by Allied bombing during the Second World War.

Nuremburg was the symbolic home of Adoph Hitler's Reichsparteitag. From 1927 until 1938 the party's rallies were held there. These rallies were extremely important, carefully constructing the cult of personality that surrounded Hitler, representing him as a formidable leader, statesman, and saviour of the German people, and for demonstrating the might and power of Germany to its uneasy European neighbours. The rallies grew over time to become enormous spectacles. Over half a million people attended the 1938 rally, listening to Hitler and swearing loyalty to him. Bombing Nuremburg was bombing the spiritual home of Nazi Germany's Third Reich.

In this chapter, Basil Spiller explains that their pilot, Bill Rabbitt, was forced to abandon the raid on Nuremburg because of severe problems with his aircraft's superchargers. Basil also refers to a previous raid on Nuremburg on the 16th/17th of March 1945. On that night, 277 Avro Lancasters and sixteen De Haviland Mosquitos were sent to bomb the city. The raid caused extensive damage to the south and south-west of the city as well as the Altstadt, the historic old town precinct, and the railway station and the gasworks were also destroyed. However German night fighters engaged the flight as it headed towards the target and inflicted severe damage on the raiders. Twenty-four Lancasters, 8.7 percent of the Lancasters involved in the mission, were destroyed.

Almost twelve months earlier on the night of 30th/31st of March 1944, 795 aircraft were sent to Nuremburg, despite a meteorological reconnaissance flight reporting that the bombing stream would be flying across Europe in moonlight and in skies clear of clouds, conditions that would normally have led to the cancellation of the mission. At the target, strong winds and continual night fighter attacks were responsible for the Pathfinders incorrectly marking their flares, and on their bombing runs the attacking force encountered heavy cloud that closed in over the city. Little damage was done.

German night fighters intercepted the bomber stream near the Belgian border attacking relentlessly for the next hour as they neared the target. Ninety five planes were shot down - sixty-four Lancasters and thirty-one Halifaxes. The toll would have been much heavier had the German night fighters not been forced to return to their bases to refuel. For bravery on this raid 4 Group Pilot Officer, Cyril Barton, was posthumously awarded the Victoria Cross.

Chapter 68: Operation 38 - Flensburg Fiord

377 Lancasters and 105 Halifaxes of Nos 3, 6 and 8 Groups to Kiel. 2 Lancasters lost. This raid was directed against the port area, with the U-boat yards as the main objective. Bomber Command rated this as 'a poor attack' with scattered bombing. 20 Halifaxes and 8 Mosquitos in a diversionary raid on Boizenburg, 87 Mosquitos to Hamburg, 20 to Stralsund and 12 to Reisa, 62 RCM sorties, 55 Mosquito patrols, 82 Lancasters and 27 Halifaxes minelaying in Kiel Bay and the Kattegat. 1 Mosquito of No 100 Group lost. *Total effort for the night:* 855 sorties, 3 aircraft (0.4 per cent) lost.
The Bomber Command War Diaries, 13/14 April 1945

After we had to abort the Nuremburg mission, N-Nan was out of action having its superchargers fixed, so for the next couple of operations we flew Halifax O-Oboe RG 503. On the 13th of April 1945 we returned to Flensburg Fiord to do some more gardening. This was my thirty-eighth operation, the sixth of my second tour. War records have us minelaying in either Kiel Bay or the Kattegat but we went to Flensburg Fiord again.

There were six Halifaxes from our squadron in the minelaying force. We carried four eighteen hundred pound Mark VI mines again and took off at 2050 in the evening on a six hour trip.

I had navigated the plane to the correct area but when I switched on the H2S set to get ready for our timed run, I found that it was unserviceable. Without H2S I couldn't find the headland from which our run was to start. I had just told Bill that we would have to take the mines back to base when Doug Young, our bomb aimer, came to the rescue.

"Hang on," he said, "I can see the headland clearly in the moonlight. Let's do a visual drop."

Fortunately it was a brilliant moonlit night and Doug in his position in the nose, looking through the perspex, could see the ground clearly. He was able identify the prominent headland that was our point of reference on our flight plan. I did not have to tell Doug that it was the right position because he was an expert map reader, and after all, map reading is all about being able to "read" the ground. I took his word for it and we started our run. Normally we would have picked up the headland on the H2S oscilloscope.

We used H2S all the time. Unless we were ordered not to, we turned H2S on immediately we crossed the enemy coast and left it on. There were rumours about the Germans being able to track H2S but they would have known we were there anyway because they had very sophisticated radar equipment.

Apparently one of the other Groups, possibly 3 Group, discontinued its use of H2S because they knew about German night-fighters homing in on their planes. 4 Group headquarters knew about it as well but they did not tell us to stop using it. The truth only emerged after the war. That was good of them, wasn't it?

If Doug hadn't recognised the headland there would have been nothing more to do except go back home with the mines. The other planes from our squadron were around but they could not have helped us as we kept complete radio silence. Even though we were all heading to the same place and at the same time, we couldn't wait around for a visual sighting and then bomb when they bombed. It didn't work that way. Waiting around would have been too dangerous. We had to get straight in, lay our mines and get out of there. We didn't want to be flying around a target with the aircraft stream coming at us either. It had to be straight in and straight out. We were all individual aircraft doing our own thing. We never worried about other aircraft. We never saw them. They might have been miles away.

While we were gardening in the Flensburg Fiord, a large force of about six hundred Lancasters and Halifaxes went back to Kiel, to have another go at the shipbuilding yards but apparently the attack was a failure. At this stage of the war, Kiel was the major Bomber Command target. There was a lot of activity in the area. In April and early May, until the end of the war, they bombed Kiel eleven times and closed the harbour with two more minelaying operations.

While we were away from base, the weather closed right in. Visibility was so poor that we were told to divert to the American airforce base at Chelveston in Northamptonshire, over a hundred miles south of Pocklington. It was the home of the 305th Heavy Bombardment Group which flew Flying Fortresses.

Pilot Officer Cyril Barton, VC

Halifax pilot, Pilot Officer Cyril Barton of 578 Squadron, was posthumously awarded the Victoria Cross for his bravery during a night time bombing operation to Nuremburg on the 30th/31st March 1944. His squadron, a 4 Group squadron, was located at Burn, a small village twenty-five kilometres south of York. He and his crew had completed sixteen operations before the Nuremburg raid.

The flight of heavy bombers was intercepted by German night fighters before it had crossed the Belgian border into Germany and the deadly attack continued to the target abating only as the night fighters left the battle to refuel. Eighty-two aircraft were shot down before the flight reached Nuremburg and thirteen more were lost as they made their way home.

Cyril Barton's Halifax, E-Easy (LK797), was attacked by a JU88 and later by an Me410 while they were on the long leg of their flight across Germany, but still approximately one hundred kilometres from the target. The Halifax was badly damaged. Two fuel tanks were punctured and the fuel lost, the rear turret was destroyed, the radio and navigation equipment was unserviceable, intercom lines were cut and worse the inner starboard engine was in flames and there was fire and smoke inside the fuselage.

Cyril Barton, posthumously awarded the Victoria Cross for bravery during a night raid on Nuremburg on the 30th/31st March 1944.

In his account of the mission in the book *Halifax and Wellington*, the mid-upper gunner, Sergeant H. D. Wood, wrote: "The starboard inner engine had been vibrating furiously and evidently had been badly damaged. Eventually its propeller, which had been red hot, tore loose and flew up and way into the night, looking like an enormous Catherine Wheel. The engine did not catch fire but sparks flew back briefly. These ceased and the engine died."

Amidst the confusion and alarm, the bomb aimer, navigator and wireless operator misinterpreted a signal from the intercall light system and bailed out. The remaining crew members extinguished the flames.

At that point most pilots would have turned back towards England which was at least three hours flying time away. But assessing the situation, Barton decided to complete the mission and bomb the target. Believing he was bombing on target indicators, he mistakenly bombed the town of Schweinfurt, ninety kilometres north-west of Nuremburg. This done he turned the aircraft towards home with reduced power from the three serviceable engines and without a navigator to keep the Halifax on course. When they approached the coast to cross into English airspace they were fired upon by coastal batteries and fearing that they would be shot down by friendly fire headed back out to sea, using up valuable fuel supplies which were already critically low. They approached the English coast again some 150 kilometres north of their airfield. The engineer, Sergeant Maurice Trousdale, believed that there was enough fuel on board to allow them to find an airfield and land safely, however he did not know that in the attack the fuel pipes from the remaining tank had been severed. He switched tanks but the fuel ran out instead of going into the engines. Nearing the coalmining village of Ryhope, Cyril Barton told his three remaining crew members to immediately prepare for a crash landing. Wrestling with the controls, he brought the stricken Halifax down and it crashed into a nearby coalmining pit.

Cyril Barton was pulled out of the wreckage alive but died while being taken to hospital. One miner on his way to work at the nearby pit was killed. The two air gunners and engineer were injured but survived.

Pilot officer Barton was posthumously awarded the Victoria Cross, the only Handley Page Halifax crewman to receive the award.

Chapter 69: Operation 39 - Heligoland

969 aircraft - 617 Lancasters, 332 Halifaxes, 20 Mosquitos - of all groups attacked the naval base at Heligoland, the airfield and the town on this small island. The bombing was accurate and the target areas were turned almost into crater-pitted moonscapes. 3 Halifaxes were lost.
The Bomber Command War Diaries, 13/14 April 1945

On the 18th of April, flying N-Nan, we were briefed to bomb the guns and military installations on the island of Heligoland. That was the British name for it. Twenty Halifaxes took off from Pocklington. We carried eleven and a half thousand pounds of heavy explosives, probably made up of nine 1,000 pound and five 500 pound bombs. We would have gone direct to the target over the North Sea. The time of the raid was only four hours and twenty five minutes so we didn't dogleg at all.

Heligoland is an island off the coast of Germany - between the German coast and the southern Denmark coast. It was a repeated thorn in the side of Bomber Command and the navy all through the war. It was very heavily defended. For a short while a Messerschmitt fighter squadron operated from Dune, the small island nearby. Heligoland had numerous ack-ack defences as well as big naval guns that could destroy any ships that approached from twenty-five miles away or more. It was right in the track of Bomber Command's attacks on Berlin and flying over it was studiously avoided. It had very steep cliffs and caves built underneath for storage. Large submarine pens had also been built into the cliffs by the Germans.

At briefing when the Wing Commander announced that we were going to bomb Heligoland a great roar of approval went up. That's what we all thought about the prospect of bombing it. Rightly or wrongly we thought it should be bombed because it was continually causing problems.

This trip took place on a sparkling sunny day. We took off at 1105 in the morning. We saw the steep cliffs of the island very clearly as we approached on our bombing run. Everything went to plan. We had a fighter escort, there was little opposition and the pathfinders put the markers down accurately.

It was a real get square operation for Bomber Command for all the troubles that Heligoland had caused during the war. It was almost a full, thousand bomber raid and we obliterated the target completely. The before-and-after photographs show that the bombing was very concentrated and everything was destroyed. It was so intense that the island looked like a lunar landscape when we had finished with it. It was well over the top but that's war!

Some war historians have made the point that there wasn't a thing that bombing streams could do when they were heading off or returning from raids except fly over Heligoland. No doubt they are referring to our targets in north-west Germany such as Wilhelmshaven, and minelaying operations in the Kattegat. I don't think this is quite right. Why would a flight plan tell us to fly over a heavily defended area when it could be avoided by a slight change of course? It doesn't make sense. We would just fly around it. It is more likely that the Royal navy were the ones whose noses were out of joint because they didn't dare let any of their warships go anywhere near Heligoland. If they did the ships would have been blown out of the water in no time. Heligoland also offered protection for German ships returning to their home ports. The British navy couldn't chase them in there. Once they were near the island they were safe from from naval attack. Heligoland was just like a big battleship moored off the coast which they couldn't sink. It was probably all of this frustration that built up during the war years and made its way into our briefing room that day.

When we returned to base one of our planes had a big hole in its bomb doors. They decided that a bomb must have come loose on the outward journey. The crew was lucky that the whole plane didn't explode before they reached the target.

Heligoland

The Heligoland Archipelago is located in the North Sea, some fifty kilometres from Germany's north-west coast. The busy waters south and east of Heligoland are known as the Heligoland Bight. In the First World War, two of the largest naval battles were fought there. The first air battle of the Second World War was also fought there.

Control of the Heligoland Bight was critical to Germany during the Second World War. It was the gateway to the immensely important shipbuilding, manufacturing and petrochemical industries in cities such as Wilhelmshaven and Hamburg. The Kaiser-Wilhelm-Kanal, which linked the North Sea and the Baltic Sea, entered the Heligoland Bight at Brunsbuttel near the mouth of the Elbe River. The canal stretched ninety-eight kilometres to Kiel on the Baltic Sea. Warships could move quickly through the canal rather than sail the extra 450 kilometres around the Jutland Peninsula. Outgoing ships and U-boats could start operations in the North Atlantic faster and returning warships and supply ships were able find shelter sooner in the better protected waters of the Baltic Sea.

In the shipyards located along the southern coast of the Heligoland Bight some of the legendary German battleships and heavy cruisers were built. In 1939, the 42,000 ton Bismark and its sister-ship, the Tirpitz were built at Hamburg and Wilhelmshaven respectively. The 35,000 ton Scharnhorst was built at Wilhelmshaven in 1936. As well, shipyards at Emden, Wilhelmshaven, Bremen, Vegesack and Hamburg were responsible for building 703 of Germany's 1,154 commissioned U-boats.

During the First World War Heligoland was arguably the world's most impregnable fortress. Its massive cannons, capable of firing a 406 kilogram shell accurately with a range of over twenty kilometres, were dismantled after the war under the terms of the Treaty of Versailles.

As the Second World War approached Heligoland was rearmed and refortified. It's radar directed cannons were capable of inflicting heavy damage on any ship that closed to within forty kilometres of the island and the withering fire from over fifty radar controlled ack-ack guns created a ferocious barrage through which approaching British and American aircraft would have to fly.

In 1938, the two islands had six batteries with eighteen cannons and eleven ack-ack guns. By 1945, there were twelve batteries with thirty-two cannons and fifty-one ack-ack guns. In January 1945, guns were still being repositioned on the island and in March, less than six weeks before Germany's surrender, a new battery of four 10.5 centimetre cannons was installed to protect the harbour breakwaters.

View of the Second World War fortress island of Heligoland, from the north-west, with the smaller island of Dune behind.

The main target for Allied operations against Heligoland was the Kriegsmarine U-boat base *Nordsee 3*. By 1941 the base had berths for the refuelling, rearming, reprovisioning and repairing of up to nine submarines at a time. If necessary, submarines could be removed from the water on a floating dry dock. The base was very well protected from heavy bombing. Reinforced concrete on the roof was three metres thick and the walls were two metres thick. The bunker was 156 metres long and ninety-four metres wide. Although the island bristled with cannons, Nordsee 3 was defended by only two 3.7 and one 2.0 centimetre flak guns and a two metre wide searchlight.

After the D-Day landings, the use of Nordsee 3 by U-boats declined and the pens were mainly used as shelter for E-boats and midget submarines. "Sprengboote", motor boats filled with explosives and driven into the target with the sailor jumping overboard before the explosion, were also operated from the island.

The "Lobster Claws Project" demonstrates the enormous strategic importance that the German war cabinet attributed to Heligoland as war approached. The project called for the reclamation of land between the islands of Heligoland and Dune, amounting to fifteen times the area of Heligoland itself, and the establishment of a naval base capable of sustaining Germany's Atlantic fleet and U-boat packs. As well, the island was honeycombed with a labyrinth of reinforced tunnels connecting storage and supply depots and bomb shelters. The map of the ambitious scheme below shows the remarkable extent of the plan, its unusual name perhaps coming from the anticipated shape of the reclaimed land.

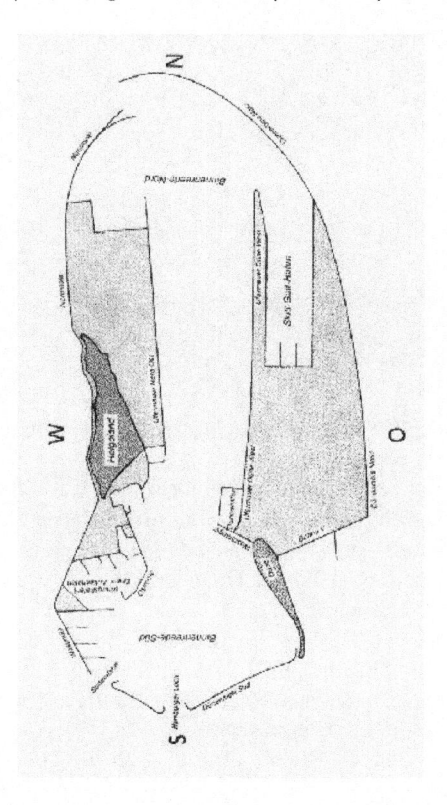

Heligoland Lobster Claws Project

As part of the Lobster Claws project a small Luftwaffe airfield was built on Dune but the short runways allowed only a small squadron of Messerschmitt Bf 109Ts, planes specially adapted for aircraft carrier deployment, to operate from the island from late 1942 until late 1944.

As the war progressed, the RAF and the USAAF took control of the skies over the North Sea. By the end of 1941, with the loss of the cruiser Blücher and the battleships Admiral Graf Spee and Bismarck, the sea-war too had turned against Germany. Heligoland was wide open to Allied attack and the Lobster Claws Project was abandoned.

From March 1944 until April 1945, Bomber Command intensified its bombing of Heligoland and minelaying operations in the surrounding seas.

A dramatic photograph taken during the 18th April 1945 attack on Heligoland. Bombs fall and bomb craters litter the north-east coast of the island. The two lines of the X on the smaller island of Dune are the runways of the abandoned Luftwaffe base.

During this time the RAF launched three bombing and seven minelaying operations against the island. The USAAF bombed the island five times. Three of these operations targeted the U-boat base.

In this chapter, Basil Spiller tells the story of his part in the RAF raid on Heligoland on the 18th of April 1945. N-Nan was part of a massive force of 969 bombers that attacked the two islands. The remarkable photograph above shows eight bombs falling towards their target. Bombs are seen exploding on Heligoland, the island in the bottom right corner of the picture. The small Luftwaffe airfield on the island of Dune stands out clearly, its two runways forming the "X" in the photograph.

The before and after photographs below, taken by reconnaissance aircraft, show the scale of the destruction wrought during the raid. According to the *Bomber Command War Diaries*, the target areas were turned "almost into crater-pitted moonscapes".

The final raid on Heligoland was conducted on the following day when twenty-two Tallboy bombs were dropped. Despite these two awesome attacks, the U-boat pens were not damaged. The war in Europe ended just eighteen days after the 18th of April raid. With the war obviously coming to a close, the two bombing operations were massive attacks on a target that had become irrelevant.

Heligoland before and after the RAF raid on 18th April 1945.

After the war Heligoland was initially used as a bombing range by the RAF. On the 18th of April 1947, two years to the day after the mission described by Basil Spiller in this chapter (and two days before the anniversary of Adolph Hitler's birth) six thousand seven hundred tonnes of explosives were packed into the U-boat pens, underground storage tunnels and remnant fortifications on the island and detonated by the British navy, from a warship fourteen kilometres from the island. The blast yield was 3.2 kilotons, an explosion one quarter the size of the nuclear bombing of Hiroshima but 1600 times larger than the 1995 Oklahoma City bombing. Film of the April 18th 1945 operation and the 1947 explosion and its aftermath are readily available on the internet.

In 1952 the Heligoland Archipelago was returned to Germany and it has since been resettled.

Chapter 70: Operation 40 – Wangerooge

Wangerooge: 482 aircraft - 308 Halifaxes, 158 Lancasters, 16 Mosquitos - of Nos 4, 6 and 8 Groups. 5 Halifaxes and 2 Lancasters lost. The raid was intended to knock out the coastal batteries on this Frisian island which controlled the approaches to the ports of Bremen and Wilhelmshaven. The weather was clear and bombing was accurate until smoke and dust obscured the target area. 6 of the 7 bombers lost were involved in collisions - 2 Halifaxes of No. 6 Squadron, 2 Lancasters of No. 431 Squadron and 2 Halifaxes of Nos 408 and 426 Squadrons (both from Leeming airfield). The seventh aircraft lost was a Halifax of No. 347 (Free French) Squadron, whose crew were all killed. *Total effort for the day:* 857 sorties, 9 aircraft (1.0 per cent) lost.

The Bomber Command War Diaries, 25 April 1945

On the 25th of April 1945 we were briefed to bomb Wangerooge, one of the Frisian Islands situated near Wilhelmshaven in the Jade Bight. Further east is the Elbe estuary which leads down to Hamburg. Wangerooge was in a very strategic position. It was another fortress island but it was smaller scale than Heligoland. No-one at the base knew that this was going to be 102 Squadron's final bombing operation and it turned out to be the last operation for most Bomber Command squadrons. At the time I remember that we had a very definite idea that the war was about to end because we all knew that the Allies and the Russians were knocking at the gates of Berlin and it was only a matter of time.

I understood from briefing that the mission was to attack U-boat pens to deter high ranking Nazi individuals from escaping to Argentina by submarine. This was a big Bomber Command effort and it was made in broad daylight. Over 450 heavy bombers went on this mission, so Bomber Command was definitely making a big statement for such a small target.

Nineteen Halifaxes left Pocklington. It was a clear, sunny day. We took off at 1440 in the afternoon and the trip lasted only four hours and ten minutes, so we were back at Pocklington at 1850 that evening. We flew a direct flight over the North Sea and carried eleven and a half thousand pounds of bombs, our maximum bomb load – all heavy explosive. There would have been nine 1,000 pound MC (Medium Capacity) and five 500 pound MC bombs.

We flew in the middle wave. I can clearly remember looking out through the nose of the plane when Doug Young was over his bombsight. I was looking at the flak. It was as intense as anything I had ever seen before. I saw two planes destroyed in the first wave. They were probably Pathfinder Force Lancasters. Each one had a wing shorn off completely and immediately exploded. I saw them both in flames by the wing root and spiralling madly down to earth in a vertical dive. The flak was everywhere. I saw no parachutes. Those guys had bought it right at the end of the war. I was despairing and very scared. My immediate reaction was: "Christ! I've come this far. Am I going to buy it here, at the end of the war?" I can still remember how I felt to this day. It is a vivid memory!

The Pathfinders marked the target well and the first waves bombed accurately but the markers were lost in the smoke from exploding bombs and the bombing became more ragged. By the time the third and fourth waves reached the target the flak had diminished completely. The Lancasters would have probably been carrying more bombs than the Halifaxes and we had 11,500 pounds, so more than 2,400 tons of bombs were dropped on Wangerooge that day. Sobering isn't it? We bombed successfully, plastered the joint and returned to base.

This was a pretty big way to go out on our last mission - with a full on Bomber Command operation. There were no fighter attacks. We had been very lucky because my crewmates and I never had a daylight fighter attack while we were on operations together.

The RAF Pocklington War Diary for this raid describes the flak as "slight to moderate" but this is totally wrong. *The RAF Elvington War Diary* at least describes the flak as "moderate heavy". I know what I saw!

Seven aircraft were lost. Officially, six of the seven planes are listed as being subject to mid air collisions but how could they tell through everything that was going on over the target? As far as I know, I saw two Lancasters shot down by flak and I saw them falling. One of the planes was a Halifax from No. 347 Squadron, the Free French squadron, at Elvington – our satellite squadron. With the Germans already driven out of France they would have been excited about going home. The seven crew members were all killed. Their Halifax, E-Easy NP921, broke in half and crashed into the sea. Four of their bodies were recovered and they were buried on the beach at Wangerooge. These men were the last heavy bomber casualties of the war.

We had no idea that this would be our last mission but the powers that be knew something that we didn't know. We didn't go on leave. We waited and we drank beer!

Wangerooge

Wangerooge is one of the Frisian Islands, an extensive line of islands that stretches some five hundred kilometres along the north-west coasts of the Netherlands and Germany, and the south-west coast of Denmark. From west to east Wangerooge is eight kilometres long and has a maximum width at the western end of just one and a half kilometres. Its area is approximately five square kilometres.

The Second World War "fortress island" of Wangerooge.

In both the First and Second World Wars, Wangerooge was heavily fortified and defended because of its strategic importance. Just thirty kilometres south of Wangerooge is Wilhelmshaven a vital North Sea port, naval base and shipbuilding centre.

German naval ships, including the legendary battleships Admiral Graf Spee, Tirpitz and Scharnhorst, were built at the Wilhelmshaven shipyards as well as twenty seven U-boats.

The raid described by Basil Spiller in this chapter came just thirteen days before the end of the war in Europe, Victory in Europe Day, on the 8th of May 1945.

News of this attack on Wangerooge was reported in the Tasmanian *Mercury* newspaper two days after the raid. Like the extract from the *Bomber Command War Diaries* at the start of this chapter, it presents a strong indication of the ferocity of this bombing raid and the damage wrought on the island.

Newspaper Report – Wangerooge

Concentrated Air Attack on Friesian Island
Australian Associated Press

London, Thurs. – Five hundred Halifax and Lancaster bombers escorted by Spitfires attacked coastal guns and fortified positions on the Friesian Island of Wangerooge near the mouth of the River Weiser yesterday.

The attack began soon after 5 pm and the bombing was so highly concentrated that the master bomber controlling the attack stopped the bombing of several targets because he considered no more damage could be done.

Smoke covered the whole island and fires were spreading throughout the entire target area as the last aircraft turned for home. Seven bombers are missing.

The Mercury **(Hobart, Tasmania). Friday 27 April 1945**

Bombing Wangerooge

Wangerooge. 25th April 1945. In the top left corner of the photograph, two Halifax bombers can be seen on their bombing runs over the island.

Chapter 71: Last Days On The Squadron

The mission to Wangerooge was 102 Squadron's last bombing operation. I was still in the squadron with the rest of my crew when the end of the war in Europe was announced. Between Wangerooge and that announcement there were only a few smaller scale bombing missions while negotiations with the Germans were taking place in earnest.

On the night after Wangerooge the last heavy bomber raid of the war was conducted when 107 Lancasters and twelve Mosquitos attacked the Tonsberg oil refinery in southern Norway. After that Bomber Command concentrated on ferrying Allied prisoners of war who had been released by the Germans back to Britain, and doing emergency food drops to starving people in the Netherlands. On several smaller raids, most of them near Kiel, Mosquitos were used.

After we bombed Wangerooge I flew six more times - one of these as a passenger. On the 28th of April, Bill and I ferried Air Commodore Walker from base to RAF Hooton Park in Cheshire in an Airspeed Oxford. There and back was a short flight of one hour and forty minutes. Hooton Park was an airfield where a lot of lend lease aircraft were assembled after they arrived from America. Unwanted aircraft were also sent there during the war to be scrapped. We left Gus Walker there and Bill and I flew back to base.

My log book then shows that Bill, Harry, John and I ferried Halifax III, MZ486, to an aerodrome called Kinloss, on the 2nd of May 1945, six days before the war in Europe ended. We didn't need a bomb aimer or gunners so Doug, Mick and Bill (Ollerton) stayed at Pocklington. The airfield was near Findhorn Bay on the north coast of Scotland and its runways ended right on the North Sea. Occasionally very high tides would flood the runways. It had been an OTU right through the war and became the home of a coastal command squadron. 102 Squadron was flying Halifax 3s to Kinloss because Maintenance Unit 45 was based there and after the war they broke them up and sold them as salvage. I can remember that for the return journey, they packed all the crews into one aircraft and flew us back to Pocklington. We all found a place on the floor. My log book says that our return flight was in a Halifax 6 piloted by Flight Sergeant Cowper but in his log, Bill wrote that he flew us back in Halifax VI, H-Harry PP171 and that Flight Sergeant Cooper was second dickie. Bill might have pulled rank. We left base at 1220 hours and the flight up took two hours and ten minutes. We left to go home at 1618 and the flight took one hour and twenty five minutes, so it looks like Bill was driving on the way back!

The next day they flew more planes up to Kinloss but we only did the one trip. As a matter of interest the Halifax that we flew back from Kinloss was sold after the war to the Lancashire Aircraft Corporation, a domestic airline company.

Our last three flights were in Halifax Mark VI's. On the 3rd of May we did a short flight that involved fighter affiliation, circuits and landings and the blind bombing of York which was a practice bombing run over York with "bombs away" and all that but without any bombs. We flew in Halifax M-Mary RG505.

After that we did our last two flights on N-Nan. On the 6th of May we did a full scale cross-country. We took off at 1515 and returned later that night at 2100. It was almost a six hour flight so looking back on this I can see that they were still keeping us on a war footing. We flew from base to Southwold, Bury St Edmunds, Cambridge, Maidstone, Reading, Bristol, Stoke-on-Trent, York and back to base. It was almost like a farewell tour of England.

Finally on the 7th of May we did a "formation cross-country". So our last flight for 102 Squadron at Pocklington, the day before the war in Europe ended, was in formation with other crews from the squadron. We did not do many of those. When I think about it now, it was a fitting way to say goodbye. The whole squadron went up together and we went out in style.

Until recently, I didn't know what had happened to our last Halifax - Mark VI, N-Nan RG532, but some recent research has explained where she ended her days. The records at the Royal Air Force Museum in London show that Halifax RG532 was flown to No. 48 Maintenance Unit which was based at the RAF Hawarden airfield near Chester in north-east Wales. The paperwork gives the date as the 30th November 1945. It probably stayed there for several months because it was included in the Home Census in March 1946.

Then it is listed as being "struck off charge" on the 10th of September 1946. This means that it was taken off the books. When this happened during the war it was because planes had been too badly damaged or were too unserviceable to repair. After the war our N-Nan must have been declared excess to requirements and its airframe stripped of anything useful and the rest scrapped.

Halifax MZ486, the plane that we left at Kinloss, was struck off charge on the 12th of February 1947, five months later than N-Nan, even though it was an older Mark III and we were still flying N-Nan when we delivered Halifax MZ486 to Maintenance Unit 45. It may have been scrapped earlier than N-Nan but that is the date that the paperwork caught up with it.

Our last N-Nan was a beautiful plane and I could not believe that the

RAF would send their most modern planes to be scrapped by maintenance units and salvage companies. The earlier Mark II's and III's yes, but not the Mark VI's. I have heard since that it was government policy to do just that – to scrap brand new aircraft.

After the First World War had finished, the British government cancelled orders for new planes and the aircraft industry collapsed. To prevent this from happening at the end of World War II, they may have allowed production to continue so that research and development would keep going and people could keep their jobs. A lot of aircraft were flown straight from the factory to the wreckers without going to squadrons first. As well, it should be pointed out that jet aircraft were starting to appear and the Canberra jet bomber was already on the drawing board as a replacement for the Mosquito.

I was at Pocklington the 8th of May when the war ended in Europe. There was huge celebration in the officers' mess. We all got drunk. It was a big party. Everyone was happy and excited.

There were almost two thousand Halifaxes still on charge with the RAF all over the country. Bomber Command could put five hundred up on an operation. That is three and a half thousand crewmen right there. Then there were the HCU's. Then there were the aircrews for Lancasters and Mosquitos, not to mention fighter planes. Then there was a ground crew for each plane and administrative personnel in every squadron.

With the war over, the last thing the RAF wanted was thousands of men hanging around the squadrons, twiddling their thumbs, with thousands of bombers parked at airfields all around the country with nothing to bomb. That was why they moved so quickly to pack up 102 Squadron.

On the 8th of May, No. 102 Squadron was officially transferred into Transport Command. They wanted us out of there as quickly as possible. A couple of days later, all the Australian airmen from Pocklington were transferred to Driffield, the base from which 466 RAAF Halifax Squadron operated. A lot of Australians from other squadrons were there too. A few days after we got there we were called on parade. The Top Brass asked for volunteers to join Transport Command. Nobody volunteered, much to their disgust. They called us for everything but everybody stood their ground. We all wanted to go home.

We'd gone up every night. We accepted that we would probably die. We had seen our mates fall. We'd been wounded and kept going. We'd signed on for the war, not the peace and now the war was over. We'd done our job and it was time to go home.

Victory In Europe Day, 102 Squadron RAF

A photograph taken at 102 Squadron's navigation section on VE Day 1945. Basil Spiller, on the right, is standing next his friend Harold Hammond of the RNZAF. In the middle is Mary, the navigation section secretary.

Part 7

Going Home

Sydney, 28th July 1945. Some of the 2000 RAAF personnel who have arrived home from England, lining the sides of the troopship SS Andes as she ties up at Woolloomooloo wharf.

Chapter 72:   Liverpool to Sydney

After a few days I was posted to report to Brighton to be embarked back to Australia. I left Driffield and travelled down by train and duly reported to the Grand Hotel in Brighton where I was once again billeted.

Every morning on the notice-board the names of the men in next draft would be posted with the names of the ships on which they would be travelling back to Australia. One morning I was standing in front of the notice-board when the fellow alongside me saw his name on the list for the next draft back home. He was upset because he'd just married an English girl and didn't want to go. I offered to take his place. He and I went to the office and got his name taken off and mine put in his place. That's why I got back so early.

By about the 20th of June, I was on a ship called the Andes, which left from Liverpool. We travelled back to Australia across the Atlantic and through the Panama Canal. The Andes was filled with aircrew from all parts of Australia. None of my Pocklington crewmates were on the voyage. We had all said our goodbyes. The only person on board I knew was Hal Slader, with whom I had gone to school. He was a good friend of mine. Miraculously, I had hooked up with him again at Brighton. It was just luck that we happened to get on the same boat. And we had both survived the war!

I can remember how good the food was on the Andes. That was the first time I'd enjoyed asparagus for lunch. I played "Five Hundred" every day for five and a half weeks all the way from England to Australia with the same three guys. We became psychic. We could read each other's minds after playing the same game over and over again.

It was the middle of summer and the voyage down the middle of the Atlantic was most enjoyable. The sea was like a millpond and the sun shone every day. After a couple of weeks we entered Limon Bay and anchored at the deepwater port of San Cristobal in Colon, the Atlantic entrance to the Panama Canal. We stayed there for three days in tropical sunlight in our heavy English winter uniforms and we all cooked and sweated like mad. We were right on the equator but we couldn't take them off because we had nothing else to put on. We stayed onboard all the time. The previous ship was filled with Australian army POWs from Greece, and they had wrecked the joint. We paid for it because we were refused leave to go ashore.

Eventually we proceeded through the locks on the Atlantic side of the Panama Canal and emerged into Gaton Lake which was eighty five feet higher than the Atlantic coastline. It was quite incongruous to me that the narrow isthmus of Panama contained such a huge lake. After anchoring for a while and being permitted to swim and cool off we proceeded through the cuts of the Panama Canal. It was an awe inspiring spectacle - a big liner moving through the jungle with nothing to spare on either side. You could almost touch the leaves of the trees on the banks. Next came the first stage of our descent to the Pacific Ocean. We moved into the Pedro Miguel Lock and were lowered thirty-one feet into Miraflores Lake. Just on dusk we arrived at the Pacific side of the canal and they lowered us down fifty-four feet in three stages, through three locks to the level of the Pacific Ocean. It had taken us all day to get through the canal. We didn't anchor at Balboa harbour and proceeded straight out into the Pacific Ocean.

We encountered beautiful weather in the Pacific until we got to within a couple of days from Wellington in New Zealand and we ran into a southerly buster. Very rough weather! Half of the guys got seasick but not me. I was a seasoned campaigner as a boy in Papua and I was quite used to it.

We arrived at Wellington and stayed there a whole day. The local RSL put on a big spread for us in one of the sheds on the wharf where we docked. Every bit of table space was occupied by a bottle of Cascade longneck beer. Cascade beer from Tasmania! We couldn't believe it. We got thoroughly plastered on good old Aussie beer. For the first time in a couple of years we were tasting real beer!

The SS (Steam Ship) *Andes*

The Steam Ship (SS) Andes was built to the highest standards at the Harland and Wolff shipyards in Belfast, Northern Ireland, for the Royal Mail Line (RML). It was to be the pride of their fleet carrying first and second class passengers, mail and cargo between the United Kingdom and South America. Coincidentally, the RML believed that its major competitor would be the *SS Pasteur*, on which Basil Spiller sailed to the UK from Halifax, Canada, to complete his airforce training and begin his tour of duty with the RAF.

Many renowned ships were built at the Belfast shipyards of Harland and Wolff Heavy Industries. The more famous ones include the Titanic, and the Royal Navy's HMS Belfast.

The Andes was launched on the 7th of March 1939, six months before the start of the Second World War. Original film of Viscountess Craigavon launching the Andes is readily available on the internet.

Its first voyage was scheduled for the 26th of September 1939 but on the 1st of September war was declared while the Andes was in the final stages of fitting out. The Andes was immediately requisitioned by the British navy to be used as a troop ship and it spent the next eight years on active service.

When returned to the company in 1947, the ship was refitted as a luxury passenger liner. Its new livery was an elegant white hull and superstructure and the traditional yellow funnel.

The Andes was a 25,689 ton steamer with powerful twin screw turbine engines capable of delivering thirty thousand shaft horsepower. Its maximum speed was twenty-one knots and it could travel up to twelve thousand miles without refuelling. The ship was almost 670 feet long, eighty four feet wide and had a draft of thirty feet.

The official postcard of the Royal Mail Line ship, the RMS Andes.

Providing food for over four thousand service men and women was a massive undertaking. Meals were plentiful and mealtimes were staggered but there was always a scramble for food. In this chapter, Basil Spiller mentions that the troops on the Andes were fed very well. He vividly remembers that it was the first time he had eaten asparagus. A quick internet search shows that sentiment is echoed by others. The bread which was baked daily on the ship is singled out for special praise.

The Andes was built to provide a luxurious and memorable cruise for up to five hundred wealthy passengers on each voyage. After being requisitioned, it was immediately fitted out for the war. Windows and expensive fittings were boarded up for protection and deluxe staterooms, dining rooms and entertainments were replaced with cramped accommodation for over four thousand troops, sleeping on mattresses on the floor or in hammocks strung from the ceilings. The troop deck alone had bunks for 2,290 men.

The Andes' first wartime voyage was to Halifax on the 9th of December 1939, and it returned to the UK with the first Canadian troops for the war. It went on to carry many thousands of troops and voyaged to ports all around the world in the Atlantic, the Pacific and the Orient for the next eight years.

Basil Spiller is uncertain about the dates of his departure for Australia. He recalls that the Andes left Liverpool in "mid June" and arrived in "late July". Research suggests that the Andes weighed anchor to begin the voyage from the Liverpool docks on the 21st of June 1945. A brief internet search revealed the story of personnel from Mobile Naval Operating Air Base No. 7 boarding the Andes and sailing from Liverpool to Australia on this date.

The Andes berthed in Sydney Harbour on Saturday the 28th of July 1945. It had taken thirty-seven days to travel across the Atlantic Ocean, through the Panama Canal, across the Pacific Ocean to Wellington and on to Sydney.

The Andes was immediately provisioned and refuelled, returning to England via Karachi and the Suez Canal, making the round trip in just seventy two days, the world record for a round the world voyage at that time.

The Andes was handed back to the Royal Mail Line by the Admiralty in 1947. After an extensive refit it entered service on the Latin America run between Britain and Brazil as a luxury passenger liner.

In 1959 it received a third major refit and reappeared as a cruise ship operating in the tourist market. At the time of its last refit in 1967 the Andes was nearing the end of its operational life. In 1971 it was sent to Ghent in Belgium to be broken up.

Chapter 73: Brisbane and Sandgate

STIRRING WELCOME TO 660 AIRMEN
Big Crowds of Relatives

Cheering crowds on the harbour foreshores on Saturday morning gave a stirring welcome to 660 repatriated R.A.A.F. men, including 150 former prisoners of war. As the ship berthed, relatives and friends eagerly scanned the decks to catch a glimpse of men they had not seen for several years. After disembarkation, the men were taken in special buses to the R.A.A.F. personnel depot at Bradfield Park. The largest crowd of civilians yet seen at Bradfield Park waited outside the parade ground to meet the men after they had completed formalities and started their leave. Addressing the men on the parade ground, the chairman of the New South Wales Recruiting Drive Committee, Sir Donald Cameron, said he had received excellent reports from overseas of the courage and exemplary behaviour of R.A.A.F. personnel. Their exploits had become world famous.

The Sydney Morning Herald. **Monday 30 July 1945**

Bradfield Park, Sydney, 29th July 1945. A section of the march-past of RAAF servicemen after their arrival home aboard the British troopship SS Andes.

After a couple of days, in late July, we arrived in Sydney. We were disembarked and taken to the holding depot at Bradfield Park, an RAAF station at West Lindfield, about eleven kilometres north-west of the Sydney CBD. At Bradfield Park we marched along the parade ground in front of a lot of people who were waiting for us there. We had an official welcome.

We were billeted overnight and the next day the Queenslanders boarded a troop train to take us back to Brisbane.

I can remember the troop train, especially because it was equipped with bunks to the ceiling. They had straw palliasses like at Cootamundra. We travelled overnight and when we arrived in Brisbane the next morning, we found a fleet of taxis waiting for us at Clapham Junction, in the southern suburbs of Brisbane, to take us through the Brisbane CBD to Sandgate. We were driven through a tickertape parade down Queen Street. It was very emotional. All the cheering crowds were there with us, welcoming us home.

When we got to Sandgate there was a big crowd and a welcoming committee – the Lord Mayor and parliamentary dignitaries. Through the crowd, I could see my own personal welcoming committee waiting for me. Betty was there! Her mother was there, also her aunts and uncles and Mrs Simpson, the mother of my mate Merv, who was killed in training at Dumfries when I was converting to Halifaxes. She came to see me too. I had not been in touch with Betty, or her family, or Mrs Simpson, so I wasn't sure how they knew I would be arriving at Sandgate that day. I found out later that my name and the names of over a hundred other Queensland airmen about to arrive in Brisbane were published in the Courier-Mail the day before. I can remember that Betty had on a pink, woollen, dress that she had knitted. She looked very beautiful. We were all drawn up in ranks until the speeches were delivered. Finally I was permitted to greet them. The memory of my welcome home is still very emotional and overwhelming. It was a very profound experience. The thought of it still is!

My father wasn't at Sandgate to meet me. As unbelievable as it may sound, he had joined the American army and he had been posted to Milne Bay in Papua to work in the stores. There would not have been many civilians travelling back there during the war and he planned to be discharged there so that he could make his way back to his coconut plantation and get it working again. Menapi was in Goodenough Bay, the next bay on from Milne bay. With his knowledge of trading along the coast he would have been a wonderful asset for the American top brass. My family was represented though. Dad's sister, Leah, and her husband, Jack Shearer, had come to Australia after being married in New Zealand and were living in Brisbane. They came to meet me too.

Our arrival at RAF Sandgate was in the papers. One of the articles about the parade says that as part of the formalities Flying Officer Bill Kaus was called out from the ranks and it was announced that he had won the DFC. I can't remember that but as a matter of interest, Bill Kaus received his DFC in November 1946 at Government House in the same ceremony as Don McLean, our bomb aimer, and me. He went on to become a member of parliament for twenty years. When Betty and I moved to our retirement village eight years ago, Bill Kaus and his wife moved here too but he died soon after. It's a small world though, isn't it?

Sity-eight years later my war experience is still a very emotional thing for me. Can you imagine what it was like? Coming home! The tickertape parade through the city! Arriving in Sandgate! Looking into the crowd! And there's Betty!"

Queensland Airmen Return

110 Qld. Airmen Return To-day

A party of 110 R.A.A.F. personnel returned from service overseas will arrive in Brisbane to-day. They include 25 ex-prisoners of war.

They will detrain at Clapham Junction at 10.10 a.m. and be transported to Sandgate along the route followed by the last party.

They are expected to cross Victoria Bridge into Queen Street between 10.45 and 11 a.m.

The ex-Prisoners of war are: W/O. A. T. Bell, Ipswich; W/O K. J. F Goulton.-East Brisbane; ....

Other returnees are:-

F/O, A. C. Warren, Ithaca; F/O. E. C. Watkins, Warwick; F/O. W. J. White, Newmarket; F/O. E. G. Wilson, Sandgate; F/O. B. J. Spiller, D.F.C., Milne Bay, Papua; .... F/O. A. Slader, Jericho....

Extract from ***The Courier-Mail*** **(Brisbane). Monday 30 July 1945**

Brisbane Street Parade

Ovation For Airmen

MANY of the R.A.A.F. returnees from Europe who arrived in Brisbane yesterday found the welcome given them in city and suburbs more overwhelming than any of their experiences.

Most of the party of 110, including 25 former prisoners of war, looked, fit and well after a comfortable journey in a luxury ship.

Flight-Lieut. J. E. Holliday (Cooparoo) said: 'The reception was marvellous. We knew all about it and dreaded it, but it has been great." His five years abroad included two years and nine months in German prison camp.

"This was well worth waiting for,' said Flight-Lieut. Gordon Given (Fairfield), referring not only to his welcome from his mother, Mrs. S. E. Given, sister Joyce, and brother Keith, but to the "good show" put on by the citizens. Two and a half years divided between three German prison camps found him ready for release from Lubeck with the arrival of the British 11th Armoured Division. Of his prison experience he said: 'It could have been worse. We had a theatre and opportunities for sport and study. We shall be eternally grateful for the parcels sent through the Red Cross."

Really Appreciated

Flying-Officer B. G. Spiller (New Guinea), back after two and a half years' flying in Halifaxes, got a thrill out of the public ovation and the greetings of relatives and friends. "We didn't expect anything like this," he said. "and we really do appreciate it!"

Flying-Officer F. T. Rabbets (South Brisbane) was greeted by his parents, Mr. and Mrs. F. L. G Rabbets, and fiancee, Miss Marjorie Bensley. Gibraltar, England, Wales, and the Hebrides provided the changing setting for his two and a half years abroad. He flew with Coastal Command. Just before he left for home he passed his staff navigator's examination with 85 per cent.

Reception committee for Flying Officer Les Tardent, D.F.C. (Wynnum), after his three years abroad included his wife, small sons Anthony and Gregory, his mother, Mrs. M. Tardent, and sister, Mrs. M. Fogarty, better known in musical circles as pianist Enid Tardent.

Freed By Tommies

Flying Officer B. D. McGill (Nundah) was very glad to meet the British Army at Boulogne last September after his plane had crashed, and he and the rest of the crew had parachuted to safety. "England was grand, but chilly," he said. "I hope Australian people give the English lads here as good a time as the English folk gave us."

"It was pretty good; we were lucky," said Flight Sergeant J. S Alexander (Atherton), who flew in Lancasters for 18 months. His brother is still in England, but the brother's fiancee, Lieut. Una Greer, A.W.A.S. was at Sandgate to welcome him.

Fruit Welcome

"I'm tickled pink to taste fruit. I had no fruit in England," said Pilot Officer Len Talty (Ipswich Road), who was greeted by his father, Mr. F. Talty, sister, Mrs. I. Mathews, and brother, W. O. Leo Talty.

The procession, in R.A.C.Q. cars from Clapham Junction to Sandgate station was frequently interrupted by enthusiastic crowds. Lines of washing in the suburb were left for the moment by aproned housewives, who waved and called greetings. School children gathered in larger groups than ever, business people waved from shops and buildings, and in South Brisbane a kerosene tin kept up a clamour. Albion reception committee again turned out with gifts of tropical fruit.

There was a special welcome for an old Albion Heights boy, Flight Lieut. John T. Rogers, D.F.C. (Toombul), who was in a car driven by his friend, driver P. V Garrett, A.I.F., whom he had not seen for four years.

At Sandgate the commanding officer, Wing Commander W. S. Walne, welcomed the men on behalf of the Air Force and gave them the Duke of Gloucester's message. The Attorney-General (Mr. Gledson) spoke for the Government. The Acting Premier (Mr. Hanlon) met the men at Clapham.

Wing Commander Walne thanked the Red Cross, Returned Soldiers' League, R.A.C.Q. and helpers from Albion for their part in the reception.

Mr. Hanlon said yesterday that when the next batch of R.A.A.F returnees arrived he would arrange to have sirens sounded at three points in the city to let people know when the men reached Victoria Bridge.

The Courier-Mail **(Brisbane).Tuesday 31 July 1945**

Arrival at RAAF Sandgate

Brisbane Airman Awarded Distinguished Service Cross
Brisbane July 31
When paraded before 6000 people at Sandgate to-day, Flying Officer Bill Kaus, of Brisbane, one of 110 men who reached Brisbane, received a "pleasant shock" when told that he had won the Distinguished Flying Cross. The award of the D.F.C. was promulgated after Kaus had left England on his way home, and he was unaware of his decoration until called out from the parade.

Among the returnees was a former inter-State cricketer and footballer, Flight-Lieutenant P.L. Dixon of Brisbane who had been a prisoner of war for nearly four years. His Wellington came down in the North Sea and he was picked up by a German seaplane.

***Cairns Post* (Queensland). Wednesday 1 August 1945**

Chapter 74: Discharge from the RAAF

After the formalities at Sandgate were over I had to decide where I wanted to stay for the ten day's leave that we had all been given. I suddenly had three alternatives. Mrs. Simpson's boarding house, Bett's uncle and aunty who lived in Cooparoo had invited me to stay with them, and Betty's parents invited me to stay at their place. Naturally I chose Betty's place because I was besotted with her and we duly proceeded to Wynham where her parents lived. It wasn't a difficult decision! I had met Bett's parents previously before I went away to Europe. I said hello to Mr Harley, Bett's father, when he came home from work. A few days after I arrived at Betty's place we were invited to go down to Palm Beach on the Gold Coast by Bett's uncle, George, who owned a block of flats there. I was reunited with wonderful Australian beaches and surf.

In the meantime I had proposed to Betty. I was pretty quick off the mark because I knew what I wanted to do. She'd accepted and we were engaged. One of George's neighbours at Palm Beach was a retired jeweller. I arranged with him to make an engagement ring for Betty. I paid fifty pounds for it, which was a lot of money when you think about what a man's wage was in Australia back then in 1945. The average weekly wage including overtime was about £5. It was about ten weeks' wages but I had plenty of money because I had been canny saving. It was worth every penny because Betty loved it.

After initially staying with Betty and her parents I felt I had to find somewhere else to live. They were hard up and I started to feel uncomfortable about living there. Betty did not want me to leave but I had sponged off them for long enough and had worn out my welcome. So I lived with my aunt and uncle, Leah and Jack Shearer for a while.

Shared story

I was discharged from the RAAF with my friend Hal Slader. His Christian and middle names were "Alfred Harold" but he liked to be called "Hal". There had been a remarkable similarity between our service histories. We knew one another really well before the war. We went to the same school in Charters Towers and were in the same class. We both enlisted in the airforce. Hal was in 29 Course and I was in 28 Course at No. 1 Air Observer's Station, Cootamundra. I explained earlier that I caught the mumps and was moved to 29 Course, and there was Hal. As well as that, we both embarked for Britain on the Mormacsea together and we travelled by rail in Pullman coaches up the western seaboard of America to Edmonton.

Halifax Navigator

Hal was one of our group of three in Edmonton with the three Canadian girls. We travelled to England together on the Louis Pasteur and after we disembarked in Liverpool we travelled by train to Brighton and stayed at the Grand Hotel. Then Hal went on leave to a Lady Ryder Scheme billet and I went to another. We lost track of each other for a while until we both turned up at Lichfield at the OTU to begin our training on Wellingtons. Like me he had to select a pilot and crew. I got posted to Halifaxes on No. 102 Squadron where I did a tour, and he was posted to Lancs on No. 463 Squadron at RAF Waddington where he did a tour. We did not meet up again until we both turned up at the Brighton embarkation depot. We travelled home to Australia on the Andes together. Two good mates who had survived the war!

Shorty Milliner

One day, not long after we returned to Australia, I met Hal in Queen Street, Brisbane. We were approached outside the main Allan and Stark door by a civilian gentleman. He wanted to know if we had come back from the UK and then he asked if we knew his son, Jack Milliner, who had been killed in an air-raid over Germany. We were able to tell him that we knew his son really well. We all called him "Shorty". It was the first we knew that Shorty didn't survive the war.

Shorty Milliner was in 29 Course with Hal and me. He went over on the Mormacsea with us, and went through Edmonton and Halifax and on the Louis Pasteur and then to Brighton with us. He was not a member of our particular group in Edmonton but he was a member of the forty odd guys that left Australia and travelled together to Brighton. He was on Lancs like Hal. He was posted as missing on his thirtieth mission. While I was looking at some newspaper clippings from that time I realized that Shorty was killed on the 25th of July 1944 on the Stuttgart raid that I was on. He was killed. I was spared. It was just luck!

Shorty was a pilot officer in RAF 75 (NZ) Squadron, which was based at RAF Mepal airfield, about ten kilometres west of Ely. It was a New Zealand Lancaster squadron operated by the RAF. He was the navigator on Lancaster HK568. It was a mixed crew. There was another Australian, two New Zealanders and three from the RAF. Counting Stuttgart I had chalked up seventeen operations, but Shorty had been really busy because Stuttgart was his thirtieth raid.

At that stage with the end of your tour in sight, you know it's almost over. They took off for Stuttgart at 2151 hours and nothing was heard from them after that. Shorty and all of his crew are buried at the Cronenbourg cemetery near Strasbourg which was a very well defended area. His plane could have been shot down by flak or a night fighter might have got them. Their flight plan would have been similar to ours. It took us near Strasbourg both on the way to Stuttgart and again heading home.

Shorty's family really missed him. Years after the war, on the anniversary of his death, his father, brother and uncle were still putting notices about him in the newspaper. It would have been the same in families all over Australia.

Discharge from the RAAF

While we were on leave, Hal and I were notified that we had to report to Redbank Military Station the next day. We were lined up and discharged from the RAAF. It was over quickly. They gave us a complete medical and paid us fully and that was all there was to it. Just like that. We were out the door! They couldn't get rid of us quickly enough. I wanted out desperately. I was sick of being in uniform and wanted to get back to civilian life. I felt relief. Hal went to university and studied civil engineering and got married. He and I played tennis together for several years. His wife became a friend of ours. He ended up as shire engineer of Balyando. His wife died suddenly at an early age and Hal then married his wife's sister.

Bett and I were married in 1946 and we had our honeymoon at Palm Beach. I was re-employed by Burns Philp and Co. and posted to their office in Lismore where we lived for a short while before I was transferred back to Brisbane.

Jack (Shorty) Milliner, Family Notices

P/O. Jack T. Milliner, son of Mr. H. T. Mlliner, O'Keefe Street, Buranda.
Previously reported missing. Now believed to have lost his life in air operations over Germany.
The Courier Mail **(Brisbane). Thursday 28 June 1945**

Milliner, **Jack**, Pilot Officer, Navigator, R.A.F., of Lancaster Bomber. – In proud & loving memory of my dear Son, previously reported missing over Germany, 25th July, 1944, now presumed dead also a tribute to the crew, who made the supreme sacrifice with him. Always remembered.
Inserted by his loving Father, Brother Keith, R.A.A.F., & Uncle Jim.
Milliner. - In fond and loving memory of our dear Pal, P.O. Jack T. Milliner (Johnnie), Navigator, Lancaster Bomber, missing from raid on Stuttgart. 25th July, 1944, believed killed.
Always remembered. Inserted by Joy & Nev (R.A.A.F., England).
Milliner. In loving memory of my very dear Friend, P.O. Jack T. Milliner. Navigator, Lancaster Bomber, missing from raid on Stuttgart, 25th July, 1944, believed

killed.
Oh, for the touch of a vanished hand. And the sound of a voice that is still.
Inserted by Miss Edith Small. Edmonton, Canada.
Milliner. - In fond memory of our dear Friend, P.O. Jack T. Milliner. Navigator, Lancaster Bomber, missing from raid on Stuttgart, 25th July, 1944, believed killed.
Inserted by McHardy Family, Wooloowin.
Milliner. - In memory of our Friend. Pilot-Officer Jack Milliner, presumed killed over Stuttgart, July 25, 1944.
Inserted by the Lund Family.
The Courier Mail **(Brisbane).** Wednesday 25 July 1945

Milliner - In loving memory of
Pilot Officer Jack Milliner, who lost his life over Germany, 25th July, 1944; also gallant Members of his Crew.
Always remembered.
Inserted by Dad. Brother, Keith, and Uncle Jim.
The Courier Mail **(Brisbane, Queensland). Friday 25 July 1952**

Basil and Betty's Honeymoon

Basil and Betty at Palm Beach on their honeymoon, 1946.

Chapter 75: Distinguished Flying Cross

Queenslanders Decorated

Decorated: Flt.-Lt. V. F. Cage, husband of Mrs. V. F. Cage, of Southport, awarded DFC.
Pilot-Officer Basil G. Spiller, son of Mr. H. Spiller, Menapi, Papua, awarded DFC.
Flt.-Lt. I. G. Durston, son of Mr. and Mrs. H. D. Durston, Rosemount Terrace, Windsor, posthumously awarded DFC. W./O. Arnold Kent, son of Mr. Allan Kent, of Brisbane, posthumously awarded DFC. Sqdron-Ldr. Allan J. Radcliffe, son of Mr. and Mrs. J. N. Radcliffe, Southport School, Southport, awarded DFC. for gallant service in the Middle East with the Desert Air Force. Gnr. R. H. Tann, son of Mr. and Mrs. R. H. Tann, Hermit Park, Townsville, awarded a Commander-in-Chief's Card for distinguished service in the South-west Pacific.
The Courier-Mail (Brisbane). Thursday 5 July 1945

My DFC was gazetted on the 27th March 1945. That was two days after our raid on Osnabrück, the first mission of my second Tour of Duty. After being told of the award I was entitled to wear the DFC ribbon but there was no investiture or celebration on the squadron. I purchased the ribbons at a menswear shop, which was designated to supply ribbons specifically for that purpose and I asked my bat-woman to sew them on my battledress and my dress tunics.

I don't know when Sandy and John received theirs but Bill had his DFC presented by King George VI on the 22nd of June 1945 at Buckingham Palace. Bill's family still have the telegram that was sent by the RAAF Air Ministry to his mother, and the letter from the palace about the presentation. They also have a congratulatory letter from Gus Walker. My father would have collected a telegram about my award while he was at Milne Bay with the US Army.

On the 20th of November 1946, Betty accompanied me to Government House at Rosalie, in Brisbane, where I was invested with my DFC in the beautiful gardens by the Governor of Queensland, Sir John Lavarack. Don McLean and I were invested together. The day after, it was incorrectly reported in the newspapers that the ceremony was performed at Parliament House. It also said that I received the DFM, not the DFC. DFM's were only awarded to aircrew below commissioned rank. An earlier newspaper report had me down as a pilot-officer when I was in fact a flying-officer.

It was a very proud moment in my life. It was good that Don and I, two friends from the same crew, were able to receive our awards at the same ceremony. We had been through a lot together.

That's the end of my story.

Distinguished Flying Cross Citation

RAAF Pilot Officer Basil Gordon Spiller, 426177

"Pilot Officer Spiller has proved himself a navigator of exceptional ability and possessed of cool courage and determination. He has participated in numerous operational sorties against targets in Germany and enemy operated territory. On one occasion his aircraft was damaged by heavy anti-aircraft fire and he was wounded in the thigh but although in pain he unhesitatingly continued with his allotted tasks while receiving first aid from another member of the crew. He navigated the aircraft to the target and back to his country. For his example of fortitude and devotion to duty Pilot Officer Spiller has won the admiration and confidence of his crew."

The Distinguished Flying Cross

The Distinguished Flying Cross is awarded to officers and warrant officers in airforces of British Commonwealth countries, for "an act or acts of valour, courage and devotion to duty performed whilst flying in active operations against the enemy."

Halifax Navigator

Awards Presentation Government House, Brisbane

Awards For Bravery In Peace and War
Presentation by Governor

Brisbane, Nov. 20. – Eighty-five awards for bravery in war and peace by members of the armed forces, policemen and civilians, were presented by the Governor (Sir John Lavarack) in an attractive setting in front of Parliament House this morning.

It was the first presentation of this nature by Sir John Lavarack, and incidentally, comprised the largest number ever made in Queensland at one function. Each recipient was congratulated by His Excellency, and thanked on behalf of the King for his bravery.

About 300 persons attended the ceremony, which was simple, but dignified. Mothers and wives of the recipients of the honours were prominent. His Excellency was accompanied by Lady Lavarack, while all service chiefs, as well as the Commissioner of Police, were present.

Air force officers received the greatest number of awards for operations against the enemy. A sad note was introduced into the proceedings when relatives of servicemen killed in action received the awards of the fallen. One mother, Mrs. A. Carver, received a decoration from His Excellency, but in the other cases, the fathers were the recipients....

The Awards
.... DFM.-Pilot Officers O. W. Dawson, G. L. Hando, R. C. Harkiss, A. J. Hughes, W. V. Kaus, R. J. Leftwich, J. D. Lewis, D. B. McLean, J. D. Marley, L. N. Rackley, N. F. Robinson, R. J. Sexton, B. G. Spiller and M. Stafford....

Extract - *Morning Bulletin* (Rockhampton). Thurs. 21st November 1946

Basil Gordon Spiller RAAF Service Record

Name	SPILLER, BASIL GORDON
Service	Royal Australian Air Force
Service Number	426177
Date of Birth	1 Oct 1923
Place of Birth	MENAPI, NEW GUINEA
Date of Enlistment	23 May 1942
Locality on Enlistment	Unknown
Place of Enlistment	BRISBANE, QLD
Next of Kin	SPILLER, HOBART
Date of Discharge	20 Oct 1945
Rank	Flying Officer
Posting at Discharge	466 Squadron
WW2 Honours and Gallantry	Distinguished Flying Cross
Prisoner of War	No

Basil Gordon Spiller RAAF Honours and Awards

Service number:	426177
Rank at the end of the war:	Flying Officer
Unit:	102 Squadron RAF
Service:	RAAF
Conflict:	Second World War, 1939-1945
Award:	Distinguished Flying Cross

Halifax Navigator

Date of London Gazette: 27 March 1945
Location in London Gazette: Page 1656, position 31
Date of Commonwealth of Australia Gazette: 12 April 1945
Location in Commonwealth of Australia Gazette: Page 855, position 66

NAME SPILLER, Basil Gordon
Award D.F.C. Reg. No. 426177 Rank P/O. Service R.A.A.F.
Recommended by Governor-General on O - R
Promulgated in *London Gazette* on 27/3/45. G. H. File R.A.A.F. 5.
Promulgated in *Commonwealth of Australia Gazette* on 12/4/45.
Citation (G. H. File RAAF 553 B)Exceptional ability as Navigator on numerous sorties
Insignia received from London 8/11/45. PN LONDON. 16/12/46. G. H. File L/65.
Insignia presented by The Governor of Queensland
At Government House Brisbane On 20/11/46 G. H. File BRISBANE/12.
Address of recipient on presentation date "Cheltenham" Berrima Street,
WYNNUM CENTRAL BRISBANE QUEENSLAND

Remarks

Other Awards

Greg Brown and Basil Spiller

Greg interviewing Basil
Stradbroke Island, Queensland, May 2012

381

Research and background information

Primary texts:
Diaries
1. Rabbitt, Bill. The Perilous Sky. The Diary of William Forsyth Rabbitt, 1943-1944. Unpublished.
2. McLean, Don. 1943 Diary. Unpublished.
3. Brabin, Harry. Diary of a WAG. Memoirs of a WW2 Wireless Air Gunner. (2001) Self Published.

Historical works
1. Bowyer, Chas & Van Ishoven, Armand. Halifax and Wellington. (1994) Promotional Reprint Company Ltd. for Treasure Press Australia. ISBN 1 85648 173 5.
2. Enright, Michael. Flyers Far Away. Australian Aircrew in Europe During World War II. (2009) Longeuville Books, Woollahra, NSW.
3. Goss, Chris. It's Suicide But Its Fun. The Story of 102 (Ceylon) Squadron 1917-1956. (1995) Bookcraft (Bath) Ltd., Great Britain.
4. Middlebrook, Martin & Everitt, Chris. The Bomber Command War Diaries: An Operational Reference Book, 1939-45. (1990) Penguin Books. London.
5. Roberts, R. N. The Halifax File (1982). Air Britain (Historians) Ltd.
6. Usherwood, Mike, The RAF Pocklington & RAF Elvington War Diaries (1993) Compaid Graphics, Lower Whitley, Warrington, Cheshire.

Covers:
Front cover photograph – site accessed 24 Feb 2013
http://www.awm.gov.au/collection/SUK12408/
Back cover photograph – site accessed 24 Feb 2013
http://www.iwm.org.uk/collections/item/object/205023321

Part 1: Training in Australia
Coming? Then Hurry poster – site accessed 9 Oct 2012
http://cas.awm.gov.au/item/ARTV04297

Chapter 1:
Burns Philp & Co. – site accessed 9 Oct 2012
http://en.wikipedia.org/wiki/Burns_Philp
Dorothy Spiller – site accessed 24 Oct 2012
http://trove.nla.gov.au/ndp/del/article/79524566
http://trove.nla.gov.au/ndp/del/article/37638707
Liela Spiller – sites accessed 24 Nov 2012
http://trove.nla.gov.au/ndp/del/article/31879063
http://trove.nla.gov.au/ndp/del/article/31879083
Japanese bombing Port Moresby photograph – site accessed 5 Apr 2013
http://www.awm.gov.au/collection/P02018.068
Gibbs, W. J. 1995 *A Glimpse of the RAAF Meteorological Service* - site accessed 9 Oct 2012
http://www.austehc.unimelb.edu.au/fam/0424.html#1280
Basil Spiller photograph from Basil Spiller collection

Chapter 2:
Sandgate and Kingaroy newspaper article - site accessed 4 July 2012

http://trove.nla.gov.au/ndp/del/article/25837523
    Flying Fortress crash and photograph - site accessed 31 Dec 2012
http://www.ozatwar.com/18apr42.htm
    Airacobras crash - site accessed 4 July 2012
http://www.ozatwar.com/15jul42.htm
    Airacobra photograph -- site accessed 10 Jan 2013
http://cas.awm.gov.au/item/P03338.002

Chapter 3:
    Empire Air Training Scheme newspaper article – site accessed 15 Oct 2012
http://www.awm.gov.au/encyclopedia/raaf/eats.asp
    Avro Anson Cootamundra photograph – site accessed 15 Oct 2012
http://cas.awm.gov.au/item/P00448.004
    Flight Sergeant John Jenkins – sites accessed 15 Oct 2012
http://www.cwgc.org/find-war-dead.aspx?cpage=1&sort=name&order=asc
http://www.awm.gov.au/research/people/roll_of_honour/person.asp?p=557360
    Sergeant Vivian Suthurst – sites accessed 15 Oct 2012
http://www.cwgc.org/find-war-dead/casualty/2244931/SUTHERST,%20VIVIAN
http://www.awm.gov.au/research/people/roll_of_honour/person.asp?p=562007
    31 Squadron RAAF – sites accessed 15 Oct 2012
http://www.awm.gov.au/units/unit_11067.asp
http://en.wikipedia.org/wiki/No._31_Squadron_RAAF
    Bristol Beaufighter – sites accessed 13 Dec 2012
http://www.awm.gov.au/units/subject_621.asp
http://en.wikipedia.org/wiki/Bristol_Beaufighter
    Bristol Beaufighter photograph – site accessed 13 Dec 2012
http://cas.awm.gov.au/item/OG3377

Chapter 4:
    New airforce bases newspaper article – site accessed 10 July 2013
http://trove.nla.gov.au/ndp/del/article/40927860
    Air to air gunnery test abbreviations – site accessed 26 May 2013
http://airforce.ca/awards.php?search=&keyword=&page=161&mem=&type=rcaf
    Fairey Battle – sites accessed 10 October 2012
http://www.pilotfriend.com/photo_albums/timeline/ww2/Fairey%20Battle.htm
http://en.wikipedia.org/wiki/Fairey_Battle
http://www.historyofwar.org/articles/weapons_fairey_battle.html
    Modern Training - newspaper photograph – site accessed 4 Dec 2012
http://trove.nla.gov.au/ndp/del/article/44904371
    Fairey Battles at Evans Head photograph – site accessed 10 Oct 2012
http://cas.awm.gov.au/item/P00869.057

Chapter 5:
    Parkes newspaper article – site accessed 10 Oct 2012
http://trove.nla.gov.au/ndp/del/article/17719025
    Bubble sextant – site accessed 10 Oct 2012
http://www.airspacemag.com/flight-today/celestial.html
    Avro Anson - site accessed 10 Oct 2012
http://www.awm.gov.au/units/subject_612.asp
    Avro Anson photograph - site accessed 10 Oct 2012
http://cas.awm.gov.au/item/045158

Chapter 6:
   RAAF Sandgate photograph – site accessed 15 Oct 2012
   http://cas.awm.gov.au/item/P00279.011
   Basil and Hobart Spiller photograph – Basil Spiller collection

Part 2: Embarkation
   London Calling. War funds poster – site accessed 10 Oct 2012
   http://www.iwm.org.uk/collections/item/object/5842

Chapter 7:
   Moore-McCormack Line – sites accessed 10 Oct 2012
   http://www.moore-mccormack.com/The-Company/Mooremack-Timeline.htm
   http://www.moore-mccormack.com/Cargo-Liners/Mormacsea.htm
   http://www.theshipslist.com/ships/lines/mormac.shtml
   Mormacsea photograph – site accessed 10 Oct 2012
   http://cas.awm.gov.au/photograph/302679
   Silver Certificate photograph – site accessed 10 Oct 2012
   http://www.moore-mccormack.com/Cargo-Liners/Mormacsea.htm

Chapter 8:
   Edmonton barracks photograph – site accessed 11 Oct 2012
   http://cas.awm.gov.au/item/P01408.001
   Blatchford Field – site accessed 11 Oct 2012
   http://www.canadianwings.com/Stations/stationsDetail.php?RCAF-Station-Edmonton-22

Chapter 9:
   The TSS Pasteur (history & photograph) – site accessed 11 Oct 2012
   http://cruiselinehistory.com/?p=7059)

Part 3: Training in Britain
   Vickers Wellingtons in formation photograph – site accessed 11 Dec 2012
   http://www.iwm.org.uk/collections/item/object/205210910

Chapter 10:
   Grand Hotel Brighton photograph – site accessed 12 Oct 2012
   http://eo.wikipedia.org/wiki/Dosiero:Grand_Hotel_-_Brighton_-_02082004.jpg
   RAAF Personnel Centre, Bournemouth – site accessed 11 Oct 2012
   http://www.454-459squadrons.org.au/ourhistory.html
   Bournemouth air-raid – sites accessed 12 Oct 2012-10-12
   http://trove.nla.gov.au/ndp/del/article/11338249
   http://www.ww2aircraft.net/forum/aviation/bournemouth-raid-1943-a-11371.html
   Metropole Hotel in ruins photograph site accessed 10 July 2013
   http://www.dorsetlife.co.uk/2013/04
   Flight sergeant Allan Kerrigan – sites accessed 12 Oct 2012
   http://trove.nla.gov.au/ndp/del/article/18191147
   http://www.cwgc.org/find-war-dead/casualty/2690978/KERRIGAN,%20ALLAN%20JOHN
      Bournemouth raid from
Beleznay, Angela. *Incident 48. Raid on a South Coast Town, 1943.* (2012) Natula Publishing, Dorset.

Chapter 11:
    Lady Ryder portrait – site accessed 12 Oct 2012
http://www.npg.org.uk/collections/search/portrait/mw71310
    The Lady Ryder Hospitality Scheme – sites accessed 12 Oct 2012
http://www.awm.gov.au/events/conference/2003/nelson.asp
http://www.awm.gov.au/collection/records/awmohww2/air/vol3/awmohww2-air-vol3-ch5.pdf
    Piccadilly photograph – site accessed 22 Oct 2012
http://www.iwm.org.uk/collections/item/object/205196821

Chapter 12:
    Vickers Wellington – sites accessed 29 Nov 2012
http://en.wikipedia.org/wiki/Vickers_Wellington
http://uboat.net/allies/aircraft/wellington.htm
    Wellington Mark III – site accessed 29 Nov 2012
http://www.raf.mod.uk/history/vickerswellington.cfm
    Aircraft engines – site accessed 29 Nov 2012
http://www.tarrif.net/cgi/production/all_engines_adv.php
    9 Squadron, RAF Honington – site accessed 11 Dec 2012
http://en.wikipedia.org/wiki/RAF_Honington
    9 Squadron Wellingtons photograph– site accessed 10 July 2013
http://www.iwm.org.uk/collections/item/object/205216453
    One thousand bomber raid on Cologne – site accessed 11 De4c 2012
http://web.archive.org/web/20050510084032/http://www.raf.mod.uk/bombercommand/may42.html
    91 and 92 Group OTUs – site accessed 11 Dec 2012
http://www.bansteadhistory.com/Memorial/2_F.html
    James Ward – sites accessed 28 Nov 2012
http://muse.aucklandmuseum.com/databases/Cenotaph/18197.detail
http://web.archive.org/web/20050510083645/http://www.raf.mod.uk/bombercommand/diary1941_2.html
http://www.cwgc.org/find-war-dead/casualty/2201083/WARD,%20JAMES%20ALLEN

Chapter 13:
    RAF Lichfield - site accessed 19 Oct 2012
http://en.wikipedia.org/wiki/RAF_Lichfield
    Swansea, Tasmania, aircraft tragedy - newspaper article – site accessed 9 Dec 2012
http://trove.nla.gov.au/ndp/del/article/36784944

Chapter 14:
    Cannock Chase Bombing Range
http://hansard.millbanksystems.com/written_answers/1947/nov/26/cannock-chase-bombing-range
    Ian Stoeckel, Wellington/Stirling collision – sites accessed 18 Oct 2012
http://www.awm.gov.au/catalogue/research_centre/pdf/rc09125z022_1.pdf   Page 324.
http://www.214squadron.org.uk/Personnel_pages/Scantleton_Vern_L/Fl_Lt_Vern_L_Scantleton_War_Experience_1.htm
    Short Stirling photograph – site accessed 19 Oct 2012
http://www.214squadron.org.uk/Personnel_pages/Scantleton_Vern_L/Fl_Lt_Vern_L_Scantleton_War_Experience_1.htm
    Crew photograph from Bill Rabbitt collection.

Chapter 15:
    HCU Training - sites accessed 1 Dec 2012
http://rafww2butler.wordpress.com/operational-training/
http://rafww2butler.wordpress.com/hcu-training-schedule/
    RAF Marston Moor - sites accessed 1 Dec 2012
http://en.wikipedia.org/wiki/RAF_Marston_Moor
http://www.airfields-in-yorkshire.co.uk/marston/
    Lichfield crew photograph from Basil Spiller's photograph collection

Chapter 16:
    Merv Simpson – site accessed 6 Oct 2012
Storr Alan (2006) <u>RAAF Fatalities In Second World War Among RAAF Personnel Serving On Attachment In Royal Air Force Squadrons and Support Units.</u> Kwik Copy, Canberra, ACT. p37
http://www.awm.gov.au/catalogue/research_centre/pdf/rc09125z023_1.pdf
    Engine data – sites accessed 13 Nov 2012
http://www.bombercommandmuseum.ca/engine_bristolhercules.html
http://en.wikipedia.org/wiki/Rolls-Royce_Merlin
http://www.tarrif.net/cgi/production/all_engines_adv.php
    No 102 Squadron – site accessed 14 Dec 2012
http://102ceylonsquadron.co.uk/history102squadron.html
http://www.raf.mod.uk/bombercommand/h102.html
http://www.raf.mod.uk/bombercommand/s55.html
http://en.wikipedia.org/wiki/RAF_Dalton
http://en.wikipedia.org/wiki/RAF_Driffield
Goss, Chris. <u>It's Suicide But Its Fun. The Story of 102 (Ceylon) Squadron 1917-1956.</u> (1995) Bookcraft (Bath) Ltd., Great Britain.
    FE2b – sites accessed 7 Dec 2012
http://www.ww1aero.org.au/pdfs/Sample%20Journal%20Articles/Night%20Bombing%20with%20the%20FE2b.pdf
http://en.wikipedia.org/wiki/Royal_Aircraft_Factory_F.E.2
http://www.greatwaraviation.com/forum/index.php?topic=3429.0
    FE2b photograph – site accessed 14 Dec2012
http://www.iwm.org.uk/collections/search?query=RAE-O+640&submit=&items_per_page=10
    Heyford and Whitley – sites accessed 15 Dec 2012
http://www.raf.mod.uk/history/handleypageheyford.cfm
http://www.raf.mod.uk/history/armstrongwhitworthwhitley.cfm
http://ezinearticles.com/?The-Armstrong-Whitworth-Whitley-MkV-Bomber&id=217166

Part 4: First Tour of Duty
    Handley Page Halifax Mk III photograph - site accessed 10 July 2013
http://www.iwm.org.uk/collections/item/object/205127113

Chapter 17:
    La Rochelle – site accessed 1 September 2013
http://www.michaelbriant.com/La%20Rochelle.htm
    No 102 Squadron – sites accessed 14 Dec 2012
http://102ceylonsquadron.co.uk/history102squadron.html
http://www.raf.mod.uk/bombercommand/h102.html
http://www.raf.mod.uk/bombercommand/s55.html
http://en.wikipedia.org/wiki/RAF_Dalton

http://en.wikipedia.org/wiki/RAF_Driffield
Marguerite Hudson - sites accessed 16 Dec 2012
http://www.cwgc.org/find-war-dead/casualty/2413856/HUDSON,%20MARGUERITE%20HESTER
http://www.ww2talk.com/forum/royal-artillery/30855-aa-units-defending-raf-station-driffield-15-aug-40-a.html
102 Squadron RAF Pocklington information from
Goss, Chris. *It's Suicide But Its Fun. The Story of 102 (Ceylon) Squadron 1917-1956.* (1995) Bookcraft (Bath) Ltd. Great Britain.
Usherwood, Mike. *The RAF Pocklington & RAF Elvington War Diaries.* (1998). Compaid Graphics, Cheshire, UK.

Chapter 18:
Colline Beaumont gun battery picture gallery – site accessed 3 Sept 2012
http://www.bunkerpictures.nl/pictures/france/pas%20de%20calais/colline%20beaumont/00.html
U-boat bases – sites accessed 4 Sept 2012
http://www.battlefieldsww2.com/Brest_U-boat_bunker.html
http://uboat.net/flotillas/bases/
Battle of Brest – sites accessed 4 Sept 2012
http://www.ww2f.com/western-europe-1943-1945/13284-fortress-brest-1944-a.html
http://en.wikipedia.org/wiki/Battle_for_Brest
Brest U-boat bunker photograph site accessed 10 July 2013
http://www.iwm.org.uk/collections/item/object/205023173

Chapter 19:
Lickey Hills Golf Course – site accessed 2 Dec 2012
http://en.wikipedia.org/wiki/Lickey_Hills
http://www.rosehill-golfclub.co.uk/

Chapter 20:
Briefing room photograph – site accessed 26 Dec 2012
http://www.iwm.org.uk/collections/item/object/205210523
Night Bombing - sites accessed 26 Dec 2012
http://en.wikipedia.org/wiki/RAF_Bomber_Command
http://www.rafbombercommand.com/master_overview.html
http://www.elsham.pwp.blueyonder.co.uk/raf_bc/

Chapter 21:
Flak and the 88 millimetre cannon – sites accessed 7 July 2013
http://www.awm.gov.au/wartime/8/articles/machines_of_war.pdf
https://en.wikipedia.org/wiki/8.8_cm_Flak_18/36/37/41
http://www.timemoneyandblood.com/HTML/weapons/german/88gun.html
http://www.achtungpanzer.com/88mm-flak-series-flugabwehrkanone.htm
http://www.constable.ca/caah/flak.htm
Operation Battleaxe, Halfaya Pass – site accessed 7 July 2013
http://www.timemoneyandblood.com/HTML/weapons/german/88gun.html
Lancaster direct hit by flak photograph – site accessed 7 July 2013
http://www.awm.gov.au/collection/P00811.034

Chapter 22:
Crash Landing Airfields – site accessed 8 Dec 2012

http://en.wikipedia.org/wiki/RAF_Carnaby
The Drem System – site accessed 2 Sept 2012
http://www.rafdrem.co.uk/lighting.html.

Chapter 23:
Massy-Palaiseau –site accessed 25 June 2013
http://en.wikipedia.org/wiki/Massy,_Essonne
Leonard Cheshire - site accessed 25 June 2013
http://en.wikipedia.org/wiki/Leonard_Cheshire
The Master Bomber – sites accessed 11 Sept 2012
http://en.wikipedia.org/wiki/Pathfinder_(RAF)
http://www.raf.mod.uk/bombercommand/peenemunde.html
Friedrichshafen - site accessed 25 June 2013
http://en.wikipedia.org/wiki/Luftschiffbau_Zeppelin
Gnome-Rhone aero-engine factory raid photograph - site accessed 11 July 2013
http://www.iwm.org.uk/collections/item/object/205023365

Chapter 24:
Evrecy - site accessed 25 June 2013
http://fr.wikipedia.org/wiki/%C3%89vrecyhttp://en.wikipedia.org/wiki/Basse-Normandie
Sergeant Roy Harris from
Goss, Chris, *It's Suicide But It's Fun. The Story of Number 102 Squadron 1917-1956*.
Crecy Books Ltd. 1995. pp 119-121.

Chapter 25:
Aviatik – site accessed 5 Sept 2012
http://www.firstworldwar.com/airwar/earlyfighters.htm
Aviatik-Doppeldecker Photograph – site accessed 5 Sept 2012
http://upload.wikimedia.org/wikipedia/commons/9/9e/Aviatik_B.I.jpg
Halifax LW192 – sites accessed 6 September 2012
http://www.aircrewremembrancesociety.com/raf1944/3/braddockeric.html
http://www.ww2museums.com/article/1614/Commonwealth-War-Graves-Buren.htm
Sergeant David Roy Fisher, London Gazette – site accessed 6 Sept 2012
London Gazette, Issue 35560. Published 12 May 1942. pp 2121 and 2122
http://www.london-gazette.co.uk/issues/35560/supplements/2122
Squadron Leader David Fisher from
Goss, Chris, *It's Suicide But It's Fun. The Story of Number 102 Squadron 1917-1956*.
Crecy Books Ltd. 1995. pp 120-121.

Chapter 26:
Austin – sites accessed 10 Jan 2013
http://www.austinmemories.com/page7/page4/page4.html
http://www.uniquecarsandparts.com.au/car_info_austin_10.htm
"The Lodger" film review – site accessed 3 September 2012
http://trove.nla.gov.au/ndp/del/article/17924991
N-Nan "Naughty Nineties" photograph – Bill Rabbitt collection
Austin 10 photograph - Bill Rabbitt collection

Chapter 27:
Noyelles-en-Chaussée - site accessed 7 Sept 2012
http://www.communes.com/picardie/somme/noyelles-en-chaussee_80150/
Duralium - - sites accessed 7 Sept 2012

http://en.wikipedia.org/wiki/Duralumin
http://en.wikipedia.org/wiki/Junkers_Motoren
http://www.roden.eu/HTML/041.htm
　　　Junkers J1 Photograph - site accessed 7 Sept 2012
http://www.aviastar.org/air/germany/junkers_j-1.php
　　　Fontaine L'Etalon Churchyard Cemetery – site accessed 7 Sept 2012
http://www.cwgc.org/find-war-dead.aspx?cpage=1&sort=name&order=asc

Chapter 28:
　　　Junkers 88 – sites accessed 9 Sept 2012
http://www.456fis.org/JUNKERS_Ju_88.htm
http://en.wikipedia.org/wiki/Junkers_Ju_88
　　　Junkers 88 photograph – site accessed 9 Sept 2012
http://www.iwm.org.uk/collections/item/object/205220374

Chapter 29:
　　　Tour of Duty – sites accessed 10 Sept 2012
http://www.elsham.pwp.blueyonder.co.uk/raf_bc/
http://www.spartacus.schoolnet.co.uk/2WWraf.htm
　　　Henry Rogers – sites accessed 9 Apr 2013
http://www.aircrewremembered.com/alliedlossesmaster.html
http://www.102ceylonsquadron.co.uk/memHenryRogers.html
http://www.cwgc.org/find-war-dead/casualty/2689323/ROGERS,%20HENRY
　　　Mimoyecques raid photograph - site accessed 11 July 2013
http://www.awm.gov.au/collection/SUK12546/
　　　Leonard Cheshire - sites accessed 10 Sept 2012
http://en.wikipedia.org/wiki/Leonard_Cheshire
http://trove.nla.gov.au/ndp/del/page/1768966
　　　Sandy Concannon - extract from
Enright, Michael. Flyers Far Away. Australian Aircrew in Europe During World War II. (2009). Longerville Books. Oxford Street, London. p224

Chapter 30:
　　　Reconnaissance Spitfire –sites accessed 7 Sept 2012
http://en.wikipedia.org/wiki/Supermarine_Spitfire_(early_Merlin_powered_variants)
http://www.historyofwar.org/articles/weapons_spitfire_PR.html
http://spitfiresite.com/2010/04/supermarine-spitfire-variants-the-initial-merlin-powered-line.html/2
　　　Spitfire photograph etc – site accessed 7 Sept 2012
http://www.airrecce.co.uk/WW2/recce_ac/RAFAR.html
　　　Mosquito – site accessed 7 Sept 2012
http://en.wikipedia.org/wiki/De_Havilland_Mosquito
　　　Mosquito PR Mk 1X photograph – site accessed 7 Sept 2012
http://www.wwiivehicles.com/unitedkingdom/aircraft/reconnaissance/de-havilland-pr-mosquito.asp
　　　Wing Commander Wilson – site accessed 7 Sept 2012
http://www.telegraph.co.uk/news/obituaries/1465771/Wing-Cdr-Douglas-Wilson.html

Chapter 31:
　　　Flying Bomb – sites accessed 7 Sept 2012
http://en.wikipedia.org/wiki/V1_flying_bomb_facilities
http://en.wikipedia.org/wiki/V1_(flying_bomb)

Operation Crossbow – site accessed 7 Sept 2012-09-08
http://en.wikipedia.org/wiki/Operation_Crossbow
Flying Bomb photographs – sites accessed 7 Sept 2012
http://cas.awm.gov.au/item/SUK12643
http://cas.awm.gov.au/item/SUK12918
Benzedrine
Enright, Michael. Flyers far Away. Australian Aircrew in Europe During World War II. (2009) Longerville Books, Oxford Street, London. p225

Chapter 32:
Butt report – site accessed 27 June 2013
http://en.wikipedia.org/wiki/Butt_Report
Oboe – sites accessed 26 June 2013
http://ww2today.com/9th-january-1943-the-raf-start-blind-bombing-with-oboe
http://www.rafbombercommand.com/tactics_naviadvances.html
http://en.wikipedia.org/wiki/Oboe_(navigation)
http://www.gyges.dk/jamming_service%20Oboe.htm

Chapter 33:
Halifax and Lancaster survival rates – site accessed 14 June 2013
http://homepage.ntlworld.com/r_m_g.varley/concise%20history%20of%2077%20sqd.html
Halifax photograph – site accessed 2 Sept 2012
http://www.iwm.org.uk/collections/item/object/205023321
Self-sealing Fuel Tanks - sites accessed 13 Sept 2012
http://en.wikipedia.org/wiki/Self-sealing_fuel_tank
http://www.dtic.mil/cgi-bin/GetTRDoc?AD=AD904092&Location=U2&doc=GetTRDoc.pdf
Inside the Lancaster - site accessed 13 Sept 2012
http://www.flightglobal.com/pdfarchive/view/1942/1942%20-%201700.html
Inside the Halifax - site accessed 13 Sept 2012
http://www.flightglobal.com/pdfarchive/view/1942/1942%20-%200877.html

Chapter 34:
Halifax MZ298 shot down – site accessed 21 Apr 2013
AWM 237 (65) NAA: A705, 166/10/277, 166/24/501 Micro Film No 463 OAFH
http://www.pocklingtonhistory.com/forum/viewtopic.php?f=5&t=1304&start=20
Robert Selth service record – site accessed 21 Apr 2013
http://www.ww2roll.gov.au/Veteran.aspx?serviceId=R&veteranId=1028222
Sandy Concannon interview – 19 April 2013
Robert Selth interviews - 22nd & 23rd April 2013 and 3rd May 2013
Albert Ball – site accessed 24 June 2013
http://en.wikipedia.org/wiki/Albert_Ball
Shrage Musik – site accessed 25 June 2013
http://en.wikipedia.org/wiki/Schr%C3%A4ge_Musik
http://www.ww2talk.com/forum/war-air/12796-luftwaffe-schrage-musik-raf-losses.html
http://www.ww2talk.com/forum/war-air/12796-luftwaffe-schrage-musik-raf-losses.html
Rudolph Schoenert – site accessed 25 June 2013
http://en.wikipedia.org/wiki/Rudolf_Schoenert
Mk 108 cannon – site accessed 25 June 2013
http://en.wikipedia.org/wiki/MK_108_cannon

Schrage Musik demonstration – site accessed 25 June 2013
http://www.youtube.com/watch?v=8gi6UOoKItY

Chapter 35:
Halifax X-Xray LL552 account of crash – site accessed 14 Aug 2012
http://www.102ceylonsquadron.co.uk/memBobLeyland.html
Bruce Johnston text and map – site accessed 8 Jan 2013
http://lancasterdiary.net/July%201944/july_24_1944.php
102 Squadron damage and Loss
Goss, Chris, *It's Suicide But It's Fun. The Story of Number 102 Squadron 1917-1956*. Crecy Books Ltd. 1995. p199

Chapter 36:
Happy Valley diary quotations – site accessed 7 Jan 2013
http://www.rusinsw.org.au/Papers/2008W02.pdf
Happy Valley
http://www.awm.gov.au/units/event_213.asp
Bombing Germany
Levine, Alan. The Strategic Bombing of Germany, 1940-45. (1992). Greenwood Press, Westport. pp51-53
Wanne-Eickel raid photograph - site accessed 7 Jan 2013
http://www.iwm.org.uk/collections/item/object/205022243

Chapter 37:
Rose Brothers (Gainsborough) Ltd – sites accessed 30 June 2013
http://www.bphs.net/GroupFacilities/R/RoseBrothersGainsborough/index.htm#1
http://www.chezfred.org.uk/University/ComputerXHistory/EarlyHistory/1950-AirPosInd-DSCN1552.htm
http://www.gainsboroughheritage.com/html/rose_brothers.html
http://en.wikipedia.org/wiki/Gainsborough,_Lincolnshire
http://en.wikipedia.org/wiki/HACS
The Air Position Indicator – sites accessed 30 June 2013
http://plane-design.com/documentation/An%20introduction%20to%20Bomber%20Command%20Navigation.pdf
http://timeandnavigation.si.edu/multimedia-asset/air-position-indicator

Chapter 38:
Great Ashfield - sites accessed 2 Dec 2012
http://en.wikipedia.org/wiki/RAF_Great_Ashfield
http://www.elmswell-history.org.uk/arch/society/airfield/airfield.html
Great Ashfield Photograph - site accessed 13 August 2012
http://www.challoner.com/aviation/airfields/great-ashfield.html
Very Pistol – sites accessed 3 Dec 2012
http://www.museumoftechnology.org.uk/expand.php?key=483
http://firearmshistory.blogspot.com.au/2011/03/utility-firearms-flare-gun-or-very.html

Chapter 39:
Paddy Heffernan – site accessed 16 Oct 2012
http://www.ww2roll.gov.au/Veteran.aspx?serviceId=R&veteranId=1206046
http://www.awm.gov.au/catalogue/research_centre/pdf/rc09125z022_1.pdf   Page 574.
No. 4 Service Flying Training School – site accessed 18 Oct 2012

Heffernan, P.G. *No.4 Service Flying Training School. Pilot Training 1941-1945.*
From *Stand To* magazine. Canberra R.S.L. Office, Oct/Dec 1966.
http://www.futurepd.org/les/Documents/PDFs/4%20SFTS%20Book%20A.pdf
    8 Squadron RAAF – site accessed 18 Oct 2012
http://www.awm.gov.au/units/unit_11033.asp
    RAAF Base Pearce – site accessed 18 Oct 2012
http://en.wikipedia.org/wiki/RAAF_Base_Pearce
    Heffernan OBE - site accessed 18 Oct 2012
http://trove.nla.gov.au/ndp/del/article/23247823
    Paddy Heffernan photograph – site accessed 17 Jan 2013
http://cas.awm.gov.au/item/SUK13845

Chapter 40:
    102 Squadron information from
Goss, Chris, *It's Suicide But It's Fun. The Story of Number 102 Squadron 1917-1956.*
Crecy Books Ltd. 1995.
Usherwood, Mike, The RAF Pocklington & RAF Elvington War Diaries (1993) Compaid Graphics, Lower Whitley, Warrington, Cheshire.pp164-170.
    Bombs on trolleys photograph – site accessed 14 July 2013
http://www.iwm.org.uk/collections/item/object/205212772

Chapter 41:
    Icing on wings – site accessed 19 Nov 2012
http://bombercommand.wordpress.com/planting-vegetables-460-squadron-style/
    Lack of Moral Fibre – sites accessed 7 Jan 2013
http://www.elsham.pwp.blueyonder.co.uk/raf_bc/
http://www.academia.edu/2023436/Malingering_and_Lack_of_Moral_Fibre_Trauma_in_the_Royal_Air_Force_during_World_War_Two

Chapter 42:
    B17 Flying Fortress – site accessed 30 Sept 2012
http://www.aviation-history.com/boeing/b17.html
    Kammhuber Line – site accessed 30 Sept 2012
http://en.wikipedia.org/wiki/Kammhuber_Line
    Venlo Photograph – site accessed 30 Sept 2012
http://www.histomil.com/viewtopic.php?f=210&t=370

Chapter 43:
    Pocklington history
Ainscough, Jim & Ainscough Margaret. *Pocklington At War.* (2010). Posthaste Printers, Pockligton.
http://www.pocklingtonhistory.com/
    Griffin Hotel, Leeds – site accessed 16 June 2013
http://www.leodis.org/display.aspx?resourceIdentifier=2007119_165247

Chapter 44:
    German 6th Military District at Münster – site accessed 17 June 2013
http://en.wikipedia.org/wiki/M%C3%BCnster
    77 Squadron information – site accessed 30 Sept 2012
http://homepage.ntlworld.com/r_m_g.varley/concise%20history%20of%2077%20sqd.html
    Halifax LW142 flight crew and ground staff photographs - Bill Rabbitt collection

Chapter 45:
    Battle of Arnhem – site accessed 17 June 2013
http://www.leesaunders.co.uk/html/world_war_II/ww2_events/arnhem.php
https://en.wikipedia.org/wiki/Battle_of_Arnhem
    Courtrai raid information from
Middlebrook, Martin and Everitt, Chris. *The Bomber Command War Diaries: An Operational Reference Book, 1939-45.* (1990) Penguin Books. London.
    Melsbroek airfield – site accessed 1 October 2012
http://www.brusselsairport.be/en/corporate/our_company/airport_history/
    Melsbroek airfield reconnaisance photograph – site accessed 1 October 2012
http://www.iwm.org.uk/collections/item/object/205023334
    Melsbroek airfield camouflaged hangar photograph – site accessed 1 October 2012
http://www.iwm.org.uk/collections/item/object/205211825
    Operation Bodenplatte – German attack on Melsbroek – site accessed 22 Feb 2013
http://en.wikipedia.org/wiki/Operation_Bodenplatte

Chapter 46:
    Wound Stripe newspaper articles – sites accessed 20 Aug 2012
http://trove.nla.gov.au/ndp/del/article/59149766
http://trove.nla.gov.au/ndp/del/article/11809728

Chapter 47:
    Gus Walker general information – site accessed 12 Sept 2012
http://www.rafweb.org/Biographies/Walker_G.htm
    Gus Walker accident – site accessed 14 Sept 2012
http://www.3bktj.co.uk/wood13.htm
    Gus Walker newspaper articles – sites accessed 14 Sept 2012
http://news.google.com/newspapers?id=YLtTAAAAIBAJ&sjid=cDgNAAAAIBAJ&pg=3101,4311494&dq=gus+walker+raf&hl=en
http://www.britishnewspaperarchive.co.uk/
    Gus Walker DFC – site accessed 14 Sept 2012
http://www.london-gazette.co.uk/issues/35389/supplements/7237
    Gus Walker photograph – site accessed 12 Sept 2012
http://squadronforum.freeforums.org/viewtopic.php?t=62&p=450

Chapter 48:
    Ruhr region - site accessed 8 Jan 2013
http://en.wikipedia.org/wiki/Ruhr
    Ruhr map created by Daniel Ullrich - site accessed 8 Jan 2013
http://en.wikipedia.org/wiki/File:Ruhr_area-map.png
    Monica – sites accessed 28 June 2013
http://en.wikipedia.org/wiki/Monica_tail_warning_radar
http://en.wikipedia.org/wiki/Flensburg_radar_detector
http://www.207squadron.rafinfo.org.uk/wesseling/wesseling_ecm.htm
    Fishpond
http://www.rquirk.com/cdnradar/Sands/Radar%20book%202.pdf
http://users.skynet.be/Emmanuel.Gustin/fgun/fgun-uf.html
http://www.rquirk.com/cdnradar/cor/chapter17.pdf
http://en.wikipedia.org/wiki/Fishpond

Chapter 49:
    Duisburg - Operation Hurricane – site accessed 7 Nov 2012

http://en.wikipedia.org/wiki/Bombing_of_Duisburg_in_World_War_II
    Damaged Halifax – site accessed 7 Nov 2012
http://www.iwm.org.uk/collections/item/object/205090448
    158 Squadron RAF – site accessed 7 Nov 2012
http://www.158squadron.co.uk/
    Neil (Mick) Starmer auction – site accessed 26 August 2012
http://www.invaluable.com/auction-lot/medals-orders-decorations-three:-flight-serge-1-c-efnismmhrb

Chapter 50:
    H2S – sites accessed 12 Nov 2012
http://cas.awm.gov.au/item/SUK14704
http://en.wikipedia.org/wiki/H2S_radar
    H2S photograph – site accessed 12 Nov 2012
http://cas.awm.gov.au/item/SUK14707

Chapter 51:
    Halifax engines photograph – site accessed 14 July 2013
http://www.awm.gov.au/collection/UK1914/

Chapter 52:
    Krupp AG- site accessed 26 Aug 2012
http://www.britannica.com/EBchecked/topic/323930/Krupp-AG
http://en.wikipedia.org/wiki/Krupp 26 Aug 2012
    James Begbie SAAF – site accessed 2 Oct 2012
http://www.aircrewremembrancesociety.com/raf1944/begbie.html
    F/O Redmond – site accessed 2 Oct 2012-09-01
http://www.pocklingtonhistory.com/forum/viewtopic.php?f=14&t=1304&start=10
    Commonwealth War Graves Commission – site accessed 2 Oct 2012
http://www.cwgc.org/find-war-dead.aspx?cpage=2

Chapter 53:
    Bochum Raid – sites accessed 17 April 2013
http://trove.nla.gov.au/ndp/del/article/81412841
http://trove.nla.gov.au/ndp/del/article/43227515
    Allan Crabb – sites accessed 6 Oct 2012
http://trove.nla.gov.au/ndp/del/article/55902711
http://trove.nla.gov.au/ndp/del/article/26661387

Chapter 54:
    Kattegat and Skagerrak Straits – sites accessed 15 Nov 2012
http://en.wikipedia.org/wiki/Kattegat
http://en.wikipedia.org/wiki/Skagerrak
    Battle of Jutland – site accessed 8 Dec 2013
http://en.wikipedia.org/wiki/Battle_of_Jutland
    Post war mines – site accessed 15 Nov 2012
http://www.thelocal.se/20102/20090616/
    Kattegat mines – site accessed 23 March 2012
http://www.cphpost.dk/news/national/88-national/48207-wwii-mines-found-in-kattegat-strait.html
    Kattegat and Skagerrak Straits map – site accessed 15 Nov 2012
http://upload.wikimedia.org/wikipedia/commons/c/c2/Carte_Skagerrak-Kattegat2.png

http://commons.wikimedia.org/wiki/File:Carte_Skagerrak-Kattegat2.png

Chapter 55:
 Jülich – site accessed 2 October 2012
http://en.wikipedia.org/wiki/J%C3%BClich
 River Rur – site accessed 2 Oct 2012
http://en.wikipedia.org/wiki/Rur
 Jülich photograph – site accessed 11 July 2013
http://wgs.cc/416/missions/mission149.html
 Hilton Beadle – site accessed 2 October 2012
http://www.london-gazette.co.uk/issues/36894/supplements/414/page.pdf
http://www.london-gazette.co.uk/issues/39767/supplements/689/page.pdf
http://www.london-gazette.co.uk/issues/37578/supplements/2511/page.pdf

Chapter 56:
 "The Tail Gunner" by Dennis Adams – site accessed 13 July 2013
http://www.awm.gov.au/collection/ART256941

Part 5: Between Tours
 Flak over Hamburg - site accessed 13 July 2013
http://www.iwm.org.uk/collections/item/object/205023205

Chapter 57:
 Halifax Bomb Bay Photograph – site accessed 8 Dec 2013
http://www.iwm.org.uk/collections/item/object/205210785

Chapter 58:
 Operation Gisella – sites accessed 7 Oct 2012
http://www.clickpress.com/releases/Detailed/266005cp.shtml
http://www.arxitecture.org.uk/lh11.htm
http://web.archive.org/web/20050510083832/http://www.raf.mod.uk/bombercommand/mar45.html
Usherwood, Mike. The RAF Pocklington & RAF Elvington War Diaries. (1998). Compaid Graphics, Cheshire, UK. pp 181-202
 Halifax 1944/45 winter - site accessed 15 July 2013
http://www.iwm.org.uk/collections/item/object/205211239

Chapter 59:
 Commonwealth War Graves – site accessed 19 Nov 2012
http://www.cwgc.org/
 Halifax LW 142 N-Nann Loss – site accessed 19 Nov 2012
http://www.pocklingtonhistory.com/forum/viewtopic.php?f=14&t=1248
 Halifax LM 149 Y-Yoke Loss – site accessed 19 Nov 2012
http://www.pocklingtonhistory.com/forum/viewtopic.php?f=14&t=1304&start=0
 RAAF fatalities in WW2
RAAF Fatalities in Second World War Among RAAF Personnel Serving on Attachment in Royal Airforce Squadrons and Support Units. AWM 237 (65) NAA : A705, 166/7/805 Micro Film No. 463 OAFH.
Commonwealth War Graves records. W R Chorley: *RAF Bomber Command Losses of the Second World War.* Page 49, Volume 1945
 Loss of N-Nan and Q-Queenie
Goss, Chris, *It's Suicide But It's Fun. The Story of Number 102 Squadron 1917-1956.*

Crecy Books Ltd. 1995. pp 139-142 and p203
P-Peter LW158 crash investigation photograph – Bill Rabbitt collection
Chapter 60:
Bill Rabbitt and Basil Spiller photograph – Bill Rabbitt collection

Part 6 – Second Tour of Duty
Halifax Mk 6 over Paris – site accessed 13 July 2013
http://yorkpress.co.uk/features/features/9155493

Chapter 61:
Bill Rabbitt – London Gazette – site accessed 11 Sept 2012
http://www.london-gazette.co.uk/issues/36997/supplements/1598/page.pdf
Second Tour crew photograph – Basil Spiller collection

Chapter 62
Bruce Johnston website – site accessed 8 Jan 2013
http://lancasterdiary.net/July%201944/july_24_1944.php

Chapter 64:
German wartime oil production - site accessed 8 Jan 2013
http://www.sturmvogel.orbat.com/ussbsnat.html
http://vanrcook.tripod.com/Germanfuelshortage.htm
Fischer-Tropsch process - site accessed 8 Jan 2013
http://en.wikipedia.org/wiki/Fischer%E2%80%93Tropsch_process
Hydrogenation process - site accessed 8 Jan 2013
http://en.wikipedia.org/wiki/Synthetic_fuel
Rhenania oil plant - site accessed 8 Jan 2013
http://www.fischer-tropsch.org/Tom%20Reels/tom_meeting/refineries_hamburg.htm
Hamburg shipyards, U-boat builders. Blohm and Voss shipyards – site accessed 8 Jan 2013
http://www.uboat.net/technical/shipyards/
Damaged Rhenania oil refinery photograph – site accessed 23 Feb 2013
http://www.iwm.org.uk/collections/item/object/205200032

Chapter 65:
Hamburg bombing
Lowe, Keith. *Inferno 1943. The Fiery Destruction of Hamburg.* (2007). Simon and Schuster.
Hambug photograph – site accessed 5 Oct 2012:
http://www.iwm.org.uk/collections/item/object/205023601
Operation Gomorah
http://en.wikipedia.org/wiki/Bombing_of_Hamburg_in_World_War_II
Firestorm
http://www.historylearningsite.co.uk/hamburg_bombing_1943.htm
Hamburg raid
Usherwood, Mike. *The RAF Pocklington War Diaries.* (1998) Compaid Graphics. pp 203

Chapter 66:
Flensburg – site accessed 21 June 2013
http://en.wikipedia.org/wiki/Flensburg
Minelaying – site accessed 22 June 2013
http://www.navweaps.com/Weapons/WAMBR_Mines.htm

http://en.wikipedia.org/wiki/Naval_mine
http://www.globalsecurity.org/military/library/policy/navy/nrtc/14313_ch5.pdf
    Aerial minelaying film – site accessed 22 June 2013
http://www.criticalpast.com/video/65675049278
    Admiral Scheer – site accessed 22 June 2013
http://en.wikipedia.org/wiki/German_cruiser_Admiral_Scheer
    Admiral Scheer photograph – site accessed 22 June 2013
http://www.iwm.org.uk/collections/item/object/205211768

Chapter 67:
    Nuremburg Raid – sites accessed 27 Aug 2012
http://web.archive.org/web/20050510083832/http://www.raf.mod.uk/bombercommand/mar45.html
http://web.archive.org/web/20050510083832/http://www.raf.mod.uk/bombercommand/mar45.html
    Nuremburg photograph - site accessed 27 Aug 2012
http://www.history.army.mil/books/wwii/Occ-GY/ch14.htm

Chapter 68:
    Cyril Barton - sites accessed 27 Aug 2012
http://www.key.aero/central/attachments/2%20Halifax.pdf
http://www.raf.mod.uk/bombercommand/halifax.html
http://en.wikipedia.org/wiki/Cyril_Joe_Barton
    Cyril Barton photograph - site accessed 9 Dec 2013
http://www.rafbombercommand.com/people_vcwinners_citations001.html
    Description of Cyril Barton's actions which earned him the VC from
Bowyer, Chas & Van Ishoven, Armand. *Halifax and Wellington.* (1994) Promotional Reprint Company Ltd. for Treasure Press Australia. ISBN 1 85648 173 5. pp 70-75

Chapter 69:
    Heligoland – sites accessed 19 Nov 2012
http://translate.google.com.au/translate?hl=en&sl=de&tl=en&u=http%3A%2F%2Fde.wikipedia.org%2Fwiki%2FHeligoland
http://en.wikipedia.org/wiki/Heligoland
    Battle of Heligoland Bight – site accessed 19 Nov 2012
http://en.wikipedia.org/wiki/Battle_of_the_Heligoland_Bight_(1939)
    Kiel Canal - sites accessed 19 Nov 2012
http://en.wikipedia.org/wiki/Kiel_Canal
http://www.kiel-canal.org/english.htm
    U-boat shipyards - site accessed 19 Nov 2012
http://www.uboat.net/technical/shipyards/blohm.htm
    Heligoland U-boat bunkers – site accessed 19 Nov 2012
http://books.google.com.au/books?id=Qo8kOmEaORYC&pg=PA119&lpg=PA119&dq
    Heligoland armaments - site accessed 19 Nov 2012
http://forum.12oclockhigh.net/archive/index.php?t-5706.html
    SK L/50 coastal defence gun - site accessed 19 Nov 2012
http://en.wikipedia.org/wiki/30.5_cm_SK_L/50_gun
    Lobster Claws project - site accessed 19 Nov 2012
http://www.bananasraras.org/Helgopalmen/History.htm
    Lobster Claws Project map – site accessed 9 Jan 2013
http://www.bananasraras.org/Helgopalmen/History.htm
    Me109 – site accessed 19 Nov 2012

http://acepilots.com/german/bf109.html
    Dune airfield – site accessed 19 Nov 2012
http://en.wikipedia.org/wiki/Jagdgeschwader_11
    Heligoland bombing – sites accessed 19 Nov 2012
http://en.wikipedia.org/wiki/Nuclear_weapon_yield
http://www.youtube.com/watch?v=Z6hKwjoKa-c
http://www.youtube.com/watch?v=LTkc7fnSaz8&NR=1
http://www.britishpathe.com/record.php?id=56942
    Heligoland photograph – site accessed 23 Feb 2013
http://commons.wikimedia.org/wiki/File:Heligoland_Vogelperspektive.jpg
    Heligoland two bombing photographs – site accessed 23 Feb 2013
http://forum.axishistory.com/viewtopic.php?f=54&t=163176
    U-boats at Heligoland
Williamson, Gordon. *Wolf Pack. The story of the U-boat in World War II.* 2005. Osprey Publishing Ltd. p119-124

Chapter 70:
    Wangerooge information - sites accessed 19 Nov 2012
http://en.wikipedia.org/wiki/Wangerooge
http://www.lancewadplan.org/Cultural%20atlas/LS/Wangerooge/wangerooge.htm
    Mercury newspaper article – site accessed 19 Nov 2012
http://trove.nla.gov.au/ndp/del/article/26061185?searchTerm="Wangerooge"&searchLimits
    Wangerooge photograph – Martina Nolte sites accessed 19 Nov 2012
http://en.wikipedia.org/wiki/File:2012-05-13_Nordsee-Luftbilder_DSCF8674.jpg
http://creativecommons.org/licenses/by-sa/3.0/de/legalcode
    Wangerooge bombing photograph – site accessed 19 Nov 2012
http://www.flickr.com/photos/nationalarchives/3010671412/

Chapter 71:
    Halifax RG532 History
Bryan Legate, Assistant Curator Department of Research & Information Services, RAF Museum London.
    Halifax photograph – site accessed 8 Jan 2013
http://www.iwm.org.uk/collections/item/object/205127078
    Navigation section photograph, VE Day 1945 – Basil Spiller collection

Part 7: Going Home
    SS Andes at Woolloomooloo wharf – site accessed 13 July 2013
http://www.awm.gov.au/collection/112250/

Chapter 72:
    Andes history - sites accessed 9 Jan 2013
http://oceantimes.weebly.com/uploads/3/0/1/1/3011162/ocean_times_09_july__v13.3-1.pdf
http://www.britisharmedforces.org/pages/nat_troopships.htm
http://www.bbc.co.uk/ww2peopleswar/stories/77/a3331577.shtml
    Andes troop accommodation - sites accessed 9 Jan 2013
http://www.mercantilemarine.org/showthread.php?3220-Andes-and-Otranto-WW2-Troopships
http://www.ovguide.com/harland-and-wolff-9202a8c04000641f8000000000166841
    Andes leaving Liverpool & MONAB - sites accessed 9 Jan 2013

http://www.fleetairarmarchive.net/squadrons/monab.html
http://www.fleetairarmarchive.net/squadrons/monab.html
    Andes voyage June/July 1945 - site accessed 9 Jan 2013
http://oceantimes.weebly.com/uploads/3/0/1/1/3011162/ocean_times_09_july__v13.3-1.pdf
    Andes broken up - site accessed 9 Jan 2013
http://www.cruiseshipodyssey.com/andes.htm
    Andes fitting for wartime - site accessed 9 Jan 2013
http://www.acstadden.co.uk/Pages/CCStadden.aspx
    Andes launch video - site accessed 9 Jan 2013
http://www.britishpathe.com/video/belfast-rms-andes
    Andes postcard – site accessed 9 Jan 2013
http://www.cruiseshipodyssey.com/andes.htm
    Andes Arrival Sydney photograph – sites accessed 9 Jan 2013
http://cas.awm.gov.au/item/112248
http://cas.awm.gov.au/item/112251
    Panama Canal - sites accessed 9 Jan 2013
http://en.wikipedia.org/wiki/Panama_Canal
http://www.eclipse.co.uk/~sl5763/panama.htm

Chapter 73:

    1945 Australian wages calculation. Institute of Public Affairs – site accessed 3 Dec 2012
http://www.ipa.org.au/library/publication/1229563340_document_3-5_wages.pdf
    Courier Mail articles - sites accessed 10 Feb 2013
http://trove.nla.gov.au/ndp/del/article/50284079
http://trove.nla.gov.au/ndp/del/article/50285279
    The Sydney Morning Herald article - site accessed 3 Dec 2012
http://trove.nla.gov.au/ndp/del/article/27920287
    Cairns Post article - site accessed 3 Dec 2012
http://trove.nla.gov.au/ndp/del/article/42448721
    Bradfield Park Photograph – site accessed 31 Dec 2012
http://cas.awm.gov.au/item/112259

Chapter 74:

    Jack (Shorty) Milliner classified articles – sites accessed 16 Sept 2012
http://trove.nla.gov.au/ndp/del/article/48940417
http://trove.nla.gov.au/ndp/del/article/50265198
http://trove.nla.gov.au/ndp/del/article/50509981
    Shorty Milliner's Stuttgart raid – site accessed 25 Oct 2012
http://www.awm.gov.au/catalogue/research_centre/pdf/rc09125z004_1.pdf
    Honeymoon photograph - Basil Spiller collection

Chapter 75:

    DFC Photograph – site accessed 10 Sept 2012
http://regimental-books.com.au/the-distinguished-flying-cross-to-australians-p-2460.html
    Honours and Awards - site accessed 11 July 2013
http://www.awm.gov.au/research/people/honours_and_awards/person.asp?p=371249
    DFC award presentation – site accessed 22 September 2012
http://trove.nla.gov.au/ndp/del/article/56408498

Printed in Great Britain
by Amazon